featuring
MUMTAZ SHANTI
DILIP KUMAR
MANORAMA, DIXIT
JEEVAN, GULAB SULEMAN
GOPE
घर की इज़्ज़त
GHAR KI IZZAT
Directed by
RAM DARYANI
Filmistan Ltd., presents
KAMINI KAUSHAL
DILIP KUMAR
CHANDRAMOHAN
and
LEELA CHITNIS
SHAHEED
शहीद
شہید
Directed by
RAMESH SAIGAL
मेला
MELA
HBOOB PRODUCTION PVT. LTD.
नर्गिस · राजकपूर
انداز
अंदाज़
ANDAZ
DILIP KUMAR
KAMINI KAUSHAL
IN
आरज़ू
ARZOO
DIRECTOR-SHAHID LATEEF-MUSIC-ANIL BISWAS
Sunny Art Productions
NARGIS, DILIP KUMAR
MUNAWAR SULTANA
بابل
BABUL
बाबुल
NAUSHAD. SUNNY
Ranjit presents
NARGIS
DILIP KUMAR
JOGAN
जोगन
DILIP KUMAR · NIMMI IN
DAAG
SHANKAR JAIKISHAN
Talwar Films
LIMITED
presents
SANGDIL
संगदिल
سنگدل
MADHUBALA
DILIP KUMAR
R.C.TALWAR
RANJIT
Presents
DILIP KUMAR
MEENA KUMARI
फुटपाथ
FOOTPATH
Written & Directed by
ZIA SARHADY
ASHA DEAP
DILIP KUMAR
NALINI JAYWANT
& OM PRAKASH
शिकस्त
شکست
SHIKAST
RAMESH SAIGAL SHANKER-JAIKISHAN
Bimal Roy PRODUCTIONS
Devdas
KUMAR
AYANTI MALA
CHITRA SEN
देवदास
Produced and Directed by BIMAL ROY
Film Group
MUSAFIR
मुसाफ़िर
مسافر
HRISHIKESH MUKHERJEE · SALIL CHOWDHURY
will remember the exciting people and their exciting
in a symphonic drama of natures many splendoured grandeur
FILMS
Naya
B.R.CHOPRA O.P.NAYYAR AKHTAR MIRZA SAHIR
Remember it's an All India Film Corp. Pvt. Ltd. Release
AF516904

With fond good wishes
&
regards to
dear 'Kakku'

[signature]

DILIP KUMAR

PEERLESS ICON INSPIRING GENERATIONS

DR. TRINETRA BAJPAI
ANSHULA BAJPAI

BLOOMSBURY
NEW DELHI • LONDON • OXFORD • NEW YORK • SYDNEY

Grateful Thanks:

Janaab Dilip Kumar Sahab, Smt. Saira Banu
Late Shri Lekh Tandon
Shri Ameen Sayani Sahab
Smt. Uma Dubey
Ali Peter John
Vishwas Nerurkar
Rehman Naushad
Deepesh Salgia
Nutan Asgaonkar
Aatmanand Golatkar
Aslam Khan
Paul Vinay Kumar
Shambhu Sahu
Jyoti Mehrotra

Inspired by

Kanika Bajpai

Production Team

Shreyas Tiwrekar
Prakash Arekar
Siddharth Patil

DILIP KUMAR

PEERLESS ICON INSPIRING GENERATIONS

BY

TRINETRA BAJPAI ANSHULA BAJPAI

AN AUTHENTIC ENCAPSULATION OF THE LIFE
TIMES AND HISTRIONIC SPLENDOUR OF THE MEGA STAR

BLOOMSBURY INDIA
Bloomsbury Publishing India Pvt. Ltd
Second Floor, LSC Building No. 4, DDA Complex, Pocket C – 6 & 7,
Vasant Kunj New Delhi 110070

BLOOMSBURY, BLOOMSBURY INDIA and the Diana logo are
trademarks of Bloomsbury Publishing Plc

First published 2019

ISBN: 978-93-88630-55-9

2 4 6 8 10 9 7 5 3 1

Printed and bound in India by Replika Press Pvt Ltd

Dedication

With immense pleasure and profound delight,
we dedicate this book to the inspiration of our lives

Kanika Bajpai
– the greatest die-hard fan of Dilip Sahab

देख पाते हैं जब फ़नकारी के वो नायाब मंज़र,
झिलमिला उठते हैं कई ताजमहल।

–कनिका बाजपेयी

CONTENTS

Anshula Bajpai with Ameen Sayani

FOREWORD

Like every young Indian of the 19th century, I too became a dedicated fan of super-star Dilip Kumar at the threshold of my youth. I always tried to dress like him, act like him and even romanticise like him ! (Of course, unlike Dilip Kumar Saheb, all the response that I ever got from girls was heaps of giggles !)

But, as I grew older and began my career of commercial broadcasting – which included deeply studying Dilip Saheb's films and publicising them on Radio Ceylon, I began to realize that even his style of speaking was matchless, and I tried hard to imbibe the greatness of his speaking in my own programmes – and it gradually helped me to improve my own popularity in radio broadcasting.

Later, I also had the good fortune of meeting him often – sometimes at his residence in Bandra – and so warm and kind was his personality, that every time I even think of him, I feel like standing up and saluting this matchless megastar !

And, now that TRINETRA BAJPAI Saheb has sent me an advance copy of his fabulous book on Dilip Kumar, I stand up and salute Trinetraji, too – because he and his daughter Anshula have brought out such a matchless book on Dilip Saheb's personality, films, co-stars, posters, photographs and songs that it has left me wonderstruck ! Read it yourself, and feel its wonderful effect - even the "Words Worth" prologue by the eminent journalist Ali Peter John is memorable !

AMEEN SAYANI

Dear Bajpai Saheb,

Your book on Dilip Kumar is surely the finest filmstar biography I've ever gone through. Congratulations!

A short introduction is sent herewith - you could use it in any manner that you like.

Warm regards - and best wishes to you and Anshula. I'm sure the book will break many records!

Ameen Sayani.

Dilip Kumar

Words Worth by ALI PETER JOHN

I HAVE LIVED WITH LEGENDS, BUT THERE WAS AND THERE WILL NEVER BE A LEGEND LIKE DILIP KUMAR

How do I begin and how can I dare to end the story of a living and immortal legend like Dilip Kumar whose very name sends shivers of joy all over my being? I will not talk about his massive contribution to Indian cinema as a one-man institution as I feel I am not as qualified as it takes to pass judgement on a legend who is the ultimate, the limitless and the endless.

I will let Mr. Trinetra Bajpai and his daughter Anshula Bajpai and their tireless and tremendous effort in adding glory to one of the most unforgettable chapters in the history of Indian cinema do what I call a genuine and dedicated labour of love. I will only talk about my encounters and experiences with Dilip Kumar which I feel will speak volumes for him...

Let me start with a believe it or not story. I lived in a slum in Bombay where they worshipped all kinds of gods. There were pictures of gods and goddesses in every home and for some strange reason there were posters and pictures of Dilip Kumar in every home. There was an 'uncle' who told us stories about Dilip Kumar. He was the man who spread the cult of Dilip Kumar in our slum called 'Lateef Ahmed Cyclewala Compound'. His little room was covered with photographs of stars more than any God. Every evening he told us stories about Dilip Kumar and his films. He aroused the curiosity of all of us of all ages to go with him and see a Dilip Kumar film. We traveled in bullock carts. Yes, bullock carts in a city like Bombay in the 60s, to the nearest theatre showing a new or an old Dilip Kumar film. The 'uncle' gave us a running commentary during the screening and held an 'uncle's darbar' in the evening when he sat on a 'charpoy' and all of us, men and boys gathered around him as he explained the film we had seen to us. The women kept away but then asked us what 'uncle' had to say about Dilip Kumar and the film we had seen.

I was just ten when my mother who had a great fascination for Dilip Kumar had enough money to take us all the way to Bandra in a taxi to Neptune Talkies (now defunct) to see 'Mughal-E-Azam' and bought tickets in the 'black market' all for her love of Dilip Kumar. Watching 'Mughal-E-Azam' was a dazzling experience for us. That was the first time I had seen the film and I have seen it at least thirty-five times and can still watch it whenever it is telecast on T V or in a theatre old or new, a madness which I am proud to pass on to my 30 year old daughter Swati who is a writer, director and cinematographer who is always busy but has never lost an opportunity to see the film and any other Dilip Kumar film. There are several evenings when we have watched his films together and exchanged notes about his performance.

I first saw Dilip Kumar in flesh and blood (I like many others believed he was more like a God-like figure than a human being) when he had come to the annual day of a Christian school. There were hundreds of people who had thronged the place. A man dressed in dazzling white arrived in a huge car and the crowd rushed towards him. That man was Dilip Kumar. He looked so very different from all the other men I had seen till then (why?). He was like a man from some other world. I could only see him from a distance but I remembered his short speech in which he had said, 'I don't know why all of you look at me as if I am some animal from a zoo. I wish you could understand that I am like anyone of you. I am a human being like you, made of flesh and blood like you. My working in films doesn't make me any different from you. I wish I was treated like a human being and not like some rare species in a zoo'. That was the time when I had decided to be either a Roman Catholic priest or a BEST bus conductor and could never ever dream of coming anywhere near a God- like man like Dilip Kumar.

The next time I saw him and heard him for an hour was at a political rally to campaign for V. K Krishna Menon, a brilliant Barrister and an envoy of India to the United Nations where he was ranked among the best speakers in the world. Everyone wanted to only listen to Dilip Kumar. There was rapt silence when Dilip Kumar rose to speak and he spoke till two am and not one man or woman in the crowd moved.

Time passed. I changed all my earlier ambitions and ended up working for 'Screen', a film weekly and was writing about films and stars and the happenings and activities associated with them. And during all the thirty-eight years with the weekly I have had the proud privilege of coming close to the 'Emperor' and the 'Shahenshah' of acting. I can write a book or two about my encounters with him but for my well-wisher Mr. Trinetra Bajpai, a devotee of Dilip Kumar who has compiled a book about the legend, I feel I must share some of my experiences I have had with him.

At this moment I feel thoroughly disappointed with the biography of Dilip Kumar which is in the market now. It is in no way the kind of tribute that should have been paid to the giant of an actor he has been and will always be...

It was the year 1995 and 'Screen' wanted to start its own awards. We needed a very big celebrity to head the jury. There could not be a greater celebrity than Dilip Kumar, I told my seniors. They said it would be very difficult to make him agree. I said I would like to try. They scoffed at me and asked me to go ahead and take the risk. I had just started knowing the legend and I realized he was very warm and affectionate with me. One evening I met him in the compound of 34 B, Pali Hill, a bungalow where he lives with his beautiful 'begum' Saira Banu. I told him I had something to talk to him about. He didn't take a second and said, 'get into my car and I will talk to you'. I did as I was told. He took me out in his red Mercedes and parked his car in a corner on the same lane where the bungalow was. I told him 'Screen' wanted him to be the chairman of the jury of our first ever awards. He paused for a while (his pauses and silences were the most interesting parts of his complete personality in and off films) and then asked his chauffeur, Kutty for same paper and a pen and started writing. I kept silent. Twenty minutes later he handed over the paper to me and said, 'These are my conditions. Tell your bosses if they agree to my demands, I am willing'. I went through the piece of paper and couldn't control my feelings. It was a menu of the kind of dishes he would like to be served during the interval of every screening. Who could have said no to the unusual and simple demands of an 'Emperor'? He has always been fond of very good food. In fact, he was caught 'smuggling' in some delicious 'tandoori chicken' into the ICU of a leading hospital. It was one great experience to have a man like him on the jury together with others great names like Dr. B.R Chopra. Hrishikesh Mukherjee, G.P. Sippy,

Gulzar and Ramesh Sippy who gave the awards the kind of prestige very few awards have ever had. The meetings of the jury were blended with some learned discussions in between some delicious snacks which Sairaji prepared under her supervision. Every day of the discussions of the jury was like a festival, thanks to the hospitality of Dilip Kumar and his 'begum'. My company was relieved as it did not have to spend any money as the films were screened at Ajanta mini theatre owned by Sunil Dutt who did not charge a rupee and the snacks came straight from one of the best kitchens, from the house of Dilip Kumar and his gracious wife, Saira Banu.

I was privileged to be invited to all his birthdays, his wedding anniversaries and Eid. He always had a crowd of people from all walks of life waiting for him. He came down around three and that was lunch time for everyone and what a feast it was!

I have had the privilege of inviting him to any number of functions and he has never said no. I remember one particular occasion when I gave him just a day's notice and he agreed to come provided I did not let Sairaji know. I was caught in a tricky situation but he said he wanted to come. What could I do? He asked me to come to the bungalow at 5.30 pm so that we could reach the venue at 6.00pm. He was not at home when I reached and I panicked. There was a crowd waiting outside the auditorium and a bigger crowd outside waiting to have a glimpse of him. I was told he was busy helping with the post-production of Sairaji's serial. I called him and he said he would be with me in ten minutes. He told me he needed ten minutes to get ready. He asked me if it was necessary to wear a suit. I said 'yes' and he said, 'Then you will have to give me twelve minutes'. He came down the staircase in a hurry and I saw his shirt hanging out of his trousers. He asked me to tuck it in for him. I was hesitant but he asked me to do it if I wanted him to go to the function. It was a small gesture, but I will remember it all my life.

On the way he asked me what the event was all about. I told him it was organized by a friend. He asked me for the name of my friend and I told him he was a man called Ram Jawharani. He asked me to give him a description of the man. I said he would be wearing a stark white suit and would have a very dark complexion and would be sitting in the center of the stage. He asked me to repeat the name Ram Jawharani several times till we reached the hall. He was still not sure and asked me to sit in the front row and make a sign when he reached my friend during his speech so that he could mention his name. The time came for him to speak and he mentioned the names of everyone on the stage but stopped when it came to my friend. He kept looking at me and I tried my best to make the signs he wanted me to make but all my efforts failed and Ram Jawharani went unmentioned by the legend which was his dream. He had lost the opportunity of a lifetime and has never forgiven me for the 'crime' I had committed.

It was the same story when Anupam Kher organized a party to mark the inauguration of his acting school 'Actor Prepares'. He had invited Dilip Kumar to be the chief guest. An excited and nervous Anupam asked me to go to the legend's house to bring him to the hotel. I reached the bungalow to find Dilip Kumar and Sairaji ready to leave. But their chauffeur Kutty had gone on leave. He asked me if I could drive his Mercedes. I told him I couldn't even drive a cycle. He asked me what car I had come in. I pointed out a second hand Maruti 800 and he said, 'Let's go in your car'. I was dumb for the moment. Fortunately, for me, one of his young nephews walked into the bungalow. He asked him if he was free and if he could drive them to 'The Leela' (the hotel where Anupam's function was to be held). The young man agreed. The couple got into the brand new

Mercedes presented to him by the Sheikh of Kuwait. I was getting into my Maruti 800. He held me and led me to the Mercedes and asked me to drive with them. My driver kept staring at 'the Dilip Kumar'. I had to bring him back to the present and asked him to lead the way to the hotel. As we drove down he asked me, 'yes, now tell me, where are you taking me and why'? I told him he was the chief guest at Anupam Kher's function. He asked me, 'kya uska janamdin hai, yaa shaadi ki saalgirah hai'? I told him it was to celebrate the opening of his school to train actors. 'Yeh acting ka school kya hota hai? Acting koi sikhaa sakta hai kya? I don't know anything about this acting school and I don't know what to say in my speech', he said. I told him to say something nice about Anupam and congratulate him on his new adventure. He spoke at the packed party and said exactly what I had told him to but in a way only he in the whole world could speak. Anupam blushed like a school boy and thanked the legend and Sairaji and when they had left, he treated me like the hero of the night.

I can never forget some of the legend's humane gestures. I cannot forget the time he saw me waiting for a bus at Haji Ali. He stopped his Mercedes, called out to me and asked, 'Chalta hai kya'? I forgot where I was going and sat with him and we drove down to his bungalow where I had some piping hot tea made by him (he is very particular about the kind of tea he has, just like another legend I knew, M. F. Husain). And this other gesture when he saw me entering his house completely drenched in the rain. He went up and brought me a huge towel and a set of kurta-pyjama and asked me to dry myself and change before I could talk to him.

He was a popular football player when he was a student but as he grew older he took a liking for cricket and saw as many cricket matches as he could. He was the captain of the film industry team which played festival matches to raise funds for various causes. He carried a huge transistor where ever he was shooting to listen to the running commentary and his comments were more interesting than the commentary by the experts (Vijay Merchant was his favourite commentator). Things became easier for him after the coming of television and he followed the game ball by ball and stroke by stroke. He was the first to publicly predict that India would be the champion of the world one day and this prediction was made long before India won the World Cup in 1983.

How can I forget the story he told me about the 'many deaths' he died? There was a time when he was supposed to die in every second film he worked in. And he took great pains to make his death scenes look as real as possible. Dying was a part of his life and a way of making a living and living up to his reputation as an actor. A stage came when he had to be treated by the best doctors in the world for depression caused by the kind of death scenes he played, and he was asked to cut down on playing of tragic roles and try comedy. He came back from London where he was treated and played comic roles in films like 'Kohinoor', 'Azaad' and 'Ram Aur Shyam' and was accepted as a great comedian, and was freed from all his depression.

The great Dilip Kumar could be child-like and mischievous at times. He could be quite harsh when describing women who played his mother. 'It was very agonizing to embrace women half my age who used to stink sometimes and call them 'maa maa maa' when my own ideal of a mother was a beautiful and gorgeous mother'. He could also be harsh on some of his directors and co-actors who he felt did not know the basics of film making 'and should not punish others because of their ignorance or sheer innocence about acting or filmmaking'.

He loves good poetry and used to have grand evenings with all the best poets during his heydays. He invited poets to his house every evening and offered them the most expensive drinks and food and presented them with rich gifts to inspire them to come up with better poetry. He lamented the lack of good poets and good poetry in the eighties and nineties 'jahaan jo bhi qalam pakad sakta hai woh shaayar ya lekhak ban jaata hai' (where anyone who can hold a pen can become a poet or a writer).

Some thirteen years ago, a poet from Pakistan came to India with the ambition to visit him and recite same of his poems to him. He did not eat for two days because he had vowed that he would eat only after he had met Dilip Kumar. I managed to arrange a meeting for him with the help of Sairaji. The poet could not believe it. Dilip Kumar did not allow him to touch his feet and when he sat on the floor, he said 'Shaayar toh bade se bade badshah se bada hota hai'. The poet recited some of his poems in a tremulous voice and Dilip Kumar listened to him keenly and told him he had a long way to go if he was interested in being a genuine poet. He handed over a very precious gift and some money to the poet and left him till the gate of his house even though he was not well and the poet could not control his tears and looked back at his idol and cried out aloud and left.

And this story about Dilip Kumar and the mobile phone. Sairaji presented him with a brand new mobile one evening. He kept looking at it and said, 'Yeh kya cheez hai? Isse main kya karoonga'? Sairaji explained all the advantages of having a mobile and taught him how to operate it. He was to go to the city the same evening. Sairaji slipped the mobile into his coat pocket. He carried it with him and hardly had he reached Mahim when the mobile rang. It was Sairaji on the line asking him, 'Where are you, Saahab'? He told her where he was and this ringing of what he called 'the damn thing' went on and on till he reached the city and then it rang again. It was Sairaji asking him the same question and he said, 'I am having tea with my friends at the Taj Mahal Hotel'. What followed was only what the husband and wife knew. She accused him of lying. Hadn't he told her that he was going to the CCI, so what was he doing at the Taj? Their arguments continued at the end of which he called his chauffeur, Kutty and gave away the mobile to him and never touched it again.

Mohammed Yusuf Sarwar Khan (the full name of Dilip Kumar) is ninety-five now and has been ailing for the last ten years. But he has Sairaji by his side all the time and he knows and believes that Sairaji is his 'Florence of Nightingale' sent by Allah, without whose love and tender care he once said, 'I would have been travelling in some other world'. What a tribute coming from such a great Saahab to his 'begum'!

I first heard about his biography being written some twenty-three years ago. There were some biographies already in the market, but they were not official and not authorized by him. He even ran down a biography written by one of his best friends, Bunny Reuben and another by a journalist called Sanjit Narvekar.

I am very confident that a Dilip Kumar *bhakt* like Mr. Trinetra Bajpai and his daughter would hate to do any kind of injustice to the 'God of acting' they have been worshiping for the last several decades.

Ali Peter John

Bajpais with Khans

ON A PERSONAL NOTE

Yours truly (Trinetra Bajpai) fell prey to the hypnotic spell cast by 'Abhinay Samrat' (Acting King) Dilip Kumar at an (admittedly) impressionable age of nine while watching Bimal Roy's timeless classic *Madhumati* (1958). Ever since, I have watched with avid interest all but two—*Jwar Bhata* (1944) and *Pratima* (1945)—of his 59 released films, with my wife Kanika Bajpai, who shares this unabashed admiration in ample measure, as does our only child Anshula Bajpai, who is the co-author of this book. Befittingly, the first motion picture Anshula saw was (no awards for guessing right) a Dilip Kumar starrer— *Paigham* (1959)—which literally makes her a born admirer.

It has been a truly fascinating journey for us to view and review numerous Dilip Kumar starrers—debate their merits/demerits and hold in-depth discussions on the nuances, subtle shades and finer points of 'Dilipian'[1] performances—that too practically as a daily chore. Honestly, we have never seen any flaws in any Dilip Kumar portrayal despite a most critical scrutiny. But, we did feel that there were a few films like *Mazdoor* (1983), *Dharam Adhikari* (1986), *Kanoon Apna Apna* (1989) and *Izzatdaar* (1990) which he could have stayed away from. These films were nowhere near the exacting standards of his other films. Nevertheless, film after film, the overwhelming impact of his tour de force performances has kept us in an inescapably bewitched trance.

We have grown up watching Dilip Kumar's films, drawn profuse inspiration from them and imbibed tremendous motivational virtues. The Bajpai clan has no hesitation in admitting that we owe a lot to Yusuf *Saheb* in shaping our personalities and honing our behavioural patterns to some levels of perfection. Dilipian films and his personal activities have deeply influenced countless professionals and personalities in all walks of life and endeavours. For example, I, in a corporate career of 46 years in the petrochemical industry, have seen champion professionals imitate Dilipian mannerisms and vocal intonations to their advantage, and a telling effect in crucial negotiations and even board meetings. Repeat viewing of his films is a habit with countless Dilip admirers to set moods; for example, if you want to feel romantic, watch *Madhumati* and if you want to chase your blues away, take a fresh look at *Kohinoor* (1960) or *Leader* (1964).

Also, I started collecting his films' memorabilia, contained in this compilation, as a 12-year-old way back in 1963, and I have kept acquiring more and preserving cuttings to this day. Kanika, who is from the histrionic world herself, and our darling daughter Anshula, who has a master's in Mass Communication (Creative Writing), gave me the idea to compile and publish this collection, adequately laced with anecdotes. Their insistence and immense contribution catalysed this collection's evolution. Anshula pitching in as a co-author truly imparted momentum to this endeavour.

---

[1] A term we have coined for anything and everything pertaining to Dilip Kumar.

Anshula / Kanika / Trinetra Bajpai with Dilip Sahab

We are truly elated to see this labour of love see the light of the day. We, proudly and with great reverence, dedicate the book to the one and only, Dilip Kumar, and present it to the readers.

Mumbai, January 2019

Dr. Trinetra Bajpai
Anshula Bajpai

PROLOGUE

Cinematic history, till date, has witnessed a million stars. Some of them are reminisced for their charm, some for their fashion sense, some for their dancing and singing, some for their wit, while others for their comic genius. All in all, they are successful entertainers and expert improvisers. Then, there are those who have the power to light up the screen while presenting their own interpretation of the art of emoting. These enigmatic beings make movie going a cathartic experience. You walk out purged and relieved, or joyful and fulfilled or even (unavoidably at times) submerged in the depths of despair. These are the idols whose posters you post on your walls or imitate them in front of a mirror and sometimes, subconsciously, infuse their styles in your own walk and talk. One such actor with a talent of monumental proportions is Yusuf Khan a.k.a. Dilip Kumar.

He is not merely a living legend striding across the celluloid firmament like a colossus over the last seven decades; he is a superstar far above the unattainable peak of fame, ensconced on a much loftier pedestal in the hearts of legions of admirers across generations. While many performers may have charmed their ways in to their fans' hearts, Dilip went far beyond. Mesmerising generations of filmgoers with his unmatched histrionics in all his on-screen portrayals, he carved a permanent niche in their inner being. Dilip Kumar lives and shall live forever in the hearts and souls of his countless fans world-over.

Cinema lovers have always had that unquenchable thirst for thespians. They have an obsessive-compulsive need to be completely enveloped by a character that reflects shades of what lies within him or her on screen. Dilip Kumar fulfils that desire of the audiences as he draws them alluringly into the world of mimeses (Greek word for art imitating reality). Though known as the tragedy king of Hindi cinema for having played many intense characters akin to the archetypal tragic Greek hero, Dilip Kumar's dramatic zeal evolved beyond just tragedy. He mastered the entire range of acting techniques which led to his superlative performances in several films ranging from tragedies to comedies to dramas and romances. We watch movies not only for entertainment but also to live someone else's life in those two and a half hours. An actor is a magician that makes us believe in his craft. Like Sir Laurence Olivier said, 'I don't know what is better than the work that is given to the actor-to teach the human heart the knowledge of itself.' Dilip Kumar has touched our souls by compelling us to completely identify with the character portrayed on screen–never larger-than-life and invariably authentic. To say that he lived those roles would be an understatement. Dilip Kumar lived the characters assigned to him, painting each emotion in colours of true life with consummate artistry and simplicity of realism.

In his glorious career of several decades, Dilip Kumar has been literally showered with awards and accolades: nine Filmfare awards (including one for Lifetime Achievement), DadaSaheb Phalke Award, Padma Vibhushan, numerous lifetime achievement awards, etc. He has also been the Sheriff of Bombay, an envoy designate and a member of the Rajya Sabha. It has been an innings studded with magnificent accomplishments, worldwide acclaim and universal adoration.

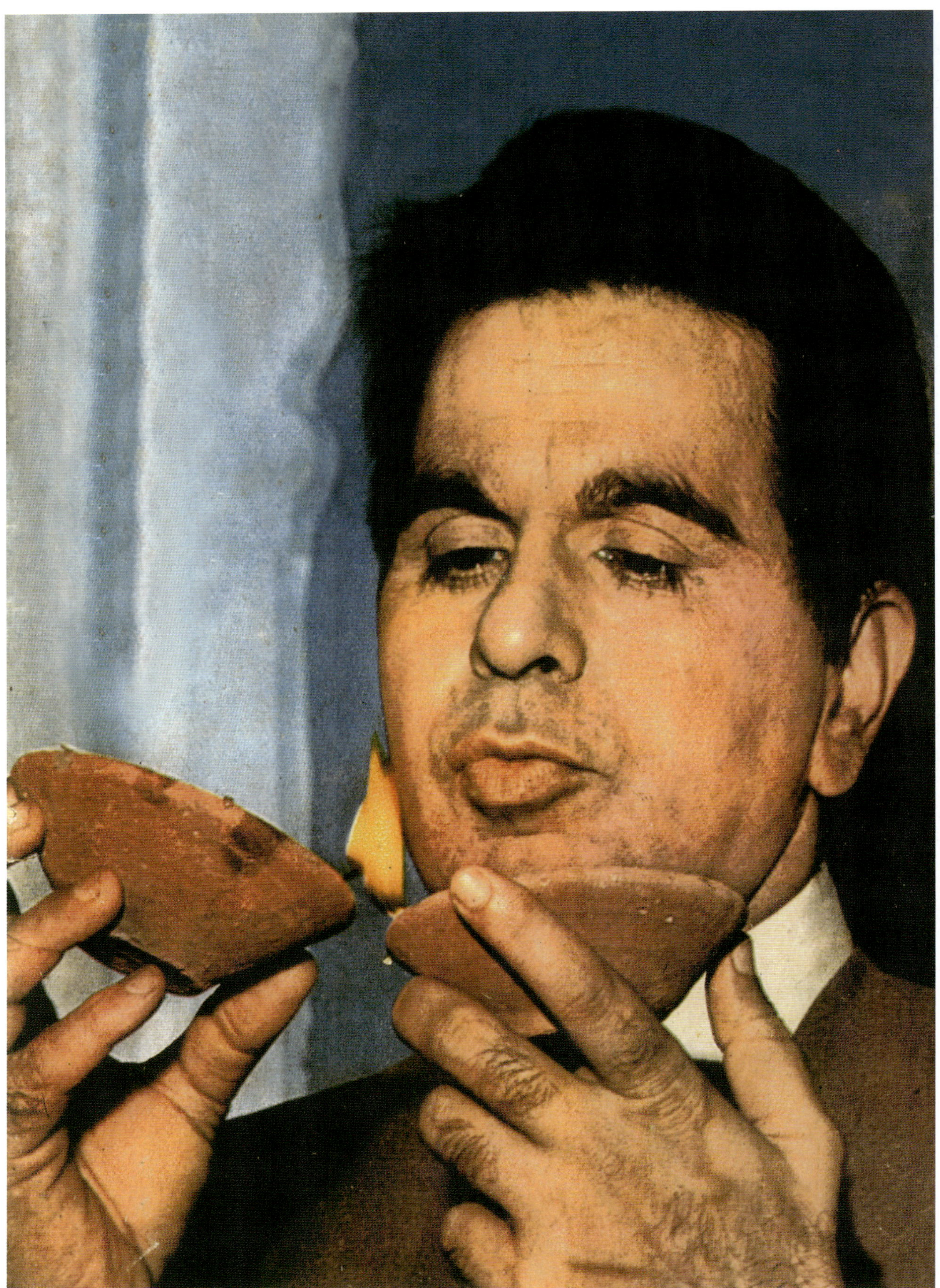

Lighting the histrionics lamps

His fans venerate Dilip Kumar as the monarch of tragedy for his splendid performances in numerous oedipal dramas. In the same breath, they adore him for giving a new meaning to cinematic comedy in films like *Ram aur Shyam* (1967) and *Azaad* (1955). He imparted a dash of subtle sophistication to the humour intended to be evoked. He essayed Sisyphean roles with effortless ease and never stooped low to raise boisterous merriment. A slight smile when happy and raised eyebrows on a furrowed forehead when melancholic—he immediately struck a rapport with his viewers. Only Dilip Kumar knew how to convey pathos without really wetting eyes and create a sheer delight without tomfoolery. Even in later times, Dilip retained the same inquiring gaze and the cultured-mellow timbre of an expressive voice.

We can go on and on to elucidate the innumerable fascinating facets of the persona of Dilip Kumar who epitomises cinematic excellence and histrionic genius. A lot will still remain unsaid for the readers to grasp as they could gauge every subtle, unstated expression in a 'Dilipian' portrayal.

Our meticulously compiled presentation, titled *'Dilip Kumar: A Peerless Icon Inspiring Generations'*—is an attempt in stating what has remained unsaid. It will make all our efforts worthwhile (it's a labour of love of over 40 years), if this compilation could, in its own modest way, take Dilip Kumar's fans through a part of what has made the legend a beacon of astonishing acting prowess. Amen!

The Authors with Dilip Sahab

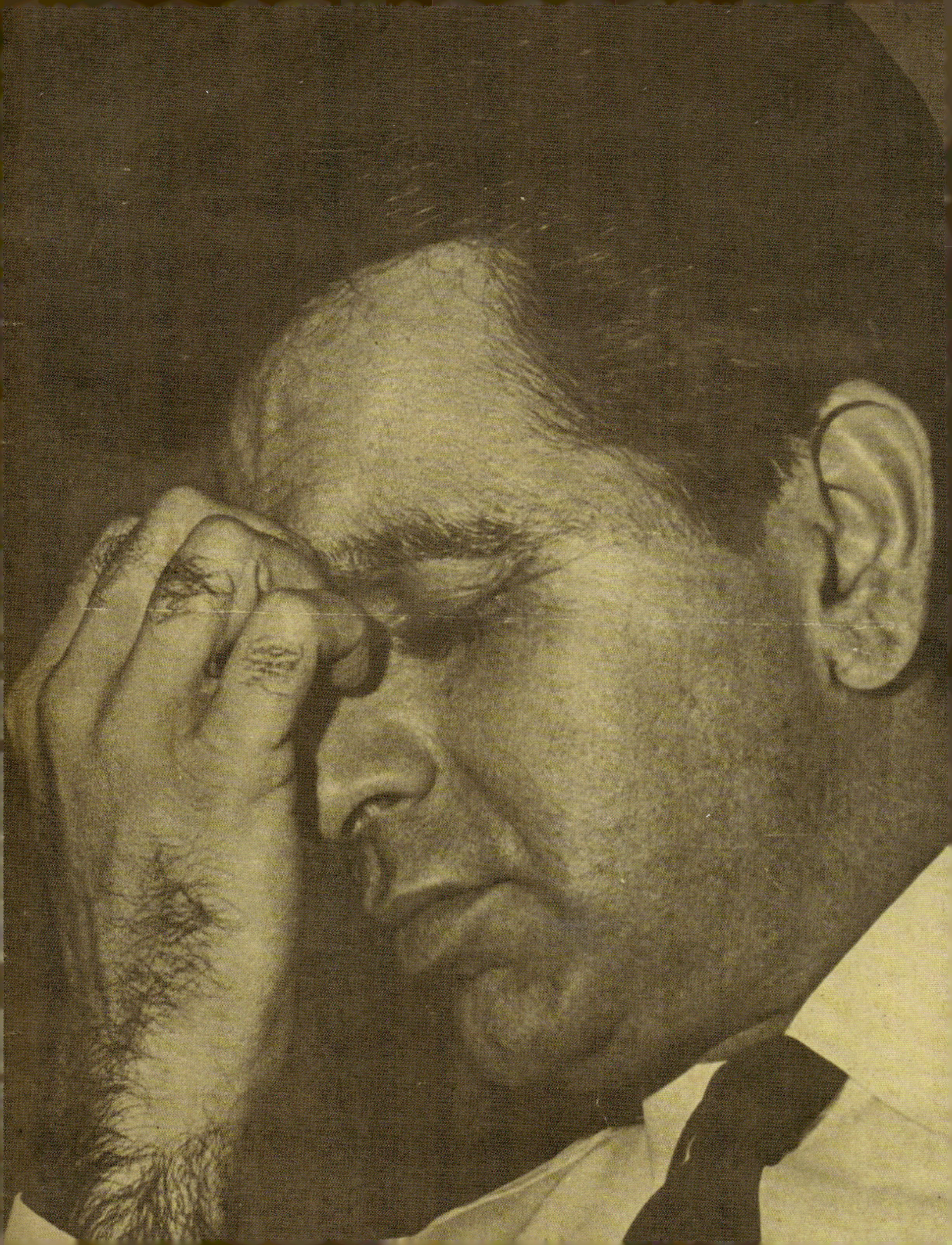

CHAPTER 1

EARLY YEARS AND FAMILY

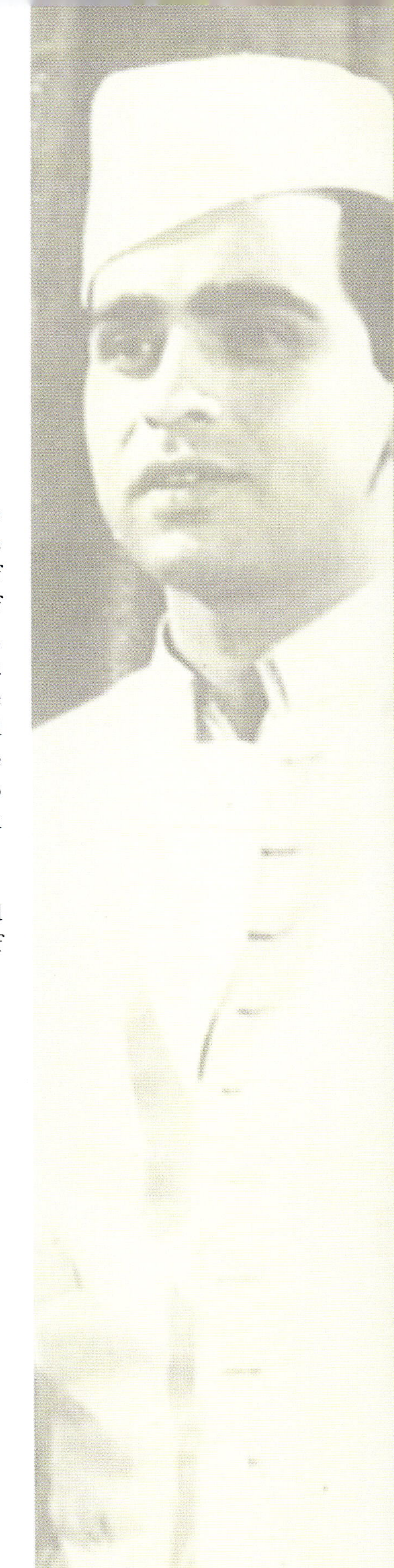

In the *Aaryavart* (undivided ancient India) of yore, the town of Pushpapura or the City of Flowers or the Lotus Land, founded over 2,000 years ago by the Kushan kings of Gandhaar, was the gateway to the hinterland of the then enormous country of subcontinental dimensions. It was also known as the City of Grain and was the seat of Buddhist Gandhaar civilisation, an important place of pilgrimage. Over later centuries, the city became the vantage-point gateway for the invaders of the subcontinent. With the inevitable decline of Buddhism, the city sank into historical oblivion until the Mughal invader Emperor Babur recognised its strategic and military significance and rebuilt it with a fort, circa 1530. The grandson of Babur, Emperor Akbar renamed the city as Peshawar (which means 'the Place at the Frontier') because of its proximity to the Khyber Pass which links the present-day Pakistan to Afghanistan. Peshawar, now in Pakistan, is an important town of its North-West Frontier Province.

Our great megastar and the greatest actor ever, Dilip Kumar was born as Mohammad Yusuf Khan, inside the walled city of Old Peshawar on the bitterly cold day of

Peshawar House

Kissa Khwani Bazaar

Yusuf with Mother

Young Yusuf

11 December 1922. He is the third son and fifth child (of thirteen children) of the fruit merchant Ghulam Mohammed Sarwar Khan (son of Haji Mohammed Khan) and his wife Ayesha Begum. The day, of course, went on to become a red-letter day in the annals of Indian motion picture industry and the world of histrionics. Dilip Saheb's father and the family lived in Mohalla Khudabad (also known as Khodadad) of Kissa Khwani Bazaar in the heart of Peshawar.

Long ago, when Dilip Kumar was a small child, his father took him to Taunsa Sharif's *mazaar* (mausoleum) for praying, offering obeisance and performing the usual rituals. His father reportedly swore that he heard a commanding voice from behind the mausoleum proclaiming, 'Sarwar Khan, this son of yours is going to grow up to become a great man.' Ostensibly, the great fame and fortune which were to come Dilip's way in later years were ordained. Grapevine also has it that once a *fakir* (singing minstrel) came to the Khans' Peshawar household seeking food and some alms. Fixing his gaze on Yusuf, he loudly declared, 'This child is made for great fame and unparalleled achievements. Take good care of the boy, and protect him from the world's evil eye.' The entire household sat up and took notice of the prophetic words.

Haji Mohammed Khan's family was traditional and deeply religious, yet pragmatic and practical. All the girls in the family were educated and could at least read and write Urdu. Haji Mohammed himself was very fond of the Persian language and spoke the same at home, often reading aloud from his collection of Persian books and then interpreting those passages in Hindko for the children. Apparently, it is from his grandfather, who loved poetry, that Yusuf inherited and developed his love of poetry and sher-o-shayri, which he uses frequently in his conversations. While the rugged terrain and cultural ethos of Peshawar tempered Yusuf Khan's character, the thespian owes his peerless proficiency in many languages (Pashto, Hindko, Hindi, Urdu and English), and also in literature and fine arts, to the educative atmosphere in his house, but particularly to the literary penchant of his grandfather.

His father Ghulam Mohammed Sarwar Khan was a prosperous fruit merchant, who decided to migrate to Mumbai (then Bombay in Maharashtra) in 1926, seeking more lucrative fortunes in the emerging commercial capital of India. He rented premises on the fourth floor of a building at Nagdevi Street, close to his shop at Crawford Market (now known as the Jyotiba Phule Market). He came with peaches from Peshawar, pears from Kandahar, grapes from Kabul, and his six sons and two daughters. In Mumbai, he added Alphonso mangoes from Ratnagiri, figs from Pune (then Poona), chikoos from Golwad, and four more daughters. But, the city's fast pace and its humid weather suffocated this Pathan family from the North-West Frontier Province. Besides, Ghulam Sarwar's wife Ayesha Begum, and one of their children, Ayub, kept poor health. At the advice of their family doctor, one Dr Parmar, the Khans shifted to Deolali, a sort of hill station (and also a military cantonment) located around 65 kms from Mumbai. Yusuf was enrolled at the prestigious Barnes School where he also learnt to play football, one of his favourite games.

The story of Dilip Kumar reads like a novel of a bygone age. As a child, Yusuf was a mischievous but natural leader. In his school, the children fell into two groups–one led by brother Nasir, and the other by Yusuf. Initially, everyone would join Nasir's group. But, Yusuf would be so boisterous–inventing all kinds of entertainment–that ultimately, he would win them all over. Ghulam Sarwar, himself only a matriculate and a classmate of Raj Kapoor's grandfather Lala Basheshar, was very particular about educating his children. They would cycle to school each day.

Yusuf joined the Anjuman-E-Islam School (founded by Badruddin Tyabji, the third President of the Indian National Congress) located opposite the Chhatrapati Shivaji Terminus (then the Victoria Terminus Station) and close enough from Sarwar Khan's shop at Crawford Market. He was fluent in English, Persian and Urdu, but an irregular student. His attendance record was filled with late marks. He spent his evenings at the Azad Maidan, playing hockey or football. His pocket money was spent on *falooda* at the Badshah Cold Drink House or on an English movie. In school, he befriended another young boy who was to become his most consistent co-star, Mukri. Actually, Mukri's elder brother was Yusuf's classmate. After matriculation, he moved to Wilson College, where he joined its literary society. His voracious reading habit improved his English and his essays were often cited as examples to emulate. His academic record, however, was indifferent. One of his classmates at the college was Ajit Merchant, who later became a well-known film critic. For intermediate, Yusuf shifted to Khalsa College where he played football for the college. There, he met the famous hockey player Ved Puri, who later worked under him as his secretary. Yusuf, whenever possible, tried to employ his old classmates.

Crawford Market

Deolali Railway Station

Barnes School

***

Deolali is the Khans and the Khans are Deolali. Every member of the Yusuf Khan's family talks of it. The older members remember it fondly and pass on the stories to the next generation. At Deolali, a railway line lay in front of the Khan bungalow. In the backyard, were an Australian spotted cow called Quest, a goat–named Bade Miyan–, buffaloes and a poultry farm. A black cobra was spotted going around the garden after midnight–thrice. Their neighbours said he guarded the ailing Ayub. After the cobra's rounds, often came a blind man singing bhajans, and then, in the early morning light, galloped a six-horse cart carrying fresh milk, butter and cream for the nearby army camp. Every fortnight a train, the Victoria Mail with its red, blue and green wagons, pulled up at Deolali. The family called it 'Father' for on it Ghulam Sarwar came from Mumbai, laden with fruits, *mithai*, dry fruits and a variety of toys. The family left the place just before the Second World War. Dilip Saheb once recalled to me, 'This *mohalla* of my childhood is where I have known immense happiness. Everything is a part of that happiness, the Dharna river, the trees, this almost desolate, brown landscape of Deolali and you want to go back to it.' Ghulam Sarwar's seventeen grandchildren know almost everything about the place. While Dilip Kumar's brothers like Nasir and Noor made the mistake of going back to the place and faced the inevitable disillusionment, he himself has been wise. When he wants to go back, he just jogs the vivid memory of the place.

In 1937, when the Second World War clouds began to loom large, the British Government promptly declared Deolali as a military cantonment; the British Army and the governmental agencies took over most of the buildings. Sarwar Khan's bungalow was among them. So, the family again shifted to Mumbai and rented a residence on Pali–Mala road in Bandra (West), a place not so far from the iconic Pali Hills Bungalow Dilip Kumar later bought for himself. At the time, Dilip Kumar was around 15 years old but had not seen even a single film by then.

Anyone dealing in commodities during the wartime should have made a fast buck, more so, Sarwar Khan as he sold the most important of commodities, that is, fruits. But, his business began to decline, primarily due to the lack of availability of transportation in those times. The number of available wagons dwindled from four to five wagons a day to two wagons a week. The stored fruits started rotting and had to be converted into marmalades and jams but that could not fill in the gap. Eventually, the fruits began to be distributed to the villagers or were just thrown away. The Khans lost heavily in their own orchards as well as those they had contracted. Dilip Saheb recalls those testing times saying, 'Our business was sold and so were our houses in Peshawar and Deolali... and the ornaments too... all of them. We could visibly see the distress in the family. My father began to do less lucrative businesses like dealing in onions but his heart was not in it.'

Young Yusuf had to take the tough decision of quitting studies and start working to contribute to the family kitty. He dropped out of college and joined the military contractors, Wazir Mohammad & Sons, in Pune as an assistant manager at a then princely salary of ₹36 per month. While working, he took the permission of the owners to open his own fruit stall in the British barracks canteen and sell fresh fruits to the British Army personnel and their families. The fruit stall made a profit of ₹22, nearly two-thirds his monthly salary on the first day itself. He further boosted the income of the stall by additionally selling tea and coffee along with sandwiches on Dancing Nights. In a short time, Yusuf started making a ₹1000 a month. Nothing exciting happened for him in Pune otherwise, except that he met a palmist who told him he would be a *Nat.* Yusuf couldn't get the word. He spent many sleepless nights wondering what the palmist meant, until one day when a friend told him that *Nat* in Hindi means *Abhineta* (an actor). Later, an ordinance that allowed only government contractors to sell in the army canteen brought all this to an end. But, Yusuf returned home on Eid, richer by several thousand rupees. Thus, Dilip Kumar, who later became one of the highest-paid Indian stars, started his working life with exactly ₹36 a month.

***

Wilson College

At this juncture, it may be worthwhile to recapitulate the filial affiliations of Dilip Kumar. As mentioned, he was the fifth–born among thirteen siblings. The first-born was a girl named Sakina Begum who remained unmarried all her life and looked after the kith and kin as a matriarch. She was addressed as *Aapa ji.* At one time, she was engaged to be married but developed some strange skin disease which resulted in the engagement being called off. Noor Mohammed was the second child who later assisted his father in the family fruit business. Although Yusuf respected him, he could never become close to him. The initially cordial relationship soured with time leading to eventual estrangement. The third–born was a son Ayub–a sensitive and physically fragile person. He went on to become a thinker, a poet and a very well-read man and was Dilip's friend, philosopher and guide. Ayub also wrote the script of a film titled *'Kala Aadmi'* (to be directed by Ramesh Saigal with music by Madan Mohan) but that was not to be. After an accident at a hill station, Ayub's health deteriorated and he died of kidney failure on 10 March 1954, which shattered Dilip. A girl was born after Ayub but she died in early childhood. Yusuf Khan was the next in the lineage followed by Nasir Khan, who also became an actor. He was seen in films like *Mazdoor, Nagina, Daera, Angaarey, Gunga Jumna*, etc. Nasir fell in love with Suraiya, a cousin of the legendary film maker K. Asif, and married her. The couple had a daughter named Naheed, who was given a break in films by the great Dev Anand (Nasir's friend). However, the Nasir Khan–Suraiya marriage did not last and they got divorced. Nasir later married the 'Oomph Girl' actress Begum Para (of *Shabnam* and *Kismat Ka Khel* fame). Actor Ayub Khan, currently seen on Television shows, is their son and he later married his cousin (daughter of Yusuf's sister Fauzia). Around 1948, Nasir Khan temporarily migrated to Pakistan and starred in the first Pakistani movie titled *Tere Liye* but hastily returned to India. Later down the years Nasir wvKhan and Begum Para launched a film titled *Zid,* starring Saira Banu and Sanjay Khan. During the film's shooting in Kulu Manali, Nasir died of a massive heart attack on 2 May 1976.

Nasir was followed by sister Taj (Mumtaz)–and two brothers, Ahsan (who has remained unmarried and produced a film titled Sangat) and Aslam (who migrated long ago to the US but returned when he and his American wife broke up). Another sister Akhtar came next, who in later years became the third wife (the first two being Sitara Devi and Nigar Sultana) of the legendary filmmaker K. Asif of Mughal-E-Azam fame. Three sisters followed Akhtar. First was Sayeeda, who married filmmaker Mehbbob Khan's son Iqbal but subsequently separated from him. Farida was next, who worked for the magazine Femina for some years and later went to New York; while the third and the youngest was Fouzia, who later became Mrs. Dilip Surve.

Dilip with Brothers Noor, Aslam and Ahsan

Dilip Kumar married the famous star, actress and 'Beauty Queen', Saira Banu, who is the daughter of star-actress Naseem Banu of Pari Chehra fame. But more about that legendary marriage later.

Dilip with Sisters Sakina, Sayeeda and Taj

CHAPTER 2

THE EVOLUTION OF DILIP KUMAR

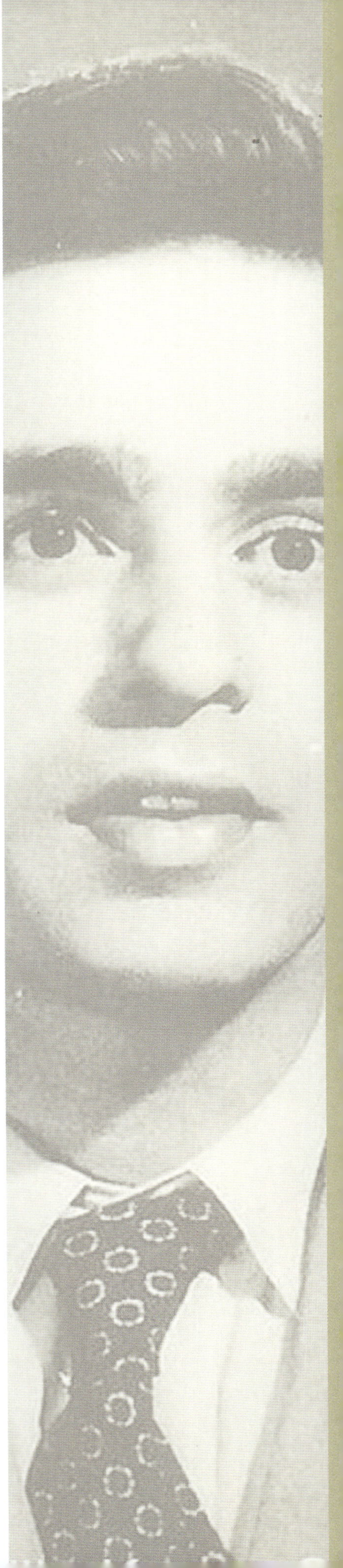

With Yusuf Khan back in Mumbai and his Pune sojourn over, his major goal was to get gainfully employed or target new avenues of earning to share the family burden. He was blissfully unaware that lady luck was about to smile on him. The turn of events propitiously sequenced by providence was to catapult young Yusuf Khan into Dilip Kumar, the megastar of the then Bombay Film Industry now dubbed as Bollywood.

There are many versions of Dilip Kumar's entry in the film industry but we shall recount here only the version we believe is the most authentic. Yusuf commenced his endeavours in the city by helping his Agha ji in his fruits business. His ageing father was becoming rather frail, so Yusuf started travelling to the orchards in the hilly regions of Dehradun and Nainital in north India. Little did the young man know that one of these trips would be his springboard to filmdom and that too with the iconic Bombay Talkies Studios of Mumbai! This was circa 1943.

Bombay Talkies was among the three legendary film studios of the country in that era–Prabhat Studios in Pune and New Theatres Studios, Kolkata (then Calcutta) were the other two. Bombay Talkies was founded by the scion of a wealthy Bengali family and London-trained lawyer Himansu Rai around mid-1930s. The studio employed well-trained British, German and Indian technicians and churned out highly successful and path-breaking films like *Achhut Kanya* (1936), *Kangan* (1939), *Bandhan* (1940), *Jhoola* (1941), *Basant* (1942), *Kismet* (1943), etc. Devika Rani, daughter of the surgeon-general of Chennai (then Madras), Colonel M.N. Chowdhury and a niece of Rabindranath Tagore, was a student of the Royal Academy of Dramatic Arts, London where she met Himansu Rai who invited her to work in his films. Devika Rani thus became the First Lady of Indian Screen. The two later got married. She acted in his films and together they founded the studio in 1935 as a joint stock company with a then huge capital base of ₹ 25 lakh. It was established on the site of F.E. Dinshaw's sprawling summer mansion in the then far-flung Mumbai suburb of Malad. The studio was designed and equipped on modern lines, complete with sound and echo-proof stages, automated laboratory, editing rooms, preview theatre, a carpentry workshop and plenty of facilities for artists and the administrative staff. The German technicians who had worked with Rai on *Light of Asia*, *Shiraz* and *A Throw of Dice* were brought together to supervise production and to train local talent. Franz Osten directed all the early Bombay Talkies films, while Hartley from Britain was the sound technician and Zollee the laboratory technician. Equipped with the latest machinery and manned by a highly-skilled staff, Bombay Talkies set a standard in technical excellence unsurpassed by any other studio at that time. Unfortunately, Himansu Rai died of a nervous breakdown at the age of 48 in 1940. The studio's reins then shifted to Devika Rani, and by 1943 when Dilip Kumar was discovered, she was the boss. Incidentally, Bombay Talkies became the grooming ground of the greatest names of filmdom including actors Ashok Kumar, Dilip Kumar, Raj Kapoor, Dev Anand, Kishore Sahu; filmmakers Shashdhar (S.) Mukerji, Amiya Chakrabarty, Nitin Bose, Gyan Mukherjee, N.R. Acharya; writers Babu Bhagwati Charan Varma, Niranjan Pal, Saadat Hasan Manto, Pt. Narendra Sharma, Krishan Chandar; and music directors Saraswati Devi, Ramchandra Pal, Anil Biswas and S.N. Tripathi just to name a few.

The iconic Bombay Talkies Studios

It so happened that by a quirk of fate while Devika Rani and director Amiya Chakrabarty were location hunting in Nainital, Yusuf also was in the same hill station for a business deal. He had a chance meeting with Devika Rani and Amiya Chakrabarty and the lady liked his tall handsome pathani looks as did Chakrabarty. Yusuf was shocked that superstar Devika Rani was taking an interest in him. She gave him her card, saying, 'Do call on me when you return to Bombay as I wish to discuss something with you.' Back in Mumbai, Yusuf was advised by his father to seek advice from one Dr Masani, a close family friend. Yusuf, in course of his conversation with Dr Masani, casually mentioned his meeting with Devika Rani in Nainital. Dr Masani, who was the personal physician of Devika Rani and her late husband as well as a family friend, advised Yusuf to meet her and offered to take him to Bombay Talkies. To cut a long story short, Devika Rani and Amiya Chakrabarty took Yusuf's screen test and subsequently signed him up for *Jwar Bhata* (1944) at a then astronomical monthly salary of ₹1000 plus ₹200 as war allowance. Rest, as they say, is history. Incidentally, Yusuf's close friend and legendary actor-director Raj Kapoor was also then employed with Bombay Talkies as an apprentice at a meagre monthly salary of ₹140 only, and he even played a bit role in *Jwar Bhata*. Dilip Saheb reminisces, 'Bombay Talkies was the best thing that happened to me at that juncture in my life. I couldn't have found a better job than the one offered to me by Devika Rani". One of the first Bombay Talkies employees to whom Yusuf was introduced was the production manager Hitendra Chowdhury who later had a lifetime friendship with the megastar.

Devika Rani

Once Yusuf was formally inducted in to the Bombay Talkies, the studio think-tank emphasised that he be given a different and more appropriate screen name. This pleased Yusuf as

Bhagwati Charan Varma

the new name would keep his joining films under wraps and Agha*ji* who disliked filmi people would not discover his son's real profession. The celebrated littérateur Bhagwati Charan Varma suggested three alternative names—Jehangir, Vasudev and Dilip Kumar. Almost intuitively and instantly, Yusuf opted for the now famous screen name of Dilip Kumar.

Devika Rani saw to it that young Dilip got the right grooming within the Bombay Talkies Studios under the tutelage of its exceedingly talented experts that were the best in the Industry. Strict discipline was enforced in the studio in terms of punctuality and adherence to the curriculum of training and work execution. Dilip Kumar was exposed to all elements of movie production which became invaluable for him. He rubbed shoulders with legends like Ashok Kumar, S. Mukerji, Gyan Mukerjee, Frank Austen and his first director Amiya Chakrabarty. Dilip Saheb recalls in his autobiography that the best and most useful acting tip he received was from Ashok *bhaiyya* (as he addressed Ashok Kumar), 'You are a handsome man and I can see that you are eager to learn. It is very simple. You just do what you would do in the situation if you are actually in it. If you act it will be acting and it will look very silly.' On his rapport with the great Ashok Kumar, Dilip Saheb adds, 'I met him every day and he treated me like a younger brother who had to be led and protected. My shyness and reticence began to recede in his company and his friendliness and affection for me were a fillip for me to be on the sets while the shooting of *Kismet* was going on.' Dilip got an opportunity to watch Ashok Kumar perform on the sets of the then under-production film *Kismet* which was a great education for him. The best talents were employed by the studio, each a master of his or her own field. They would all sit together and share their thoughts and exchange views on the songs, dialogue, music, filmmaking, camera handling, editing, direction, lighting, etc. It was a stimulating experience for young Dilip who got to learn about filmmaking in all its varied facets including, of course, acting.

Dilip, Ashok Kumar and Raj Kapoor

Ashok Kumar introduced Dilip Kumar to his brother-in-law S. Mukerji, a doyen of filmmaking who later founded of the iconic studios—Filmistan and Filmalaya—and made innumerable box office hits. Dilip Saheb's proficiency in the Urdu language came handy in impressing Mukerji, an intelligent, well-read and polished gentleman, who taught him finer nuances of filmmaking. Dilip Saheb regaled Ashok Kumar and S. Mukerji with Urdu as well as Farsi (Persian) verses after pack-up. A deeply impressed S. Mukerji then insisted on Dilip participating in the story-dialogue sessions of the studio with legends like Amiya Chakrabarty, Gyan Mukherjee, Krishan Chandar and others. This experience was very enriching for the young Dilip. He got the *mool mantra* (basic principles) of emoting effectively which was that he would have to arrive at the business of simulating feelings and conveying emotions on his own. Seeds of the evolution of the later much-eulogised Dilipian brand of histrionics were sown. Surprisingly, until this point in time, Dilip Kumar had not seen a single full-length Hindi feature film. At the advice of S. Mukerji, Dilip started viewing movies particularly those made in Hollywood. He especially liked the performances of legendary actors and actresses like Paul Muni, Clark Gable, Ingrid Bergman, Jimmy Stewart, Charles Laughton, etc. Studying their acting styles by minute observation, Dilip Kumar got ample exposure to the different approaches of the past masters of the craft and began shaping his own acting methods.

S. Mukerji

After this protracted training stint, Dilip Kumar finally donned make-up for the first time and started shooting for his debut film *Jwar Bhata* in May 1943, under the expert watchful eyes of director Amiya Chakrabarty. The evolution of the actor Dilip Kumar had commenced.

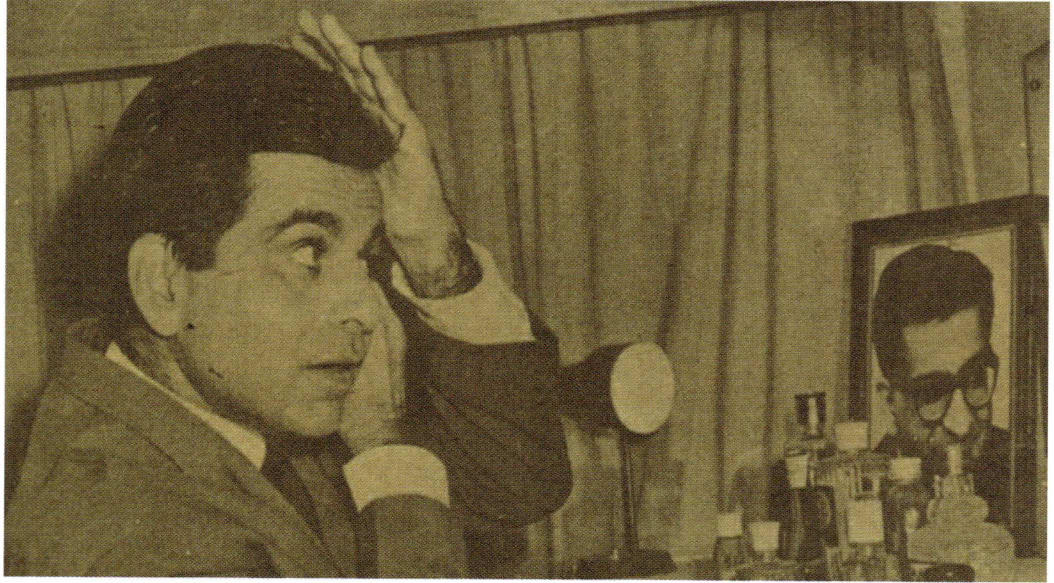

Dilip Kumar in His Make-up Room

In a candid interview published by *Filmfare* on 17 January 1969, Dilip Saheb went on to state the following regarding the evolutionary phase of his career:

> **'In Bombay Talkies where I started my career, we had to do much more than just don make-up and report for work. We had to frequently and often repeatedly see good films, discuss the work of other artistes, read books on acting, drama, criticism. We were all a very close-knit family—writers, directors, producers, technicians and artistes. Often there would be a lively debate and we could always take our problems to our more experienced seniors. Those institutions are, alas, no more. Filmmaking today has become the forte of dealmakers. Younger artistes are being nurtured in a highly mercenary and ruthless climate. They are relatively smarter and shrewder than we were but their efforts are stunted and they fail to set new standards of their own. The number of assignments is today considered an actor's prestige symbol.'**

CHAPTER 3

THE HISTRIONIC SPLENDOUR OF THE INCREDIBLE ACTOR AND HIS MAGNIFICENT MOVIES

Dilipian films have always celebrated some paradoxical theme which invariably showcased a unique blend of interplay of emotions and conflict of characters. The captivating appeal of the narrative was unmatched in its profundity. Accentuating this enigmatic charm was Dilip Kumar's impactful facial anatomy, magical dialogue delivery in whispered tones, emphasis of lucid gestures and those tousled hair which made the moviegoers swoon in sheer admiration. His face had a mirror-like honesty in which generations of fans found a reflection of their own emotions. Dilip Kumar's histrionic triumphs exuded a prismatic emotive brilliance in very carefully chosen roles. Dilip Saheb created a myriad set of vividly cubistic portrayals of utterly credible onscreen characters and engineered his own growth beyond perfection. He had developed his own brand of complex histrionics while mastering the art of spectroscopic projection of emotions. He gave emotions a colour and humour a rare subtlety, raising the level of acting to that of a fine art. He is the actor of actors who personified the yearnings, joys and sorrows of the people to exercise a magnetic command on and off screen.

There are characters played by actors who are eventually consumed by them. Then there are actors that consume the very character they play. Dilip Kumar is blessed with the uncanny knack of reaching right beneath the skin of the character and absorbing its traits imbued in its internal landscape and assimilate/absorb the entire gamut of its personal attributes within him. With such an extensive preparation, he then literally explodes on the screen, projecting the character with incredible conviction and clarity of expression. Dilip delineates the characters with such fluid lucidity that they remain unforgettably etched in the memory of cinemagoers. Dilip Kumar's characterisations have never been larger than life; rather they have been utterly humane, down-to-earth and real. The actor dissolved himself in the character so imperceptibly that the differentiation between the actor and his character became difficult. For example, the viewers of *Devdas* (1955) left the theatre overwhelmed with Dilip's masterly portrayal of the protagonist. For them, Dilip is Devdas and Devdas is Dilip. So much so that when they read Sarat Chandra Chattopadhyay's classic book, the emerging image of Devdas unquestionably is that of Dilip (and not of a K.L. Saigal or Pramathesh Barua or Shah Rukh Khan). Dilip has played all his characters with immense ease and ingenuity. Be it the silently-suffering lover in *Andaaz* (1949); the twinkle-eyed postmaster of *Babul* (1950); the lovelorn doctor of *Tarana* (1951); the blind singer of *Deedar* (1951); the aggressive chieftain who tames a wild, haughty princess in *Aan* (1952); the lust-driven coward of *Amar* (1954); the dark-eyed doomed Heathcliff in *Arzoo* (1950), *Hulchul* (1951), *Dil Diya Dard Liya* (1966); the frustrated zamindar in *Shikast* (1953), the depressed alcoholic in *Daag* (1952), the Robin Hood of *Azaad* (1955); the pathos-filled lover of *Devdas;* the intense rustic of *Insaniyat* (1955); the voice of the downtrodden in *Naya Daur* (1957); the dying lover of *Musafir* (1957); the star-crossed lover of *Madhumati* (1958); the deeply-involved Jewish prince of *Yahudi* (1958); the rebellious prince in the epic *Mughal-E-Azam* (1960); the principled union leader of *Paigham* (1959); the dare-devil prince in *Kohinoor* (1960); the honest villager-turned-dacoit of *Gunga Jumna* (1961); the charming, frolicsome Vijay Khanna in *Leader* (1964); the ebullient Shyam and gloomy Ram in *Ram Aur Shyam* (1967); the tycoon lover with split personality in *Aadmi* (1968); the conscience-burdened lover of *Sunghursh* (1968); the iron-willed trade union leader in *Sagina* (1974); the village idiot devoted to his elder brother in *Gopi* (1970); the tougher-than-nails DCP of *Shakti* (1982). The list is endless. No actor on either side of the Suez Canal has essayed such a variety of roles with such dextrous aplomb.

All the above listed roles are landmarks of acting prowess in the annals of Indian motion pictures. Dilip's long film career is replete with myriad acting accomplishments, which themselves represent a celebration of the very best in Indian cinema. His portrayals resonated in the minds of audiences as it wasn't just the character he played that appealed to our cinematic sensibility but also his sincerity that reached straight to our hearts. His fabled dialogue delivery–lowered at times to a mere whisper with telling effect–contained a multitude of bewildering vocalisations which were proficiently incorporated to suit every portrayal. His stylistic technique has been subtle yet suffused with potent weaponry to send many a heart a-flutter. A lean build, an intense countenance, piercingly communicative eyes, skilled voice modulations, the unrivalled ability to effortlessly express pain and pleasure, an engagingly disarming smile all contributed to the incandescent persona of Dilip Kumar. There are examples galore of the thespian's sheer magical brilliance contained in numerous scenes craftily enacted by him. As per us, following are the top thirty acting milestones (a scene or a song sequence) in the thespians illustrious film career:

1 The staircase confrontation with Raj Kapoor in *Andaaz.*
2 *Mera jeevan saathi bichhad gaya* in *Babul.*
3 The jail scene with Leela Chitnis in *Shaheed.*
4 *Huey hum jinke liye barbaad* in *Deedar.*
5 The secluded picnic episode with Madhubala in *Tarana.*

6. *Yeh hawa yeh raat yeh chandni* in *Sangdil.*
7. The rape scene in *Amar.*
8. *Aye dil mujhe aisi jagah* in *Arzoo.*
9. The drunken altercation with screen mother Lalita Pawar in *Daag.*
10. *Takra gaya tum se dil hi to hai* in *Aan.*
11. His dialogue *'Jis dil mein aag lagi ho, wo waqt nahin dekhta Shobha'* in a scene with Meena Kumari in *Azaad.*
12. His dialogue *'Na jaane kitna dukh hua tou maine peena shuru kiya'* in a scene with Vyjayantimala in *Devdas*
13. The death scene with Shobhna Samarth in *Insaniyat.*
14. His powerful dialogue *'Hamara tumhara kaisa jhagda babu, yeh jhagda toh haath aur machine ka hai'* in a scene with actor Jeevan in *Naya Daur.*
15. *Toote huey khwabon ne* in *Madhumati.*
16. *Yeh mera deewanapan hai* in *Yahudi.*
17. The pond-side romantic interludes with Vyjayantimala in *Paigham.*
18. The mirror imitation scene with Jeevan in *Kohinoor.*
19. The confrontations with Prithviraj Kapoor and Durga Khote in *Mughal-E-Azam.*
20. The banter with Vyjayantimala, *'In haathon mein bhi...'* in *Gunga Jumna.*
21. The Udaipur lake sequences with Vyjayantimala and the *'Mujhe duniyawalon sharabi na'* scene in *Leader.*
22. His dialogue *'Dil ne bahut dhokhe diye hain ab dimaag se kaam leta hoon'* with Waheeda Rehman, Shyama and Rehman in *Dil Diya Dard Liya.*
23. The Kodaikanal love scenes with Waheeda Rehman and breakfast confrontation scene with Pran in *Ram Aur Shyam.*
24. The *'Teen ka dibba'* banter with Waheeda Rehman and his dialogue scene *'Mat socho ki tum ek aadmi ho'* in *Aadmi.*
25. His dialogue *'Jiyo Dwarka, kya cheez pilai hai'* banter with Vyjayantimala in *Sunghursh.*
26. The 'Gentleman, Gentleman' sequence with Saira Bano, Om Prakash, Nirupa Roy and Lalita Pawar in *Gopi.*
27. The–restaurant card game–scene in *Dastaan.*
28. The–public meeting–scene in *Sagina.*
29. The–Lover's Point/Lands End–sequence with Amitabh Bachchan in *Shakti.*
30. The rivulet side challenge to Raaj Kumar in *Saudagar.*

The list, again, is endless. We can cite a hundred other equally powerful scenes. They all ooze pure celluloid magnificence. How unforgettable is the scene in *Devdas* where the hopeless alcoholic protagonist, who is on the threshold of his death, asks, *'Aur kitni door hai gadiwale'* (How far is the destination, driver?). A simple dialogue, delivered with such intensity of pain, turmoil and undying hope of being able to see his beloved one last time before death devours him. In fact, some of the characters played by him like in the films *Ram Aur Shyam, Amar, Devdas, Musafir, Daag,* etc., are inimitable. It would be sacrilegious to even consider attempting to recreate his powerhouse performances in original films. It has now become fashionable to reproduce his films in Bollywood, which is fast running out of ideas. They rationalise such gratuitous attempts and call it personal interpretation. With all due respect, any such endeavour is futile because grandiose cannot replace authenticity. So, let's just politely accept these as nothing but amateurish tributes to Dilip Saheb.

There are so many words one can use to describe a good actor but when you start running out of words the actor obviously is not merely good but great. When you think of Hollywood greats, names like Clark Gable, Humphrey Bogart, Gary Cooper, Cary Grant, Gregory Peck, Marlon Brando, Peter O' Toole, Sean Connery, Dustin Hoffman, Robert De Niro and Jack Nicholson reflexively spring to mind. Each of these great actors embodied distinctive attributes. A brief elucidation of these mammoth giants of the American film industry, clearly outlines their exclusive stylistic attributes:

Clark Gable: Charming and incredibly handsome. He often played the hero that tamed the shrew (*Gone With The Wind, It Started in Naples*).
Humphrey Bogart: Ruggedly handsome, "Bogey", (to his fans) has been ranked as the greatest male star of American cinema and a brilliant stage actor, who charmed the viewers with his magical screen presence and overpowering zeal to perform (*Casablanca, To Have or Have Not, Big Sleep, Sabrina*).
Gary Cooper: Stylish American actor known for his natural, authentic, understated acting style and screen performances (*High Noon, Meet John Doe, Desire, Love in the Afternoon*).
Cary Grant: The English-American actor, known as one of classic Hollywood's definitive leading men, became known for his transatlantic accent, debonair demeanour, light-hearted approach to acting, and sense of comic timing. (*Philadelphia Story, Suspicion, North by North West, To Catch a Thief, Charade*).
Gregory Peck: Subtlety was the name of the game for him, the one with that famous arched brow (*To Kill a Mockingbird, Man in the Gray Flannel Suit, Roman Holiday*).
Marlon Brando: Iconic American actor and film director regarded for his cultural influence on the 20th-century films (*On the Water Front, A Street Car Named Desire, The Saboteur, Julius Caesar, Godfather*).
Peter O'Toole: British–Scottish actor known for memorable performances rendered with panache and engaging realism (*Lawrence of Arabia, Beckett, How to Steal a Million, Goodbye Mr. Chips*).
Sean Connery: The suave, polished, magnetic and stylish Scottish actor known as the best ever 'James Bond' (*Dr No, To Russia With Love, Goldfinger, Thunderball, Marnie, The Man who Would be King*).
Dustin Hoffman: His face was expressionless like Lake Placid but one could feel the bubbling frustration seething within his core (*The Graduate, Rain man*). He surprised the world with his comic genius in *Tootsie*.
Robert De Niro: He epitomised Martin Scorsese's street violence, playing the neurotic unsung hero of the masses (*Taxi Driver*), Mafia King (*Goodfellas*), Psychotic killer (*Cape Fear*), etc.
Jack Nicholson: American actor and filmmaker known for playing a wide range of roles, including satirical comedy, romance, and dark portrayals of anti-heroes and villainous characters (*One Flew Over Cuckoo's Nest, China Town, Bucket List, As Good as It Gets*).

We all know these great performances and these actors' accomplishments which catapulted them to worldwide fame. These are the stars of the west but in the east we have our own sun shining as brightly as ever on the horizon in the names and styles of greats like Ashok Kumar, Motilal, Balraj Sahani, Yaqoob, Pran, Dev Anand, Raj Kapoor down to Shammi Kapoor, Amitabh Bachchan, Sanjeev Kumar, Aamir Khan, et al.

Imagine an amalgamation of all the earlier-mentioned acting talents and their emotive attributes and the result would be Dilip Kumar as an actor, who deserves all the adjectives you can think of in his praise–a star, a thespian, a matinee idol, a crowd-puller and, last but not the least, a peerless performer in every sense of the word. His amazing forte as an actor has inspired the lives of many. His sublime portrayals are engraved in our cinematic memory. His powerful screen presence is no less (and in fact even more overpowering) than an Ashok Kumar, a Robert De Niro or a Dustin Hoffman or any actor worth his salt. When he first emerged as an actor, overtly dramatic acting was ubiquitous in the industry. Dilip Kumar developed his own natural style, which was path-breaking in its originality and stunningly effective on celluloid.

Economics of movement on screen is the hallmark of Dilipian histrionics. His face mirrored the emotions and the eyes effortlessly conveyed them. He could establish an instant rapport with his audiences merely with a hint of a knitting of eye brows–a brooding gaze–a twitch of a lip quiver or just a dejected walk. Only Dilip Kumar knew how best to convey internal turmoil and emotional pathos of his characters without shedding a tear or welling up of eyes. As far as his impeccable comic timing is concerned, the actor never stooped to raise a laugh or two–the endearing mirth came as effortlessly as the depth of tragic emotions.

Dilip Kumar's talent is a school in itself and he has had innumerable imitators over past six decades. The list of imitators is endless from film stars like Rajinder Kumar, Manoj Kumar, Rajesh Khanna, Amitabh Bachchan, Shah Rukh Khan, etc. The Dilipian method of acting has become an inseparable part of Bollywood histrionics–scripts are written structuring scenes in a manner that would facilitate today's performers to relate them to previous Dilipian celluloid triumphs that still go down so well with movie buffs. Dilip Kumar is an institution for acquiring cinematic excellence and would remain the alma matar of all budding and established talents for all time to come. Amusingly, some time ago, the Al-Mansoor video of Dubai had released a VHS/DVD titled 'Copy Cat Amitabh', which showed Dilip Kumar's influence on Amitabh's performances. Imitation of acting mannerisms apart, numerous scenes from Dilip Kumar films have often been copied in various later movies; for example, the mirror scene in *Kohinoor* was copied in *Amar Akbar Anthony* (1977) and *Kasme Vade* (1977) and the famous Amitabh death scene in *Deewar* (1975) is an unabashed rehash of Dilip Kumar's death scene in *Insaniyat* (1955). Several films have liberally borrowed the basic structure of scenes from Dilip Kumar's iconic movies.

In an era when egos have more often than not prevented performers from openly pitting their talents against equally proficient actors, Dilip never ever shied away from crossing histrionic swords with contemporary star performers. Thus, it was a treat to watch such emotive rivalry on screen with him taking on Ashok Kumar (*Deedar*), Dev Anand (*Insaniyat*), Raj Kapoor (*Andaaz*), Chandra Mohan (*Shaheed*), Motilal (*Devdas, Paigham*), Yaqub (*Hulchul*), Jayant (*Amar, Sunghursh*), Balraj Sahani (*Hulchul, Sunghursh*), Raaj Kumar (*Paigham, Saudagar*), Manoj Kumar (*Aadmi*), Pran (*Madhumati, Dil Diya Dard Liya, Ram Aur Shyam* and *Aadmi*),Sanjeev Kumar (*Sunghursh, Vidhaata*) and Amitabh Bachchan (*Shakti*), etc.

From the initial phase of his career itself, Dilip Kumar set very high standards in terms of acting and overall presentation as well as the appeal of his films. *Milan* (his third film) onwards, release of a Dilip Kumar starrer would be a major cinematic event with his countless fans waiting for his films with bated breath and expectations building up to a crescendo. To be associated with a Dilip starrer became a status symbol for artists, directors, producers, music directors, scriptwriters, cinematographers, et al. Obviously, Dilip had to be very choosy in selecting scripts, co-stars and technical crews, so as to ensure maintaining the high standards he had set out to achieve in his movies.

Critical acclaim, public adulation and commercial success have always courted Dilip. His movies (with a very few exceptions) were major hits not only at the time of their original releases, but also in repeat runs. We remember *Gunga Jumna* celebrating a silver jubilee during its umpteenth re-release at Prakash Cinema (Varanasi, Uttar Pradesh) in 1970-71 and *Leader* doing huge business in numerous repeat runs. It may be pertinent to recapitulate the success story of the Dilipian films as tabulated:

S. No.	Category	Movies
1.	SUPERHITS (17 films with Golden Jubilees)	*Jugnu, Shaheed, Shabnam, Nadiya Ke Paar, Mela, Andaaz, Babul, Deedar, Aan, Azaad, Naya Daur, Madhumati, Paigham, Gunga Jumna, Ram Aur Shyam, Sagina Mahato* and *Kranti.*
2.	MAJOR HITS (13 films with Silver Jubilees)	*Milan, Daag, Uran Khatola, Amar, Insaniyat, Devdas, Kohinoor, Aadmi, Gopi, Shakti, Vidhaata, Karma* and *Saudagar.*
3.	SUCCESSES (Six films)	*Jogan, Tarana, Footpath, Yahudi, Leader* and *Sunghursh.*
4.	AVERAGE GROSSERS (Eight films)	*Jwar Bhata, Ghar Ki Izzat, Arzoo, Hulchul, Sangdil, Dil Diya Dard Liya, Bairaag, Mashaal* and *Izzatdaar.*
5.	FLOPS (12 films)	*Pratima, Anokha Pyar, Shikast, Musafir, Dastaan, Sagina, Mazdoor, Duniya, Dharm Adhikari, Kanoon Apna Apna* and *Qila.*

Table 3.1 Success of Dilipian Films.

From the earlier list, Dilip Kumar's forty-three films out of a total of fifty-seven (excluding special appearances), were successful, recording a strike rate of 75.40 per cent—a success rate still unmatched by any other star. Dilip Kumar gave his best in his films as an actor irrespective of the fate of the film. Thus, it is virtually impossible to shortlist even a dozen best performances of the peerless legend. Still, we share the posters of Dilip Kumar's films which are our favourites in terms of the thespian's performance in them:

1952

1952

1954

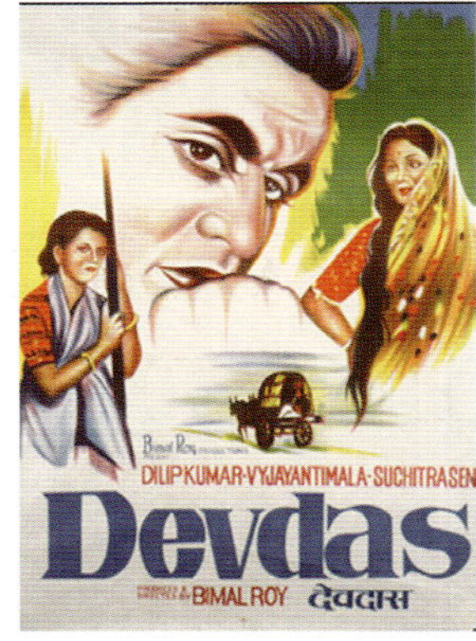

1956

1957

1958

1960

1960

1961

1967

1968

1982

The authors consider it prudent to encapsulate the salient features, thematic content and histrionic attributes of Dilipian motion pictures in this chapter. So, let's begin with the completed films of the megastar.

CHAPTER 3.1

EVOLUTION OF THE TRAGEDY KING–THE FORMATIVE FORTIES

JWAR BHATA

DATE / YEAR OF RELEASE: 1944
BANNER / PRODUCER: BOMBAY TALKIES
DIRECTION: AMIYA CHAKRABARTY
MUSIC: ANIL BISWAS
LYRICS: Pt. NARENDRA SHARMA
STORY / SCREENPLAY: AMIYA CHAKRABARTY
DIALOGUE: BHAGWATI CHARAN VERMA
CINEMATOGRAPHY: R. D. MATHUR
EDITING: J.S. DIVADKAR
CHOREOGRAPHY: MUMTAZ ALI
ART: L.H. CHORIDIA
COSTUMES: R.H. KUBAL
CAST: DILIP KUMAR / MRIDULA / SHAMIM / AGHA JAAN / K.N. SINGH / PEETHAWALA / BIKRAM KAPOOR / KHALIL / MUMTAZ ALI / ARUN KUMAR

Jwar Bhata was a Bombay Talkies' film with which several legendary luminaries were associated. The celebrated novelist Pt. Bhagwati Charan Verma (of *Chitralekha* fame) wrote the dialogue and the famous poet Pt. Narendra Sharma penned the lyrics. Amiya Chakrabarty (he made the classic *Daag* with Dilip later) directed the movie while "*Guru*" cinematographer R.D. Mathur (who also later shot the Dilip classics *Mughal-E-Azam* and *Sunghursh*) filmed the movie. Doyen composer emeritus Anil Biswas crafted the musical score.

Bombay Talkies searched for a hero and found Dilip Kumar. You can see his anaemic self in "Jwar Bhata", a social picture.

It was the keen eyes of Devika Rani who could spot the boundless talent in the handsome aspiring young actor even when he had no previous experience and hand him over to the astute director Amiya Chakrabarty (who too was a stubborn individual known for making his own decision and must have seen the spark in Dilip as well to accept him) to hone his talent and initially shape him for making celluloid history. It was also an amazing quirk of fate that the third assistant of Amiya Chakrabarty in the film was the prodigal son of the illustrious Prithviraj Kapoor–the legendary actor-producer-director-to-be Raj Kapoor. The families of Dilip Kumar and Raj Kapoor were very close (both hailing from Peshawar) with the two legends-to-be being college-mates who played football together. Raj also played a bit role in *Jwar Bhata* and it was indeed fateful that two of the greatest megastars in the film world commenced their illustrious careers together at Bombay Talkies. *Jwar Bhata* also marked the debut of comedian Mukri (erstwhile collegemate of Dilip Kumar) who continued to perform in many later Dilip Kumar film.

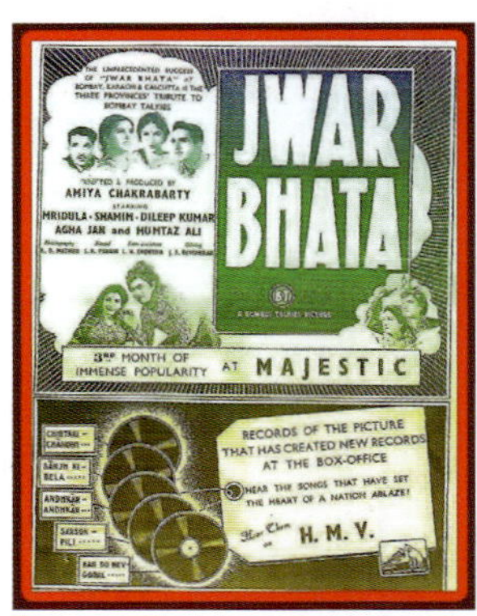

Jwar Bhata was a film with a muddled triangular romantic angle the leading lady Mridula (later a character actress), played the role of Renu, opposite Dilip Kumar's Narendra and Agha Jaan (later a famous comedian Agha) who played a dance troupe owner (Jagdish) opposite Shamim (Rama). The film prominently showcased the debut of heroine Mridula who somehow could not make much headway in the industry later.

The movie released at Bombay's Majestic Cinema on 29 November, 1944 and ran for twenty weeks. Thus, the film was a moderate success but its reviews virtually wrote Dilip Kumar off as an acting prospect–what a colossal error of judgement! The acid-pen of the powerful editor of *Film India,* Baburao Patel, was highly critical of Dilip Kumar in his review. He wrote: '**Dilip Kumar the new hero of the Bombay Talkies is an anaemic addition to our film artists. He needs to lot of vitamins and a prolonged treatment of proteins before another picture can be risked with him. He looks gaunt and famished and strikes one as a long ill-treated convict who has escaped from a jail. His appearance on the screen creates both laughter and disappointment. His acting effort in this picture amounts to nil.**'

However, *The Times of India* on 9 December 1944 noted that the film had 'some of the best acting seen on the Indian screen for years'. Today, *Jwar Bhata* is best remembered for being Dilip Kumar's debut film.

The film was embellished with music by Anil Biswas and he did come up with some enchanting numbers such as *Sanjh ki bela panchhi akela* (Arun Kumar Mukherjee), *Bhool jaana chahti hoon bhool paati nahin* (Parul Ghosh–Chitalkar), *Prabhu charanon mein deep jalao* (Parul–Ameerbai), *Sarson peeli dhaan sunehle* (Parul Ghosh–Arun Kumar), *Sa ra ra ra, Kabir Kabir udao abeer – a Holi song* (Anil Biswas) and *More aangan mein chhitki chandni* (Parul Ghosh). *Bhool jaana chahti hoon* was also sung as a solo by Parul Ghosh in the film with captivating violin/piano interludes. Composer C. Ramchandra sang (under the pseudo name Chitalkar) in the film for the first time as did the celebrated Manna Dey in the duet *Bhoola bhatka path haara* with Parul Ghosh. The exquisite title music of the film was also released on the other side of the 78 RPM disc containing the title music of *Chaar Aankhein.*

Anil Biswas

DATE / YEAR OF RELEASE: 21 JULY 1945
BANNER / PRODUCER: BOMBAY TALKIES / M. I. DHARMSEY (DESIGNATED)
DIRECTION: JAIRAJ
MUSIC: ARUN KUMAR
LYRICS: NARENDRA SHARMA
STORY: BABU BHAGWATI CHARAN VERMA
AUDIOGRAPHY: M.I. DHARMSEY
CAST: DILIP KUMAR / SWARNALATA / JYOTI / MUMTAZ ALI / PITHAWALA / MUKRI / ZEBUNISSA / SHAH NAWAZ

Despite the not-so-favourable response to *Jwar Bhata,* Devika Rani, S. Mukerji and Ashok Kumar retained their faith in Dilip Kumar. They cast him in Bombay Talkies' next venture *Pratima,* opposite the emerging star Swarnalata. Her last outing *Rattan* was a diamond jubilee hit (she later married actor S. Nazir). Originally, the think-tank of Bombay Talkies wanted to film Leo Tolstoy's *Resurrection* or Munshi Premchand's *Godaan* (adapted as a Rajput love story titled *Dussera* by writer Krishan Chandar). But the designated producer, M.I. Dharmsey, opted for a new story by Bhagwati Charan Verma titled *Pratima.* Actor Paidi Jairaj, who had made his debut in films in the last phase of silent era and was the leading man in several B-grade movies for decades, impressed the Bombay Talkies, management to become the director for the movie. In the years to come, Jairaj became a fast friend of Dilip Kumar.

Swarnalata

Pratima was based on an unusual storyline featuring two wealthy men who are fond of acquiring rare antique artefacts and outbid each other at auctions. The plot hinged around putting together of an extremely valuable artefact which is split in two parts. The wealthy men, who share a love-hate relationship, assigned a young man to find the two halves. The film was released on 21 July 1945 in Mumbai with the publicity campaign

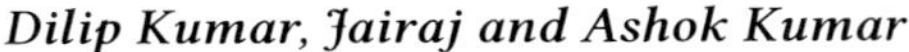

Dilip Kumar, Jairaj and Ashok Kumar

Dilip Kumar, Jairaj, M.I. Dharmsey and Swarnalata

hailing Dilip Kumar's performance saying— 'His second role will be first in your mind'. Nevertheless, the film was a damp squib at the box office. *Film India* editor Baburao Patel called the film 'a chain of still photographs stuck together for film purposes'. In his review in the magazine, Patel was again very severe on Dilip Kumar: **'Dilip Kumar seems to have gone more anaemic since his last picture. He now presents a hollow chest, limp arms, shaky legs and a woebegone look, suggesting a patient illness of several years. When a man with these looks plays the hero, it must be the end of motion picture glamour. Dilip Kumar does not act at all and we doubt whether he will ever act in future.'** This was another colossal error of judgement.

Arun Kumar, a relative of doyen Anil Biswas, scored the music of the film with songs like *Aata hai labon pe naam tera baar baar, Chand uga re man ke gagan mein, Bhool gaye tum pyas bujhana* (Parul Ghosh) and *Aayi re roop nagar ki chhori* (Arun Kumar), penned by Pt. Narendra Sharma, being moderately popular.

As mentioned earlier, the film was no great shakes at the box office, nor did it lead to any recognition for Dilip Kumar as an actor except that his intensity was noticed.

DATE / YEAR OF RELEASE: 14 JUNE 1946
BANNER / PRODUCER: BOMBAY TALKIES
DIRECTION: NITIN BOSE
MUSIC: ANIL BISWAS
LYRICS: P.L. SANTOSHI / ARZOO LUCKNOWI
PLAYBACK: PARUL GHOSH / SHANKAR DAS GUPTA
STORY: BASED ON RABINDRANATH TAGORE'S *NOUKADUBI* (THE BOAT-WRECK)
SCREENPLAY: SAJNIKANTA DAS
DIALOGUE: P.L. SANTOSHI
CINEMATOGRAPHY: R. KARMAKAR
ART: BRATIN TAGORE
EDITING: KALI RAHA
AUDIOGRAPHY: MUKUL BOSE
CAST: DILIP KUMAR / MIRA MISRA / RANJANA / PAHARI SANYAL / MONI CHATTERJEE / SHYAM LAHA

Dilip Kumar's next film for Bombay Talkies was *Milan*, which was directed by doyen Nitin Bose and co-starred Mira Misra and Ranjana. It was based on 'Gurudev' Rabindranath Tagore's story *Noukadubi* (The Boat-wreck). The film came to be heralded as a classic and years later was remade as *Ghoonghat* (1962) by Ramanand Sagar for Gemini Productions. In *Milan,* Dilip Kumar played the character of Ramesh, a youth in love with a petite and well-educated woman Hemanalini, played by actress Mira Misra. However, Ramesh is forced by his landlord father to marry some other girl chosen by him. While returning from his marriage to the girl, whom Ramesh had not yet seen, there is an accident in which their boat capsizes. Ramesh mistakenly takes another surviving bride Kamala (played by Ranjana), instead of his own, due to a misunderstanding. Kamala believes Ramesh is her husband (having never ever seen her husband before marriage). But, Ramesh knows she is not his wife as his bride had a different name. Ramesh has a perplexing dilemma since he cannot accept Kamala as his wife despite her being a willing partner. Ramesh has to find Kamala's husband while ensuring that her reputation remains immaculate. Ramesh succeeds in reuniting Kamala to her husband, simultaneously retrieving the affections of Hemanalini, who is on the verge of marrying Kamala's lost husband. It was an intriguing storyline which captivated the audiences.

Nitin Bose

As has been previously mentioned, Nitin Bose (26 April 1897–14 April 1986) was a pioneering film director, cinematographer and screenwriter of the Indian film industry. He was born in Kolkata (then Calcutta) and died in the same city. In the 1930s and early 1940s, he worked with New Theatres, which made bilingual movies–in both Bengali and Hindi. Among the notable New Theatres films were classics *Bhagya Chakra* (First Indian film with playback singing), *President, Dharti Mata, Dushman, Kapal Kundala, Lagan, Kashinath,* etc. *Bhagya Chakra* (1935) was later remade in Hindi the same year as *Dhoop Chhaon.* Kolkata had, traditionally, displayed deeper social awareness in its films than Mumbai. And New Theatres, the studio that was to Kolkata what Bombay Talkies was to Mumbai, reflected this awareness in its films, many of which were made by Nitin Bose. Bose left New Theatres owing to a misunderstanding with its owner (B.N. Sircar) and moved to Mumbai and continued direction under the banners of Bombay Talkies and Filmistan. *Milan* was made under Bose's direction for Bombay Talkies. The film succeeded and is heralded as a classic till date.

Mira Misra and Dilip Kumar in Milan

The unit of Milan

Bombay Talkies had taken a decision to make *Milan* as a bilingual (Bengali and Hindi) and had requisitioned the services of popular Bengali actor Abhi Bhattacharya in Mumbai. The Bengali version was titled *Noukadubi* and as the shooting progressed, it became obvious that the Bengali hero had no flair for Hindi diction. Nitin Bose decided to make the two versions with different leading men. Abhi was assigned *Noukadubi* as its hero and Dilip got the lead role in the Hindi version, *Milan.* Abhi, nick named Gobindo, later became a close friend of Dilip Kumar due to their common guru and Abhi's uncle, Hiten Choudhary.

As described earlier, director Nitin Bose brought out the latent histrionic of Dilip Kumar, imparting him a unique natural and intense acting style which captivated the audiences. *Milan* brought Dilip Kumar his first big box office success and recognition as an actor with many film critics lauding his natural performance. Dilip Kumar came to the fore as a sensitive natural actor of immense potential. However, inexplicably Baburao Patel drastically differed from the general opinion in his overall view of both *Milan* as well as of Dilip Kumar. The headline of Patel's review of *Milan* in the *Film India* edition on 14 June 1946 read: *"Tagore 'Wreck' Wrecked On Screen! Milan Becomes Lousy, Boring Stuff!'* Quite erroneously, the acidulous pen of Baburao Patel once again spewed venom as reproduced below:

'If you have the nerve to keep awake till the interval, you may probably see the end of *Milan* on the screen. The picture has a terrifically hypnotic value and it takes all your will power to keep your eyes open throughout the marathon lengths of the ruins of this Tagore story .... as to old Tagore, death has silenced his protest and knowing very well that dead men tell no tales, Nitin Bose can consider himself safe from reproach for wrecking "The Wreck" beyond all recognition. .... as the picture suffers badly in its two main characterisations. Dilip Kumar in the role of Ramesh and Mira Misra in the role of Karuna ruin all prospects of the picture becoming popular. In a motion picture, it is always essential that a hero should primarily look a hero whatever grim realism of life a director may seek to portray. Dilip Kumar is a heart-rending choice for the hero's role. The boy looks anaemic and though he seems to make an honest attempt to deliver the goods as an artist, he sadly fails to convince. Dilip Kumar has come to the screen with an unfortunate face and no one is going to imagine a hero's portrait on the screen with that face. Mira and Dilip Kumar, who are seen more often than the others, take all the entertainment out of the picture and *Milan* fails as an entertainer no sooner those two make an appearance. Nitin's direction of the emotional contents of the story fails miserably. The way we find Dilip Kumar constantly twitching fingers, as if constantly in epileptic convulsions. When the boy had a face on his shoulder one wonders why the fingers were used so often and so clumsily to portray inner emotions.'

We have seen *Milan* which, till date, appears to be a decent and rather well-made picture. The review of Baburao Patel was inexplicably harsh.

Noticeably, *Milan* was Anil Biswas' last film for Bombay Talkies. Anil Biswas's score with hits like *Gungun gungun bole bhanwarva* (Parul Ghosh), *Oopar hai badariya kari maujon mein hai naav hamari* (Shankar Dasgupta), *Suhani beliya beeti jaaye* (Parul Ghosh) with enchanting clarinet interludes and the *Raag Bhairavi*-based *Jisne banadi bansuri* was very well appreciated. Arzoo Lakhnavi and P.L. Santoshi penned the lyrics for *Milan.*

DATE / YEAR OF RELEASE: 2 OCTOBER 1948
BANNER / PRODUCER: SHAUKAT ART PRODUCTIONS
DIRECTION: SHAUKAT HUSSAIN RIZVI
MUSIC: FEROZ NIZAMI
LYRICS: M.G. ADEEB / ASGAR SARHADI B.A.
PLAYBACK: NOORJEHAN / MOHD. RAFI / SHAMSHAD BEGUM / ROSHAN ARA BEGUM
STORY / SCREENPLAY: A.S. USMANI
DIALOGUE: A. S.USMANI
CINEMATOGRAPHY: ISSAC
CHOREOGRAPHY: P. ENGINEER
ART: SYED IMAM
EDITING: MOHSIN BANGRIWALA
AUDIOGRAPHY: MISRA
CAST: NOORJEHAN / DILIP KUMAR / GULAM MOHAMMAD / SULOCHANA / LATIKA / JEEYA / LADDAN / AAGHA MIRZA / SENGAR / PRAVIN / SHASHIKALA / NAZEER KASHMIRI / MUNWAR AAGHA / JILLOBAI

The first major commercial success of Dilip Kumar was *Jugnu* with which the future megastar entered the purple patch of his career with a string of hits to follow. Legendary singing star and *Malika-E-Tarannum* Noor Jehan was Dilip's co-star in this immensely popular film. Released on 2 October 1948, the movie had a light romantic subject revolving around college students (with Dilip Kumar playing a student named Suraj) and their revolt against certain established practises. The film firmly ensconced the legend in the top stars' bracket. Its tragic ending was also the beginning of Dilip wearing the mantle of the 'Tragedy King'.

New Shahnoor Studios
On the set of Film Jugnu-8.jpg

Initially, the conservatives wanted the film banned because they felt it could lead young college students to go astray. Baburao Patel of *Film India* once again spewed venom in his review of the film headlined 'Jugnu [is] a Dirty, Disgusting, Vulgar Picture! Students and Colleges Slandered!' Among other comments featured in the review was the observation that 'Dilip Kumar looks the average college boy as Suraj but a poor hero–indeed, very poor. He tries to do his bit but he doesn't match well with Noor Jehan. Dilip, however, speaks his dialogue well.' Patel sent an advance copy of his review to Morarji Desai, who was then Home Minister of the erstwhile Mumbai state. Morarji saw the film on 26 October 1948 and promptly banned it under Section 21 of the General Clauses Act of 1897.

Feroz Nizami

The ban was eventually lifted and the film went on to become a big box office hit. The film's songs also became very popular. The delectably melodious Rafi–Noor Jehan duet *Yahan badla wafa ka bewafai ke siva kya hai* became an all-time hit. Feroz Nizami's musical score sells even in the millennium. Other popular songs of the film were *Umangein dil ki machalin* (Noor Jehan), *Aaj ki raat saaz-e-dil-e-purdard na chhed* (Noor Jehan), *Hamein to sham-e-gham mein kaatni hai* (Noor Jehan), *Loot jawani phir nahin aani* (Shamshad Begum) and *Woh apni yaad dilane ko* (Mohd. Rafi). Interestingly, Mohd. Rafi appeared on the screen during the last mentioned song, in a brief cameo.

Mohd. Rafi in Jugnu

Notably, the well-known scribe Clare Mendonca reviewed the film in *The Times of India* on 16 October 1948 and commented about Dilip Kumar saying, '[He] improves with every picture. He plays his role with an unconscious art which creates an impression of naturalness that is great acting'. The movie was a super-duper hit and established Dilip Kumar's credentials as a star of immense potential.

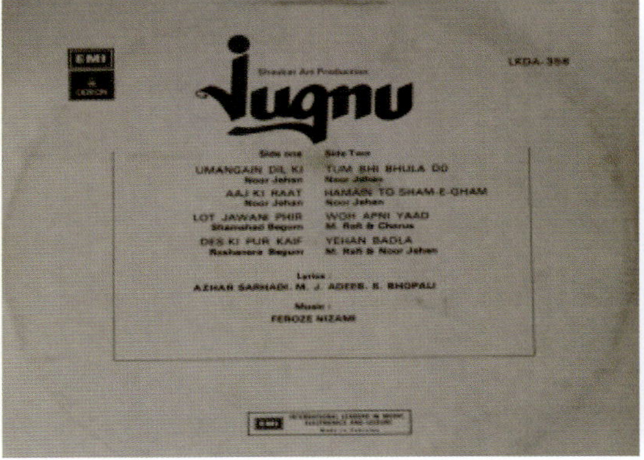

Poster / Stills / LP Disc of Jugnu

FILMISTAN LIMITED
presents
NADIYA KE PAR
CAST
KAMINI KAUSHAL & DILEEP KUMAR
with
SUSHIL SAHU • RAMESH GUPTA • DAVID • MAYA BANERJI • GULAB • S. L. PURI
HARI SHIVDASANI • SAMPSON • KANTA KUMARI • SATYANARAYAN • TIWARI
JULIET • RANI BALA • ANANT PRABHU

Produced & Directed by: KISHORE SAHU

CREDITS

Story, Screenplay & Dialogues	Kishore Sahu	Music	... C. Ramchandra	Make-up	... Ram Tipnis
Sound	... M. M. Kaka	Editing	... Kantilal B. Shukla	Hair Dresser	... Hilda Nathan
Photography	... K. H. Kapadia	Dance Direction	... Satyanarayan	Production Manager	Anant Prabhu
Lyrics	... Moti	Settings	... D. Malwankar		

ASSOCIATES & ASSISTANTS

Story Screenplay & Dialogues	Radha Kishan, Ramesh Gupta, Sushil Sahu & Kantilal B. Shukla	Photography	Braz Braganza & Prakash Chander	Make-up	Gregory & Pemgirikar
Sound	.. Kuldip Singh	Editing	Babu Lavande & V. Narvekar	Directors	Ramesh Gupta, Sushil Sahu, Madhu
		Settings	... N. R. Mistry		

Produced at—THE BOMBAY STUDIOS LTD., GOREGAON, BOMBAY.
Processed at—THE FAMOUS CINE LABORATORY, BOMBAY.
Recorded on—R. C. A. PHOTOPHONE.
Songs of "NADIYA KE PAR" are available on H. M. V. Records.

All rights of printing and publishing or producing on mechanical or electrical equipment any of the songs, dialogues or pictures of "NADIYA KE PAR" have been reserved by Filmistan Limited.

Hind Printing Works, Bombay 4. Booklet Price Annas 4/- (Incl. E. Tax.)

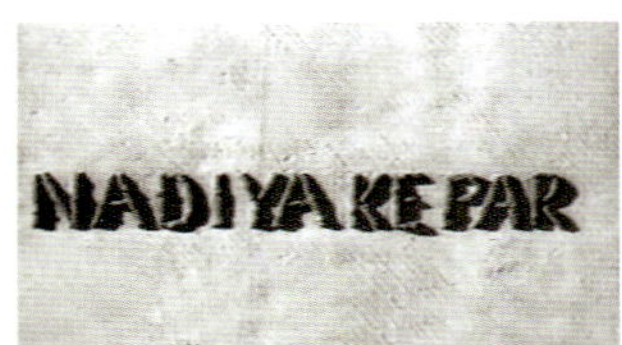

DATE / YEAR OF RELEASE: DECEMBER 1948
BANNER / PRODUCER: FILMISTAN LTD.
DIRECTION: KISHORE SAHU
MUSIC: C. RAMCHANDRA
LYRICS: MOTI B.A.
PLAYBACK: LALITA DEWOOLKAR / SHAMSHAD BEGUM / CHITALKAR / SURENDAR KAUR / P. CHANDAR / S.L. PURI
STORY / SCREENPLAY: KISHORE SAHU
DIALOGUE: KISHORE SAHU
CINEMATOGRAPHY: K.H. KAPADIA
EDITING: KANTILAL B. SHUKLA
AUDIOGRAPHY: M.M. KAKA
CHOREOGRAPHY: SATYANARAYAN
SETTING: D. MALWANKAR
CAST: DILIP KUMAR / KAMINI KAUSHAL / SUSHIL SAHU / RAMESH GUPTA / DAVID / MAYA BANARJEE / GULAAB / S.L. PURI / HARI SHIVDASANI / SAMPSON / KANTA KUMARI / SATYANARAYAN / TIWARI / JULIET / RANI BALA / ANANT PRABHU

This was Filmistan's third film with Dilip Kumar and ended the year 1948 on a most successful note for the actor, with three super hits in his kitty. *Nadiya Ke Paar* was directed by actor–producer Kishore Sahu, who made his acting debut opposite Devika Rani in Bombay Talkies' *Jeevan Prabhat* in 1937. He was a prolific writer of short stories and went on to become a very successful actor, producer and director, and co-starred the beautiful Kamini Kaushal in the female lead opposite Dilip Kumar in *Nadiya Ke Paar*.

Nadiya Ke Paar was the story of a young zamindar who meets and falls in love with a village belle, serenades her in the salubrious surrounding only to encounter stiff local opposition from the villagers. The lovers eventually meet a tragic end in the raging river in the vicinity. The film could manage to capture the attention of its audiences throughout after a sensational opening in which the souls of the lovers are shown to be enjoying

a river ride on specific days. Dilip Kumar's character, wearing his heart on his sleeves, dauntlessly romanced Kamini Kaushal's alluring village belle to the utter delight of the filmgoers who thronged the theatres to applaud their favourite star pair. The onscreen chemistry of Dilip Kumar and Kamini Kaushal matched their off screen fondness for each other. However, Baburao Patel in his *Film India* review commented that, *Nadiya Ke Paar* is a technically attractive picture with sparkling performance by Kamini Kaushal...Dilip Kumar, who plays the hero, gives his stereotyped performance and becomes boring, being seen in too many pictures recently. The boy has no new tricks left, it seems'. *The Times of India* reviewer Clare Mendonca had a piquant observation in her review dated 25 December 1948: 'Dilip Kumar as the young zamindar's brother meanders casually through a role which has no meat for an actor of his calibre.' The easy-going natural performance of Dilip Kumar in the picture was strangely not given its due. Such reviews notwithstanding, the film was an instant hit with college students who could empathise with the theme of prohibited love. Kamini Kaushal and Dilip Kumar became the new hot onscreen lovers. The rumours that they were madly in love off-screen only added to the pair's mystique.

A major contribution to this golden jubilee hit was its super hit music score by C. Ramchandra. The composer showcased his resplendent rhythmic capabilities in creating uniquely lilting folk tunes such as *Oh gori oh chhori kahan chali* (Lata-Chitalkar), which was Lata's first song under C. Ramchandra's baton, *Dil leke bhaaga daga deke bhaaga* (Lalita Dewoolkar), *Ankhiyan milake* (Surinder Kaur), *Najariya mein aayi ho* (Chitalkar-Lalita Dewoolkar), *Do chaar din pyar se* (Shamshad-Rafi), *Maar gayo re* (Shamshad-Chitalkar) and *More raja ho le chal nadiya ke paar* (Rafi-Lalita Dewoolkar). Moti B.A. wrote the film's songs.

C. Ramchandra

This musical super hit is still nostalgically viewed by old timers and vintage music lovers, as evidenced by the availability and popularity of DVD prints. Recently, in an interview for Tata Sky's *Classic Cinema* TV channel, Kamini Kaushal candidly gave a left-handed compliment to *Nadiya Ke Paar* and its director, saying, 'Kishore Sahu *ne badi hi pyari* film *banayi thi.'* (Kishore Sahu had made a lovely film).

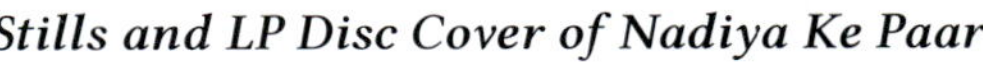

Stills and LP Disc Cover of Nadiya Ke Paar

DATE / YEAR OF RELEASE: 1948
BANNER / PRODUCER: FILMISTAN LTD.
DIRECTION: RAMESH SAIGAL
MUSIC: GHULAM HAIDER
LYRICS: RAJA MEHNDI ALI KHAN / QAMAR JALALABADI / J. NAQSHAB
PLAYBACK: LALITA DEWOOLKAR / MOHD. RAFI / KHAN MASTAAN / SURINDER KAUR / GEETA ROY
STORY / SCREENPLAY: RAMESH SAIGAL
DIALOGUE: RAMESH SAIGAL
CINEMATOGRAPHY: MARSHAL BRAGANZA
AUDIOGRAPHY: J.B. JAGTAP / M.M. KAKA
CAST: DILIP KUMAR / KAMINI KAUSHAL / CHANDRA MOHAN / LEELA CHITNIS / V.H. DESAI / RAM SINGH / S.L. PURI / PRABHU DAYAL / RAJ ADEEB / SHASHI KAPOOR

The year 1948 dawned as a landmark year for Dilip Kumar as glorious success came the legend's way as his film after film stormed the box office.

Rai Bahadur Chunilal and S. Mukherji left Bombay Talkies in 1943, and established Filmistan Studios (Goregaon, Mumbai). S. Mukherji along with his brother-in-law and legendary actor Ashok Kumar was a friend and mentor to Dilip Kumar. They were instrumental in the actor signing a three-film deal *(Shaheed, Nadiya Ke Paar* and *Shabnam*) with Filmistan Studios. Dilip Kumar's first release in 1948 was *Shaheed*, co-starring the talented and beautiful Kamini Kaushal. Kaushal had made her debut in 1946 with Chetan Anand's *Neecha Nagar*–the first Indian film to be awarded at the Cannes Film Festival. Meanwhile, *Shaheed* was a golden jubilee hit and with the film's spectacular success, Dilip Kumar achieved superstardom which has stayed with him lifelong.

The film was written and directed by Ramesh Saigal, who himself had started as a clapper boy with Pancholi Art Productions in Lahore and worked his way up to become an assistant director. He had turned up in Mumbai after the partition and co-authored (with Inder Raj Anand) the stage-play *Deewar* for Prithvi Theatres. *Shaheed* was only his second film but he was destined to become a major filmmaker in the 1950s.

Shaheed was an intensely romantic story set in the backdrop of the 1942 freedom struggle. It was a sure-fire formula of heady romance laced with measured doses of patriotism. In the film, Dilip played a young freedom fighter Ram who sacrifices both his love and his life. His portrayal was loved by the public. Kamini Kaushal played the role of a young woman who marries a police officer in order to save her beloved's life. It was a contemporary subject, and very much in tune with its times as India had just achieved independence from the British rule. *Shaheed* showcased Dilip's powerful histrionics. His dramatic scenes with Chandra Mohan–who played his lawyer-father initially siding with the British and later changing sides to defend his son in court–and Leela Chitnis, as his mother, were truly memorable. The mother-son jail meeting scene was brilliantly performed by Dilip and Leela Chitnis, taking poignancy to new emotive heights. But the tour de force feature of the film was the scintillating chemistry between its lead pair–a charming youthful Kamini Kaushal and Dilip Kumar who in spite of his tousled hair (or maybe because of it!) was as handsome as they came. Naturally, rumours started doing the rounds that the pair was hopelessly in love and had eyes only for each other. It is on record that Dilip Kumar and Kamini Kaushal did have an off-screen chemistry, but more about that later. Girls started wearing Kamini-style blouses and copied her hairstyle and the public thronged the movie halls to see its favourite star pair. Also, very importantly Master Ghulam Haider's musical score found its echo in every heart. Dilip Kumar with the evergreen song *Watan ki raah mein watan ke naujawan shaheed hon* on his lips became a national hero.

Leela Chitnis and Dilip Kumar

Baburao Patel reviewed *Shaheed* with the headline 'At last, a Decent Film from Filmistan!' and commented :

'So far as acting is concerned, Dilip Kumar steals the picture with his deeply felt and yet perfectly natural delineation of the main role. Sensitivity and intelligent under-statement are the

Stills from Shaheed

outstanding characteristics of his acting. Kamini Kaushal is somewhat overshadowed by Dilip and while giving a fairly balanced performance, fails to rise any histrionic heights. But the two of them act some of the most tender, most intimate and most moving love scenes that have ever been seen on the Indian screen.'

Since S. Mukerji had rejected Lata's voice, Ghulam Haider did not call her while recording the super hit music of *Shaheed.* Nor did he call his regulars like Shamshad Begum and used different voices such as Surindar Kaur, Lalita Dewoolkar (later day wife of composer Sudhir Phadke) and Geeta (Roy) Dutt. Surinder Kaur's *Badnaam na ho jaaye mohabbat ka fasana, Aana hai to aa jao* were super hit songs alongside Lalita's *Bachpan ki yaad dheere dheere* and Geeta's *Aaja bedardi balma.* But it was the Mohd. Rafi–Khan Mastana duet *Watan ki raah mein watan ke naujawan shaheed hon*–a nationalistic call for sacrifices–that took the nation by storm. Notably, Master Ghulam Haider had demanded ₹100,000 for the music of *Shaheed* and eventually accepted it at a then record price of ₹75,000.

Master Ghulam Haider

DATE / YEAR OF RELEASE: 8 OCTOBER 1948
BANNER / PRODUCER: WADIA FILMS LTD.
DIRECTION: S.U. SUNNY
MUSIC: NAUSHAD
LYRICS: SHAKEEL BADAYUNI
PLAYBACK: ZOHARABAI AMBALEWALI / SHAMSHAD BEGUM / MOHD. RAFI / MUKESH
STORY / SCREENPLAY: AZM BAZIDPURI
DIALOGUE: AZM BAZIDPURI
CINEMATOGRAPHY: FALI MISTRY
ART: V. JADHAV
EDITING: MOOSA MANSOOR
AUDIOGRAPHY: ROBIN CHATTERJEE
CAST: NARGIS / DILIP KUMAR / JEEVAN / AMAR / ROOP KAMAL / ALAUDDIN / ABBAS / CHANDABAI / REHMAAN / NURJAHAN / KHALIL / ZUBEIDA (BABY)

Dilip Kumar followed up the huge success of *Shaheed* with another mega hit of 1948–Wadia Movietone's *Mela*–with Nargis, who was already a big star by then. It was the first time that the legendary pair of Nargis–Dilip Kumar came together and eventually starred in a record seven movies together.

Those were the volatile days of post-partition India and music director Naushad and director S.U. Sunny were staying with J.B.H. Wadia at his palatial bungalow at the Worli

Sea Face for safety reasons. Hilla Wadia came up with an idea that her husband make a film with the then most popular composer Naushad, who accepted but suggested S.U. Sunny's name as the director. Sunny in turn brought in story-writer Azm Bazidpuri, who went on to write many of Dilip's starrers in the 1950s. Nargis was signed to play the female lead. Since the hero was the last to be signed, Sunny did not tell Dilip Kumar anything about the film but just played two songs for him: Mukesh's *Mera dil todne wale* and *Gaaye ja geet milan ke*. Dilip was hooked to the songs, and he did the unthinkable–he signed the film without even hearing the story. Dilip Kumar's faith in Naushad and Sunny as well as Naushad and Wadia's faith in Dilip, both were vindicated with the movie breaking all box office records. It later turned out that the main story line of the movie was inspired by Emily Bronte's celebrated classic novel *Wuthering Heights* and Dilip Kumar played a loose and toned-down adaptation of the character of Heathcliff which he was to subsequently repeat in three other films. But, more about that later.

S.U. Sunny, Naushad

There is nothing as beautiful as a well-told love story. There are popular sayings about true love, like Ralph Waldo Emerson's famous 'All mankind loves a lover'. Indian films have always been infatuated by love stories and most of them revolved round love. But the elusive spirit of real love has somehow always escaped them. Among the handful of films which succeeded in capturing this essence was *Mela*. When the film was released in October 1948, the audience loved it so much that it became a stupendous hit, enjoying a straight jubilee run in many places. Also, whenever the film was re-released, it drew Full Houses and the film is watched till date.

Mela had something of the *Romeo and Juliet* charm in its story with a background of the Indian village. It starts from the childhood days of Mohan and Manju as innocent playmates. They tie themselves in bonds which are to last a lifetime or more, but without fulfilment. This childhood sequence trick has been tried by many films, but in *Mela* it had a quaint charm of its own. Their love then runs its course, never smooth and always full of aches, except for a few hopeful moments of a possible marriage. Mohan goes to town for buying the wedding jewels but meets with an accident and lands up in a hospital. Manju's step-mother and a villain who hated the lovers get her married to an old man with many children. The tragedy has Mohan returning to find her taken away forever. One day, he saves the life of her husband who is suffering from epilepsy and she sees him. Then the old man dies, but the social barriers are too harsh. The lovers meet only once at their favourite tryst, but a storm takes Manju's life as she falls off a cliff and Mohan is wrongfully imprisoned for her murder. The story is told in flashback as Mohan comes out of jail and in the end answers the call of love (as the song *Dharti ko aakash pukare* plays) by jumping over a cliff.

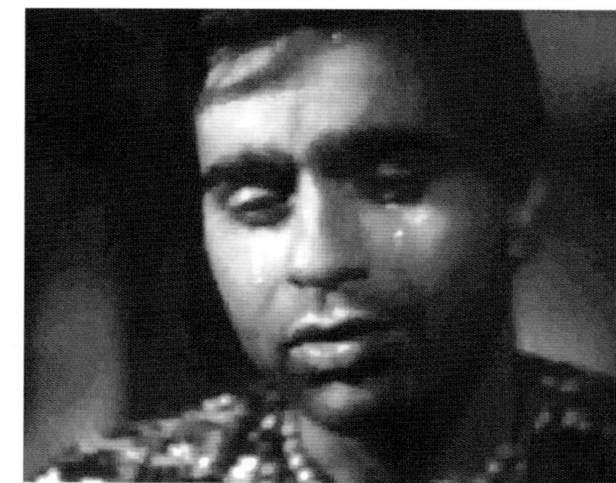

Dilip in Mela

Mela had a handpicked cast and crew of the flowering talents giving their best–Nargis, Dilip Kumar and Jeevan, Naushad, Shakeel, Mukesh, Fali Mistry–who soon became top names. The film was an integrated combination of their inspired work. Nargis and Dilip won immense popularity as the lovers and almost brought today's star-pair system into vogue. Fali's camera and lights created romantically haunting images with the rural background. In *The Times of India* review dated 23 October 1948 Clare Mendonca wrote: **'Dilip Kumar puts over a really fine performance, natural as he is permitted to be in a role so greatly misconceived, Dilip Kumar is convincingly realistic as the country lad. He should counter the tendency to keep his mouth half open. With his facial configuration, it gives him an adenoidal look which sits ill in heroes. And for a word of personal advice, he should resist all directorial blandishment in future and decline to commit suicide for all the tea in China – for some time at any rate.'**

Baburao Patel was, as usual, very caustic in his review of *Mela* in *Film India*, which read:

'After seeing Mela one feels that the 'Rattan' formula is still very much in vogue. In fact, Mela is a bad rehash of 'Rattan' and as such presents a very familiar story which the spectators themselves can complete at any stage of the picture without the Bazidpuri writer taking the trouble to do so. Mela is far from being sensible. It is at once stupid and reactionary with the story being anti-social. From the players, Nargis plays her part well, especially in pathetic scenes, though she looks unconvincing in sequences of her synthetic motherhood. Dilip Kumar plays the hero Mohan and does the job well. As the picture is anti-social in its theme, it does not provide suitable entertainment to the masses, though the music is an attractive feature of the picture. It is such a picture of which the educated Wadias should be ashamed [of].'

Nevertheless, damning all sceptics *Mela* won the hearts of millions of Indians to become a top grosser and firmly established Dilip Kumar on the pedestal of a superstar.

But credit must also be given to music director Naushad and lyricist Shakeel Badayuni, singers Shamshad Begum and Mukesh who gave the songs of *Mela* its spellbinding quality. All the ten songs of the film were gems and great hits of their time. Naushad created evergreen melodies which were chartbusters–*Pardes balam tum jaoge* (Shamshad), *Mohan ki muraliya baaje* (Shamshad), *Main bhanwra tu hai phool* (Shamshad-Mukesh), *Mera dil todne wale* and above all the most popular number *Gaaye ja geet Milan ke* (Mukesh), et al. The film also had an immortal Mohd. Rafi number *Yeh zindagi ke mele duniya mein kam na honge* and an unforgettable Zohrabai Thumri *Phir aah dil se nikli.* The film's title track

Stills from Mela

(almost lover's call couplet then) *Dharati ko aakash pukare* (Shamshad–Mukesh) became so popular that a 78 RPM record disc of the same (along with a dance music track from the film) had to be released by HMV.

Mela was director S.U. Sunny's maiden triumph with Dilip Kumar. He later earned the distinctions of directing a record four number of Dilipian films. But, singularly the most salient feature of *Mela* is that it launched the matchless actor–music director team of Dilip Kumar and Naushad which has extremely popular musical scores in fifteen films to its credit.

The handsomeness of young Dilip Kumar of *Mela* reflected in his facial anatomy, his forehead, his expressions, his magical voice, and his whole being. It created a fresh image of the screen hero which at once caught the fancy of the audiences. Thus, out of *Mela* came a youthful screen image of a hero passionately in love with love, life and tragedy —all of which Dilip Kumar, then just 25 years old, came to personify. A star was born, a legend began taking shape.

LP Disc of Mela

EP Disc of Mela

DATE / YEAR OF RELEASE: 28 MAY 1949
BANNER / PRODUCER: AMBICA FILMS
DIRECTION: M.I. DHARMSEY
MUSIC: ANIL BISWAS
LYRICS: ZIA SARHADY / BEHZAD LUCKNAWI / GOPAL SINGH NEPALI / SHAMS AZIMABADI
PLAYBACK: LATA MANGESHKAR / MUKESH / MEENA KAPOOR / IRA NAGRATH
STORY / SCREENPLAY / DIALOGUE: ZIA SARHADY
CINEMATOGRAPHY: JAL D. MISTRY
EDITING: FAQIR MAHOMED SHEIKH
AUDIOGRAPHY: R. CHATTERJEE (RCA SOUND SYSTEM)
FILM ARCHITECH: V. JADHAVRAO
ART: Y.L. JADHAV / RANDHIR
CAST: NARGIS / NALINI JAYWANT / DILIP KUMAR / AMIRBAI / SANKTHA PRASAD / MUKRI / VED / KESARBAI / UMA DUTT / HABIB / SHEIKH / MUNSHI MUNAKKA

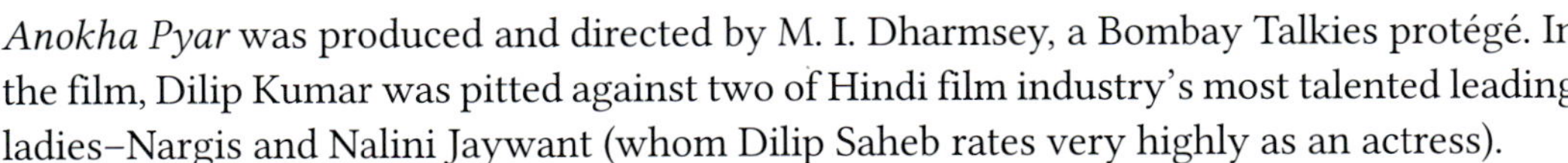

Anokha Pyar was produced and directed by M. I. Dharmsey, a Bombay Talkies protégé. In the film, Dilip Kumar was pitted against two of Hindi film industry's most talented leading ladies–Nargis and Nalini Jaywant (whom Dilip Saheb rates very highly as an actress).

ANOKHA PYAR

(SYNOPSIS)

The phases of our life are governed by circumstances. You and I feel these circumstances every day, every hour, every minute and every second, so much so that they rule the strings of our feelings, sentiments and actions. We simply can not avoid them.

Bindiya, the innocent, simple, active yet charming young girl used to stay in a hut and maintained her living by selling flowers. She used to pluck her flowers from the garden created by Nature on the bank of the rippling river. It was adorned by the ruins of the ancient palace. The scanty shadows designed by the sunbeams on the cracked floor of the palace and the reflections of the crystal clear water on the broken walls bounded by the luxuriant growth of the flowers made it an ideal spot. Ashok, a young dreamer, a thinker and a writer selected this secluded spot to inspire him to write his novel. Bindiya, thinking this handsome youth as her customer, approached him and asked him in her childlike voice, 'Babu, wouldn't you buy the flowers from me?' Ashok looked at her and said, 'No.' Bindiya told him that she could not find any customer to buy her flowers on that day. Ashok felt his pockets. They were almost empty. He had hardly a two anna piece in it. He placed it in her shapely hands. Bindiya threw away the piece and said, "What do you think I am?" Ashok admired her. He smiled and took from her a glowing bud of rose. She thought he was grand. She began to like him. Yes, then she began to love him.

In the meantime Bindiya while returning home, met a tramp who used to take away her earnings. He began to harass her. She cried and shouted for help. Ashok heard her cry and ran to help her. A herculean fist of the tramp sent him reeling on the ground, depriving him of his eyesight.

The circumstances sometimes behave with us very mathematically. Bindiya took him to the nearest doctor, who was a very kindhearted social worker. He admitted him in his small hospital-which was incidentally his home-and began to treat him for his eye trouble. Ashok met Geeta the doctor's daughter, refined and cultured. Her chisel carved face and the graceful body impressed him as an angel of sublimity and beauty. In the absence of her father, she nursed his physique and soul. She sang a song which inspired Ashok to work on his novel.

The circumstances play the game of chess in man's life. Ashok thought of his weakness of economic condition and felt it too bad to visit Geeta. He resolved to meet her after getting sufficiently rich to stand with her family on the same level. He began to work on his novel with vigorous spirit and enthusiasm.

He often met Bindiya while he was writing his novel on the river bank. He liked to talk to her and listened to her innocent, lovely, chirping voice. She imagined the world too beautiful. He liked her for her fancies and dreams. She loved him sincerely, truly. She thought he also loved her. Ashok loved Geeta, the paragon of beauty, culture and learning.

Sometimes circumstances play the game of hide and seek with human beings. Once Bindiya and Geeta met at the river bank. They went sentimental over their 'boy'. Their emotions clashed. There was a mighty storm in their hearts. Ultimately, Sublimity gave way to Innocence.

But the fate calculated their lives to be different. Ashok loved Geeta. He liked Bindiya but never loved her. But Geeta had given him up and had never shown a sign of remembering him. Once she very politely turned him out of her house. Ashok was flabbergasted, stunned. He couldn't read his future. It was all darkness.

The circumstances were playing with him. They were responsible for many tears and blood. They alone can determine the shape of the lives of Bindiya, Geeta and Ashok. Let us watch them.

As can be seen in the synopsis, the film was the story of a writer struggling to make a name and find his place in the world while being in love with Nargis. Nalini Jaywant played a poor flower seller who also was in love with Dilip and eventually died in the film sacrificing her love. Interwoven in the story was a false murder charge on male protagonist. *The Times of India*'s Clare Mendonca comment about the film in the newspaper's 25 June 1949 edition as:

'As far as acting (is concerned), I frankly found no attempt, at any rate on the part of Dilip Kumar and Nargis, both of whom appear to have been content to merely amble through their none-too-exacting roles. Dilip can clearly do better, but is content to act what he probably is building up for a formula of success for the type of romantic lead for which he is constantly in demand. He is typecasting himself with his dishevelled locks worn the peek-a-boo way, his down-at-heel clothes and lacklustre air, his staccato speech, and his formless emoting. Into this particular role he has put nothing, whatever he may have got out of it.'

Stills from Anokha Pyar

We have seen the film and find the above criticism quite unjustified and so did the filmgoers in those times. Dilip rendered an underplayed and natural performance, excelling in the tragic scenes with his expressions of pathos earning him public accolades heralding him as the 'Prince of Tragedy'. Celebrated actresses Nargis and Nalini Jaywant were apt foils to Dilip, rendering equally natural performances. Nevertheless, the lacklustre directorial treatment of a trite tale resulted in the film being a damp squib at the box office.

The film won its music director Anil Biswas universal acclaim for his enchanting compositions, which over decades have come to be acknowledged as immortal classics.

The advent of 'Melody Queen' Lata Mangeshkar in the musical domain of Anil Biswas came about in *Anokha Pyar,* which also featured songs by Meena Kapoor (Anil's later day wife) and Mukesh. Lata's peerless range opened up new vistas of musical composition for Biswas, as it did for most other composers of the golden era. But, Biswas's contribution in the evolution and shaping of Lata's voice, which attained unmatched glory, is next to none. It was Anil Biswas who brought her out of the shadow of Noor Jehan, imparting her fabulous voice its own magnificent identity. Lata sang like a champion for Biswas in *Anokha Pyar,* a fragrant bunch of blooming melodies par excellence including the classic *Yaad rakhna chand taaron is suhani raat ko, Ghadi ghadi poochhona re, Ek dil ka lagana baaki tha, Mere phoolon mein chhupi hai, Jeevan sapna toot gaya, Mere liye woh gham-e-intezar, Aye dil meri wafa mein koi asar nahi hai* (with Ira Nagrath, Roshan's wife), *Ab yaad na kar bhool bhi ja sapne suhane* (with Mukesh) and *Bhola bhala re*–what a collection of immortal classics. The songs *Mere liye woh gham-e-intezaar, Ab yaad na kar bhool bhi ja* and *Ek dil ka lagana baaki tha* appear in the film in the voice of Meena Kapoor and grapevine has it that after recording the songs for the film version, Meena Kapoor fell sick and the 78 R.P.M. disc versions were recorded by Anil Biswas in the voice of Lata Mangeshkar. Grapevine also has it that around that time Biswas had composed the song *Jeevan sapna toot gaya* for K.L. Saigal, to be used in a Shaukat Hussain Rizvi's (then husband of Noor Jehan) film starring Saigal and Noor Jehan. The film got shelved as Rizvi and Noor Jehan migrated to Pakistan and Saigal was no more. Anil Biswas recorded the song in the voice of Mukesh and later Lata in two versions for *Anokha Pyar.* The musical score gave a boost to the career of Mukesh.

Anil Biswas with Lata

DATE / YEAR OF RELEASE: FEBRUARY 1949
BANNER / PRODUCER: MURLI MOVIETONE / K.S. DARYANI
DIRECTION: RAM DARYANI
MUSIC: Pt GOBIND RAM
LYRICS: ISHWAR CHANDRA KAPOOR
PLAYBACK: SHAMSHAD BEGUM / ZOHARABAI AMBALEWALI / MOHD. RAFI / MEENA KAPOOR / G.M. DURRANI
STORY / SCREENPLAY: K.S. DARYANI
DIALOGUE: ISHWAR CHANDRA KAPOOR
CINEMATOGRAPHY: KUMAR JAYWANT
CHOREOGRAPHY: K.S. MORE
ART: PANDURANG KRISHNA SHINDE
EDITING: M.D. MALEKAR
AUDIOGRAPHY: P.S. MISRA
CAST: MUMTAZ SHANTI / DILIP KUMAR / JEEVAN / MANORAMA / DIXIT / SULEMAN / GULAB / GOPE

Daryani brothers owned Eastern Art Syndicate, a pioneering film production company. They also founded their production concerns Murli Movietone and Krishin Movietone with K.S. Daryani and Ram Daryani handling the production and direction departments respectively. They signed up the highly successful actress Mumtaz Shanti of the super hit *Kismat* fame (and wife of Wali Saheb) in the lead opposite Dilip Kumar in a family

Still from Ghar Ki Izzat

social titled *Ghar Ki Izzat*. The film also had the comical duo of Gope and Dixit. The story featured an improbable family melodrama which pitted an uneducated mother-in-law (played by Gulab) against her educated daughter-in-law (Mumtaz Shanti) with the leading man (Dilip Kumar), unable to withstand the persecution of his wife by his mother, takes to alcoholism. The film however had a happy ending.

Clare Mendonca commented in her review in *The Times of India* dated 5 February 1949 that 'Dilip, who gets better with each performance, acts more naturally as the hero, and is completely convincing'. *Film India* panned the film as 'Trash Supreme' with the comment that it was 'another of those idiotic stories with reactionary content'. The review opined that Mumtaz Shanti gave a usual good performance, but it was extremely critical of Dilip Kumar. The film did not do well at the box office.

Pt Gobind Ram

Pt Gobind Ram's name is mentioned with awe in musical circles even today. He had a deep knowledge of Indian classical music and was a highly accomplished and versatile music composer of great repute. He had a long association and friendship with Roop K. Shorey, lyricist Ishwar Chandra (I.C.) Kapoor (father of veteran actor Bharat Kapoor, the authors' family friend), Ram Daryani and comedian Gope. Many may not be aware that Pt. Gobind Ram was the original choice as music director of *Mughal–E–Azam* when it was launched by K. Asif way back in 1944. But, the film got stalled after its producer (Shirazi) migrated to Pakistan. By the time it was revived Pt Gobind Ram had virtually quit the film Industry. Although *Panditji* belonged to the so–called Punjabi school of music, he was an all-rounder composer of rare merit. The music of *Ghar Ki Izzat* featured some popular song such as *Bagh me koyaliyan yahi gaye* (Shamshad Begum, Zorabai), *Taron ki toliyon pe kaisa yeh nikhar* (Shamshad Begum, G.M. Durrani) and *Wah re zamane kya rang dikhaye* (Mohd. Rafi). Ishwar Chandra Kapoor penned the lyrics and the dialogue of the film.

DATE / YEAR OF RELEASE: 15 JULY 1948
BANNER / PRODUCER: FILMISTAN LTD
DIRECTION: BIBHUTI MITRA
MUSIC: S.D. BURMAN
LYRICS: QAMAR JALALABADI
PLAYBACK: SHAMSHAD BEGUM / GEETA ROY / LALITA DEWOOLKAR / MUKESH
STORY / SCREENPLAY: C.J. PAVRI
DIALOGUE: AKHTAR-UL-IMAN
CINEMATOGRAPHY: DALI DAROOWALA
EDITING: KAMLAKAR
AUDIOGRAPHY: Y. SHINDE
CAST: DILIP KUMAR / KAMINI KAUSHAL / JEEVAN / PARO / MUBARAK / HAROON / RAJENDRA SINGH / SHYAMA / CUKKOO

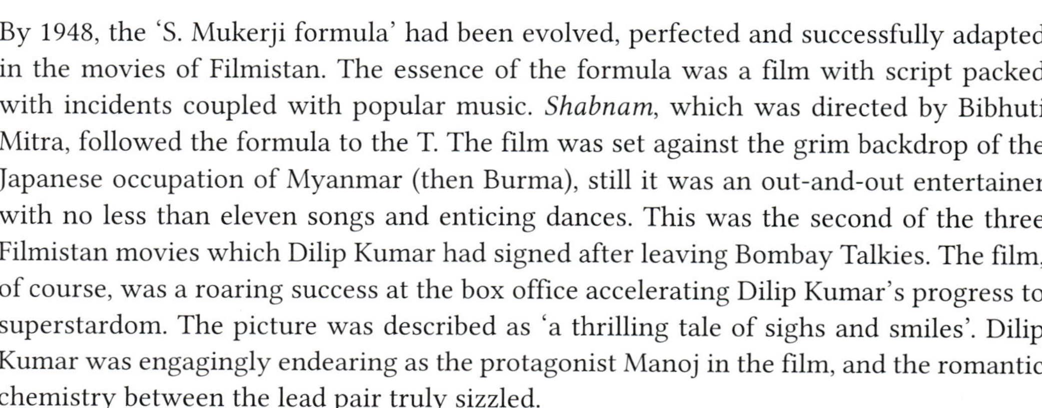

By 1948, the 'S. Mukerji formula' had been evolved, perfected and successfully adapted in the movies of Filmistan. The essence of the formula was a film with script packed with incidents coupled with popular music. *Shabnam*, which was directed by Bibhuti Mitra, followed the formula to the T. The film was set against the grim backdrop of the Japanese occupation of Myanmar (then Burma), still it was an out-and-out entertainer with no less than eleven songs and enticing dances. This was the second of the three Filmistan movies which Dilip Kumar had signed after leaving Bombay Talkies. The film, of course, was a roaring success at the box office accelerating Dilip Kumar's progress to superstardom. The picture was described as 'a thrilling tale of sighs and smiles'. Dilip Kumar was engagingly endearing as the protagonist Manoj in the film, and the romantic chemistry between the lead pair truly sizzled.

Dilip in Shabnam

Morarji Desai was the Home Minister of Bombay Presidency when *Shabnam* had released. He saw the film on 23 July 1948 at Roxy theatre and said to the filmmaker, 'I have no quarrel with you if people are not actually benefited by your films. So long as you give them harmless entertainment, I have not the least objection.' *Shabnam* thus passed Morarji's strict scrutiny. Meanwhile, the *Film India*'s headline of for the film's review was: '*Shabnam* draws huge crowds at Roxy, Minister Morarji sits through the picture!' Baburao Patel in the review observed:

'*Shabnam* made under the banner of Filmistan, starring Kamini Kaushal and Begam Para, is a fun film and S.D. Burman scores some melodious tunes with Mukesh and Geeta Roy as playback singers. The love story is enacted within the backdrop of the exodus of Indians from Burma and the escapades and adventures of Kamini Kaushal (disguised as a boy) and Dilip Kumar. Finally his discovery, that she is a girl after all, ends [up] in their romance. Dilip Kumar is very good in the lighter moments as well as the romantic scenes. Kamini Kaushal looks charming as Shanti and gives an excellent performance. And so does Dilip Kumar in the role of Manoj. Their love scenes give glimpse of realism and both artistes seem to enjoy their romantic scenes.' Clare Mendonca in her review of the film in *The Times of India* dated 30 July 1948 had an uncharitable unjustifiable comment on the actor: **'Dilip who is just good in the first half, sharing honours with Kamini, falls away hopelessly in the latter portion, giving a performance that is tame and as unrecognisable as he is himself in his painted gypsy face and strange attire.'** Those who have seen *Shabnam* would not agree with the uncharitable comment on Dilip Kumar's smooth performance in the film.

S.D. Burman's first super-duper hit music came with *Shabnam.* The music won nationwide popularity. As he did for Dev Anand in *Vidya* (1948), Dada Burman used Mukesh as the playback voice for Dilip Kumar. Many of the songs of the film were runaway hits, including *Tumhare liye huye badnaam* (Shamshad-Mukesh), *Tu mahal mein rahne wali main* (Shamshad-Mukesh), *Mera dil tadpa kar kahan chala* (Geeta), *Pyar mein tumne dhokha seekha* (Shamshad-Mukesh), the multilingual *Yeh duniya roop ki chor* (Shamshad), *Qismat mein bichhadna tha* (Geeta Roy-Mukesh) and *Hum tum ko sunaye haal haal yeh duniya* (Lalita Dewoolkar). The film went on to become a golden jubilee hit and the grand success of the music of *Shabnam* established S.D. Burman as a successful music director in Mumbai film industry.

S.D. Burman

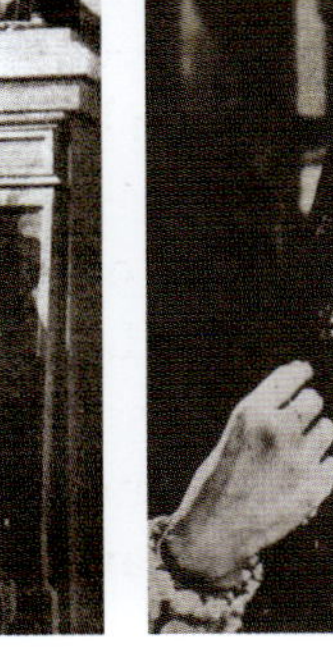

Stills from Shabnam

DATE / YEAR OF RELEASE: 21 MARCH 1949
BANNER / PRODUCER: MEHBOOB PRODUCTIONS
DIRECTION: MEHBOOB
MUSIC: NAUSHAD
LYRICS: MAJROOH SULTANPURI
PLAYBACK: SHAMSHAD BEGUM / LATA MANGESHKAR / MUKESH / MOHD. RAFI
STORY / SCREENPLAY: SHUMS LUCKNOWI
DIALOGUE: S. ALI RAZA
CINEMATOGRAPHY: FAREDOON IRANI
EDITING: SHAMSUDDIN KADRI
AUDIOGRAPHY: KAUSHIK
CAST: NARGIS / DILIP KUMAR / RAJ KAPOOR / MURAD / V. H. DESAI / KUKKOO / ANWARI BHAI / AMIR BANO / JAMSHEDJI / ABBAS / VASKAR

By the start of 1949, Dilip Kumar with five super hit films under his belt had already made giant strides towards becoming a superstar with enormous fan following. But, the lady luck had further plans as Mehboob Khan's *Andaz*, one of Indian cinema's most memorable films, catapulted Dilip Kumar in the league of one of the finest actors in the country. *Andaz* released on 21 March 1949 at the famous Liberty Cinema in Mumbai, which was inaugurated with this picture. The film went on to be a mega hit collecting a whopping ₹7 lakh (a huge amount in those days) in its first 28-week run at the theatre.

Clare Mendonca wrote on 26 March 1948 in *The Times of India*: '**Dilip Kumar runs away with acting honours in the central role, which he portrays with an inimitable grace of which his entire naturalness and spontaneity are the chief ingredients. He does not act but lives the role, displaying the rare genius of the born actor, who is unaware that he is acting. He will go far, this young man if he retains this priceless gift of spontaneity which characterises him today.**' Baburao Patel's review was effusive in its praise of the actor's performance in its review which was headlined: *''Andaz Draws Crowds at Liberty! Dilip Kumar Gives his Greatest Performance'*. In his review, Patel said: '**Dilip Kumar improves beyond recognition under Mehboob's direction. He casts off his usual mannerisms and becomes versatile in the role of Dilip, the frustrated lover. The way he portrays his struggle of suppressed emotions is a fine piece of histrionic art. This is easily Dilip Kumar's greatest performance so far.**'

Stills from Andaz

Mehboob Khan was influenced by Hollywood as in those days the only school that was seen as worthy of emulation was Hollywood. *Andaz* was thus India's first archetypal Hollywood-influenced motion picture. Thanks to the high-key cinematography of Fardoon Irani, excellent editing and powerful storytelling, *Andaz* rewrote the ground rules of Hindi cinema. It is important to remember Mehboob's fondness for 'a message', for saying something significant between the lines, in his films. In *Andaz* too, he was saying something of significance to the youth of the mid-1940s, who were then aping the western culture. His 'message' in *Andaz* was conveyed through a poignant scene between the father and daughter, played by Murad and Nargis. The father says, in so many words, 'Do not be so free and overfriendly with other young men if you have already given your heart to one and promised to marry him. Overfriendliness can be misunderstood for love, and sometimes leads to tragic consequences.' For Mehboob, it was a matter of walking the razor's edge all the time in balancing the performances of all three stars with regard to their motivations, emotions and dialogue. The timeless *Andaz* was shot in just sixty-eight days and the actors were paid moderate amounts. Reportedly, Nargis was paid ₹35,000, Dilip Kumar: ₹25,000 and Raj Kapoor only ₹15,000.

While Naushad's music was a definite high point of the film, it was the absorbing plot revolving around two men in love with the same woman that struck a chord with the audience. The film's tragic climax became a trendsetter. A triangular love story, *Andaz* was about a carefree modern girl (Nargis) who is the tomboyish daughter of a rich man who employs Dilip Kumar as his manager. Nargis spends a lot of time with him, and he mistakenly assumes, so does the audience, that she is falling in love with him, and has begun to reciprocate his feelings. Nargis's father warns her many times about the impression she may be giving to him and to others', but she disregards it. Then, one day, she tells Dilip Kumar that her fiancé is returning from England—the news which comes like a bolt from the sky for Dilip Kumar. He wants to leave but Nargis's father dies at the same time. She insists that, for the sake of her father's memories, he stays back and continues to look after their interests and Dilip agrees. As Raj Kapoor and Nargis get married, Dilip Kumar finds it increasingly difficult to cope with his unrequited state. He again begs Nargis to let him go, but she again refuses him. Meanwhile, due to some minor misunderstandings, Raj Kapoor begins to suspect that she is having an affair with Dilip Kumar. In an intelligently crafted scene, at a party at Nargis' house, she comes to talk to Dilip Kumar and just then the lights go off. She pleads with him to go away and then a match is struck, Raj Kapoor's face becomes visible and the lights come back, shocking Nargis when she sees that she was talking to Raj Kapoor instead. Their marriage develops problems and soon matters come to a head. Nargis is widely pilloried, she goes to confront an injured Dilip Kumar (hit on the head by Raj Kapoor), and in a moment of frenzy shoots him. Meanwhile, Raj Kapoor learns that he had been mistaken in suspecting his wife and the misunderstanding is cleared, but Nargis is sentenced for life imprisonment for the murder of Dilip.

It was an author-backed role for Dilip who was called upon to display a wide range of emotions from a confident young man in love, turning into a vulnerable and unsure lover. The emotions that Dilip is able to summon on his face–first of fun and laughter and then of controlled anger, frustration, hurt and finally, of vulnerability–are awe-inspiring. Dilip's natural acting style suited the role to perfection and astutely the director allowed him a free rein. In fact, Dilip's brilliant underplay of emotions attained hitherto unscaled peaks of acting excellence, as he stole the show in the unforgettable staircase confrontation scene between him and Raj Kapoor.

The effortless performances of the three greats–Dilip Kumar, Raj Kapoor and Nargis–added magic to the film. The undercurrents of a rivalry between the two male stars gave the drama an added edge. Every actor's trick, known and unknown, every subterfuge of scene-stealing, every device of action and gesture, under-play and over-play was employed by the two in an all-out 'prestige effort'. The way the two actors filled their roles was also important for the emergence of the personae of Raj Kapoor and Dilip Kumar as we know them today. For Dilip Kumar, it was the beginning of maturity where histrionics must come from a mystic fusion of brain and heart and economy of physical movement. With *Andaz*, he created a language of acting and style, where a gesture, an expression, a flutter of an eyelid, a disarming smile, a vocal intonation lent profound meaning to words. For Raj Kapoor, it was the emergence of an individual set of mannerisms, overdone

Nargis, Dilip Kumar and Raj Kapoor in Andaz

for effect, with flamboyant gestures, facial expressions and physical movement placing him in stark contrast with Dilip Kumar's understatement and subtlety with his very ebullience and overplay. Till date, the two styles dictate the acting scene in Indian cinema.

Naushad's classy score in the film is one of his best, if not the best. Naushad's songs such as *Tu kahe agar jeevan bhar main geet sunata jaoon* (*Raag Bhairavi*), *Hum aaj kahin dil kho baithe* (*Raag Jhinjhoti*), and *Toote na dil toote na* (*Raag Bhairavi*), became the ultimate symbol of love. These songs were sung by Mukesh. Majrooh Sultanpuri wrote the lyrics. Regardless of the magnum opus canvas of the film, Naushad chose the then fresh voices of Lata Mangeshkar, Mukesh and Mohd. Rafi against the established voices such as Zohrabai, Ameerbai, Nirmala, G.M. Durrani and Uma Devi. A bold move indeed, but these fresh voices sang like champions and resultantly become the most sought-after playback voices for the next four–five decades. Even Shamshad Begum was given just one duet with Lata (*Dar na mohabbat kar le*) in which her voice was not used for the leading lady Nargis but Kukkoo. Lata Mangeshkar's *Raag Kedar*-based *Uthaye ja unke sitam aur jiye ja* (rendered on screen by Nargis with rare sensitivity) ranks among her best ever. The album heralded Lata first major association with Naushad. Her other popular songs in the album include *Koi mere dil mein khushi ban ke, Meri laadli bani hai* and *Tod diya dil mera toone arey bewafa.* In fact, Lata Mangeshkar soon surpassed the competition with her immensely successful songs in the year 1949 which included *Aayega aane wala* (*Mahal*), *Chup chup khade ho* and *Chale jaana nahin* (*Bari Behen*) and the songs of *Andaz.*

One of the highlights of *Andaz* was those mesmerising Mukesh numbers picturised on Dilip Kumar which included *Tu kahe agar jeevan bhar main geet, Hum aaj kahin dil kho baithe, Toote na dil toote na* and *Jhoom jhoom ke nacho aaj* (based on a *mukhda* sung by Prem Dhawan at the Independence Day function at the Taj Mahal Hotel). Dilip Kumar behind the piano expressing emotions of a lover became a symbol of love, making *Andaz* a nationwide rage. A lesser known fact is that *Andaz* had another beautiful Mukesh number, *Sunaoon kya main gham apna*, which remained unused in the film. Naushad had also recorded a second Rafi–Lata duet (*Suno dil ka afsana*) for *Andaz*, which too remained unused. After *Andaz*, the Naushad–Majrooh Sultanpuri team broke up for decades (their next film together was *Saathi* in 1969). Apparently, Naushad had a misconception about communist Majrooh being an atheist.

Mehboob Khan adopted a unique marketing trick for his prized creation, *Andaz.* As the time of the film's all-India release date approached and its pre-release publicity peaked to a fever pitch, Mehboob made a deal with Habib Hussein, whose Liberty Cinema was coming up at Marine Lines, that *Andaz* would be the film with which his theatre would be inaugurated. People had never seen such crowds outside any cinema house as they saw when the advance booking counters of the theatre opened for *Andaz.* The manager of Liberty Cinema, Mahboob Ali, had to summon the police and there was lathi charge time and again to disperse the frenzied fans. It is now history that *Andaz* went on to become one of the biggest box office hits of all time.

CHAPTER 3.2

THE CLASSIC CINEMA PHASE– THE FASCINATING FIFTIES

ARZOO

DATE / YEAR OF RELEASE: JANUARY 1950
BANNER / PRODUCER: INDIAN NATIONAL PICTURES
DIRECTION: SHAHID LATEEF
MUSIC: ANIL BISWAS
LYRICS: PREM DHAWAN / MAJROOH SULTANPURI / JAN NISAAR AKHTAR
PLAYBACK: LATA MANGESHKAR / DHAWAN / ANIL BISWAS / MAJROOH / SUDHA MALHOTRA / SHAMSHAD / S.D. BATISH / AKHTAR / MUKESH
STORY / SCREENPLAY: ISMAT CHUGTAI
DIALOGUE: ISMAT CHUGTAI
CINEMATOGRAPHY: S. SRIVASTAVA
EDITING: J.S. DIWADKAR
AUDIOGRAPHY: MOOLGAONKAR
CAST: DILIP KUMAR / KAMINI KAUSHAL / GOPE / CUCKOO / AARIF / PREM DHAWAN / SHASHIKALA / SEETA BOSE / NEELAM KHAN / GAJJOO / CHANDABAI / ZAIDDI / RAM SHASTRI /HAMEED / KAMLAKAR

Ismat Aapa

Shahid Lateef

Ismat Chugtai and her husband Shahid Lateef (fresh from Talkies' *Ziddi* which was the Dev Anand) signed the highly Kumar and Kamini Kaushal for very fond of Dilip Kumar and her as *'Aapa'.* With *Andaz* the history of Indian Cinema sterling performance in the film being praised all around, it was now a challenge for the actor to live up to his fabulous reputation. The Ismat Chugtai–Shahid Lateef home production with Hiten Chowdhury was based on Emily Bronte's classic novel *Wuthering Heights.* Interestingly, Heathcliff was reportedly Dilip Saheb's favourite character and he attempted to portray it in quite a few films–*Mela, Aarzoo, Hulchul* and *Dil Diya Dard Liya.* Dilip Saheb fancied this character and was able to effectively bring out the anguish of Heathcliff time and again albeit in toned down romanticised versions, minimising the negative traits in the beastly character. *Arzoo* had all the ingredients of a fine film but did not attain the expected box office success. The film nevertheless won plaudits from cinegoers for the performance of its leading man and its soulful music.

The story hovered around the trials and tribulations of a young man who is treated badly because he is not able to earn enough to marry the girl he loves. He thinks of leaving the scene but his love for her makes him stay and suffer the indignities inflicted by her family. Finally, he does go away and returns a rich man only to find the woman he loves is already married to another man. He then begins to woo another woman just to make his beloved jealous. *Arzoo* is still remembered since it further consolidated Dilip's image as the tormented lover who loses his sweetheart to the onslaughts of social propriety.

The Times of India review dated 11 February 1950 by Clare Mendonca read as follows: **'Dilip proves an excellent foil rather than a teammate for (Kamini Kaushal) for with all his naturalness, his greatest asset, which he brings to the role, his studied, typed mannerisms rob his performance of all freshness and spontaneity, even in the earlier village sequence. He is getting to dramatise himself too much and he does it too consciously. He is more himself than the hero of this film.'**

Baburao Patel was very critical about the theme of the film and wrote in the *Film India* review:

'Distortion of Hindu married life! Hindu marriage is primarily a spiritual bond with gods as witnesses. Its sanctity is not only felt by the parties to the marriage but also by every Hindu in the whole of India! Defiance of the spiritual sanctity of the Hindu marriage is scoffed at in the narrative and it is this disgusting aspect of *Arzoo* that has made the picture unpopular and caused it to fail at the box office. The direction of Shahid Lateef is amateurish. From the players, Kamini Kaushal, who plays the heroine, does the bubbling sequences very well. Her reflective work, however, fails to be impressive. Dilip Kumar plays Badal very indifferently. He seems miles away from his situations even though Kamini sits so near to him. The embracing situations between the two are, however, quite effective.'

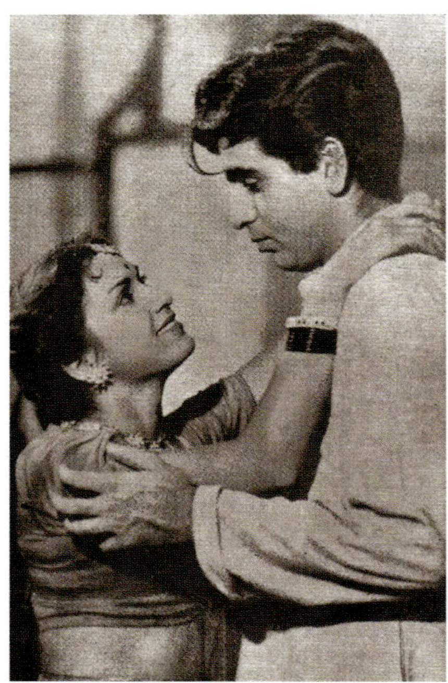

Most of the people, however, enjoyed the film and were of the opinion that Dilip performed the emotional scenes with rare sophistication. This was the fourth and last film of Dilip Kumar and Kamini Kaushal together due to some serious personal developments–but more about that later.

Arzoo came with ten bewitching melodies aesthetically sculpted by Anil Biswas. Singer Talat Mahmood, in those days, had been singing non-film songs in Bengali in Kolkata and a few Hindi non-film numbers under the pseudonym of Tapan Kumar. The credit of bringing Talat to Mumbai and giving his velvety voice its first big break in Hindi films with the *Raag Darbari*-based song *Aye dil mujhe aisi jagah le chal* goes to Anil Biswas. The Talat number apart, the score of *Arzoo* was an out-and-out Lata session with golden melodies like *Kahan take hum uthayein gham (Raag Asavari), Mera naram karejwa dol gaya* with enticing flute interludes, *Aayi bahar jiya dole, Jaana na dil se door aankhon se door jaake* with its exquisite musical structure and the haunting *Unhein hum jo dil se bhulane chale.* The other songs like the *nautanki*-style comedy number *Humein maar chala yeh khayal yeh gham* (Anil Biswas), *Mil gaye nain gaya such chain* (Sudha Malhotra) and *Jao sidharo hey Radha ke Shyam* (Shamshad–Mukesh–S.D. Batish) were also notable. It was yet another musical landmark in Anil Biswas' illustrious career. Majrooh Sultanpuri penned the lyrics for the first time for an Anil Biswas film, with the other song writers being Prem Dhawan and Jan Nissar Akhtar (also credited as Jan Nisar Akhtar).

Under their banner of Film India Corporation, the Ismat Chugtai and Shahid Lateef duo made several more films including *Lala Rukh, Do Raha* and *Sone Ki Chidiya,* etc. But, *Arzoo* remains their most remembered celluloid venture to this date.

Dilip in Shabnam

DATE / YEAR OF RELEASE: OCTOBER 1950
BANNER / PRODUCER: SUNNY ART PRODUCTIONS / NAUSHAD
DIRECTION: S.U. SUNNY
MUSIC: NAUSHAD
LYRICS: SHAKEEL BADAYUNI
PLAYBACK: SHAMSHAD BEGUM / LATA MANGESHKAR / TALAT MAHMOOD / MOHD. RAFI
STORY / SCREENPLAY: AZM BAZIDPURI
DIALOGUE: AZM BAZIDPURI
CINEMATOGRAPHY: FALI MISTRY
EDITING: MOOSA MANSOOR
AUDIOGRAPHY: ROBIN CHATTERJI / ISHAN GHOSH
ART: V. JADHAV RAO
CAST: NARGIS / DILIP KUMAR / MUNAWAR SULTANA / AMAR / A. SHAH / JANKIDAS / H. PAHADI / VINOD / ISMAIL / JUGNOO / CHAND BALA / SEEMA / MEHAR / RAJBALA / KHURSHID

Naushad and his director friend S.U. Sunny established their own company Sunny Art Productions and gave the super-duper hit *Babul* (1950), starring Nargis, Dilip Kumar and Munawar Sultana. Having broken off with Kamini Kaushal, Dilip Kumar teamed up with his other favourite heroine Nargis to do four films in a row, beginning with *Babul*. The film went on to become a golden jubilee hit, running for 104 weeks simultaneously at several theatres in Mumbai alone.

The story of the film was about a man Ashok (Dilip Kumar) who comes to a small town on being appointed as a postmaster. He meets Usha (Munawar Sultana), the comely daughter of the town's affluent rich man and falls in love with her while giving her music lessons (remember the memorable song *Milte hi aankhen dil hua deewana kisi ka?*). Usha reciprocates his love. Bela (Nargis), a village belle who cooks and keeps house for Dilip, is secretly in love with him. Things come to a head when Bela learns of the love of Usha for Ashok and accuses the latter of stealing her man. Usha sacrifices her love deciding to give up on Ashok and marries some other man chosen by her father. Ashok is heartbroken but Bela is happy. Bela dies when a tree (from atop which she was watching the wedding party of Usha approaching the town) falls. The film thus had a tragic end. The main artists' credible performances and an evergreen lilting musical score made the film a super hit.

Stills from Babul

Fali Mistry's stunningly alluring cinematography was another major highlight of the film. We, who have seen *Babul* a couple of times, can vouch for this. The picturisation of one particular song sequence–*Nadi kinare saath hamare*–remains indelibly etched in our minds. Dilip Kumar, who was at his handsomest best attired in a suit with a loose tie, and a shy and wistful Munawar Sultana were splendidly photographed while serenading to the spectacular Talat Mahmood–Shamshad Begum number. The song shot in the backdrop of boatmen humming a stunning Rafi *alaap* was sheer cinematic magic. Equally effective was the death scene of Nargis when Dilip's sings the sad version of *Chhod babul ka ghar* (by Talat), followed by the heart-wrenching call of the heavens *Aao sajan khade hain duaar* (Mohd. Rafi).

Clare Mendonca's review of *Babul* in *The Times of India* dated 14 October 1949 read: ' **Dilip Kumar also acts extremely well as the *Dak Babu*–kindly, honest, blunt and dignified even in the moments of his keenest pain and sorrow. He has shed most of his irritating mannerisms, and if he would only enunciate clearly–a primary consideration in any actor–he would be near perfect.**' In his film review, Baburao Patel commented: '**The role of his life, Dilip Kumar, a master in portraying morbid characterisation of a spineless frustrated lover, lives the role of Ashok,**

the postmaster. Even his natural humour takes the hue of his helpless sex and soul starvation and he strides through the picture with a pathetic poverty of a licked spineless lover who has neither the courage to love nor the guts to ask and take what he wants. It is a great work and the ease with which Dilip Kumar portrays the role makes one wonder whether the man himself has lived through similar moments of pathos and frustration in his private life!'

Bringing in Talat Mahmood's velvet voice as the playback voice for Dilip Kumar, using Lata and Shamshad for Nargis and Shamshad alone for Munawar Sultana's voice, Naushad came up with a dream score. The title song *Chhod babul ka ghar,* a *Bidaai Geet* sung evocatively by Shamshad Begum, is played at some weddings even today. Shamshad and Talat, who had contrasting styles of singing, came together brilliantly to give us evergreen duets *Milte hi aankhen dil hua diwana, Duniya badal gayi meri* and *Nadi kinare saath hamare* (with Mohd. Rafi's lead support). Lata made her mark with super hit solos–*Panchhi ban mein piya piya* and *Lagan more man ki,* as did Shamshad with her solos *Dhadke mera dil, Jadoo bhare nainon mein* and *Na socha tha humne.* Shamshad and Lata together rendered a sad duet *Kisi ke dil mein rahna tha* with rare effect. Talat, despite rendering splendid solos such as *Husn walon ko na dil do, Mera jeevansaathi bichhad gaya* and *Chhod babul ka ghar,* somehow never found much favour with Naushad in the time to come and rarely got his patronage. Grapevine has it that Talat had once dared to smoke in Naushad's presence, ruffling a few feathers.

LP Disc of Babul

With *Babul,* a number of romantic tragedies had come in quick succession which used Dilip Kumar's image as an embodiment of unrequited love. Millions of hearts throbbed when Dilip suffered a rejection, separation or betrayal in love. Millions of eyes became moist with him in the darkness of the movie theatres. No actor had so intensely involved the audiences in his portrayals, as Dilip did. Adoring the actor, millions copied him with unconcealed pride. Dilip Kumar on the other hand went on making such films, not only because these came his way but also because he wanted them. Film after film, Dilip Kumar the actor became a phenomenon–ever deeper and enigmatic. No one but he alone knew what he was doing, where he was going.

Talat and Naushad

EP Disc of Babul

JOGAN

DATE / YEAR OF RELEASE: MAY 1950
BANNER / PRODUCER: RANJIT MOVIETONE
DIRECTION: KIDAR SHARMA
MUSIC: BULO C. RANI
LYRICS: MEERABAI / PT. INDRA / BUTA RAM SHARMA / HIMMAT RAI SHARMA / KIDAR SHARMA
PLAYBACK: GEETA ROY / TALAT MAHMOOD / SHAMSHAD BEGUM
CINEMATOGRAPHY: D.C. MEHTA
EDITING: Y.G. CHAVAN
AUDIOGRAPHY: K.V. SHAH
ART: S.A. WAHAB
CAST: NARGIS / DILIP KUMAR / MANJOO / PRATIMA DEVI / PESI PATEL / PURNIMA / BABY TABASSUM / ANWARI / RAMESH THAKUR / DARPAN / RAJENDRA KUMAR

Directed with rare sensitivity by Kidar Sharma, *Jogan* had outstanding portrayals from the lead actors Nargis and Dilip Kumar. The Sadhvi of *Jogan* was brought alive onscreen by Nargis with immaculate subtlety. Dilip Kumar's flawless subdued exhibition of internal landscape is a landmark in Indian cinema. The lead player acted merely with expressive eyes and communicative facial emotions.

This was the second Nargis–Dilip Kumar movie which turned out to be an all-time classic. The telling portrayal of emotional turmoil in interplay of characters and the director's enchanting static frames made for a compelling storytelling. The film was made with rare sensitivity, imbued with understated emotional drama.

Kidar Sharma

Sardar Chandulal Shah

The story behind the making of this film is quite interesting. Once Sardar Chandulal Shah, the owner of Shree Ranjit Studio and a silver bullion magnet, was sitting in the veranda of his studio with actress Gohar Bai (his long-time friend and confidante) and directors Nitin Bose, Mahesh Kaul and Kidar Sharma. He threw a challenge at them–to make a movie out of a one-line story concept: a music lover is so smitten by a sonorous singing that he goes all out to woo the voice. Gohar Bai, Bose and Kaul opined that it would be a hare-brained idea to translate such an abstract subject into a motion picture. Thus, Bose and Kaul refused to pick up the gauntlet, but Sharma was game and said, *'Huzoor, main beeda utha loon?'* (Sir, Shall I take it forward?).Chandulal Shah and Gohar Bai immediately agreed. Bose sceptically said, 'Fools rush in where angels fear to tread.' Kidar Sharma gave a tongue-in-cheek rejoinder saying, 'Yes, we will see who the angels are.' Sharma went on to convert the abstract subject into this memorable movie called *Jogan*, arguably his best film.

Chandulal Shah had Nargis and Dilip Kumar in mind for the main leads. While Nargis accepted the role immediately, Dilip Kumar had some reservation due to its inherent contradictions and for some time avoided meeting Shah. Mehboob Khan got wind of Dilip's reluctance and prevailed upon the actor to meet Chandulal and accept the role. Dilip Kumar immediately complied and a happy Chandulal Shah rang up Mehboob to thank him. 'How much did you sign Dilip for?' asked Mehboob. 'For ₹40,000,' said Shah, to which a surprised Mehboob asked, 'Did you know that his current price is ₹60,000?' Chandulal Shah did not comment but on the occasion of next Eid, he called Dilip, embraced him and gave him a packet containing an additional ₹20,000.

Nargis as Sadhvi

Ranjit Studio was in some financial difficulties at that time and hence *Jogan* was shot and completed in a straight schedule of just twenty-nine days. The film went on to become a super hit giving a good boost to the sagging fortunes of the studio.

The story of *Jogan* (originally titled *Sadhvi*) turned out to be a captivating one and just right for Dilip Kumar's image. It centred around Vijay, a dissolute atheist, and Meeradevi, a female ascetic (*jogan*). Vijay is a music lover and visits the notorious houses of dancing girls so as to savour the music. Once, while visiting his village, he hears a *bhajan* being sung by a *jogan* in a temple. Mesmerised, he waits outside the temple till she catches a sight of him. She asks him not to come there ever again but he returns the next day and all the other following days. The unrequited love remained largely unexpressed with the feelings conveyed through very expressive eyes of the lead pair, throughout the film which had a tragic end in which the *jogan* dies. The beautifully-narrated tale of love and sacrifice came alive on celluloid with the exceptional histrionics of Nargis and Dilip Kumar. It was a woman-oriented subject and Nargis excelled in the titular role. Dilip Kumar's role was equally substantive and the thespian performed it with rare sensitivity, infusing vibrant life in the author-backed role requiring portrayal of unspoken emotions.

To set the mood and elicit quietude from Dilip Kumar for specific scenes, Sharma used to recite *shers* (Urdu couplets) on the sets before shooting the particular scenes. For example, the *sher* Sharma recited when Vijay was brooding immersed in Meeradevi's thoughts was, '*Nikle huye hai lahet se khade hain bulaiye, Saheb kahan chale gaye humko pukar ke.*' Similarly, for the scene when after Meeradevi's departure from the town of Kalunagar, Vijay lies on the mat in her small cottage reminiscing about her, Sharma recited, '*Meri jabeen ne jhuk jhuk ke kar diye sajde, jahan jahan pe taqaza-e-husn-e-yaar hua.*'

Stills from Jogan

Glowing tributes were paid to the lead pair of Nargis and Dilip Kumar by Clare Mendonca in the review in *The Times of India* dated 6 May 1950: '**Nargis, who appears here in a role utterly different from anything she has done before, gives a wonderful performance which marks her (as a) dramatic actress of the highest merit. The same goes for Dilip Kumar, who, also in a different role than any of his before, acts with a true sympathy and a dignity which lifts the character to a high level of the heroine and the story.**'

Bulo C. Rani created his career-best musical score for *Jogan*. The album had the immensely popular numbers especially Geeta Dutt's *Ghoonghat ke pat khol re tohe piya milenge* (based on *Raag Darbari*), *Mat ja mat ja jogi* (*Raag Bhairavi*), *Daaro re rang (Raag Tilak Kaaamod), Zara tham ja tu aye sawan, Jin aankhon ki neend, Pyare darshan deejo aay* and *Sakhi ri chitchor nahin aaye.* Apart from these splendid Meera Bai songs, the film also had some other classic numbers like *Sundarta ke sabhi shikari* (Talat Mahmood), *Uth to chale avadhoot* (Mohd. Rafi) and *Kaahe nainon mein kajra daale ri* (Shamshad Begum).

Bulo C. Rani

Actor Rajendra Kumar, later a superstar himself, played a small cameo (debut) in the film, fulfilling his ambition of working with Dilip Kumar. Also, later day's celebrated director Lekh Tandon was an assistant to Kidar Sharma in the film.

DATE / YEAR OF RELEASE: 1951
BANNER / PRODUCER: FILMKAR LTD
DIRECTION: NITIN BOSE
MUSIC: NAUSHAD
LYRICS: SHAKEEL BADAYUNI
PLAYBACK: SHAMSHAD BEGUM / MOHD. RAFI / LATA MANGESHKAR / G.M. DURRANI
STORY / SCREENPLAY: AZM BAZIDPURI
DIALOGUE: AZM BAZIDPURI
CINEMATOGRAPHY: DILIP GUPTA
EDITING: BIMAL ROY
AUDIOGRAPHY: MUKUL BOSE
CAST: ASHOK KUMAR / NARGIS / DILIP KUMAR / NIMMI / YAQOOB / BABY TABASSUM / PARIKSHIT / BABY ANWARI / MURAD / JAL MERCHANT / NIHARIKA DEVI / UMA DEVI / SURENDAR / AGHA MIRAZ

Dilip Kumar's next was *Deedar*, his sixth film with Nargis, which stormed the box office. Produced by Makhanlal Jain's Filmkar banner, the film had a star-studded cast of Ashok Kumar, Nargis, Dilip Kumar, Nimmi and Yaqoob. Directed by Nitin Bose, Dilip Kumar's mentor director who also gave this super hit film a unique photographic treatment, *Deedar* featured one of the actor's most applauded portrayals as a blind singer. Despite sharing screen space with seasoned actors, Dilip excelled in his role.

Ashok, Nargis, Dilip and Yaqoob

Azm Bazidpuri's story was actually very simple but the twist and turns of the love triangle created a unique dynamics in the script which prove to be a novelty. The narrative centred around childhood sweethearts Shyam (Dilip Kumar) and Mala (Nargis) who get separated owing to their belonging to different strata of the society. Shyam gets blinded due to a freak accident and is adopted by a family comprising Yaqoob (who performs on the streets) and his sister Champa (Nimmi). Shyam grows up harbouring Mala's love in his heart and becomes an accomplished singer performing on the streets with Yaqoob. Champa too harbours love for Shyam in her heart. While Shyam keeps pining for Mala, she has blissfully forgotten her childhood friendship. Mala gets betrothed to Dr Kishor (Ashok Kumar) who is a famous ophthalmic surgeon. One day Shyam sings at the doorsteps of Dr Kishor who gets very impressed and promises to treat the eyes of Shyam, who discovers that its childhood sweetheart Mala is with Dr Kishor. Shyam recovers his eyesight under the treatment of Dr Kishor, but when he realises that Mala has totally forgotten him, he blinds himself again and goes away with Champa and Yaqoob. The intrigue in the plot that Mala till the very end does not remember her childhood crush was a strong point of the screenplay. Terrific performances by all actors and a super hit musical score made the film a golden jubilee hit.

Dilip as blind singer

Eager to excel in playing a blind man, Dilip sought acting tips from the veteran matinee idol Ashok Kumar. He asked him, 'How should I play a blind man?' Ashok Kumar said, 'Close your eyes and you will not be able to see anything, Dilip's counter question was, 'But I have to keep my eyes open and with open eyes I can see everything.' Ashok Kumar thought for a few moments and advised, 'Go to Mahalaxmi and where the bridge ends, you will see a blind beggar who begs with his eyes open. Observe him carefully.' And Dilip actually drove down to Mahalaxmi to observe the beggar in action. A case of art imitating life! Dilip Saheb recounted the experience saying: **'I spent quite a few days with him to get an insight into the world within him. He was very pleasant and would laugh at the darkness inside him. From him, I learned to be cheerful and had that beatific smile on my face in *Deedar*. It would have been far too run-of-the-mill to play a blind man with my eyes closed. It would have been an easy way out.'** No wonder, the result was a stupendous performance which remains etched in the memories of cinemagoers.

The film's unforgettable music featured some all-time hit of Mohd. Rafi, Lata Mangeshkar, Shamshad Begum crafted by maestro Naushad with unmatched dexterity. Apart from creating the film's musical score, Naushad also wrote the story and reportedly contributed in the making as well. The film's music, its brilliant performances and its cinematography are remembered to this day. Mohd. Rafi, by now having virtually monopolised Naushad's male singer slot, infused heart warming feelings in the numbers he sang for Dilip Kumar – *Huey hum jinke liye barbaad (Raag Bhairavi), Meri kahani bhoolnewale (Raag Tilang) and Naseeb dar pe tere.* Lata too was assigned dream numbers *Le ja meri duayein leja (Raag Maand)* and a delectable duet with Rafi, *Dekh liya maine kismat ka tamasha.* Shamshad Begum too got her piece of cake rendering the immortal *Chaman mein rah kar veerana* for the leading lady Nargis and the duet *Nazar phero na humse* (with G.M. Durrani) for Nargis and Ashok Kumar. Very thoughtfully, Naushad deployed Shamshad's seasoned voice for the songs on Nargis and Lata's fresh voice on a relative newcomer Nimmi. Nevertheless, the all-time great Lata–Shamshad duet *Bachpan ke din bhula na dena* (also sung in a solo version by Rafi) became the hottest chartbuster. Shakeel Badayuni yet again wrote the songs for Naushad in the film.

Stills from Deedar

Veteran director Nitin Bose had a special fondness for his creation *Deedar* and had these observations in an article: **'Dilip and I got together once again in *Deedar* and everyone knows how well the film was received. It was a multi-starrer of those days with Dilip, Nargis, Nimmi, Ashok Kumar, Yaqoob and others. But, they were all chosen because of their suitability for the roles, rather than that they were big names. In those days, though you could sign for two films at a time, you could not start shooting for two films at the same time. So all the artists and technicians from the director down concentrated on the job in hand. In the four years gaps between Milan and Deedar, I noticed how Dilip had grown as an artist by leaps and bounds. Dilip was never over sure of himself and could understand my needs with a minimum of explanation. I have never come across any other artist who could absorb everything as well.'**

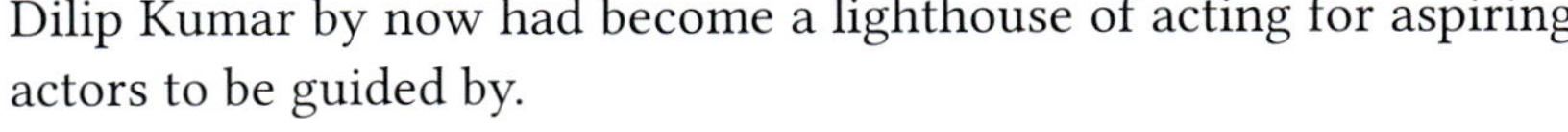

Dilip Kumar by now had become a lighthouse of acting for aspiring actors to be guided by.

HULCHUL

DATE / YEAR OF RELEASE: FEBRUARY 1951
BANNER / PRODUCER: K. ASIF PRODUCTIONS
DIRECTION: SHUBH KARAN OJHA
MUSIC: SAJJAD / MOHD. SHAFIE
LYRICS: KHUMAR BARABANKVI
PLAYBACK: SHAMSHAD BEGUM / RAJKUMARI / MOHD. RAFI
STORY / SCREENPLAY: HASRAT
DIALOGUE: HASRAT
CINEMATOGRAPHY: V.N. REDDY
EDITING: VITTHAL BANKAR
AUDIOGRAPHY: SHAIKH AKRAM / B.N. SHARMA / MINOO KATRAK / KAUSHIK
ART: S.N. DESAI
CHOREOGRAPHY: CHOBEY MAHARAJ
CAST: NARGIS / DILIP KUMAR / SITARA / BALRAJ SAHANI / YAQOOB / K.N. SINGH / JEEVAN / CUCCOO / NEELAM / GEETA NIZAMI / FAIZI / BABY ANWARI / N. KABIR / JUNIOR BALRAJ

Hulchul was produced by K. Asif, who later made the magnum opus *Mughal-E-Azam*, and directed by Shubh Karan (S.K.) Ojha. Later, Ojha also directed India's first film shot abroad – *Naaz,* an Ashok Kumar–Nalini Jaywant starrer, which flopped). Reportedly, Dilip Kumar's fondness for Emily Brontë's *Wuthering Heights* manifested itself again as he tried another interpretation of the character Heathcliff and essayed his part with amazing brilliance in the distinguished company of great actors Nargis, Balraj Sahani and Yaqoob. Famous danseuse Sitara Devi (who was married to K. Asif at that time) was featured in a vampish role of a ballerina. Jeevan also played a villain. Dilip–Nargis reportedly had a kissing scene in the film, which was, their last film together. Grapevine has it that the kissing scene (which was anyway deleted by the censors) was filmed without the consent of Nargis and that caused some misunderstandings between the lead pair. Although, there never was any romance between Nargis and Dilip Kumar, but their relationship was a cordial and friendly one.

The story featured a young orphaned man Kishore (Dilip Kumar) who has been brought up by a loving tycoon friend of his father. The tycoon has a daughter Asha (Nargis) and a son (K.N. Singh). Kishore and Asha are in love from childhood. After the demise of the tycoon, Asha's tyrannical elder brother frowns upon the Asha–Kishore love affair. He tells Kishore to first stand on his own feet and become worthy of seeking Asha's hand in marriage. Kishore leaves the house promising to come back after attaining some status on the condition that Singh should wait for his return for a year. Kishore first finds work as a stunt artist and then is given shelter by a stage ballerina Madam Neelam (Sitara Devi). In the meantime, Asha is married off to a jailor (Balraj Sahani). Kishore (still in love with Asha) spurns the advances of Neelam, who is murdered by Jeevan (her co-worker). Kishore is wrongly convicted of Neelam's murder and is jailed in the same prison where Balraj Sahani is the jailor. He meets a happy-go-lucky convict Gurudev (Yaqoob) in jail who becomes very fond of him and gets him exonerated of his wrongful conviction. While in jail, Kishore saves Balraj's life during an attempted prison break. The dramatic film had a tragic end with Dilip Kumar dying. The movie took more than two years to complete and K. Asif, who was actively pursuing his dream of making *Mughal-E-Azam* at that time, faced umpteen challenges from all quarters in completing the movie. He also had a lot of trouble in getting the film censored. These troubles compelled him to insert an ironical slide in the credits of the picture, which read: 'Respectfully and affectionately this picture is dedicated to those dear friends, comredes (sic) and well-wishers who had implicate faith in us ... never to complete this picture!', The movie was a moderate box office success.

In her review, Clare Mendonca in *The Times of India* dated 17 February 1951 commented, 'Dilip Kumar, despite touches of stolidity, gives a remarkably good performance which is deeply stirring in its expression of pathos, grief, gratitude and despair.' The film was described by Baburao Patel in *Film India* as 'a touching tale of love told in songs and sighs and wound up in tragedy'. Calling it 'a classic performance', Patel's review gave a great compliment to Dilip Kumar mentioning, 'He lives his role from scene to scene and attains frightening realism in the final climax.' In fact, Dilip Kumar's portrayal of the hungry job-seeking youth was so profoundly steeped in realism that the performance stood head and shoulders above those of his co-actors in the film.

Hulchul saw music director Sajjad reach the zenith with his compositions. Although, he recorded only three songs for this film (he reportedly walked off thereafter due to a tiff with director S.K. Ojha), they are all golden nuggets like Lata's *Aaj mere naseeb ne* or *Luta dil mera*. The classic *thumri, Koi kis tarah raaz-e-ulfat chhupaye* (sung by Rajkumari) remains unparalleled and any classically-trained singer could include the same in his/her *Riyaaz*. Any singer who can accomplish the task of exercising his/her voice with the various complicated intonations and *'murkis'*, expertly rendered by the great Rajkumari in this *'Thumri'*, will get the appropriate vigorous training required for pursuing sonorous perfection. Sajjad personally rated *Aaj mere naseeb ne* as his best ever composition. Khumar Barabankvi wrote the lyricis. Mohd. Shafi, Naushad's assistant, completed the score and the qualitative distinction was glaring.

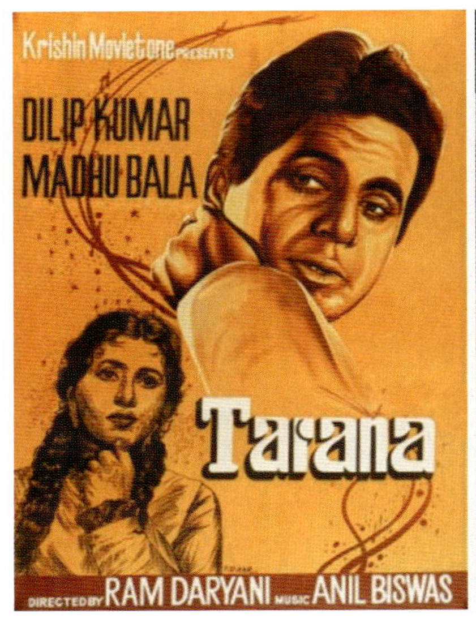

DATE / YEAR OF RELEASE: 1951
BANNER / PRODUCER: KRISHIN MOVIETONE
DIRECTION: RAM DARYANI
MUSIC: ANIL BISWAS
LYRICS: PREM DHAWAN / KAIF IRFANI / D.N. MADHOK
PLAYBACK: LATA MANGESHKAR / TALAT MAHMOOD / SANDHYA MUKHERJEE
STORY / SCREENPLAY: DWARKA KHOSLA / K.S. DARYANI
DIALOGUE: D.N. MADHOK
CINEMATOGRAPHY: KUMAR JAYWANT
EDITING: M.D. MALEKAR
AUDIOGRAPHY: INDRAVADAN DESAI
ART: M.K. SYED
CAST: DILIP KUMAR / MADHUBALA / SHYAMA / KUMAR / GOPE / JEEVAN / GULAB / BIKRAM KAPOOR / DEVASKAR / CHANDU / GIRDHARI

Madhu and Dilip in Tarana

Dilip Kumar is known to have rewarded all those who did him a favour in his initial years. He did *Tarana* for the Daryanis, who had cast him in *Ghar Ki Izzat* (1948) at the beginning of his career. *Tarana* was a beautiful romantic film with Anil Biswas providing a lilting musical score. Above everything else, the film holds a special significance in the life of Dilip Kumar as it triggered a legendary romance which is remembered even to date. On the first day of the shooting of this film, a single rose arrived in Dilip Kumar's make-up room. The bearer of the rose was the make-up artist of the leading lady. The message stated, *'Agar aap mujhe chahte hain to yeh gulab qubool farmaiye, varna isse wapas kar dijiye.'* (If you love me, please accept this rose. Else, return it). The sender of the rose, the film's nubile heroine–all of 17 years but already a veteran with thirty odd films to her credit. Interestingly, she had nearly become Dilip Kumar's heroine in *Jwar Bhata,* But she received Devika Rani's invitation to come down to Mumbai from Delhi a little late, and by the time she arrived, the film's cast had already been finalised. Meanwhile, Dilip Kumar smiled after reading the message and tucked the rose in the button hole of his suit, launching the legendary but tumultuous romance. The romantic scenes in *Tarana* are simply unforgettable and a live testimony to the fond affection shared by the lead pair.

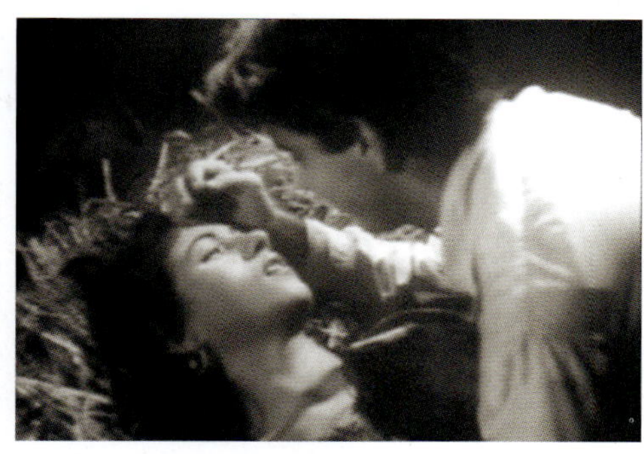

Stills from Tarana

Written by Dwarka Khosla, a veteran director in his own right, *Tarana* is a romantic tale interspersed with the usual villains and coincidences which prove the dictum that the path of true love never does run smooth, particularly when one of the lovers in Dilip Kumar. It was the love story of a young doctor Motilal (Dilip Kumar) whose airplane crash lands in a small village where he meets a nubile village belle Tarana (Madhubala) and the two fall in love. Dilip's father (played for a change by villain Jeevan) wanted him to be married to a city-bred girl (Shyama) who also loves Motilal. Complications are created in the love story by a village suitor (Gope) of Tarana. Several twist and turns in the story lead eventually to the lovers getting re-united in the happy end of the film. The narrative was enlivened by the sparkling Madhubala–Dilip Kumar romance in the salubrious backdrop of a village locale. The lovely and lively romantic chemistry between the lead pair has to be seen to be believed. The movie got rave reviews and an excerpt from Baburao Patel's review in *Film India* is reproduced below:

TARANA, A SCINTILLATING LOVE STORY, MADHUBALA AND DILIP KUMAR TRIUMPH TOGETHER! BORN TO BE A TEAM

Talking of performances, it is difficult to separate Madhubala and Dilip Kumar. Both have almost lived their roles and their romantic sequences seem to take their hues from the real canvas of live. Incidentally, Madhubala gives the best performance of her screen career in this picture. She seems to have discovered her soul at last in Dilip Kumar's company.'

Packed with passionate love scenes, the film (and obviously its new pair) caught the fancy of the audience which made the film a success.

Anil Biswas once again scored music for his old friends the Daryanis and gave his best in *Tarana.* Grapevine has it that the 'reel' romance of the lead pair turned into 'real' romance as they took the viewers into romantic ecstasy emoting Anil *Da*'s heart-stealer *Nain mile nain huey bawre* (Lata–Talat). Anil Biswas touched truly sublime levels of excellence while creating immortal melodies such as *Woh din kahan gaye bata jab is nazar mein pyar tha* (Lata), *Bol papihe bol re tu* (Lata-Sandhya Mukherjee), *Beimaan tore nainva nindiya na aaye* (Lata), *Mose rooth gayo mora sanwariya* (Lata), *Ek main hoon ek meri bekasi ki shaam hai* (Talat), *Yoon chhup chhup ke* (Lata) and *Wapas le le yeh Jawani* (Lata). The *Raag Kaafi*-based *Beimaan tore nainva* was so evocatively rendered by Lata and so very lovingly enacted on screen by Dilip and Madhubala that it became a milestone in the Indian cinema. But, of course, the greatest musical embellishment of the film was the exquisitely crafted *Seene mein sulagte hain armaan* (Lata–Talat), based on *Raag Yaman Kalyan,* which epitomised star-crossed love. Dilip Kumar and Madhubala look to be at their emotional best in the song. Veteran D.N. Madhok, Prem Dhawan and Kaif Irfani penned the lyrics of the album.

AAN

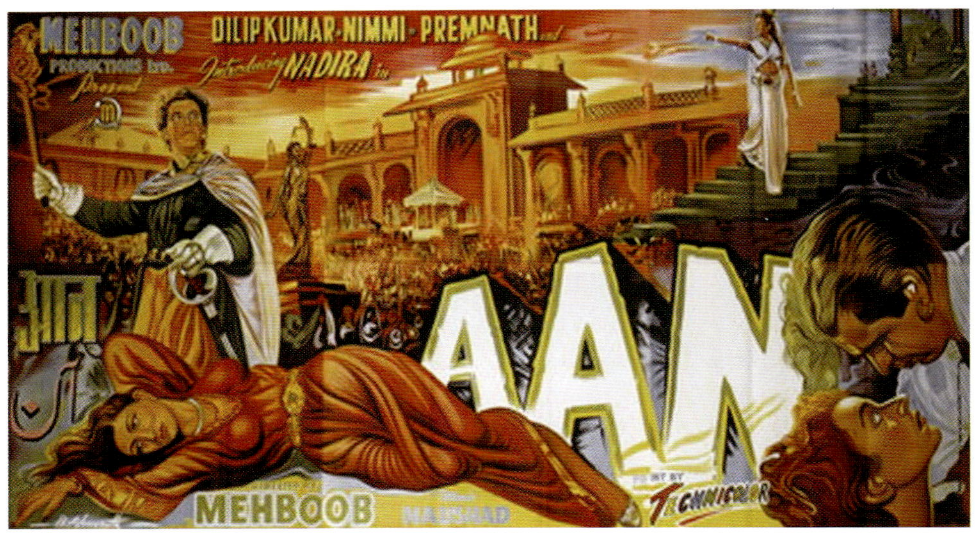

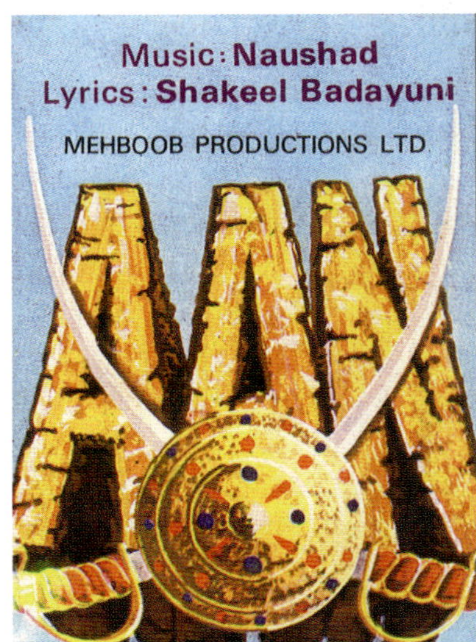

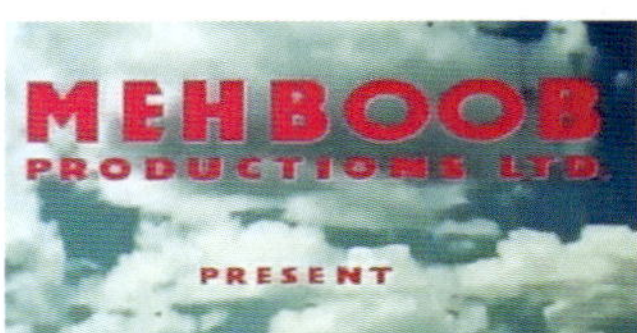

DATE / YEAR OF RELEASE: 1952
BANNER / PRODUCER: MEHBOOB PRODUCTIONS LTD
DIRECTION: MEHBOOB KHAN
MUSIC: NAUSHAD
LYRICS: SHAKEEL BADAYUNI
PLAYBACK: SHAMSHAD BEGUM / MOHD. RAFI / LATA MANGESHKAR / SHYAM KUMAR
STORY / SCREENPLAY: R.S. CHAUDHARY / S. ALI RAZA
DIALOGUE: S. ALI RAZA
CINEMATOGRAPHY: FAREDOON A. IRANI
EDITING: SHAMSUDDIN KADRI
AUDIOGRAPHY: KAUSHIK
CHOREOGRAPHY: KRISHNA KUMAR / SURYA KUMAR
ART: M.R. ACHREKAR
CAST: DILIP KUMAR / NIMMI / PREMNATH / NADIRA / SHEELA NAIK / MUKRI / MURAD / KUKKOO / MAYA / ABDUL / AGHA MEHRAJ / NILAMBAI / AMIR BANOO

With super successful *Andaz* under his belt, Mehboob Khan was itching to surpass his success with a bigger accomplishment. *Andaz* had not only become virtually the biggest box office hit ever in India but had also touched new heights of technical perfection. The era of colour films had already dawned sometime back in Hollywood but no one had really made a successful full-length colour film (V. Shantaram's *Sairandhri* made in the early 1930s was an abysmal failure). Mehboob Khan and his dearest friend and ace cinematographer Faredoon Irani were of the opinion that after *Andaz,* the time had come to go for a big box office bonanza in colour. But there were deterring odds in realising this dream as no facilities existed in India to process a colour film. It was thus decided to collaborate with the Technicolor company in London. Taking due note of the cost factor, they decided to shoot the film on 16mm Gevacolour negative and have it blown-up to 35mm at the Technicolor Ltd. laboratories in London. George Gunn of Technicolor Ltd. was a great help to Mehboob Khan in setting-up the entire procedure. By now Mehboob

Khan had already finalised the purchase of a very large tract of land (on which the famous Mehboob Studio now stands) in Bandra to build his own studio. His two prized projects – the establishment of his studio as well as the pre-production of *Aan* – were going on simultaneously. Influenced by the larger-than-life films of producer Cecil B. DeMille, whom he had met on his first visit to Hollywood, Mehboob Khan wanted to make a spectacular film which would take India and the world by storm. He went for a sword-and-dagger Ruritanian-type adventure swashbuckler plot, full of Robin Hood heroics and thrilling duels a la Errol Flynn, Douglas Fairbanks and others who had risen in Hollywood via similar acts. The film's story was written by one-time writer-director of silent films, R.S. Choudhury and scripted by S. Ali Raza (later-day husband of Nimmi). The story of a kingdom and its populace had a strong socialistic message and content. This was going to be the first film to be shot in Hindi, Tamil and English, though the English version was shelved later largely because the logistics and economics were just not working out. After signing Dilip Kumar for the main lead, Mehboob Khan approached his protégée Nargis to play the role of the haughty princess and the first poster of *Aan* announced the star cast to be Nargis, Dilip Kumar, Nimmi and Nadira. However, Nargis politely declined as she had committed her shooting dates to Raj Kapoor for his *Awara* (a script which Mehboob had earlier rejected), the film which got worldwide fame. An infuriated Mehboob vowed to create another Nargis and assigned the role to a rank newcomer Farhat (aka Florence) Ezekiel, a Jewish girl after renaming her as Nadira for the silver screen. The role of Dilip Kumar's village sweetheart (Mangala) remained with Nimmi and that of the villainous senapati and brother of the King (Murad) with Prem Nath. The spectacular 'Arena' set of the film was erected on a land which extended over an area of 5,000 square yards in order to accommodate thousands of extras plus hundreds of horses and other animals. The mahurat of the film was held on the grounds on which Mehboob Studio currently stands on 26 October 1949. The film was shot in 450 days of working shifts and the rest is history.

Director Mehboob and the Magnificent Sets of Aan

One of the biggest blockbusters golden jubilee hit of all times and India's first magnum opus Technicolor motion picture *Aan* became a landmark in the country's film history. Leading man Dilip Kumar, the star-crossed romantic was given a sword to brandish and a temperamental horse to ride in his new avatar in the film. From the lovelorn young hero, Dilip Kumar was made to switch to the character of Jai Tilak Hada, the romantic action hero, a tough act which he effortlessly pulled off without a trace of self-consciousness. Against his basic nature, Dilip acted as an extrovert with felicity. He gave a bravura performance wielding his sword with the same flourish as those delicate emotions of a unique role. This was a new role of a daredevil, confidence-oozing, farmer performed with consummate ease and astonishing dexterity, by the thespian. Women gushed as he lipped Rafi's *Maan mera ehsaan arey nadaan* and *Dil main chupa ke pyar ka*. Kanika Bajpai even today swoons watching Dilip sing *Takra gaya tumse dil hi to hai.* Nimmi gave a superlative performance as Mangala, which won her worldwide acclaim. Nadira's arrogant princess was equally convincing. Prem Nath gave a polished performance as the villainous brother of the king.

Dilip as Jai Tilak Hada

Naushad used his midas touch to the hilt in delivering a truly outstanding score for the film. He gave array of timeless melodies including *Aaj mere man mein sakhi* (Lata), *Tujhe kho diya humne paane ke baad* (Lata), *Takra gaya tumse dil hi to hai* (Rafi), *Aag lagi tan man mein* (Shamshad), *Dil mein chhupa ke pyar ka* (Rafi), *Main Rani hoon Raja ki* (Shamshad), *Maan mera ehsaan arey nadaan* (Rafi), the Holi song *Khelo rang hamare sang* (Shamshad) and *Gao tarane man ke* (Rafi-Shamshad). A Rafi number, *Tera husn maange,* remained unused in the film and has hence been irretrievably lost. *Aan,* was quite a risky experiment which worked at the box office. It also had a successful international release. Interestingly, the music of *Aan* was re-recorded in London. *Aan* was also the first film in which Naushad, considering the vast canvas of the film, had used a hundred-piece orchestra.

Dilip, Nadira and Amir Banoo

Nimmi as Mangala

Nadira as the Princess

Prem Nath as the rebel Prince

After successful re-processing of the 16mm print of *Aan* in 35mm Technicolor in London, producer-director Mehboob Khan—the unlettered and yet practical visionary from Billimora who had arrived in Mumbai with a net capital of three rupees twenty-six years ago—drew up different plans for the release of this picture. Returning to India, as soon as

Dilip and Nadira

Music Recordings for Aan in London

he finished with his distribution arrangements, he flew back to London with the colour negative of *Aan* and got going with his language of gestures punctuated by some English words often wrongly pronounced. But the practical, shop-keeping Englishmen knew this language for centuries. With that language they had conquered an empire on which the sun never set for two centuries. The Englishmen liked Mehboob. They understood him perfectly. The Technicolor people in London lionised him. Sir Alexander Korda, the shrewd film magnate of Britain, signed up *Aan* for his distribution circuits in Germany and the United Kingdom. On 18 July 1952, *Aan* was released at the Rialto in London, the first Indian film to achieve this unique distinction. *Aan* ran for twelve weeks at the Rialto, that is, ten weeks more that the average English or American picture.

Overseas Exhibition Contract

Aan at Rialto Theatre (London)

Those who attended the world premiere did not even realise then that they were witnessing an Indian picture that was going to take India to fifty countries and the Indians into the hearts of millions of people. This film thus was in reality the foundation ceremony of India's cultural contact with over fifty countries of the world.

Aan thus became the first Hindi film ever to be commercially released in the United Kingdom. It was subsequently released in eighteen countries in Europe, four countries in South East and far East Asia, nine countries in the Arab world and six countries in the USA, netting around ₹25 lakh of overseas revenues, a first for a Hindi film. The film was released in London as *The Savage Princess*, in France as *Mangala, fille des Indes* and *Maya* in the rest of Europe. In the Eastern bloc countries of Europe, the film was released as *Mangala KCI Indije.*

A delighted Mehboob returned to India for the premiere at Liberty Cinema in Mumbai on 1 August 1952 only to witness an overwhelming response for his film. *Aan* was a spectacular hit all over India and Mehboob and Dilip Kumar became the cynosure of all eyes. People said that Mehboob Khan had pulled off the impossible. But Mehboob had just begun. He flew back to London to push the film further in that territory and also started looking at other countries. Within a few months, Mehboob Khan discovered many other countries where *Aan* was subsequently released with subtitles in about seventeen leading languages of the world. These countries included France, Belgium, Spain, Italy, Luxemburg, Greece, Norway, Portugal, Cyprus, Holland, Finland, Sweden, Austria, Switzerland, Bulgaria, Hungary, Yugoslavia, Egypt, Algeria, Iran, Japan, Malaya, the Africas, South America, Madagascar, Mauritius, Indonesia, Indo-China, Siam et al. Even today, the men and women folk of Algeria fondly remember Nimmi's character *Mangala.*

Aan is one of the major milestones in the career graph of Dilip Kumar which catapulted the actor to the *Numero Uno* position in the Mumbai filmdom. Most importantly, it also proves the profound versatility of the actor in performing diverse roles.

DATE / YEAR OF RELEASE: 1952
BANNER / PRODUCER: MARS & MOVIES
DIRECTION: AMIYA CHAKRABARTY
MUSIC: SHANKAR–JAIKISHAN
LYRICS: SHAILENDRA / HASRAT JAIPURI
PLAYBACK: LATA MANGESHKAR / TALAT MAHMOOD
STORY / SCREENPLAY: AMIYA CHAKRABARTY / RAJENDRA SHANKAR
DIALOGUE: RAJENDRA SINGH BEDI
CINEMATOGRAPHY: V. BABASAHEB
EDITING: D.B. JOSHI
AUDIOGRAPHY: J.M. BAROT / MINOO KATRAK
CHOREOGRAPHY: PARBATI KUMAR / SATYA NARAYAN
CAST: DILIP KUMAR / NIMMI / LALITA PAWAR / USHA KIRON / JAWAHAR KAUL / KANHAIYALAL / C.S. DUBEY / KRISHNKANT / CHANDRASHEKHAR

Dilip Kumar's widely-acclaimed portrayal of an alcoholic in *Daag* fetched him his first Filmfare Award for Best Actor in the inaugural year (1953) of the awards. Veteran director Amiya Chakrabarty, who had directed Dilip Kumar's debut film, produced and directed this classic under his own banner, Mars & Movies, as its maiden venture. Shankar–Jaikishan gave super hit music for the movie, tunefully sung by Lata and Talat Mahmood to achieve a stupendous melodic triumph.

The three principle characters of the alcoholic son, mother and the sweetheart of the alcoholic were played with consummate aplomb by Dilip Kumar, Lalita Pawar and Nimmi respectively. Their portrayals were so effective that they have remained etched in the memories of the cinemagoers for posterity. The utterly sensitive mother and son scenes between Lalita Pawar and Dilip, enacted with rare aplomb, are truly unforgettable. The scene in which Nimmi fakes drunkenness to wean Dilip away from the bottle as well as her imperceptibly romantic interludes with Dilip remains memorable till today. Dilip's drunken scenes and his down-to-earth portrayal of a much-wronged young man harbouring deep-seated misery within are Hindi cinema's triumphant moments. The great Kanhaiyalal also played Nimmi's father with his usual dexterity. Usha Kiron and Jawahar Kaul played the second romantic pair in the film. Few would recall that initially Madhubala was announced as Dilip Kumar's leading lady in the film (discussed in later chapter).

Lalita Pawar and Dilip

Nimmi and Dilip

Amiya Chakrabarty

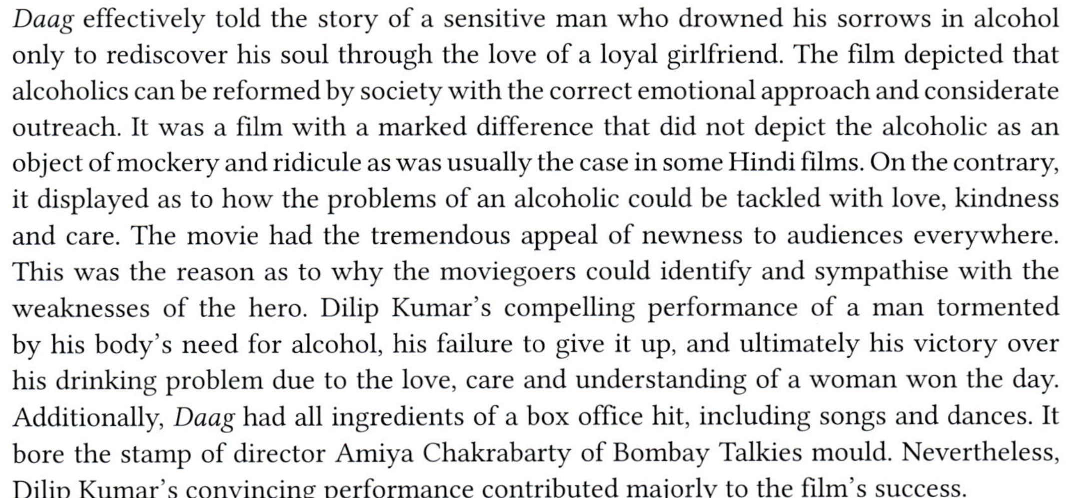

Daag effectively told the story of a sensitive man who drowned his sorrows in alcohol only to rediscover his soul through the love of a loyal girlfriend. The film depicted that alcoholics can be reformed by society with the correct emotional approach and considerate outreach. It was a film with a marked difference that did not depict the alcoholic as an object of mockery and ridicule as was usually the case in some Hindi films. On the contrary, it displayed as to how the problems of an alcoholic could be tackled with love, kindness and care. The movie had the tremendous appeal of newness to audiences everywhere. This was the reason as to why the moviegoers could identify and sympathise with the weaknesses of the hero. Dilip Kumar's compelling performance of a man tormented by his body's need for alcohol, his failure to give it up, and ultimately his victory over his drinking problem due to the love, care and understanding of a woman won the day. Additionally, *Daag* had all ingredients of a box office hit, including songs and dances. It bore the stamp of director Amiya Chakrabarty of Bombay Talkies mould. Nevertheless, Dilip Kumar's convincing performance contributed majorly to the film's success.

At this point in time, music directors Shankar-Jaikishan were going from strength to strength. Thus, time was ripe for them to compose music for a film starring the reigning superstar Dilip Kumar. *Daag* became the duo's first film with the thespian. Making the most of it, Shankar-Jaikishan (SJ) gave music of a lifetime for the movie. The chartbuster song, *Aye mere dil kahin aur chal,* took the nation by storm, and the evergreen number is sung even today. Penned by Shailendra, the unmatched *Raag Bhairavi* song was recorded in two Talat Mahmood versions (one slow and other fast) and another in Lata Mangeshkar's voice. The accordion played by Goody Seervai was the highlight of the film and its music. Lata and Talat ruled the roost in this evergreen SJ score with melodies like *Hum dard ke maaron ka itna hi fasana hai* (Talat), *Preet yeh kaisi bol ri duniya* (Lata), *Koi nahin mera is duniya mein* (Talat) and *Kaahe ko der lagayi re* (Lata). Talat's euphonious singing accentuated Dilip Kumar's magnificent histrionics as the alcoholic Shankar. Amiya Chakrabarty and SJ hit it off so well that the duo ended up doing six films for his banner Mars & Movies, namely *Daag, Patita, Seema, Badshah, Kathputli* and *Apne Huey Paraye.*

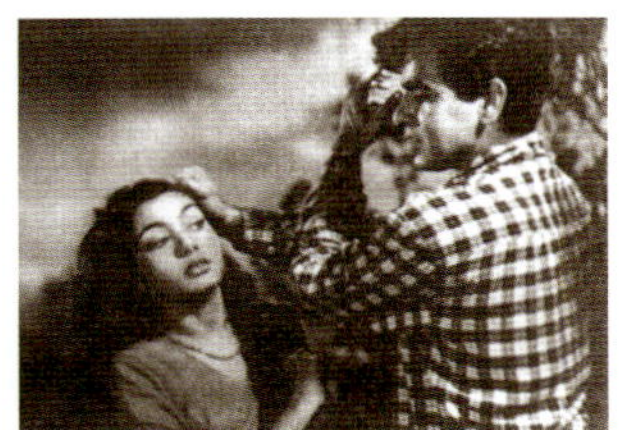

Stills from Daag

SANGDIL

DATE / YEAR OF RELEASE: 1952
BANNER / PRODUCER: TALWAR FILMS LTD.
DIRECTION: R.C. TALWAR
MUSIC: SAJJAD
LYRICS: RAJENDRA KRISHNA
PLAYBACK: LATA MANGESHKAR / GEETA DUTT / SHAMSHAD BEGUM / TALAT MAHMOOD / ASHA BHOSLE
STORY / SCREENPLAY: RAMANAND SAGAR
DIALOGUE: RAMANAND SAGAR
CINEMATOGRAPHY: PRAKASH MALHOTRA
EDITING: RANVIR
AUDIOGRAPHY: B.N. SHARMA
ART: KAMESHWAR SEGAL
CHOREOGRAPHY: GOPI KRISHNA
CAST: DILIP KUMAR / MADHUBALA / KULDIP KAUR / ANWAR HUSSAIN / SHAMMI / LEELA CHITNIS / PRATIMA DEVI / AMIR BANU / SHIVRAJ / H. PRAKASH / RAM AVTAR / BABY ROSHNI / SURENDRA JUNIOR

R.C. Talwar's *Sangdil* was an adaptation of Charlotte Brontë's classic novel *Jane Eyre*. The film starred Dilip Kumar and his favourite Madhubala. Dilip played the protagonist tormented by a secret which he does not disclose to the girl he loves. Eventually the secret is discovered–a deranged wife whom he has kept locked in an attic. It was a powerful Gothic tale, full of mystery and intrigue, but the film's producer-director R.C. Talwar could not do justice to the captivating tale despite sparkling performances by the lead pair. *Film India* called it 'a dull, boring and stupid picture', but there was a generous praise for Dilip Kumar, which had by now become a routine: '**Dilip Kumar puts to good use that famous face of his with its fixed tragic expression. He is quite faithful to the role and we certainly do not mind his whispers for a change in this loud industry.**' Critical response apart, it was an out-and-out romantic film with the famous Dilip–Madhubala pair excelling in putting forth their chemistry on the silver screen with a

telling effect. The film is also remembered for one of Talat's greatest songs (under Sajjad Hussein's music direction, picturised on Dilip Kumar) *Yeh hawa, yeh raat, yeh chandni, teri ek nazar pe nisar hai* and Lata's classic blue mood number *Woh to chale gaye aye dil* movingly enacted onscreen by Madhubala. For the first time, R.C. Talwar used a trolley shot in picturising the Talat song. The exquisite Talat–Lata duet *Dil main sama gaye sajan* was enacted by Dilip Kumar and Madhubala with immense feeling, like a couple truly in love. If only R.C. Talwar had been imaginative enough to create a different situation, one in which Madhubala (and not Shammi) would have been the object of the sensuous verses of *Yeh hawa yeh raat,* it may well have made a world of difference to the eventual box office fate of *Sangdil.* Also the scene in which Madhubala's *dupatta* envelops Dilip and the undercurrent of subdued interplay of emotions in the quasi-romantic interludes remain imprinted in the audiences' memory. Marvellous music and brilliant enactment of the songs were the tour de force of *Sangdil.*

Yeh hawa, yeh raat

Sangdil opens with Shankar (Dilip Kumar), the son of an affluent zamindar, and Kamal (Madhubala), daughter of a housemaid, serenading to the lilts of *Dharti se door gore badlon ke paar* (Geeta Dutt-Asha Bhosle) in their childhood and getting separated. Years later Shankar, the zamindar's heir, and Kamal, now a sadhvi who has renounced the world to join a God-worshipping sect, meet in the same haveli where they had spent their childhood. Memories come flooding back to rekindle the childhood romance as Shankar is mesmerised to see Kamal perform a religious dance to the strains of the melody *Darshan pyasi aayi daasi.* The rekindled romance leads to Kamal leaving her sect and agreeing to marry Shankar. As the marriage is about to be performed, a dark secret of Shankar's life is revealed that he has a deranged wife (Kuldeep Kaur) living in the same haveli. Her brother (Anwar Hussain) stops the wedding. Eventually, the lovers reunite after the deranged wife sets the haveli on fire (in which Dilip gets blinded) only to die. The inept directorial treatment of the narrative and its rather loose script prevented the film from rising to the heights of a classic.

Woh to chale gaye

Dil me sama gaye

We have long been admirers of Gothic literature and *Jane Eyre* is one of our favourite novels. A Gothic classic, it encompasses one of the most endearing, most passionate love stories of all time against the dark, mysterious, shadowy backdrop of Mr Rochester's mansion and its underlying horrifying secret. We have also seen the various Hollywood film versions of the great classic novel and the musical score of many leaves a lot to be desired. We can say with great conviction that the musical score of the film *Sangdil* is the one score that adeptly captures the Gothic nuances of the timeless love story that is *Jane Eyre.* Sajjad Hussein's unusual masterly musical score was the highlight of this film. Arguably, it is Sajjad's best score with Lata Mangeshkar, Talat Mahmood, Geeta Dutt, Asha Bhosle and Shamshad Begum putting their best foot forward for his magnificent tunes. The cadence of the amorous melodies continues to play in your head long after one has actually heard them. The music aptly captured the uncanny drama, the passion and the trembling uncertainty of the Gothic backdrop of the film.

Kahan ho kahan ho

The fascinating performances of Dilip Kumar and Madhubala and their captivating romantic interludes still invite the fans of Dilip–Madhu to enjoy repeat viewings of the movie. Undoubtedly, the splendorous musical score of Sajjad is a big draw too.

Madhubala, Dilip Kumar and R. C. Talwar

FOOT PATH

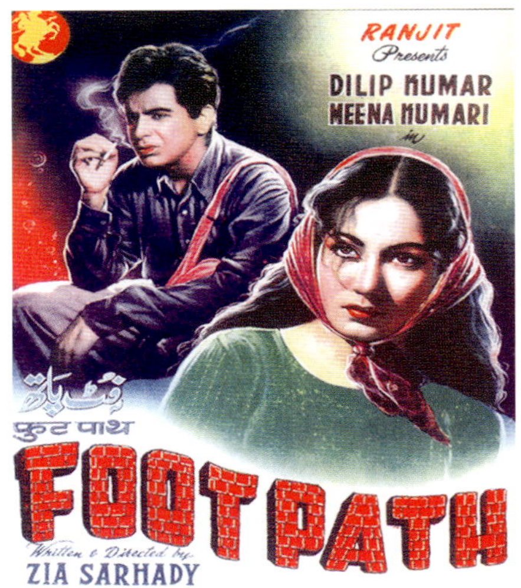

Dilip Kumar & Meena Kumari, in Footpath (1953)

DATE / YEAR OF RELEASE: 1953
BANNER / PRODUCER: RANJIT MOVIETONE / SARDAR CHANDULAL SHAH
DIRECTION: ZIA SARHADY
MUSIC: KHAYYAM
LYRICS: MAJROOH SULTANPURI / ALI SARDAR JAFRI
PLAYBACK: ASHA BHOSLE / TALAT MAHMOOD / PREMLATA / ASHIMA BANERJEE
STORY / SCREENPLAY: R.S. CHAUDHARY / S. ALI RAZA
CINEMATOGRAPHY: M. RAJARAM
EDITING: SHIVAJI AVDHUT
AUDIOGRAPHY: K.V. SHAH
ART: J.S. POPHALY
CAST: DILIP KUMAR / MEENA KUMARI / ROMESH THAPAR / ACHALA SACHDEV / ANWAR / KULDIP AKHTAR / RAMESH THAKUR / P. KAILASH / JANKIDAS / KAMLESH THAKAR / MASTER ROMI / SUMATI / MARUTI

Foot Path was an avant garde film directed by Zia Sarhady (a leftist of *Awaaz* and *Humlog* fame, who later migrated to Pakistan) for Sardar Chandulal Shah's Ranjit Movietone. Meena Kumari was Dilip's co-star in the film, marking the start of the unique 'Tragedy King–Tragedy Queen' pairing which continued through four fascinating films. This was a film in the parallel cinema genre much ahead of the dawn of that era (late 1960s–early 1970s). Dilip gave a measured but intense performance climaxing in a stunning monologue at the police station scene in the last reels. This was celebrated music director Khayyam's first major release and Talat Mahmood's solo *Shaam-e-gham ki qasam* remains an all-time favourite and one of the best songs ever picturised on Dilip Kumar. Meena Kumari's portrayal was an apt foil to Dilip's brilliant histrionics in the film, which sadly, did not do too well at the box office.

In the movie, Dilip Kumar played Noshu Sharma, a struggling writer who is unwittingly sucked into the vortex of the world of black marketeers. He becomes affluent and gets

used to the good life till a quirk of fate gives him a rude shock (the untimely death of his elder brother due to consumption of spurious medicinal drugs) which jolts him out of his life of comforts. Dilip Kumar's character had shades of gray–a self-centred man's role is not generally accepted by the audiences of Hindi film. But he performed the same with admirable aplomb. *Tarana* and *Foot Path* are the only films in which Dilip Kumar is shown smoking on the screen–that too, in just a few scenes. There is a powerful scene in *Foot Path* in which the black marketeers do not want to let go of Dilip and warn him of dire consequences.,*Marwa do agar marwa sakte ho to* (If you can, try getting me killed), he says laconically and walks down the staircase with a cigarette in the corner of the mouth. The film laid emphasis on moralistic values of the early post-independent era and denounced the black marketing practises and sale of spurious medicinal drugs. This was a typical Zia Sarhady film with subtle propagation of communistic ideology. It was Dilip's sterling underplayed performance, which prevented the film from becoming melodramatic or maudlin. Surprisingly, Meena Kumari had a rather sensual bathing scene in the film, but she succeeded in lending her dignified touch to it in her own inimitable style. The scenes between the lead pair were a treat to watch. In a surprise casting, the well-known journalist Romesh (also Ramesh) Thapar played Dilip's elder brother.

Bibi Jaddanbai was immensely pleased with Khayyam's work in *Pyar Ki Baatein* and one fine morning took him to meet Sardar Chandulal Shah and sang praises of his music. Later actor Anwar Hussain (brother of Nargis) also took Khayyam to Shah to recommend him as the music director of *Foot Path.* Shah had four or five composers in mind for the film including Khayyam and decided to test them all by getting a song–*Shaam-e-gham ki qasam aaj ghamgeen hain hum* – tuned by each of them. Khayyam used a tune rejected earlier by Wali Saheb and set the words on it. Each composer submitted his own version of the song. Majrooh Sultanpuri, Ali Sardar Jafri, Zia Sarhady, Dilip Kumar, Ayub Khan (elder brother of Dilip Saheb), Anwar Hussain and Shah himself heard all the compositions and unanimously chose the version prepared by Khayyam. Thus Khayyam signed his first big banner, big star cast movie. *Foot Path* was released at Mumbai's prestigious Liberty Cinema and ran for about 13–14 weeks. But the song *Shaam-e-gham ki qasam* took the nation by storm and went on to become an immortal classic, one of Talat Mahmood's timeless melodies. Connoisseurs sat up and took notice of the beautiful song and hailed its unique orchestral format (and Talat's mellifluous rendition). In the song, no *Dholak* or *Tabla* was used and percussion was created by double bass and Spanish guitar. Khayyam also used a new electronic instrument called Solovox, which was as small as a tape recorder. Notably Kalyanji Bhai (of the famed music director duo Kalyanji-Anandji) played the Clavioline in the song. Khayyam's choice of the female voice was Asha Bhosle and she rendered charming songs like *Soja mere pyare soja, Kaisa jadoo daala re balma* and *Piya aaja re dil mera pukare* for the film along with her first Cabaret number *Aaraaraa rum suhana hai yeh mausam.* The other songs in the album included *Taare hanse roun balma nahi na aye re* (Sandhya Mukherji) and *Thandi pawan chale sanjh dhale* (Talat-Premlata–Ashima Banerji). But, all the other songs paled into insignificance in front of the spectacular success of *Shaam-e-gham ki qasam.* At the behest of Zia Sarhady, the composer for the first time officially used his real name Khayyam (and not Sharmajee) in the credits of the film.

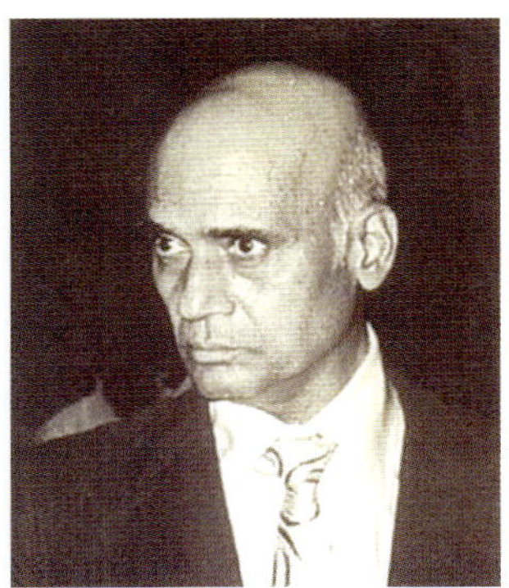

Khayyam

DATE / YEAR OF RELEASE: 1953
BANNER / PRODUCER: ASHA DEEP
DIRECTION: RAMESH SAIGAL
MUSIC: SHANKAR–JAIKISHAN
LYRICS: SHAILENDRA / HASRAT JAIPURI
PLAYBACK: MOHD. RAFI / LATA MANGESHKAR / TALAT MAHMOOD
STORY / SCREENPLAY: WAJAHAT MIRZA
DIALOGUE: WAJAHAT MIRZA
CINEMATOGRAPHY: KRISHAN SAIGAL / K.H. KAPADIA
EDITING: PRATAP DAVE
AUDIOGRAPHY: V.N. CHAUDHARI / MINOO KATRAK
ART: D. MALVANKAR
CAST: NALINI JAYWANT / DILIP KUMAR / DURGA KHOTE / K.N. SINGH / LEELA MISHRA / OM PRAKASH / HEMAVATI / SHAMLAL / MASTER KAPOOR / BABY LAXMI / MOHAN CHOTI

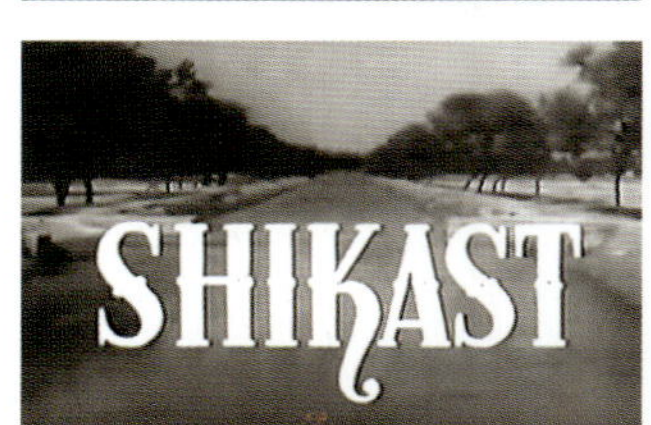

A railway train chugs into a railway station, a young man (Dilip Kumar – playing Dr Ram Singh) alights from it to join his bhabhi (Durga Khote) in a bullock-cart to travel to his village after a gap of seven years. A close-up of the great actor looms large on the screen and the expression on the face of Dilip Kumar instantly conveys his inner pathos and turmoil–an instant rapport is established with the cine-goers. *Shikast,* features one of the most gripping and celebrated performances of the actor and is an absolute must for Dilip Kumar fans and students of histrionics. Ramesh Saigal, who directed Dilip Kumar in his first golden jubilee hit *Shaheed* and struck a lifelong friendship with the actor, produced and directed *Shikast.* Saigal imbued the movie with rare sensitivity and unique interplay of emotions, coupled with fascinating conflict of characters. Nalini Jaywant was the leading lady of the film and her performance of an embittered widow was equally outstanding. In a candid conversation with us, Dilip Saheb was effusive in the praise of Nalini Jaywant's calibre as an artist and gave her the ultimate compliment quipping, *'Unke saath bahut sambhal ke kaam karna padta tha'* (You had to be very careful while working with her)'.

Dilip's Pathos, Turmoil

As Dr Ram Singh, Dilip Kumar gave a life-like performance portraying the doctor who angrily leaves his village when the villagers do not allow him to marry his childhood sweetheart Sushma, played by Nalini Jaywant. Ram returns to the village after a gap of seven years intending to sell his zamindari to his cousin (K.N. Singh), a ruthless man who is only too pleased to buy Ram's share of the huge property for a pittance. Before the transaction is completed Ram discovers that his sweetheart of yore (Sushma) is now a widow with a child and has cultivated a hardened disposition. The poor labourers tilling the village farms are undergoing untold sufferings at the hands of K.N. Singh. An embittered Sushma allows him to run her part of the zamindari also and is totally unconcerned about the hardships of the exploited labour. The sufferings of the poor labourers incite Ram into deciding not to sell his share of property. In fact, Sushma has carefully planned that Ram does not leave the village and provokes him by exploiting his compassion for the downtrodden. In order to improve the lot of the poor, Ram starts a school and a hospital for the villagers. Ram is still in love with Sushma but does not express the same due to circumstantial compulsions. He realises that Sushma too feels the same but is unable to express either her feelings of love or her support for his work because of prevalent social rigidities. Interwoven with the main emotional plot is the scourge of the deadly plague which strikes the village causing much misery. The film was in fact about widow re-marriage and the need to effectively combating plague. The movie had a tragic end with Sushma while trying to save the village, drowning in the surging waters of the local canal which has been breached due to sabotage by K.N. Singh. Ram saves her son to look after him ever after. Ramesh Saigal made a beautiful film till interval up to which the accent of the narrative was on the emotional conflicts. However, our personal opinion is that if the writer and director would have concentrated on the emotional drama and kept the morbidity associated with plague out of the equation, the film would have been a super hit.

Mahurat of Shikast

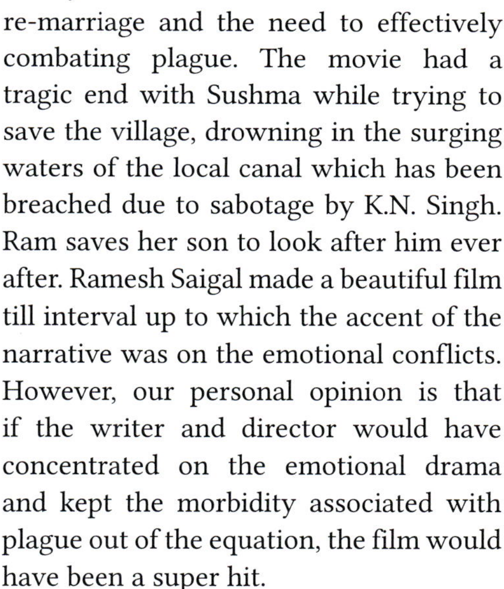

Stills from Shikast

The emotional scenes between Nalini Jaywant and Dilip Kumar are some of the most celebrated moments of Indian cinema with their histrionic *jugalbandi* attaining unscaled heights. Dilip's portrayal of a man who cannot comprehend the embitterment in the sensitive, loving girl he knew since childhood is a high watermark in acting. Moreover, Dilip Kumar was at his performing best when depicting the anger and frustrations of a man in love but unable to defend his beloved, mutely watching her destroy herself. There are classic scenes galore in the delineation of the characters among which mention must be made of a powerfully enacted scene in which Ram gets angrier and angrier at Sushma's behaviour towards a kid girl servant; he refuses to sign the property sale papers and in a fit of rage hurls the pen away which hits Sushma on her forehead leaving an indelible mark. Sushma merely smiles as this is the victory for her machination to prevent Ram from leaving the village. There is also the famous veranda scene in which Ram comes to persuade Sushma to be softer towards the village labourers, implores her not to fight with him, but ends up doing the opposite and having an altercation with her which she enjoys–it was sheer powerful histrionics of a kind. Ram's slipping on the staircase and recovering to see whether anybody has noticed it (blissfully unaware that Sushma has amusedly been watching) was also superbly done. Then there was that heart-tugging scene when Sushma, who opposes him in front of the village, comes to his house at night to give him money for the poor. On seeing Ram playing the sitar and singing (to the lilting Talat number *Sapnon ki suhani duniya ko*), Sushma sits down unnoticed. Ram realising that she is there looks at her with an expression of compassionate tenderness and sheer helplessness of being bound by shackles of society that it brings a lump in one's throat. Dilip was also absolutely brilliant in the scenes with Nalini's young son; with his face lighting up while spending time with the child and talking to him.

In those days, Shankar–Jaikishan (SJ) used to compose on the accordian or harmonium. Grapevine has it that the sublime melodies of the sensitive classic *Shikast* were composed by the inimitable duo on sitar and what an elegant score it turned out to be. Lata's *Raag Charukeshi*-based evergreen charmer *Kaare badra tu naja naja* stormed the charts. The film's music must be rated to be among SJ's best ever with several all-time classics such as *Sapnon ki suhani duniya ko aankhon mein basana mushqil hai* (Talat), the uniquely sculpted mesmerising duet *Jab jab phool khile tujhe yaad kiya humne* (Lata–Talat), the melancholic *Toofan mein ghiri hain meri taqdeer ki raahein* (Talat), the philosophical *Hum to hain khel khilaune* (Hemant Kumar) and the chorus of hope *Nayi zindgi se pyar kar ke dekh* (Rafi–Lata).

The film, despite unforgettable portrayals by Dilip Kumar and Nalini Jaywant, an outstanding musical score by SJ and deft direction of Ramesh Saigal, failed at the box office. Its distributor Gulshan Rai (later day famous producer and owner of Trimurti Films) lost heavily. As mentioned earlier, the film was marred by the extreme morbidity of its narrative in the second half. All said and done, *Shikast* would find a pride of place in the list of the best films of Dilip Kumar, Nalini Jaywant and also Shankar–Jaikishan.

SJ with Lata and Talat

DATE / YEAR OF RELEASE: 1954
BANNER / PRODUCER: MEHBOOB PRODUCTIONS
DIRECTION: MEHBOOB KHAN
MUSIC: NAUSHAD
LYRICS: SHAKEEL BADAYUNI
PLAYBACK: LATA MANGESHKAR / MOHD. RAFI / ASHA BHOSLE
STORY / SCREENPLAY: S. ALI RAZA / MEHRISH / S.K. KALIA / B.S. RAMIAH
DIALOGUE: AGHA JANI KASHMIRI / S. ALI RAZA
CINEMATOGRAPHY: FAREDOON IRANI
EDITING: SHAMSUDDIN KADRI
AUDIOGRAPHY: KAUSHIK
ART: V.H. PALNITKAR
CAST: DILIP KUMAR / MADHUBALA / NIMMI / JAYANT / ULHAS / MUKRI / AMAR / HUSNBANU / MURAD / SIDDIQI / PANDEYJI / HAROON / AGHA MIRAZ / SHAKEEL NOMANI / SHAHEEN / NAWAB KHAN

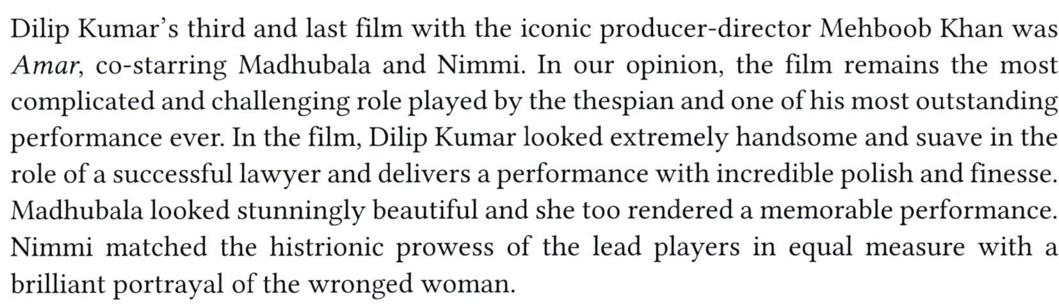
Dilip Kumar's third and last film with the iconic producer-director Mehboob Khan was *Amar*, co-starring Madhubala and Nimmi. In our opinion, the film remains the most complicated and challenging role played by the thespian and one of his most outstanding performance ever. In the film, Dilip Kumar looked extremely handsome and suave in the role of a successful lawyer and delivers a performance with incredible polish and finesse. Madhubala looked stunningly beautiful and she too rendered a memorable performance. Nimmi matched the histrionic prowess of the lead players in equal measure with a brilliant portrayal of the wronged woman.

Stills from Amar

The story of the film revolved around famous lawyer Amarnath or Amar (Dilip Kumar) who falls in love with a beautiful girl Anju (Madhubala) after some initial tiffs. In fact, Anju's father (Ulhas) had already decided on the match and proposed the alliance to Amar. Meanwhile, a village belle Soniya (Nimmi), on whom the villain Shankar Chhaila (Jayant) has set his eyes, has a crush on the lawyer. Everything is going well when one night Soniya while trying to escape the advances of Shankar Chhaila ventures into Amar's house. Amar, in a moment of surging passion overtaking his senses, seduces the poor girl to have a physical relation. Later, he is shocked at his own indiscretion and is in no position to accept or atone for it. The story goes on to relate to Amar's pangs of guilt, his fear of being discovered. Soniya is to be married to Shankar Chhaila but divulges before marriage that she is carrying somebody's child. Shankar Chhaila suspects Amar and gets killed by his own knife in a scuffle with the lawyer, witnessed by Soniya. The village belle is arrested on charges of murder. Amar finally musters courage to own his indiscretion in court–the self-inflicted death of Shankar Chhaila is proved and Soniya exonerated. Amar owning his mistake agrees to marry Soniya who is carrying his child. In a shattering climax, Anju, at a temple, renounces her love and hands over the locket presented by Amar back to him. In an utterly moving sequence, Anju walks away under strain of the following couplet of the film's famous title song *Insaf ka mandir hai yeh bhagwan ka ghar hai*:
Mayoos na ho haar ke taqdeer ki baazi, pyara hai woh gham jisme ho bhagwan bhi razi.
Dukh dard mile jisme wohi pyar Amar hai, yeh sochle har baat ki data ko khabar hai.

Anju's sacrifice

With *Amar*, Dilip became perhaps the first and the only screen hero to have raped a girl on screen. The scene, however, was shot with much care and there was no premeditated lechery. The passion was instantaneous. All we saw was Nimmi's expression of helpless fright, her clenched teeth, Dilip's dilating eyes and the falling of a burning lamp, accompanied by Naushad's effective background score. Soniya's agony is suggested in her dragging her woe-laden feet to her home, with her head lowered. Mehboob was a master director who attained sublime cinematic heights particularly when having actors of the caliber of Dilip Kumar, Madhubala, Nimmi and Jayant at his disposal.

Initially, Mehboob Khan had promised to assign the direction of the film to his assistant Mehrish. But, he got so fascinated by the film's subject–based on an intriguing script carefully crafted by Mehrish, Agha Jani Kashmiri, S. Ali Raza, S.K. Kalia and B.S. Ramaiah–that Mehboob ended up directing it himself. It is also rumoured that at one stage Dilip Kumar himself wanted to direct the film. Also, Meena Kumari was signed to play the female lead opposite Dilip Kumar. However, after the first six days of shooting, Meena's writer-director husband Kamal Amrohi apparently had a big quarrel with Mehboob, which resulted in the then budding actress withdrawing from the film. Whether Kamal Amrohi asked Meena Kumari to withdraw from the film or Mehboob Khan dropped her is not clear. But the grapevine has it that Dilip Kumar recommended Madhubala as the replacement to Mehboob who promptly signed her.

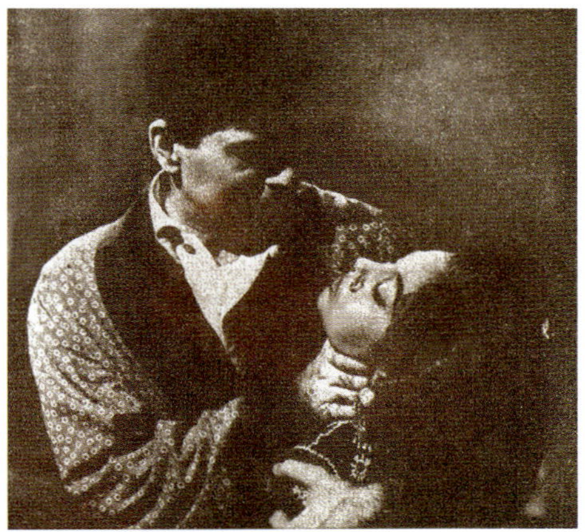

Dilip, Nimmi and the rape scene of Amar

As Mehboob Khan had reached the pinnacle of glory with his blockbuster films *Andaz* and *Aan*, there was tremendous expectation from *Amar*. The film was premiered at the Liberty cinema on the auspicious day of Dussehra in 1954. The response had been tremendous from the day the advance booking opened. The film also got rave reviews. The *Filmfare* magazine (then growing in popularity vis-à-vis *Film India*) wrote in its review in the 29 October 1954 edition: '**...*Amar*, which puts Mehboob among the greatest directors of the Indian screen, is embellished with finely sympathetic and powerful portrayals by Dilip Kumar, Madhubala and Nimmi, highlighted by a rich music score by Clare-winning maestro Naushad and the excellent, at times inspired, photography by Faredoon A. Irani. Superbly directed and acted with flawless perfection, the picture is a masterpiece of film craft and a real triumph for Mr. Mehboob's direction which displays his deft command of technique in every department of filmmaking. As a result *Amar* is a brilliant as well as an absorbing and entertaining picture with everything it takes to make one, from story to screen.**' In his *Film India* review, Baburao Patel wrote: '**This tale of a good man's degeneration, his conflict with his conscience and his final courage to confess and atone for his wrong provides the picture with a strong theme and a basis for powerful drama dealing with human sins and sacrifices, strength and frailty, dignity and depravity. But the moulding of the tale into a screenplay and its visual translation are characterised by thematic confusion and irrelevance and**

Initial and Final Choices of the Leading Lady: Meena Kumari and Madhubala

Stills from Amar

what ensues is weakening of the theme's force and befogging of the story. A clearer enunciation of the theme and development of the story, more in tune with the theme, would have invested the picture with greater force, appeal and perspicuity. But this time Mehboob seems to have contented himself with forceful flashes instead of a forceful whole... Technically the picture maintains Mehboob's usual standard. Faredoon Irani's photography being particularly outstanding. Mehboob's direction is confident and sometimes confident to a fault. Dilip Kumar as Amar performs with his usual polish and confidence though his role cried for some cogent psychological development. He is, however, easily the best among the three principal artists... It could have been a more effective and forceful picture had it not been portrayed so nebulously. And finally *Amar* proves that Mehboob needs better writers and a fully criticised scenario before he goes on the sets if he is not to repeat the attractive confusion that *Amar* is.'

The film initially did not fare well at the box office despite strong performances, fabulous music and deft direction. However, it did very well in repeat runs over the years. Quite interestingly, *Amar* (1954) was the first film in which Dilip Kumar played a lawyer. The only other film in which he played a lawyer is his last movie *Qila* (1998), co-starring Rekha. *Amar* showcases Dilip Kumar at his suave, dapper, elegant and handsome best, which adds a unique panache to the actor's sterling performance. Of course, Mehboob Khan was one of Dilip Saheb's favourite directors. Dilip Saheb has said, 'Mehboob Khan was an intuitive director with a flair for visual compositions and a dynamic narrative... it was always a pleasure to work with him.'

EP Disc

LP Disc

Amar had yet another classic Naushad score. The film's bold theme was way ahead of its times and Naushad's music matched the mood of every frame of *Amar,* right from the word go. The movie opened and ended with Rafi's immortal song *Insaf ka mandir hai yeh bhagwan ke ghar hai* (based on *Raag Bhairavi*). Otherwise, it was a Lata Mageshkar-dominated score with her several evergreen hits – *Na milta gham to, Na shikwa hai koi* (*Raag Tilak Kaamod*), *Umango ko sakhi pee ki, Oodi oodi chhayi ghata, Jaane wale se mulaqaat na* (*Raag Yaman*), *Khamosh hai khewanhaar mera* (*Raag* Bhairavi), and of course, *Tere sadqe balam na kar koi* (*Raag Bhimpalasi*). Another newcomer–Asha Bhosle – boarded the Naushad bandwagon in *Amar* with songs like *Ek baat kahoon mere piya* and *Radha ke pyaare* (*Raag Darbari*). We effectively re-picturised song *Insaaf ka mandir hai* for an episode of our super hit teleserial *Bikhri Aas Nikhri Preet,* truly embellishing the sequence.

AZAAD

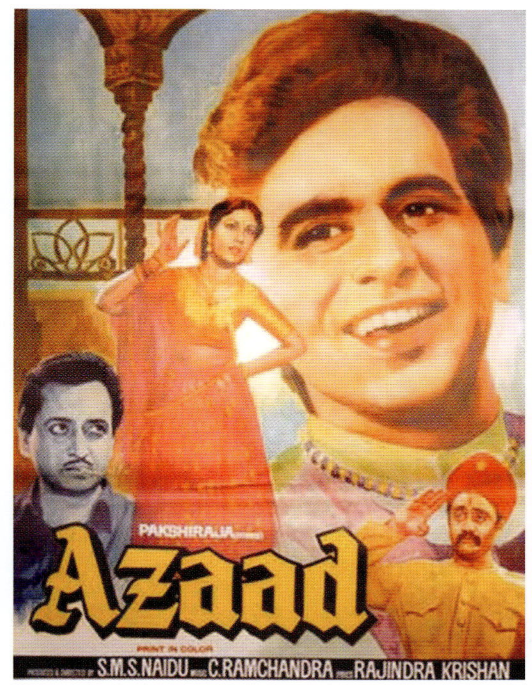

DATE / YEAR OF RELEASE: 18 MARCH 1955
BANNER / PRODUCER: PAKSHIRAJ STUDIOS LTD.
DIRECTION: S.M.S. NAIDU
MUSIC: C. RAMCHANDRA
LYRICS: RAJENDRA KRISHAN
PLAYBACK: LATA MANGESHKAR / CHITALKAR / USHA MANGESHKAR / RAGHUNATH JADHAV
STORY / SCREENPLAY: NAMAKKAL POET
DIALOGUE: RAJINDER KRISHNA
CINEMATOGRAPHY: SAILEN BOSE
EDITING: VELUSWAMY
AUDIOGRAPHY: JEEVA / B.N. SHARMA
ART: M.R. ACHREKAR / CHELLIAH
CHOREOGRAPHY: HIRALAL
CAST: DILIP KUMAR / MEENA KUMARI / PRAN / OM PRAKASH / RAJ MEHRA / BADRI PRASAD / S. NAZIR / RANDHIR / MURAD / RAMESH SINHA / BALAM / SHAMMI / ACHLA SAJDEV / DEEPA / MASTER NISAR / SAI AND SUBBU LAKSHMI

Performing complex, emotionally-charged and tragic roles in a string of highly successful films such as *Mela, Andaaz, Babul, Jogan, Hulchul, Deedar, Daag* took a toll on Dilip Kumar's health. While performing his most intense role in Bimal Roy's *Devdas,* he was advised by his psychoanalysts (Dr W.D. Nichols, Dr Woolf and Dr Raman Lal Patel) to refrain from doing sad films as it was having an adverse effect on his personal life and health. Dr Nichols was introduced to Dilip Saheb by Dame Margret Rutherford and Dame

Sybil Thorndike with whom he had a long discussion when he met them through a drama coach in London. Dr Nichols suggested a quick change of the genre of films he was doing. Dr Nichols explained to him that most actors who repeatedly worked in the same genre of films found it difficult to overcome the dichotomy that confronted them between the two lives they were leading. The unreal, sometimes, or rather most of the time, became so overpowering that the real called for protection from caving in and getting submerged. Dilip had been playing characters who were ill-fated. A morbid outlook had seized him as a result of his extreme involvement with his characters and living them beyond the working hours. Dilip Saheb took the advice seriously and his first flirtation with a change of genre was while performing the tragi-comic role of a swashbuckling prince in *Aan.* But, his first real foray in the light-hearted comic genre came about in Pakshiraj Studio's *Azaad*, which interestingly was virtually thrust upon him.

Dilip Kumar as Azaad

This attempt of Dilip to depart from the melancholic image brought him his second Filmfare Award for Best Actor. His portrayal of a daredevil Robin Hood in the fun-filled film blazed a new trail in screen projection of such characters. It was a sort of double role and his portrayal of Khan Sahib (in disguise) too was outstanding, appropriately hailed as a textbook lesson in acting by some critics. It became a landmark in Dilip's career which came at a fortuitous time as he was trying to break away from his tragic characters.

Dilip and Meena in Azaad

The film came about when South Indian film producer S.M.S. Naidu came to Mumbai in December 1954, with the print of his Tamil film *Malaikallan* (Bandit of the Hills). On a Sunday morning, he showed the film to Dilip Kumar and wanted Dilip to act in its Hindi version. Dilip Kumar and Baburao Patel looked at each other in disbelief that Naidu wanted the tragedy king to play a daredevil. But before Dilip could refuse, Naidu said, 'Don't look at each other like that! I have made ₹25 lakh from the picture which you saw now and I want to make another ₹40 lakh from its Hindi version. That is why I want Dilip Kumar.' Naidu looked at their sceptical expressions and added, 'How many Dilips and Patels are going to see my pictures? I don't produce pictures for folks like you. The masses see my pictures and I want to entertain them.' Dilip Kumar consulted his mentors and friends like Mehboob Khan, Naushad, S. Mukerji and K. Asif, et al. Most of them were unable to grasp his dilemma and his need to get a comforting approval from them. They thought Dilip was crazy to go and seek advice from psychiatrists and drama coaches in England. They named other actors who were sticking to the same genre and had no problems whatsoever. K. Asif virtually threw the gauntlet at Dilip Saheb saying provocatively, '*Kar ke dikhaiye*' (Let's see if you can do it). However, S. Mukerji had no second thoughts and said: 'Go ahead and do it. An actor's business is acting and it should not matter to him whether he is doing tragedy or comedy. What counts is the actor's ability and enterprise.' Still, Dilip Kumar tried to avoid Naidu for the next few days but the latter pursued him relentlessly till the contract was signed. The actor silently prepared for the role realising that comedy required an exceptional sense of timing, which was a carefully honed than a gifted skill. He came out with flying colours as the film was a huge success and the rest as they say is history.

S.M.S. Naidu and the Cast of Azaad

Consummate actor Meena Kumari, who had earlier worked with Dilip in *Foot Path* and had the dubious distinction of being heralded as the 'Tragedy Queen', was chosen to play the lead opposite Dilip Kumar in the film. She matched his immaculate comic timing with her own fascinating flair for comedy. The chemistry between the lead pair was magical and the Dilip Kumar–Meena Kumari team went on to do other landmark films like *Yahudi and Kohinoor* (another movie with large dosage of rib-tickling comedy). It is rather fascinating to note that the serious genre films of the 'Tragedy King' and the 'Tragedy Queen' (*Foot Path* and *Yahudi*) were comparatively average runners whereas their light-hearted romantic films (*Azaad* and *Kohinoor*) were runaway hits at the box office. Other members of the cast of *Azaad* like Pran, Om Prakash, Raj Mehra, Badri Prasad, et al were more than apt histrionic foils. Om Prakash's amusing rendition of the blundering Constable No. 442 was also a highlight of the movie. The film was completed in a record non-stop shooting schedule of just three months at Pakshiraj Studios (Coimbatore, Tamil Nadu) and nearby locations. The fabulous performances and lilting musical score by C. Ramchandra and lyrics of Rajendra Krishan reaped rich dividends for S.M.S. Naidu who struck gold with this golden jubilee hit–*Azaad.*

Still from Azaad

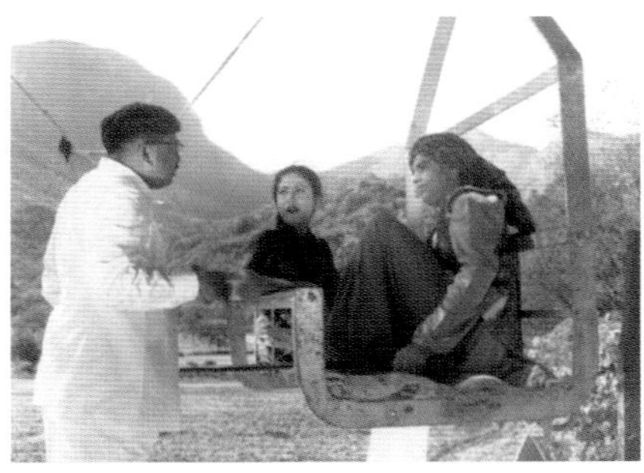

Cable Trolley Sequence

The filming of *Azaad* proceeded at a break-neck pace. One of the key sequences in the film shows the lead pair crossing a long aerial path across a deep valley aboard a cable trolley. Meena Kumari and Dilip Kumar were both initially scared to do this scene. However, being thorough professionals, they sportingly agreed to travel the dangerous aerial path. Unfortunately, the cable on which the trolley was travelling snapped and the actors had a narrow escape. Dilip and Meena were dazed as was Naidu and the whole unit, but they all thanked God that the artists had escaped a potential mishap, albeit by the skin of their teeth.

Azaad opened with a big bang on 18 March 1955 and there were a thousand guests for its premiere at Minerva in Mumbai. The film was simultaneously released in Excelsior (Mumbai) as the second main theatre. All well-known people of the film industry were there to see the miracle; the film had been completed in a record-breaking time of three months. Normally, Dilip Kumar took three months simply to get acquainted with the nuances of the script and other artists working in any of his films. Dilip's fans were thrilled to see him in a different role and *Azaad* which proved to be a great hit. Dilip also proved that he was a truly versatile actor who could perform light, fun-filled roles with the same ease and mastery as he did the complex, emotional and tragic ones. With this film, Dilip brought a new sophistication to light films. He showed that one did not have to play the buffoon to do a comic role. He was very good in all the three characters he played in *Azaad* –Abdul Rahim Khan or Khan Sahib, Azaad (the bandit) and Kumar, the good Samaritan in village elder disguise who saves the heroine from kidnappers sent by villain Pran.

C. Ramchandra, Naidu, Rajendra Krishan and Dilip Kumar–The Musical Team of Azaad

In that era, it was considered a prestigious assignment to compose music for a film starring one of the Big Three or the Trinity, that is, Dilip Kumar, Dev Anand and Raj Kapoor. But C. Ramchandra had already worked with the–'Trinity'–quite early on–composing music for Dilip Kumar's *Nadiya Ke Paar,* Dev Anand's *Nirala* and *Namoona* and Raj Kapoor's *Sargam.* In his second film with Dilip Kumar, C. Ramchandra created a super-duper hit musical score in *Azaad.* The producer wanted to make *Azaad* as a quickie and wanted all the songs to be recorded in just one week. Naushad was offered the film, but he refused saying that he needs at least a month or more to do justice to the musical score. C. Ramchandra accepted the challenge on the condition that he be paid one rupee more than Naushad (who was then charging a whopping ₹1 lakh per film) for this coveted assignment. The producer S.M.S. Naidu agreed. Naushad's loss was C. Ramchandra's gain and the great composer churned out a dazzling array of outstanding melodies. Lata Mangeshkar, who was in a superb form, sang her heart out in *Jaa ri jaa ri oh kaari badariya, Radha na bole na bole na bole* (*Raag Bageshri*)*, Kitni jawan hai raat koi yaad aa gaya, Dekhoji bahar aayi baagon mein khili kaliyan* (*Raag Bhairvi*)*, Pee ke daras ko taras rahi ankhiyan* and the dream dance duet *Aplam chaplam chaplayi re* (with sister Usha Mangeshkar). The dance number was picturised on Bharatnatyam experts Sayee and Subbalaxmi, both nieces of

P.A. Perimayaki, the famous ghost voice of the South Indian films. They always danced together, whether on stage or in films. After their dance in *Azaad,* they came to be known as 'The *Aplam Chapalam* girls'.

Then there was this terrific *Kitna haseen hai mausam kitna haseen safar hai (Raag Darbari Kanhda),* which became an evergreen romantic number. The song, picutrised on Dilip Kumar leading a horse-mounted Meena Kumari, was to be originally sung by Talat and Lata. Grapevine has it that Talat could not turn up at the recording reportedly due to a preponed foreign concert tour. Rajinder Krishan's lyrics had already been composed by C. Ramchandra and Lata's date was confirmed. Dilip too was very keen on Talat singing the song. S.M.S. Naidu was in a tearing rush as the Bengaluru (then Bangalore) location had been booked. Naidu in fact was to fly that very evening with his busy lead stars (Dilip Kumar and Meena Kumari) carrying the tape of the song recording. C. Ramchandra phoned Dilip Kumar and explained the situation saying that he would sing the song himself giving as much '*Talatian effect'* as possible and later dub it in Talat's voice when the singer is available. Dilip Saheb agreed. The song was recorded and Dilip Kumar was so very pleased with the result that he insisted on C. Ramchandra's (credited as Chitalkar) voice being retained. So, that is the story behind Chitalkar sounding so "Talatian" in the hit duet. *Azaad* also had a remarkable Qawwali–*Marna bhi mohabbat mein kisi kaam na aaya* (Raghunath Jadhav and party).

The music of *Azaad* is one of the tallest landmarks in the career of C. Ramchandra. The fact remains that no composer–lyricist combination had churned out such a popular musical score in just seven days. Lyricist Rajendra Krishan had then quipped: **'I have written songs under all sorts of conditions–while sitting in my car, sitting in my bedroom, sitting at a harmonium. But have you ever heard of a lyricist writing his songs with a producer's heavy hand on his neck? I was the lyricist and the heavy hand belonged to producer S.M.S. Naidu!'**

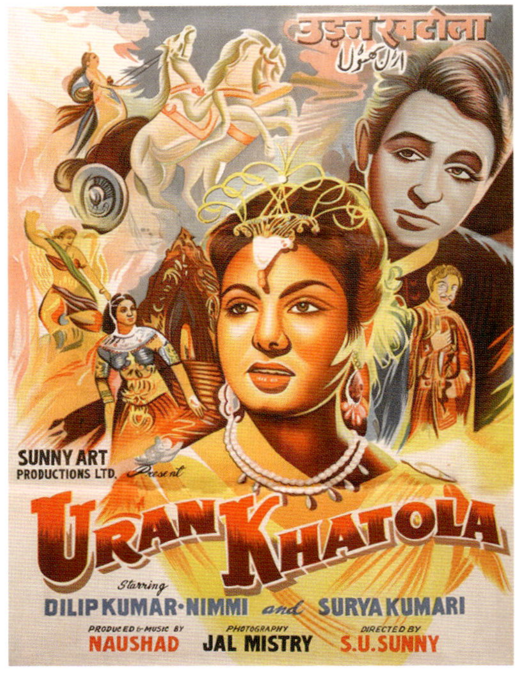

DATE / YEAR OF RELEASE: 20 MAY 1955
BANNER / PRODUCER: SUNNY ART PRODUCTIONS LTD / NAUSHAD
DIRECTION: S.U. SUNNY
MUSIC: NAUSHAD
LYRICS: SHAKEEL BADAYUNI
PLAYBACK: MOHD. RAFI / LATA MANGESHKAR
STORY / SCREENPLAY: AZM BAZIDPURI
DIALOGUE: AZM BAZIDPURI
CINEMATOGRAPHY: JAL MISTRY
EDITING: VASANT BORKAR
AUDIOGRAPHY: ROBIN CHATTERJEE
CHOREOGRAPHY: SURYA KUMAR
ART: V. JADHAV RAO
CAST: DILIP KUMAR / NIMMI / SURYA KUMARI / AGHA / JEEVAN / ROOPMALA / AMAR / NAWAB / SAYYAD JAAN / BABA / TUNTUN

Uran Khatola was another Dilip Kumar starrer (with Nimmi as the leading lady) and a yet another silver jubilee in 1955, bringing him fresh laurels in the film world. This time, Dilip had accepted to do a movie in a completely different genre–Fantasy–for his dear friends S.U. Sunny and Naushad, under their banner Sunny Art Productions (the makers of *Babul*). This is the only fantasy movie done by Dilip Kumar, and it too hit the bulls eye at the box office. It was an out-and-out musical with an unusual backdrop of an island kingdom ruled by a cruel queen (southern actress Surya Kumari) on which a suave polished gentleman (Dilip Kumar) crash lands and falls in love with the daughter (Nimmi) of the exalted head priest of the kingdom. The queen also falls in love with

Uran Khatola Playing at Imperial, Mumbai

Dilip. The film's popular musical score, its breathtaking cinematography, deft direction and superlative performances made it a super-duper hit after it released all over India on 20 May 1955.

Stills from Uran Khatola

Majority of the reviews of the film highlighted the unusual setting of is narrative and the fact that being a fantasy film, it had no references to any particular place, era or persons. The reviewers were also very appreciative of the exotic atmosphere created in the film, unusual directorial treatment and the rich design as well as the lavish mounting of the production. The reviewers, in unison, lauded the film for its alluring dances and melodious songs, which are popular to this day. Some reviewers also emphasised the fact that the performances of the main artists were of such a high standard that they almost overshadowed Sunny's superb direction. Dilip Kumar was especially highly impressive in infusing his role with rare charm, stately dignity and intense feelings. Deservedly, Nimmi too won high critical acclaim for her effortless performance in this film. Surya Kumari looked fetching and Jeevan as the menacing villain was credible.

S.U. Sunny

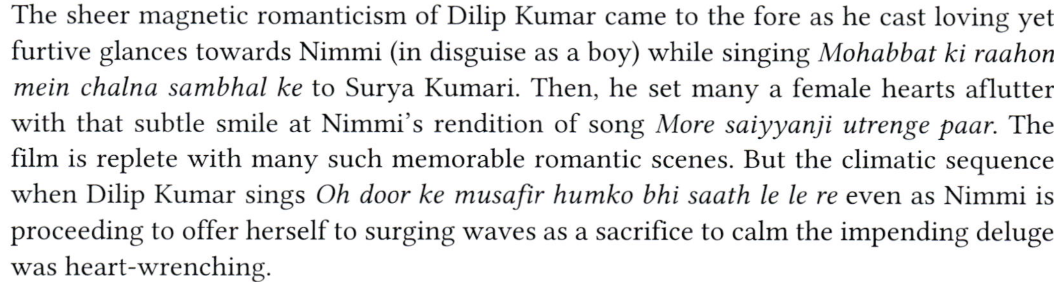

The sheer magnetic romanticism of Dilip Kumar came to the fore as he cast loving yet furtive glances towards Nimmi (in disguise as a boy) while singing *Mohabbat ki raahon mein chalna sambhal ke* to Surya Kumari. Then, he set many a female hearts aflutter with that subtle smile at Nimmi's rendition of song *More saiyyanji utrenge paar.* The film is replete with many such memorable romantic scenes. But the climatic sequence when Dilip Kumar sings *Oh door ke musafir humko bhi saath le le re* even as Nimmi is proceeding to offer herself to surging waves as a sacrifice to calm the impending deluge was heart-wrenching.

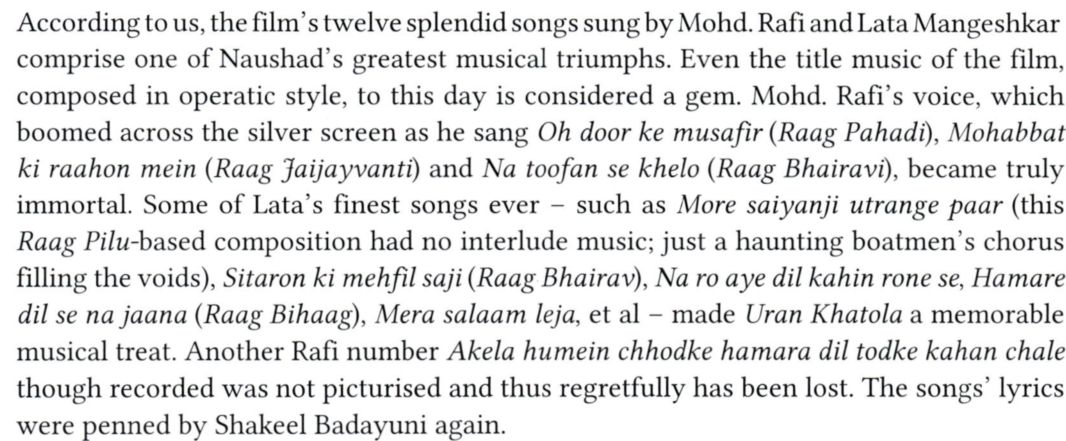

According to us, the film's twelve splendid songs sung by Mohd. Rafi and Lata Mangeshkar comprise one of Naushad's greatest musical triumphs. Even the title music of the film, composed in operatic style, to this day is considered a gem. Mohd. Rafi's voice, which boomed across the silver screen as he sang *Oh door ke musafir* (*Raag Pahadi*), *Mohabbat ki raahon mein* (*Raag Jaijayvanti*) and *Na toofan se khelo* (*Raag Bhairavi*), became truly immortal. Some of Lata's finest songs ever – such as *More saiyanji utrange paar* (this *Raag Pilu*-based composition had no interlude music; just a haunting boatmen's chorus filling the voids), *Sitaron ki mehfil saji* (*Raag Bhairav*), *Na ro aye dil kahin rone se, Hamare dil se na jaana* (*Raag Bihaag*), *Mera salaam leja,* et al – made *Uran Khatola* a memorable musical treat. Another Rafi number *Akela humein chhodke hamara dil todke kahan chale* though recorded was not picturised and thus regretfully has been lost. The songs' lyrics were penned by Shakeel Badayuni again.

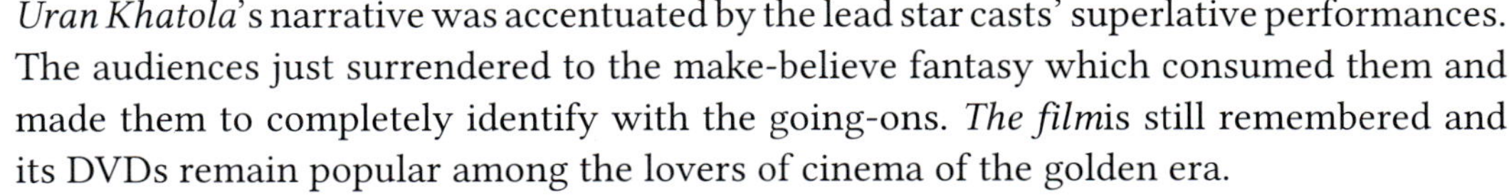

Uran Khatola's narrative was accentuated by the lead star casts' superlative performances. The audiences just surrendered to the make-believe fantasy which consumed them and made them to completely identify with the going-ons. *The film*is still remembered and its DVDs remain popular among the lovers of cinema of the golden era.

DATE / YEAR OF RELEASE: 10 NOVEMBER 1955
BANNER / PRODUCER: GEMINI PICTURES
DIRECTION: S.S. VASAN
MUSIC: C. RAMCHANDRA
LYRICS: RAJENDRA KRISHNA
PLAYBACK: MOHD. RAFI / LATA MANGESHKAR / CHITALKAR / ASHA BHOSLE / USHA MANGESHKAR / HEMANT KUMAR / TALAT MAHMOOD / MANNA DEY
STORY / SCREENPLAY: GEMINI STORY DEPT.
DIALOGUE: RAMANAND SAGAR
CINEMATOGRAPHY: P. ELLAPPA
EDITING: M. UMANATHA RAO
AUDIOGRAPHY: C.E. BIGGS / S.C. GANDHI
CHOREOGRAPHY: BHASKER ROY CHOWDHURY
ART: M.S. JANKIRAM
CAST: DILIP KUMAR / DEV ANAND / BINA RAI / VIJAYLAKSHMI / JAYANT / KUMAR / AGHA / BADRIPRASAD / SHOBHANA SAMARTH / T. MUKHERJEE / MOHANA / ISHWARLAL / G.V. SHARMA / VIJAY RAO / G. BHATT / ZIPPY THE APE

Legendary filmmaker S.S. Vasan, who was known as the 'Showman of the South Indian film industry', became the elected president of the Film Federation of India in 1954. He had produced some Hindi films such as the super hit *Chandralekha* (1948), *Nishan* (1949) and *Mangla* (1951). Vasan felt that it was about time that he made his mark in a big way in the Hindi film industry, targeting nationwide audiences, by launching a major motion picture with a top star cast. That's how Dilip Kumar's *Insaniyat* came about. Ramanand Sagar, later a renowned writer-producer–director, wrote the film. Vasan signed the dream cast of Dilip Kumar, Dev Anand and Bina Rai for the main roles. It was the first and last time that two of 'The Big Three', Dilip and Dev, came together in a film.

Insaniyat was shot at Vasan's Gemini Studios in Chennai (then Madras), and was completed in less than six months and released nationwide to a thunderous audience response.

For the film's shooting, a number of actors had to shuttle between Mumbai and Chennai with hardly any advance notice. But, those were the happy days of carefree air travel–no heavy security checks and long queues.

Dilip's Pathos, Turmoil

The film was based on a mass revolt against the tyrant Jangoora (played menacingly by Jayant) led by a farmer Mangal (Dilip Kumar) who is in love with the village girl Durga (Bina Rai). Unable to put up with the unjustified tyranny unleashed by Jangoora on his subjects, his army commander-in-chief Bhanu (Dev Anand) defects and joins the famers on revolt. Bhanu and Durga fall in love and on knowing this development, Mangal sacrifices his love and gets Bhanu and Durga married. In the climax, the farmers' revolt under the leadership of Bhanu and Mangal triumphs and Jangoora is defeated and eliminated. Mangal gives away his life in the battle, saving Bhanu. The film had many stellar performances from Agha (playing Dilip's friend), Shobhna Samarth (playing Dilip's mother), Vijayalaxmi (playing the kind hearted queen–wife of Jangoora), Kumar (heroine's father), Jairaj (the second commander-in-chief of Jangoora's army), etc. But it was Zippy, the chimpanzee brought in from abroad specially for this film, who hogged the limelight, winning the hearts of audiences everywhere.

Stills from Insaniyat

The film was released at the Roxy theatre in Mumbai on 10 November 1955 to a tumultuous public response and went on to become a huge hit. As usual, Dilip Kumar was fabulous in his role as the man who loves but loses his girl. It was one of Dilip's initial attempts at playing a rustic, which proved to be immensely successful. He literally sang his way in to the cinemagoers' heart emoting Rafi's *Apni chhaya mein bhagwan bitha le mujhe* with astonishing depth of feeling. Then, the scene where Dilip discovers that his beloved is involved with Dev Anand, and he offers the jewellery he had been collecting for her in a temple, left the audience in tears. Of course, there is that famous scene where Bina Rai accuses him of sacrificing her husband Dev Anand's life because of his own interest in her. Dilip's expressions of pain at the realisation that his beloved did not even trust him any more were superbly acted. Furthermore, Dilip's scene with Jayant in his palace, his death scene in the end and the jail scenes with Dev are extraordinary. Notably, the now-famous death scene of Dilip Kumar in *Insaniyat* was extensively copied in the climax of Gulshan Rai-Yash Chopra's *Deewar* (1975) as Amitabh Bachchan repeated even the dialogue *Maa mujhe neend aa rahi hai* in his death scene.

As mentioned earlier, the film was shot in Chennai's Gemini Studios. Dev said that Dilip would go to Chennai at least one week before a shooting and discuss everything—the script, music and costumes—in great detail. In fact, he not only discussed his own costumes, but those of the other artists as well. Dev Anand vouched for Dilip's sincerity and hard work when he said: **'Whenever I would go to meet the director, Dilip would already be there before me discussing his scenes. He had a tremendous fervour to get things done the way he wanted them and it had stood him in good stead. But there was no question of any interference on the sets by Dilip; he was always very correct.'**

Most of the press reviews of the film highlight the gorgeous, spectacle and thrilling entertainment values of the film, while lavishly praising Dilip Kumar for his outstanding performance. *Film India* hailed *Insaniyat*as as 'a mighty entertainer' and its review read as follows: **'From the players, no one comes within a mile of Dilip Kumar. In the rustic and sympathetic role of Mangal, this great artistgives one of his best portrayals on the screen. Living the rustic role from foot to foot of this fast action drama, Dilip Kumar is paid a tribute of tears from the audience as he lies dying in the lap of his mother. The intense sincerity with which he has portrayed Mangal's role deserved better support from his co-artists. But this support never comes even once and at several places the wound of fury of Mangal's characterisation adds only to the artist's individual stature without contributing to the intensity of the drama.'**

S.S. Vasan signed the highly successful composer of that era, C. Ramchandra to compose seventeen songs for his ambitious multi-starrer. The exquisite line-up of hit songs created by C. Ramchandra included *Chup chup chup hone laga kuchh* (Lata), *Aayi jhoomti bahar laayi dil ka qaraar* (Lata-Talat), *Gori kar le too aaj singaar* (Rafi), *Tere sang sang piya* (Lata) and *Bansuria bole madhur ras ghole* (Lata). But Rafi's plaintive rendering of *Apni chhaya mein bhagwan bitha le mujhe* was the pick of the album. Rajinder Krishan again wrote the lyrics for this golden jubilee hit.

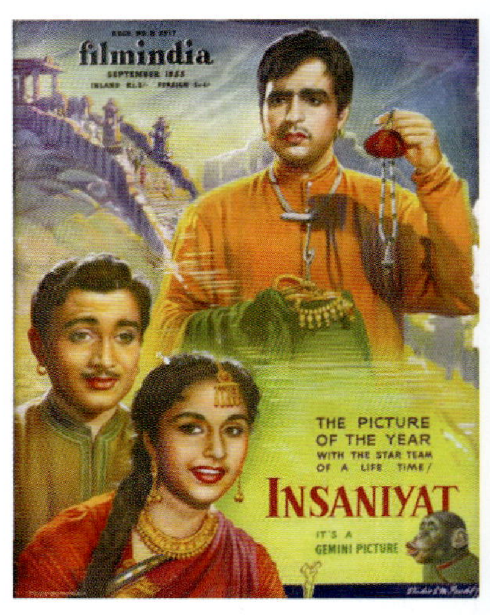

Insaniyat, which closely followed on the heels of *Azaad*, proved Dilip Kumar's all-round versatility which he had prudently decided to prove by accepting assignments in all genres. He proved that his acting range was far wider than the restrictive limits imposed by dying morbidly on the screen a la *Devdas*, which was coming to completion in 1955. Dilip Saheb enjoyed his southern sojourn in his long career and worked in numerous films with southern filmmakers such as *Paigham, Ram Aur Shyam, Aadmi, Gopi, Azaad* and *Insaniyat* (all super hits) and *Dharam Adhikari*. On the other hand, Dev Saheb did not particularly relish his south Indian sojourn and worked in only one film down south , that is, Sivaji Ganesan's *Amardeep* (1959) after *Insaniyat*.

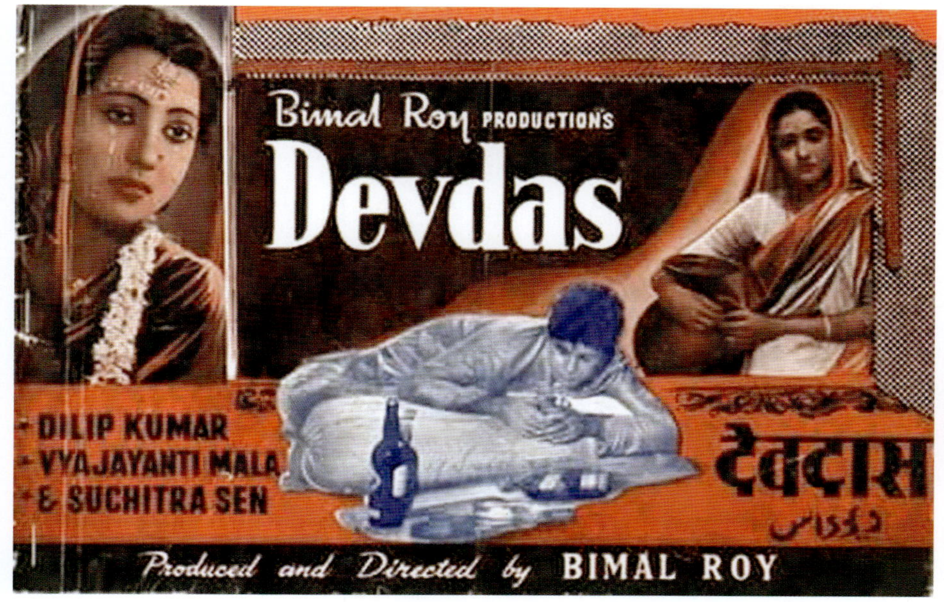

DATE / YEAR OF RELEASE: 30 MARCH 1956
BANNER / PRODUCER: BIMAL ROY PRODUCTIONS
DIRECTION: BIMAL ROY
MUSIC: S.D. BURMAN
LYRICS: SAHIL LUDHYANVI
PLAYBACK: LATA MANGESHKAR / TALAT MAHMOOD / MOHD. RAFI / MANNA DEY / ASHA BHOSLE / MUBARAK BEGUM / USHA MANGESHKAR
STORY / SCREENPLAY: NABENDU GHOSH
DIALOGUE: RAJINDER SINGH BEDI
CINEMATOGRAPHY: KAMAL BOSE
CHOREOGRAPHY: HIRALAL
ART: SUDHENDU RAI
EDITING: HRISHIKESH MUKHERJEE
AUDIOGRAPHY: P.S. MISRA
CAST: DILIP KUMAR / SUCHITRA SEN / VYJAYANTIMALA / MOTILAL / BABY NAAZ / NAZIR HUSSAIN / KAMMO / KAMALA MUKHERJI / KAMAL / PROTIMA DEVI / ASHIM KUMAR / RAMKUMAR / BABY CHAND / KANHAIYA LAL / MURAD / IFTIKHAR / MONI CHATERJEE / DULARI / NANA PALSIKAR / SHIVRAJ / SARITA DEVI / SHAKUNTALA / RUBI PAL / BIKRAM KAPOOR / SHIVJI BHAI / JANI BHAI / GIRDHARI LAL VAIDYA / PRAN / JOHNY WALKER (GUEST ARTISTS)

By now, Dilip Kumar was scaling new heights in the art of acting with one great performance after another. His next film *Devdas* immensely added to his stature and is widely rated as one of Dilip's best films and (arguably) one of his best performances. Dilip Saheb too considers *Devdas* among his most favourite films. Sarat Chandra's famous and popular novel of the same name had been filmed earlier and there have been around twenty-seven versions in several Indian languages. The 1936 celebrated version made by

Bimal Roy

Kolkata's New Theatre and directed by the legendary Pramathesh Chandra (P.C.) Barua was a super hit bi-lingual with K.L. Saigal playing *Devdas* in the Hindi version and Barua himself playing the lead role in the Bengali version. Interestingly, Bimal Roy was the cinematographer of both the Hindi and Bengali versions for Barua and therefore the subject held a special fascination for him. Besides, it was a part of the 'Sarat Chandra Phase' in Bimal Roy's career when the legendary director successfully converted Sarat Chandra's novels into classic cinema–*Parineeta* (1953) and *Biraj Bahu* (1954). It was but natural for him to work on *Devdas* to complete his trilogy. On Sarat Chandra's novel's, Bimal *Da* had said: '**Any Sarat Chandra story is an asset because there is good plot construction, convincing characterisation, truthful yet dramatic situations and telling dialogue, the sum total of which strikes a deep human note. These strong points are good material for the filmmaker. Also any Sarat Chandra classic is a difficult job for any filmmaker. It means controversies. But who can resist the temptation to film this writer's works? Any Sarat classic is good box office for the filmmaker and provides the audience with first-class entertainment. In spite of the controversies that filming Sarat classics arouses, the works of this famous Bengali author continue to attract filmmakers.**' The character of *Devdas* had truly fascinated him since he had first read the novel but he must have also developed definite ideas about how the novel was to be filmed. Now was his chance to show it and he decided to take the plunge.

The famous story of *Devdas* centred around the characters of Devdas, Paro and Chandramukhi. Devdas and Paro are childhood friends who cannot bear to be parted from one another. Devdas is sent to Kolkata for studies and returns to the village as a handsome, well-educated young man, while Paro has blossomed into a pretty damsel. The childhood fascination of Devdas and Paro has developed into deep-seated love for each other, while the two have been growing up. It is suggested that Devdas wants to marry Paro but his father turns down the proposal. The reason being that Paro is from a lower caste and hence, unworthy of the zamindar family of Devdas. Strangely enough, Devdas's father can accept Paro as his son's friend but not as his daughter-in-law. One night, Paro secretly visits Devdas and suggests that they elope but the vacillating lover remains indecisive. Back in Kolkata, Devdas writes to Paro expressing his inability to turn against his family. Overnight he regrets the decision and rushes to the village, but by that time the letter has already been delivered to Paro. Spurned by the man she loves, Paro agrees to be married to an old zamindar leaving a shattered Devdas to drown his sorrows in alcohol. Devdas's friend Chunni Babu (played brilliantly by the great Motilal) introduces him to Chandramukhi, a prostitute, who falls in love with him but he cannot offer her any hope in return. Devdas remains wrapped up in his love for Paro which takes him into a downward spiral of alcoholic despair and self-destruction. Nothing can bring solace to the tormented soul of Devdas. Eventually, Devdas makes that one final journey to Paro's doorstep, and in a heart-wrenching climax, he dies there. As a powerful story and captivating motion picture, *Devdas* ends as a sublime tragedy.

The Climax

The subject demanded sensitive directorial treatment and strong performances by the cast, the selection of which posed some challenges. Bimal Roy was convinced that Dilip Kumar was the only actor who could justice to the complex character of *Devdas* (imbued with inner contradictions and self-destroying weaknesses). He approached the superstar accompanied by their common friend Hiten Chowdhury. After some discussion and Dilip Saheb's usual introspection, the thespian accepted to do the film at an unusually low price which Bimal *Da* could afford, to the utter surprise of Hiten Chowdhury. Next Bimal Roy signed the Bengali beauty and fine actress Suchitra Sen to play the character of *Paro* since she matched his vision of a woman deeply valuing self-esteem. For the character of the prostitute-dancer, the then singing superstar Suraiya as well as Dilip Kumar's favourite Madhubala were approached. But they declined the role on the ground that it was the second lead. The role eventually went to Vyjayantimala. *Devdas* kick-started two most rewarding cinematic collaborations. First, of the director and actor, Bimal Roy–Dilip Kumar, which lasted through three fabulous films—Devdas, Madhumati and Yahudi—until Bimal Da's untimely death in 1964. Dilip Saheb rates Bimal Roy as one of the finest directors he has worked with and candidly admitted some years back that he has sorely missed him. The second was of the the leading man and leading lady, that is, Dilip Kumar–Vyjayantimala. This pair created sheer histrionic magic on the celluloid in seven wonderful films—*Devdas, Madhumati, Naya Daur, Paigham, Gunga Jumna, Leader* and *Sunghursh.*

Stills from Devdas

For the role of Chunni Babu, Bimal Roy selected the redoubtable Motilal who did a great job as Devdas's friend. His scenes with Dilip Kumar were a treat to watch, especially the heart-rending last scene between them in the train, when Chunnilal bids good-bye to Devdas saying, '*Achchha* Devdas, *phir milenge*' (Ok Devdas, see you again), to which Devdas says, '*Zinda rahe to phir milenge.'* (Sure, only if I survive to meet again)'

Bimal Da, Suchitra and Dilip

Motilal with Bimal Da and Dilip Kumar

Bimal *Da* crafted the new version of *Devdas* displaying his consummate directorial brilliance in every respect to create an unforgettable classic. Bimal Roy's *Devdas* gave Sarat Chandra's novel a new lease of life. Dilip Kumar as the doomed lover Devdas, the beautiful Suchitra Sen as Paro, the lissom dancer Vyjayantimala as Chandramukhi and Motilal as Chunilal were all brilliant in their respective roles. The music composed by S.D. Burman did full justice to the thematic requirements and also had popular appeal. *Devdas* was released on 30 March, 1956 at the Roxy Cinema in Mumbai and went on to be heralded as one of Indian cinema's most enduring classics. *Film India* hailed the movie as 'a picture of artistic grace and great appeal'. Commenting on Dilip Kumar's performance, Baburao

Patel wrote: '**Dilip Kumar plays the coveted but complex role of Devdas and he fits the role very well. This is the first time that Dilip has made an almost perfect attempt to merge himself into the role and at places, it is extremely difficult to separate the two.**' The greatest compliment for him came from the celebrated writer Sarat Chandra himself who went on record to state that Dilip Kumar exactly matched his vision of Devdas.

Dilip Kumar as Devdas

Dilip Kumar touched new heights in his acting career by bringing this fictional character of Devdas to life. Scenes depicting the tormented Devdas undertaking a desperate long journey in order to reach Paro's house before his impending death are unforgettably poignant. Talat Mahmood's voice as the playback singer matched Dilip's expressions to such a great extent that people thought it was Dilip himself singing the songs *Mitwa laagi re yeh kaisi* and *Kisko khabar thi.* Meanwhile, Dilip won the Filmfare Award (his third by then) for his mind-blowing performance; the public too loved him as Devdas and critics gave the film excellent reviews.

Living Devdas

Dilip Kumar rates his experience of doing *Devdas* as highly rewarding. He said: '**I found it difficult to do *Devdas* during the first eight to ten days of shooting. I gradually drifted into it, bringing Devdas closer to my own personality. Often an actor has to divorce his personality from the character but that wouldn't have worked. No actor is bigger than the material he is essaying, he has to give it an interpretation from his own understanding of life, he has to blend his experiences with the alien's. Bimal *Da* made me render Devdas on screen so very effectively by making me drift and ease into the character without excessive preparation and overplaying emotions. In the process I was greatly helped by a meticulously crafted screenplay and matching pithy dialogue. I think Bimal *Da* knew from his own sources that I was a stickler for making the writing base of a film strong. So he made it comfortable for me to participate in the writing work along with his formidable team comprising Nabendu Ghosh and Rajinder Singh Bedi, among others. The lines from *Devdas*, I must mention here, are some of the most responsible and sensitive ever written for a Hindi film hero. In fact, the dialogues of *Devdas* are replete with a haunting sensitivity, spontaneity and meaning. They came from the pen of Rajinder Singh Bedi, one of those rare writers whose syntax was so perfect that the simple lines he wrote inspired actors to build up deep emotions in their rendering. Being myself not given to superfluous speech, I appreciated the precision and brevity of the lines he wrote for *Devdas*. They were lines of profound meaning at times, but they were so simply and sensitively worded that generations of viewers have found pleasure in repeating them lovingly.**'

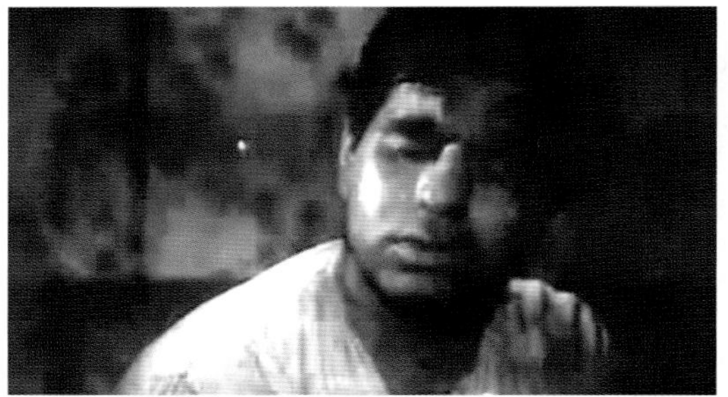

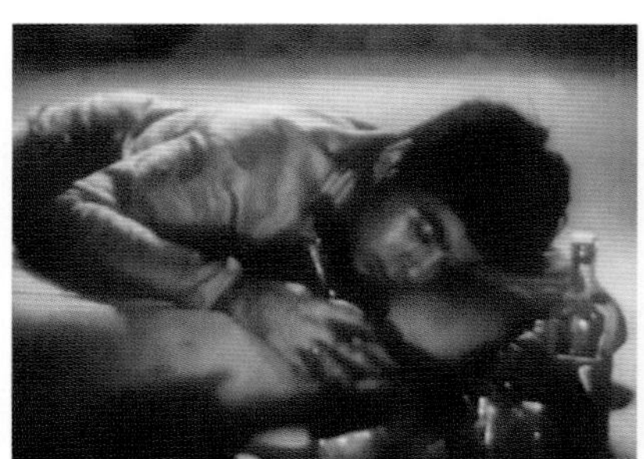

Sheer Melancholic Intensity of Dilip's Devdas

Suchitra Sen

Suchitra Sen did full justice to the character of Paro, despite her heavy Bengali accent, and emerged as an apt foil to Dilip Kumar. The famous scene at the pond where Devdas reprimands Paro; the scene in which Paro visits Devdas in the night; and the closed door scene in which the married Paro exhorts Devdas to give up drinking and get married are cases in point. She was beautifully picturised in the film and looked every bit like Paro. The only scene between Paro and Chandramukhi was also superbly emoted by Suchitran Sen and Vyjayantimala.

Dilip Kumar and Suchitra Sen in Devdas

Vyjayanti as Chandramukhi

Twinkle-toed dancing star Vyjayantimala until then was known for her roles in escapist films such as *Bahar, Nagin, Taj, Anjan,* etc. Playing Chandramukhi catapulted her into the big league of actors and changed the course of her career. Dilip Kumar has said: '**Vyjayanti and I carried forward the professional understanding and bonhomie we had developed during *Devdas* to the six films we worked in thereafter. She emerged as a capable *artist* and a quick learner while portraying Chandramukhi.**' Vyjayantimala rendered a brilliant performance doing full justice to the character. She says this about the coveted role: '**When I was offered the role of Chandramukhi, it was the first time I was being given a role that recognised my acting talent and not just my dancing skills. Bimal *Da* explained the role to me and I was thrilled about it. Chandramukhi, in my opinion, was a great woman. I thought her love was pure, noble and what I loved about the character was her humility. That was her best facet. Her transformation from a courtesan to the simple, pious woman, who loved Devdas so selflessly that she wanted nothing in return, intrigued me. The turning point in the film is also very beautiful. It was the role of a lifetime, it gave me tremendous scope. And I was geared up to portray it to the best of my ability. I poured my heart and soul into Chandramukhi. In my opinion, Chandramukhi's was the greater character. Towards the end of the film, she manages to gain Devdas's confidence. He tells her this when they say their final goodbye. She touches his feet and asks when she will see him again. And he says that she will always be in his mind and that if they cannot meet again in this birth, they will in the next. It was a very poignant leave-taking. Devdas had such a great impression of Chandramukhi. He admits as much to her when he mentions her nobility and humility as compared Paro's arrogance and pride. The wonderful thing about the film was its realistic approach. Everything was so believable, that is why the role could be identified with. That sort of realism lingers on even till today.**' This is well said and straight from the heart. Vyjayantimala won the coveted Filmfare Award for Best Supporting Actress for *Devdas* but declined it as she felt that her status in film was that of the leading lady.

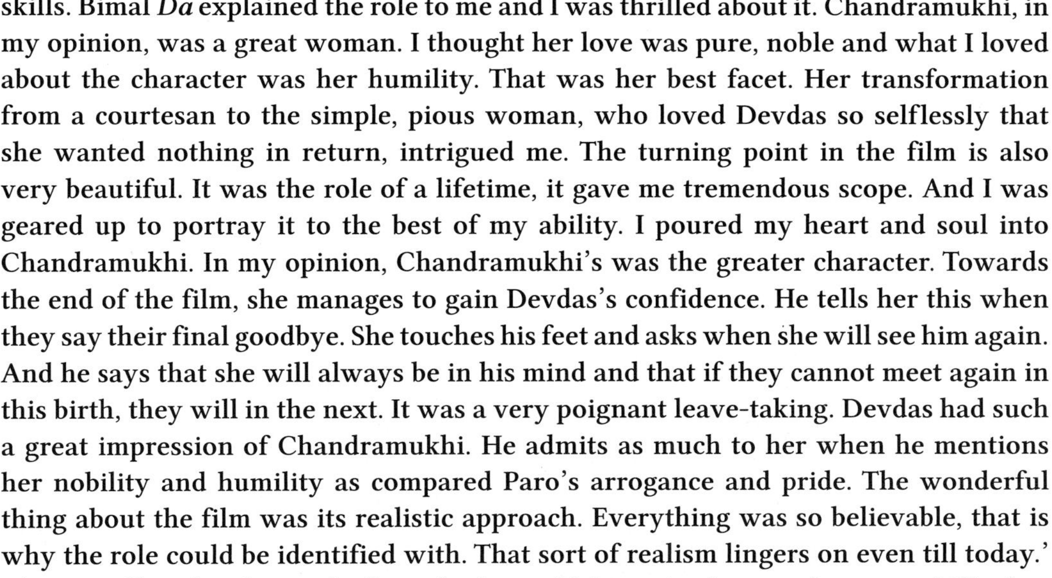

Dilip Kumar and Vyjayantimala in Devdas

P.C. Barua's *Devdas* had music by the great Timir Baran. So, when Bimal Roy decided to remake the film, he wanted a composer who could create music worthy of standing up to the original version. Instead of his regular composer Salil Chowdhury, Bimal *Da* thus opted for S.D. Burman, who fulfilled the high expectations with an evergreen score. Also, Dada Burman once again proved his versatility by composing songs in every musical milieu (children's playful number, melancholic solos, *Bidai Geet,* folk songs, *Mujra,* dance number, etc.) for *Devdas.* Dilip Kumar's magnificent portrayal was ably backed up by the heart-tugging melancholy conveyed by Talat in *Kisko khabar thi kisko yakeen tha* and *Mitwa laagi re yeh kaisi.* Vyjayantimala's *Chandramukhi* came alive with Lata's soulful numbers *Jise tu qubool kar le woh adaa kahan se laoon, Ab aage teri marzi oh rasiya* and *Oh Aanewale ruk ja koi dum.* The juxtaposition of mutual curiosity about each other among Paro and Chandramukhi was brilliantly captured in Rafi's folk song *Manzil ke raste pane ke waaste.* Similarly, Paro's emotional turmoil was splendidly captured in the backdrop of *Saajan ki ho gayi gori* (Geeta Dutt-Manna Dey). Even the other situational songs such as *Woh na aayenge palat kar unhein lakh hum bulayein* (Mubarak Begum), *Aan milo aan milo Shyam sanware* (Manna Dey-Geeta Dutt) and *Oh albele panchhi tera door thikana hai* (Asha-Usha) were splendidly crafted numbers. Sahir Ludhianvi again had penned the beautiful lyrics for this outstanding Dada Burman score. It was a landmark score for a landmark film.

Bimal Roy's impeccable direction, Dilip Kumar's fabulous performance, Motilal's histrionic brilliance, Suchitra Sen's immense talent and rare beauty, lovely Vyjayantimala living her role, the captivating musical score of S.D. Burman, Kamal Bose's mood cinematography and Hrishikesh Mukherjee's sharp editing—all contributed in making *Devdas* one of Hindi cinema's all-time classics. *Devdas* was not only a milestone for Dilip Kumar but it also established an 'acting school' to which many have sought to gain entry and learn. It signaled, in no uncertain terms, the actor's maturity, his oneness with characters who were ever so vulnerably human. *Devdas* is a prime example of what a director and his actor can achieve with simplicity, with the pristine purity of unspoken words in love scenes. No wonder, they cannot be ever erased from the memories of cinemagoers.

Bimal Da, Talat, Rafi, Burman Da

MUSAFIR

DATE / YEAR OF RELEASE: 1957
BANNER / PRODUCER: FILM GROUP
DIRECTION: HRISHIKESH MUKHERJEE
MUSIC: SALIL CHOWDHURY
LYRICS: SHAILENDRA
PLAYBACK: LATA MANGESHKAR / SHAMSHAD BEGUM / MANNA DEY / KISHORE KUMAR / SHYAMAL MITRA / DILIP KUMAR
STORY / SCREENPLAY: RITWIK GHATAK / HRISHIKESH MUKHERJEE
DIALOGUE: RAJENDER SINGH BEDI
CINEMATOGRAPHY: KAMAL BOSE
EDITING: DAS DHAIMADE
AUDIOGRAPHY: ESSA M. SURATWALA
ART: SUDHENDU ROY
CHOREOGRAPHY: SHARAD SHUKLA
CAST: DILIP KUMAR / USHA KIRON / KISHORE KUMAR / NIRUPA ROY / SUCHITRA SEN / SHEKHAR / DAISEY IRANI / DAVID / DURGA KHOTE / BIPIN GUPTA / RASHID KHAN / NAZIR HUSSAIN / RAJLAKSHMI / PAUL MAHENDRA / HEERA SAWANT / KESHTO MUKHERJI / MOHAN CHOTI / BABY NAAZ

Director-editor Hrishikesh Mukherjee, who made acclaimed films like *Anari, Anuradha, Asli Naqli, Chhaya, Satyakam, Anand, Guddi, Namak Haram, Mili* and *Khubsoorat,* made his debut with his own production *Musafir* in 1957. Hrishi *Da,* apart from being the assistant of the legendary Bimal Roy, was also an extremely accomplished editor and edited all Dilip Kumar films made by Bimal *Da.* While *Devdas* was being edited, Dilip Kumar used to often visit the editing studio and have discussions with the quiet and bespectacled editor Hrishikesh Mukherjee. Dilip Saheb was deeply impressed with the way Hrishi *Da* operated and his fine cinematic sense, and suggested to him, 'Why don't you direct a film?' Hrishi *Da* did not even look up from his work and quietly replied, 'I want to but who will finance me? I am keen to make a very different kind of film.' Dilip Kumar was curious about the storyline and Hrishi *Da* invited him to his one room paying-guest accommodation to hear the story. A curious, Dilip went over to Hrishikesh Mukherjee's pad where he was showed the walls of the room which were scribbled with names and dates and, sometimes, small graffiti. 'This,' said Hrishikesh,'is the story I want to make. A film about a house which has been home to three different sets of people ... each with their own story to tell.' Dilip Kumar was fascinated and confirmed that he would do the film free of cost and was paid a pittance of ₹5,000 only when his market rate was in lakhs. With Dilip Kumar on board, Hrishikesh Mukherjee had no difficulty in raising the money to start *Musafir*.

The film's story was written by Ritwik Ghatak, who also co-scripted the film along with the director. He related three different episodes which take place in one house, symbolising marriage (Suchitra Sen and Shekhar with Bipin Gupta and Durga Khote), birth (Nirupa Roy and Kishore Kumar with Nazir Husain and Heera Sawant) and death (Dilip Kumar and Usha Kiron with Daisey Irani and Paul Mahindra). Dilip Kumar starred in the third segment. He played a lover who meets his estranged beloved and her child while suffering from an incurable disease, but brings happiness in the life of her and her child (the child miraculously regains his ability to walk). Dilip's role in *Musafir* was tailor-made for him–a man who has loved and lost, and near his death meets his beloved again. Those scenes of Dilip and Daisy Irani, as the child, were like a breath of fresh air. Dilip is sick and looks ill but his face lights up with a half-smile when he talks to the child in a voice filled with tenderness. Daisy later said in an interview that Dilip helped her with her acting in both *Musafir* and *Naya Daur* (1957). He made her feel at ease and checked her from overacting.

Special appearance by Shailendra

A special highlight of *Musafir* was a song sung by Dilip Kumar with Lata Mangeshkar–*Laagi nahi chhute chahe jiya jaaye*– under the baton of music director Salil Chowdhury. This was the first and last time Dilip Kumar sang for a film, though Dilip is fond of singing ghazals (Urdu love songs). His voice has so much lilt and sweetness that it is a wonder he never took to playback singing seriously. Years later, in a good mood, Dilip Kumar broke into a Marathi song at a gathering. Asked why he hadn't ever cut a disc, the thespian reminded those present of the song he sang years ago for *Musafir*. When it was suggested that he should record an album, he smiled, saying, 'Oh it's too late for such indulgences now. I am much too old for all that.' Meanwhile, Salil Choudhury considered Dilip Kumar's only playback song as one of the most significant achievements of his career.

Another highlight of *Musafir* was a special appearance by the poet–lyricist Shailendra who played a street singer in the song *Tedhi tedhi hum se phire saari duniya.*

Salil Choudhury and Kishore Kumar

Like C. Ramchandra, Salil Chowdhury is among the few composers who have the distinction of composing music for the films of 'The Big Three'—Dilip Kumar (*Madhumati* and *Musafir*), Raj Kapoor (*Jaagte Raho*) and Dev Anand (*Maya*). The narrative of *Musafir* centred around its theme song *Ik aaye ik jaaye musafir duniya ek saraye re,* which was sung by Shyamal Mitra. All the songs were unique including Shamshad–Manna Dey's *Tedhi tedhi hum se phire saari duniya* (based on the *Nautanki style*), Lata's lilting bhajan *Man re hari ke gun gaa* (in *Raag Bhairav*) and Kishore Kumar's Binaca Top chartsbuster *Munna bada pyaara mummy ka dulara* (inspired by a Konkani folk song). But, as mentioned, the song that really made the score special was the Lata Mangeskar–Dilip Kumar classic *Laagi nahin chhoote rama chaahe jiya jaaye* in two parts. The trade papers' headlines screamed, 'Tragedy King sings with Melody Queen' and enormous public expectations were aroused. Grapevine has it that Dilip Kumar downed three Brandy pegs before negotiating the *murqi*s like *Taaron mein muskaan hai teri.* To hear Dilip and Lata sing together was the ultimate musical treat for film aficionados and fans lapped up the song as soon as it was released on disc and was also heard over Radio Ceylon. Shailendra penned the lyrics of the film's songs.

Composer emeritus Salil Choudhury is on record to state the following about the coveted opportunity of being the only music director to have Dilip Kumar's playback for Dilip Kumar himself: '***Musafir* was a trilogy in which Dilip Kumar had a tragic role by the name of "Pagla Chacha" alias "Raja". He also played the violin in the film. It occurred instantly to me to try Yusuf for a song in the film. I told this to Hrishi-*Da* who also liked the idea. We met Dilip Kumar at his home at Pali Hill–he was flabbergasted! He gracefully refused, saying: "Humming a tune is different but rendering it as a singer requires aptitude and skill." I told him that it was my responsibility as a music director to finalise the tune which would have the final okay by Hrishi-Da as the producer-**

director. I further added that until such time that Dilip himself was not satisfied, the tune would not be finalised. With great hesitation, Dilip agreed. I told Dilip that he should sing the tunes with an open voice but Dilip Kumar felt very shy. He opened up with the note 'Shadj' and slowly started singing with his eyes closed, a tune based on '*Raag Peelu*'. We liked his style of singing and also the tune. I accompanied Dilip on the harmonium while he was giving us the demonstration of his singing. The song was originally planned as a solo but Dilip felt that his actual singing should be restricted to the bare minimum that is he would render only a few lines of the song and suggested that there should be either more orchestration, or chorus, or an inclusion of another voice who could also sing a few lines with him. So, in order to oblige Dilip, I told poet Shailendra to shorten the song. However, Dilip's other suggestion of using a chorus, or more orchestra, could not quite convince me. I therefore thought of arranging for a female voice and in those days, who else could come to anybody's mind except the inimitable Lata Mangeshkar? After discussing it with Dilip, I contacted Lata to sing along with Dilip Kumar and she gladly consented. We three then got together and rehearsed the song a number of times. By that time Dilip's confidence soared and, great perfectionist that he is, he came very well prepared. On the day of the final take, Dilip Kumar came in his usual jovial mood but intermittently, he would revert and become serious. Purposely, I did not set any complicated tunes for him but only a few *murkis* at his insistence. The *alaaps* were set for Lataji. Everything went well and the song was recorded without many rehearsals. All of us present praised Dilip yet again for his new achievement as a singer and dispersed. While leaving the studio, when Dilip came to shake hands the inimitable actor could not hide his emotions. I too felt very happy. I became the only music director to date to record a song in the voice of Dilip Kumar. This I regard as one of the most significant achievements in my career.'

Hrishikesh Mukherjee credited Bimal Roy and Dilip Kumar for his first film as a director. However, despite the unique story, some pithy dialogue, a talented star cast and good music, the movie flopped. The theme of *Musafir* was his own, a page from his life. When he first came to Mumbai he lived in a building on Andheri–Kurla road. He used to wonder about his fellow tenants– where they came from, where they went. As indicated earlier, the three separate stories revolved around marriage, birth and death, a typically Bengali approach. As for the climax, Hrishikesh admitted he had been influenced by French writer Guy de Maupassant's famous story *The Painted Leaf.* On why the film did not do well at the box office, Hrishi *Da* said, 'People came to see big stars in big roles and were perhaps put off by their brevity. The three short stories didn't quite appeal.' Interestingly, years later Dilip Kumar made a special appearance in another Hrishikesh Mukherjee directed film *Phir Kab Milogi* (1976), to save the over delayed production from being a disaster.

The Famous Lata / Dilip Recording

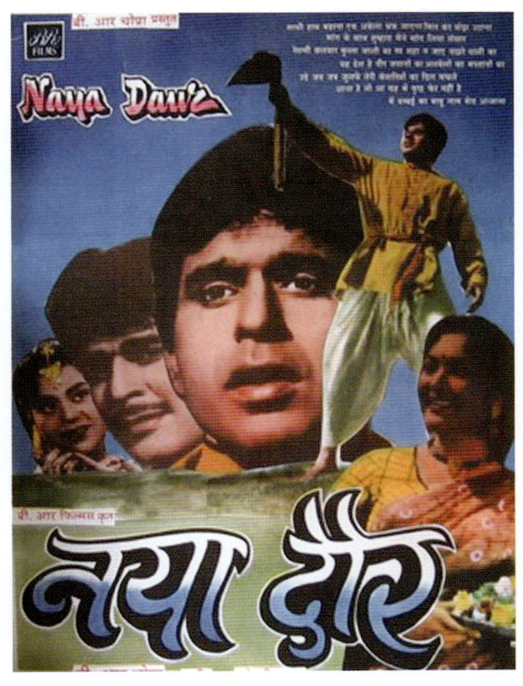

DATE / YEAR OF RELEASE: 1957
BANNER / PRODUCER: B.R. FILMS
DIRECTION: B.R. CHOPRA
MUSIC: O.P. NAYYAR
LYRICS: SAHIR LUDHIANVI
PLAYBACK: MOHD. RAFI / S. BALBIR / ASHA BHOSLE / SHAMSHAD BEGUM
STORY / SCREENPLAY: AKHTAR MIRZA
DIALOGUE: KAMIL RASHEED
CINEMATOGRAPHY: M.N. MALHOTRA
EDITING: PRAN MEHRA
AUDIOGRAPHY: ISHAN GHOSH / MINOO KATRAK
ART: SANT SINGH
CHOREOGRAPHY: PREM DHAWAN / MANOHAR DEEPAK
CAST: DILIP KUMAR / VYJAYANTIMALA / AJIT / CHAND USMANI / JOHNY WALKER / JEEVAN / MANMOHAN KRISHAN / LEELA CHITNIS / NAZIR HUSSAIN / PRATIMA DEVI / S.N. BANERJI / RADHA KISHAN / DAISY IRANI / S. NAZIR / MUNSHI MUNAQQA / NAZIR KASHMIRI / UMA DUTT / RAVIKANT / C.L. SHAH / RAJU / RAFIQ ARABI / LAXMAN / KATHANA / SHASHIRAJ / LALA NAZIR / KUM-KUM / MINOO MUMTAZ (GUEST ARTISTES)

Baldev Raj (B.R.) Chopra was a journalist in Lahore and came to India at the partition time to settle in Mumbai and went on to become a legendary filmmaker. He started his career with films like *Karwat* (Geeta Nizami and Satish), *Afsana* (Ashok Kumar and Veena) and *Chandni Chowk* (Meena Kumari and Shekhar) and then launched his own iconic banner of B.R. Films. The banner tasted great success with its first film itself, *Ek Hi Rastaa* (1956, Ashok Kumar and Meena Kumari). The fabulous success of B.R. Films and its epoch making motion pictures is history but one of the finest films to come out of the banner was the super-duper hit *Naya Daur* starring Dilip Kumar and Vyjayantimala. The film is known for Dilip Kumar's fantastic performance in the role of a (tongawalla) which fetched him his fourth Filmfare Award completing a hat-trick of awards–for *Azaad, Devdas* and *Naya Daur* in the years 1955, 1956 and 1957 respectively.

The making of *Naya Daur* is a story in itself. Writer Akhtar Mirza had penned a story on the subject of Man versus Machine in the climax of which a *tanga* (horse cart) defeats a bus in a race. The subject was offered to famous makers like Mehboob Khan, K. Asif, Raj Kapoor and Bimal Roy, etc. who turned it down saying that it was unviable. Mehboob Saheb found no meat in the story for entertainment and thought that it was fit only for a documentary highlighting the doomsday awaiting the labour force once machines replaced them. But, the subject appealed very much to B.R. Chopra. He was fascinated by the underlying message of the subject that 'progress is welcome as long as it is not at the cost of human aspiration'. Chopra Saheb offered the male lead to the great Ashok Kumar. The thespian told Chopra that the only actor who can do justice to the forceful role of the *tangewala* was Dilip Kumar and he actually phoned Dilip to recommend him to do the film. B.R. Chopra approached Dilip Kumar who initially refused, saying that he had heard the same story from Mehboob Saheb and did not entirely like it because of the climax in which originally the bus was to be beaten by a tonga by some kind of manipulation, which did not seem logical. Moreover, at that point in time, Dilip Saheb had accepted to do a film for producer-director Gyan Mukherji and did not want to divide his time between the two movies. Undaunted, Chopra Saheb decided to go ahead with writing the script in association with Akhtar Mirza and Kamil Rashid (dialogue writer). With the untimely passing away of Gyan Mukherji, his project got shelved and Dilip Kumar's interest in *Naya Daur* was revived. Chopra Saheb narrated the subject scene by scene to Dilip Kumar with the narration lasting four hours. Dilip Kumar asked for time until next morning to decide. To his utter surprise, early morning on the next day, B.R. Chopra saw Dilip Kumar at his doorstep wearing the full garb of a tangewala to discuss the subject in greater detail, fine tune the contours of the narrative and sign on the dotted line. Dilip Kumar made many suggestions–he wanted to emotionalise the narrative whereas B.R. Chopra had contemplated dramatising the scenario. Dilip's suggestions were accepted and rest as they say is history.

Asif / Chopra / Mehboob / Raj Kapoor / Bimal Roy

The underlying message of the film that 'it is wrong to misuse the immense potentialities of the machine to create prosperity, for the sake of a few, and generate unhappiness and misery for thousands'. This message was in sync with the Nehruvian dream of making India a technological utopia. Apart from the Man versus Machine conflict, the film had other very strong elements such as a triangular romance, upholding of democratic socialism norms in terms of bridging the rich–poor divide, dramatic turn of events and the eventual triumph of good over evil—all of which intrinsically made it an appealing human story. The fight of a man for a cause that seemed to be lost and his subsequent victory were the USP of *Naya Daur* which made the movie a stupendous hit.

The narrative was set in a hamlet nestling in a valley of hills and timber forests where taking pilgrims to a famous nearby temple by tongas and bringing forest wood for a timber factory were the only sources of livelihood for the villagers. The timber factory was owned by a kind-hearted zamindar Seth Madanlal (Nazir Husain) who was also the father-figure of the village community. Two prominent and righteous members of the community were Shankar, the tangewala (Dilip Kumar) and the woodcutter Kisna (Ajeet); both of them were fast friends. Shankar's sister Manju (Chand Usmani) silently loved Kisna. In this quiet and serene village, a beautiful girl Rajni (Vyjayantimala) returns with her mother (Pratima Devi). Shankar and Rajni are childhood friends and in the intervening years their juvenile affection blossomed into love. Kisna also falls in love with Rajni. As Seth leaves for a long pilgrimage, his greedy son Kundan (Jeevan) arrives and temporarily takes over the business and wants to mechanise the timber factory/sawmill. He brings modern machines to the factory and mill and also introduces a bus services from the village railway station to the pilgrimage site of the famous temple. This very adversely affects the livelihood of the tongawallas and the woodcutters. Against the backdrop of this Man versus Machine tussle, the love romance of Shankar-Kisna-Rajni and Manju-Kisna also has its own conflict. It was a highly emotional drama coupled with the conflict of good versus evil, which is eventually resolved upholding righteous human values and the Nehruvian socialism. A highlight of the film was the climax in which a very convincingly picturised race between the tonga (driven by Shankar) and the bus (driven by Kundan) takes place to resolve a bet between Shankar and Kundan in which the tonga wins. This story of highly-charged emotions and conflict of values was brilliantly enacted by its star-studded cast which was the most salient feature of this deftly directed picture. The scintillating musical score by maestro O.P. Nayyar was another high point.

Stills from Naya Daur

In 1956, one of the hottest onscreen pair was of Dilip Kumar and Madhubala who also had a personal affair going. This highly successful pair of *Tarana, Sangdil, Amar* and then in-production *Mughal-E-Azam* was signed up to play the leads in *Naya Daur*. Shooting commenced in right earnest and quite a chunk of the indoor scenes were picturised. Those who have seen the film would recall that around 60 per cent of the movie was shot outdoors. Madhubala's stern father Attaullah Khan at this point had created a conflict between the legendary pair of Dilip-Madhubala and did not allow his daughter to work at outdoor locations. Khan insisted on the film being shot at indoor locations only, when at the same time Madhubala was shooting on outdoor locations for Shakti Samanta's *Insaan Jaag Utha* and Bibhuti Mitra's *Phagun*. B.R. Chopra had already erected an outdoor set in a village called Budhni, around 250 km from Bhopal in Madhya Pradesh. He sacked Madhubala and signed Vyjayantimala instead, sacrificing the signing amount of ₹30,000

Dilip–Madhu the original choice

and announced the film in trade papers in a big way with Dilip Kumar and Vyjayantimala as the main leads. Not to be outdone, Attaullah Khan gave an advertisements in the same trade papers giving a list of Madhubala's in-production starrers with the title *Naya Daur* crossed out. Matters would still have remained within the confines of the industry had not an enraged Attaullah Khan filed a case against B.R. Chopra for sacking Madhubala on flimsy grounds. Chopra retaliated with a criminal case against Madhubala claiming that she returns his signing amount. The case came up for immediate hearing. Judge R.S. Parekh saw the film and eventually B.R. Chopra won the case. This is the same case where Dilip Kumar famously confessed his love for Madhubala in the courtroom, declaring in the open court, 'I love this woman and shall love her till my dying day.' The newspapers had a field day reporting all this. But, more about Dilip–Madhubala romance later.

A 300-member strong unit went to Budhni and shooting went on smoothly except a near mishap that occurred during the course of the climax race between the tonga driven by Dilip Kumar and the bus driven by Jeevan. Recalled the legendary Yash Chopra (then an assistant director to his brother B.R.), 'The horse cart was being driven at a breakneck speed with Dilip Kumar holding the reins. At a crucial moment, the reins slipped out of his fingers and we thought that was the end! We abandoned the camera ... all set to go to Dilip Kumar's help but he had managed to keep his cool all through. He kept his footing, leaned out and managed to get back the reins. We all breathed a sigh of relief. The scene was retained in the film.' Yash Chopra also recalled that Dilip Kumar at that time was working simultaneously in *Madhumati* and *Naya Daur* and allotted bulk dates of one month each alternatively to the two productions. He was therefore always available at the outdoor location of *Naya Daur* and assisted in every which way even when he was not required for shooting. He entertained the unit, played badminton and even cooked for everyone. Earlier, before commencement of the shooting, Dilip Kumar had enacted the entire film for the Chopra brothers at his then Juhu shack, in the manner he had visualised it to facilitate easy execution of the actual filming. No wonder that the results on silver screen were marvellous.

Dilip gave a stupendous performance for his well-scripted role with robust dynamism coupled to riveting sensitivity. His love scenes with Vyjayantimala, confrontation scenes with Jeevan and interactions with friend Ajeet are histrionic milestones. Vyjayantimala aptly complimented Dilip's tour de force portrayal. Johny Walker came up with a brilliant

Stills from Naya Daur

cameo playing a journalist and played to the gallery emoting *Main Bambai ka babu naam mera Anjana.* The film's theme aptly was summed up in a single dialogue, '*Yeh jhagda to haath aur machine ka hai*' (This fight is between man and machine). Kamil Rashid's dialogues (like '*Jab pet ki roti aur jeb ka paisa chhin jata hai to gharib ka dimaag hi kharaab hota hai*– (When the poor's food and little money is snatched away, of course he goes mad) and B.R. Chopra's direction were the other major contributing factors to the film's success. Akhtar Mirza also won the Filmfare Award for Best Story.

Dilip Kumar and Vyjayantimala in Naya Daur

Dilip with his fans

During the Kolkata Premiere of Naya Daur

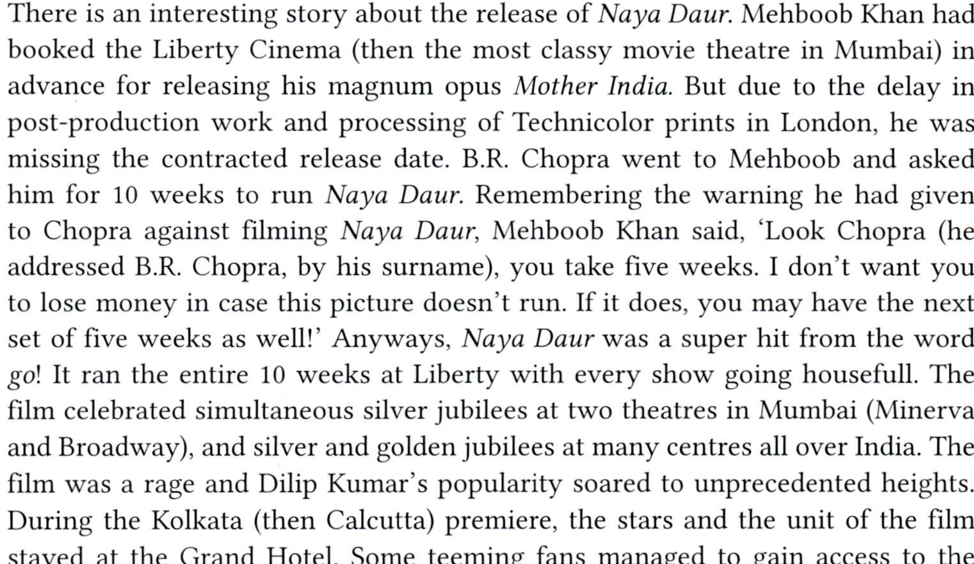

There is an interesting story about the release of *Naya Daur.* Mehboob Khan had booked the Liberty Cinema (then the most classy movie theatre in Mumbai) in advance for releasing his magnum opus *Mother India.* But due to the delay in post-production work and processing of Technicolor prints in London, he was missing the contracted release date. B.R. Chopra went to Mehboob and asked him for 10 weeks to run *Naya Daur.* Remembering the warning he had given to Chopra against filming *Naya Daur,* Mehboob Khan said, 'Look Chopra (he addressed B.R. Chopra, by his surname), you take five weeks. I don't want you to lose money in case this picture doesn't run. If it does, you may have the next set of five weeks as well!' Anyways, *Naya Daur* was a super hit from the word *go*! It ran the entire 10 weeks at Liberty with every show going housefull. The film celebrated simultaneous silver jubilees at two theatres in Mumbai (Minerva and Broadway), and silver and golden jubilees at many centres all over India. The film was a rage and Dilip Kumar's popularity soared to unprecedented heights. During the Kolkata (then Calcutta) premiere, the stars and the unit of the film stayed at the Grand Hotel. Some teeming fans managed to gain access to the hotel and the corridors were jam-packed. Crazy fans were loitering outside Dilip's room to get autographs and photographs. Outside the hotel, it appeared as if entire Kolkata had turned out to greet the star. With no hesitation Dilip mixed with the seething mass of humanity shaking hands and giving autographs, as a great roar of applause floated in the air. The crowd lifted Dilip and seated him in the convertible car. With difficulty B.R. Chopra and a couple of others also managed to get into the same vehicle. And then something incredible happened. The seething crowd surrounding the convertible lifted it off the ground, and literally carried it like a palanquin all the way from the Grand Hotel to the theatre where the premiere was to be held. Today such incredible scenes are mere nostalgic reminders of the massive sway the megastar Dilip Kumar held over the masses.

There is another interesting anecdote related to its silver jubilee celebration. In those days when silver jubilees of films were celebrated, customarily the chief guest's name was not printed on the card but somebody present at the function was selected on the spot. After the '*Naya Daur* Silver Jubilee Celebration' invitation cards went out, B.R. Chopra got a phone call from Mehboob. 'Aye Chopra,' he said, 'Is function *ka* chief guest *main banoonga*.' A delighted B.R. Chopra agreed saying, 'You be the chief guest. We'll feel honoured.' Mehboob Khan entered the celebration venue (Taj Mahal Hotel), declaring at the top of his voice the famous Urdu couplet which is a part of the Mehboob Productions' emblem–*Muddaiyee lakh bura chahe toh kya hota hai, wohi hota hai jo manzoor-e-khuda hota hai.* He stood up on the stage as the chief guest and openly confessed in public, the grievous error of judgement he'd made about a script which he had not only turned down himself, but which he tried to persuade Chopra to turn down too. Mehboob Khan was like that–a man of guts, who could publicly own up to his mistakes.

The Famous Temple Scene

In 1957, O.P. Nayyar had his maximum releases–nine films. But the jewel in his crown was *Naya Daur* for which he won the Filmfare Award with stiff competition from Shankar–Jaikishan (*Kathputli*) and S.D. Burman (*Pyaasa*). In a score of a lifetime, Nayyar's rhythmic music seamlessly blended with the film's overall atmosphere. Abundant use of boisterous Punjabi folk helped O.P. Nayyar create eight immortal hits matching the requirements of one of the finest scripts ever written. The captivating romanticism of the lead pair was splendidly accentuated by the glorious Rafi–Asha duets *Maang ke saath tumhara* and *Udein jab jab zulfein teri* as the peerless Dilip–Vyjayanti pair performed with great verve. The album has many other chartbusters–the enticingly rhythmic Shamshad–Asha's dance number *Reshmi salwar kurta jaali ka,* Rafi's comedy song on Johnny Walker *Main Bambai ka babu,* the fabulous situational bhajan by Rafi *Aana hai to aa raah mein,* the inspirational Rafi-Asha call for endeavour *Saathi haath badhana* and the pulsating bhangra *Yeh desh hai veer jawanon ka* (Rafi–Balbir). The O.P. Nayyar–Sahir Ludhianvi combination created an evergreen classic score with even the deleted Asha number *Ek Deewana aate jaate humse* being remembered for its quality alongside the Rafi two-liner *Dil leke daga denge.* After *Naya Daur,* O.P. Nayyar became the highest-paid composer. He even demanded and got a royalty from HMV which was unheard off. Some producers took an affront to this and O.P. Nayyar and B.R. Chopra parted ways on this score, never to work together again. Nayyar did not re-record the *Naya Daur* tracks, even when the colour version of *Naya Daur* was released, of late.

Saathi haath badhana

Yeh desh hai veer jawanon ka

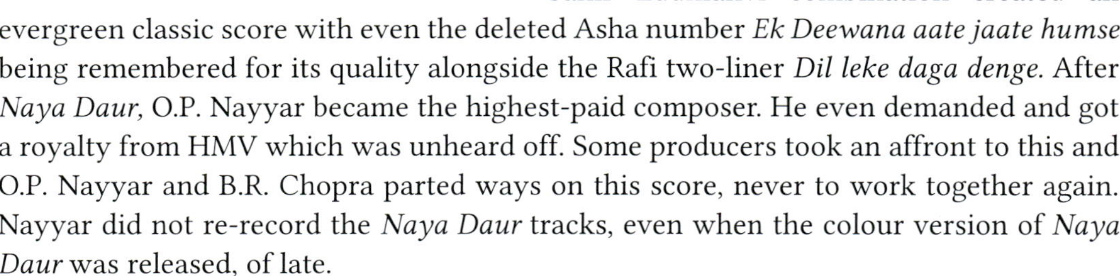

EP Disc of Naya Daur

'Naya Daur' 1957 Filmfare Awards for Dilip / Nayyar

LP Disc of Naya Daur

DATE / YEAR OF RELEASE: 12 SEPTEMBER 1958
BANNER / PRODUCER: BIMAL ROY PRODUCTIONS
DIRECTION: BIMAL ROY
MUSIC: SALIL CHOWDHURY
LYRICS: SHAILENDRA / MAJROOH SULTANPURI
PLAYBACK: MOHD. RAFI / LATA MANGESHKAR / MUKESH / MANNA DEY / SABITA BANERJI / MUBARAK BEGUM / DWIJEN MUKHERJI
STORY / SCREENPLAY: RITWIK GHATAK / RAJINDER SINGH BEDI
DIALOGUE: RAJINDER SINGH BEDI
CINEMATOGRAPHY: DILIP GUPTA
CHOREOGRAPHY: SOHANLAL / SATYANARAYAN / SACHIN SHANKA
ART: SUDHENDU ROY
EDITING: HRISHIKESH MUKHERJEE
AUDIOGRAPHY: DINSHAW BILLIMORIA
CAST: DILIP KUMAR / VYJAYANTIMALA / PRAN / JOHNY WALKER / JAYANT / TIWARI / MISRA / JAGDISH RAJ / BHUDO ADVANI / BAIJ SHARMA / SAGAR / RANJIT SOOD / SHIVJI BHAI / TARUN BOSE

The Book

Dilip Kumar, the intense actor, and Bimal Roy, the creator of eclectic cinema, had a successful collaboration in the timeless classic *Devdas.* At this point of time, the two were virtually a 'mutual admiration society'. Dilip Saheb rated Bimal *Da* as one of the finest directors ever and Bimal Roy considered Dilip Kumar the greatest actor he had worked with. Bimal *Da* was keen to make a commercially successful hit film with Dilip Kumar on a new subject would have the stamp of his cinematic excellence as well as all the trappings of a box office hit. Bimal *Da* and Dilip Saheb decided to base their new film on a Ritwik Ghatak story which dealt with the theme of reincarnation and transmigration of the soul. It was a surprising choice but the gamble paid off. *Madhumati* not only became a super-duper hit but was also heralded as an immortal classic. Like in Hollywood where the reincarnation always worked, it did here too, reaping rich dividends for Bimal Roy Productions.

Madhumati: The Surreal Dream

A surreal dream that flits across the sensibility of the viewer to cast a magical spell on his or her being—that is the captivating appeal of *Madhumati.* The film as such is based on a rather clichéd idea of 'love transcending lifetimes' but is told in a compelling manner that casts a spell on the viewer's imagination. Truly, the film had everything–top stars, brilliant performances, compelling scenario (Ritwik Ghatak), remarkable dialogues, outstanding music, flawless camera work (Dilip Gupta)–and, above all, Bimal *Da*'s unmatched craftsmanship which created poetry on celluloid. Ritwik Ghatak's story, set in the backdrop of Nainital and Kumaon Hills underlining the theme 'love rises above death's barrier' encompassed a sublime romanticism and incredible appeal which helped Bimal Roy create poetry on celluloid.

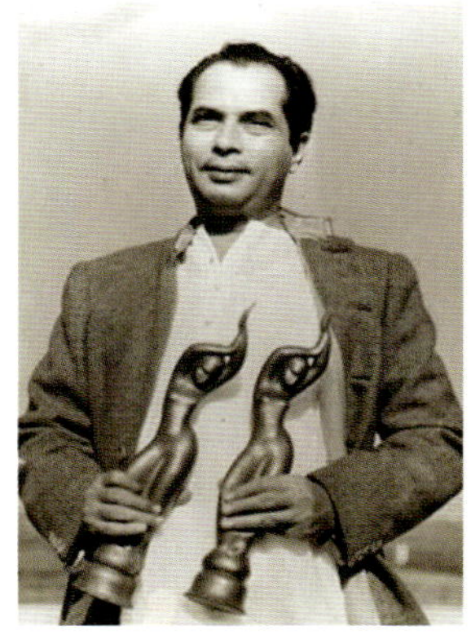

According to us, *Madhumati* could, on several counts, be easily adjudged the best Hindi motion picture ever produced–a perfect movie–a true celebration of cinema at its very best. It is like a fascinating dream, which allures, enchants, captivates and holds the viewer spellbound all through its narrative. This hauntingly beautiful celluloid masterpiece became Bimal Roy's biggest box-office success and literally swept the cinegoers off their feet with its quaint charm. The movie bagged a record nine Filmfare Awards in 1958, including Best Picture, Best Director (Bimal Roy), Best Supporting Actor (Johny Walker), Best Music (Salil Chowdhury), Best Photography (Dilip Gupta), Best Art Direction (Sudhendu Roy), Best Editing (Hrishikesh Mukherjee), Best Screenplay (Rajinder Singh Bedi) and Best Playback (Lata Mangeshkar). Dilip Kumar and Vyjayantimala matched their histrionic prowess to create an unforgettable romance on screen, which is timeless even after 60 years of the film's release. Johny Walker's was a truly hilarious cameo, which deservingly fetched him the Filmfare Award. Pran and Jayant too lived their roles.

The tenor and texture of the uniquely crafted screenplay of the film was evolved equally uniquely, in a state of complete inebriation or drunken stupor by the maverick genius Ritwik Ghatak when he was summoned from Kolkata to Mumbai by Bimal *Da* to write a much needed hit film for his banner. Ensconced in his Ambassador Hotel suite, Ritwik *Da* was consuming bottles galore but had not come up with a hit film concept to be fashioned. Running out of patience, an anxious Bimal *Da* sent his trusted lieutenants Hrishikesh

Pran as Ugra Narayan

Johny Walker as Charan

Dilip and Tarun Bose

Jayant as Pahan Raja

Mukherjee, Asit Sen and Moni Bhattacharji to plead with Ritwik to concentrate on and finish the work at hand. A completely sizzled Ritwik pointed to a thick bound register on the table to pompously announce that he had completed the full screenplay and the script, in all its details, was in that register. He also offered to narrate the script which the lieutenants gleefully accepted. What followed was a mind-boggling narration, scene by scene (of course, over more and more rounds of drinks) which left the listeners spellbound. Delighted lieutenants left with the register and handed it over to Bimal Roy, only to find the thick bound register completely empty. Anyway, they narrated the subject to Bimal *Da* who was completely floored. Rushing to Ritwik the following morning, the lieutenants asked for the register containing the script and were startled by a sober Ritwik Ghatak's retort, '*Kaun si Madhumati? Kaisi* script*? Maine to likhna shuru bhi nahin kiya!*' Eventually, the classic *Madhumati* was made from whatever the lieutenants remembered of that fateful evening's narration. Most interestingly, Ritwik Ghatak thought the whole film was a big joke and even went around saying, 'I have written such a ghost story that Bimal Roy Productions will vanish forever.' On the contrary, *Madhumati* turned out to be the long-term saviour of the iconic production house.

Stills from Madhumati

The story of the film opens on a rain-soaked night on the hilly roads to Nainital. On receiving a telegram from his wife Radha (Vyjayantimala), Devendra (Dilip Kumar), accompanied by his doctor friend (Tarun Bose), rushes to the station in his car to meet her. On the way, they find that the road is blocked by a landslide caused by heavy rain. While waiting for the road to be cleared, they go up to an old palace in the vicinity which was once owned by the local rajas. In the palace, Devendra gets an eerie feeling. The surroundings seem familiar to him. He feels he has been there before. Then, he speaks of a painting which used to be on one of the walls. The caretaker of the palace, an old man, confirms that this was indeed so. But, Devendra's friend says those are the imaginings of a worried mind. Images fly past and Devendra realised that he had come there before–as Anand (Dilip Kumar), manager of a timber company working on the estate of Raja Ugra Narayan (Pran). One day, when he had gone out to paint, he met the sprightly, nimble-footed Madhumati (Vyjayantimala), daughter of Pahan Raja (Jayant), the banished chief of a hill tribe.

Ugra Narayan's Haveli

Madhumati and her Ghost

Madhavi

Radha

Anand

Devendra

Nature provides a perfect setting for the love which grows between Anand and Madhumati. Then, their bliss is shattered by the wily Ugra Narayan. He sends Anand away on an errand and shortly afterwards asks his henchman Bir Singh (Tiwari) to tell Madhumati that Anand has met with an accident and is lying injured in Ugra Narayan's haveli. The simple village belle hurries to the Haveli, only to find herself in the clutches of Ugra Narayan, who starts making advances towards her. Returning from his mission, Anand goes straight to Madhumati's house, where he finds her father grief-stricken and under the impression that his daughter is dead. An unconvinced Anand continues to make a frantic search for Madhumati. When it proves fruitless and he is in despair, his servant Charan (Johny Walker) informs him that Madhumati had gone to Ugra Narayan's haveli on that fateful night when Anand was away. An infuriated Anand goes to the haveli to confront Ugra Narayan and demands that Madhumati be set free. Ugra Narayan's men overpower him and beat him until he is unconscious. Regaining consciousness in a hospital, Anand's life becomes one of constant vigil searching for Madhumati. One day as he is about to go to the haveli again to confront Ugra Narayan, he meets a beautiful young woman named *Madhavi* (Vyjayantimala in a triple role), who resembles Madhumati. Anand at first takes the young woman to be Madhumati only to be apprised by Madhavi's police inspector brothers (Misra and Jagdish Raj) of the reality. Anand recounts the tale of the missing Madhumati to Madhavi and her relatives, and seeks their assistance in locating his missing beloved. Seeing that Anand is grief-stricken, Madhavi offers to help him, and both try to find Madhumati's whereabouts. They learn that Madhumati had, in fact, committed suicide by jumping from the terrace of the haveli preferring death to dishonour. Anand, Madhavi, her relatives and the police hatch a carefully-crafted plan to trap Ugra Narayan and deliver justice. The plan unfolds in the film's chilling climax (brilliantly scripted, directed and enacted) leading to the arrest of Ugra Narayan. The audience is bewildered to learn that actually the ghost of Madhumati had come to the haveli (instead of Madhavi, who had got delayed due to torrential rains) to trap Ugra Narayan alongside Anand. Eventually, Anand follows the ghost to the terrace of the haveli and meets with his death by falling from the same spot from which Madhumati had committed suicide. As Devendra comes to the end of the narration of his previous birth's tale, news arrives that the train in which his wife (Radha) is travelling has met with an accident. He rushes to the station immediately and is overwhelmed with joy to find his wife, Radha and their newborn child safe and sound. He tells Radha that *'Hum to janam janam ke saathi hain' (We are soulmates for many lifetimes)* and that a new life has been granted to them–one of everlasting love which rises above the barriers of death and life. Filmgoers were stunned by the intriguing screenplay unfolding on the silver screen and overwhelmed by the majestic sweep of this motion picture masterpiece. The unusual theme and its unique execution enticed the cinegoers to go for several repeat viewings and the film is remembered and viewed even to date.

To impart the right feel matching the demands of the intriguing screenplay, the movie was shot extensively in and around Kumaon and Nainital region over a period of forty-five days. To make the village fair scene more authentically colourful, Bimal Roy announced a competition with an appropriate price for the best dressed and local people came to witness and participated in the sequence. Villagers from far and near came dressed in their traditional finery and Bimal *Da* got the desired essence and authenticity of a mountain village fair. Additionally, some scenes with the feel of a hill station heightening the mystery of the story had to be re-shot in the hilly locale of Igatpuri. Thanks to the long schedule, the film went over-budget by around ₹8–10 lakh. Dilip Kumar realised that Bimal Roy was tense and decided to do something about it. He asked Bimal Roy to call all his distributors for a preview followed by lunch. After the lunch, he told the distributors that the film had gone over-budget and that he would forgo ₹70,000 of his remuneration to make up for it. Chotubhai Desai, a Delhi distributor, was the first one to come forward. He said that he would match whatever Dilip had to forgo. One by one, all the distributors came forward to contribute to the kitty and the deficit was made up.

Lobby Cards of Madhumati

Poet and lyricist Shailendra and music director Salil Chowdhury had similar social convictions and shared a lifelong close friendship. They had an unbelievable musical tuning, until the poet's untimely demise in 1966. They created soulful music for nineteen films with numerous all-time great songs. Their greatest creation together was the music of *Madhumati,* which was at par with the best-ever created for any film by any composer. The enchanting love story of star-crossed lovers and rebirth was appropriately accentuated by the mesmerising compositions of Salil Chowdhury. He employed folk treasurers of Kumaon and Assam moulded in classical ragas with a telling effect. As per us, the greatest song sung by the melody queen Lata Mangeshkar is *Aaja re Pardesi main to kab se khadi is paar* (based on *Raag Bageshri-Kaharva Taal)* with captivating flute pieces by Manohari Singh. Grapevine has it that at Lata's suggestion, Salil Chowdhury got her to sing from *Pancham* (the words *Main to kab se khadi is paar, yeh ankhiyan thak gayeen panth nihaar* which form the take-off of the number, are actually the second written lines of the *mukhda)* which added to the enchantment. Apparently, lyricist Shailendra presented a bouquet of flowers to Lata, and Bimal *Da* held her hand for a long time–so impressed they were by the song. The interlude piece *(Ma Ma Ga Ma Ma Ga Ma Pa Dha Pa Dha...)* was so effective that Salil used it as the tune for the *mukhda* of another *Raag Bageshri* classic–Lata's *Ghadi Ghadi mora Dil dhadke,* which with Vyjayantimala's alluring dance in the Nainital locale, became a highlight of the film. So enamoured was the composer by this *Bageshri* interlude that he used it beautifully in two other songs *(Baag mein kali khili* in *Chanda Aur Sooraj* and *Saathi re tujh bin jiya udaas* in *Poonam ki Raat)* composed for other films. Then there was this astounding folk melody in *Raag Sarang* by Lata and Manna Dey, *Chadh gayo paapi bichhua* which became a raging hit. The song also had an exquisite choral version (not available on Disc/CD), with *Drut gat,* which appears alluringly in the later part of the film. Talat Mahmood was to originally sing the delectable melody *Suhana safar aur yeh mausam haseen,* but since he was away on a foreign concert tour, the choice fell on Mukesh. Reportedly, Dilip Kumar had some reservations on Mukesh singing this all important opening song of the film, but Salil Chowdhury persuaded him. The song became a national favourite. *Madhumati* was a complete score having virtually all shades of emotional melodic compositions. Mohd. Rafi was in his peak form to evocatively render the *Darbari Kanhda* based sad song *Toote huey khwabon ne humko yeh sikhaya hai,* which till date is remembered as one of the greatest expressions of melancholic love with lines like *Hum dhoondte hain unko jo mil ke nahin milte.* Mubarak Begum's *Mujra* in *Raag Asavari* (which appeared as a flash only in the film), *Hum haal-e-dil sunayenge suniye ki na suniye* recorded with just the sarangi, harmonium and table also became memorable. Then, of course, there was this ingeniously sculpted folk number *Zulmi sang aankh ladi re* sung like a champion by Lata and performed on screen with endearing exuberance by Vyjayantimala. Another *Kumaon* folk number *Kaancha re kaanchi re lagyo* (Asha–Sabita Banerji–Ghulam Mohd.), which appeared as a short flash in the film was also exquisitely tuned, as was the deleted Dwijen Mukherji chorus, *Tan jale man jalta rahe.* But then not to be outdone by any other number in the film was the gem of a duet *Dil tadap tadap ke kah raha hai aa bhi ja* (Lata–Mukesh). Inspired by *Hungarian/Czech* folk and brilliantly tuned with rave lilt, the song set many a lovers' heart aflutter in those days, and still does. Lyricist Naqsh Lyallpuri (Naqsh*ji*– our well-wisher and family friend) met Salil Chowdhury at the Andheri Railway Station when *Madhumati* was running in its fourteenth housefull week. Salil *Da* appeared a little distraught and Naqsh*ji* after congratulating him on the huge success of *Madhumati,* asked as to what was bothering him when his film had become a superhit. Salil *Da* said that he had received not even a single film offer despite the film doing so well. Naqsh*ji* replied– *'Just wait and watch'* True to his words, from the fifteenth week run of the film, Salil Chowdhury was flooded with film offers and collected around ₹4.5 lakh (a very big sum in those days) as signing amounts shortly after. Shailendra penned all the songs of the film except one (*Tan jale man jalta rahe*) which was written by Majrooh Sultanpuri. *Madhumati,* the film and its music are still loved by connoisseurs.

LP Disc of 'Madhumati'

Salil / Shailendra

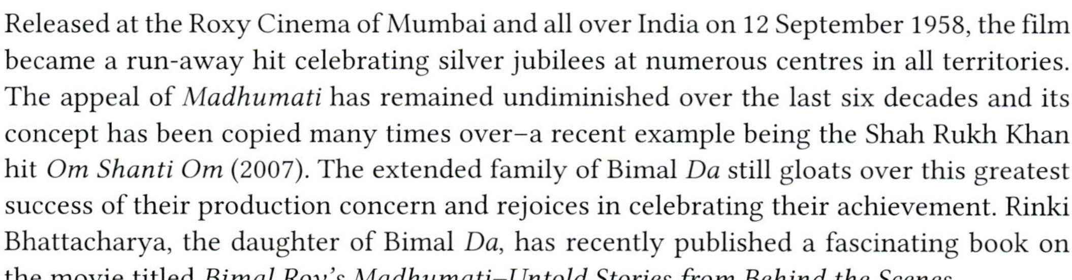
Released at the Roxy Cinema of Mumbai and all over India on 12 September 1958, the film became a run-away hit celebrating silver jubilees at numerous centres in all territories. The appeal of *Madhumati* has remained undiminished over the last six decades and its concept has been copied many times over–a recent example being the Shah Rukh Khan hit *Om Shanti Om* (2007). The extended family of Bimal *Da* still gloats over this greatest success of their production concern and rejoices in celebrating their achievement. Rinki Bhattacharya, the daughter of Bimal *Da*, has recently published a fascinating book on the movie titled *Bimal Roy's Madhumati–Untold Stories from Behind the Scenes.*

Salil / Lata

Suhana safar

Aaja re pardesi

Zulmi sang aankh

Dil tadap tadap ke

Ghadi ghadi mera dil

Phir wohi raat andhera

Toote huye khwabo ne

Chadh gayo papi bichhua

DATE / YEAR OF RELEASE: 1958
BANNER / PRODUCER: BOMBAY FILMS / SAVAK B. VACHA
DIRECTION: BIMAL ROY
MUSIC: SHANKAR–JAIKISHAN
LYRICS: SHAILENDRA / HASRAT JAIPURI
PLAYBACK: LATA MANGESHKAR / MOHD. RAFI / MUKESH
STORY / SCREENPLAY: AGHA HASHR KASHMIRI / NABENDU GHOSH
DIALOGUE: WAJAHAT MIRZA
CINEMATOGRAPHY: DILIP GUPTA
EDITING: HRISHIKESH MUKHERJEE
AUDIOGRAPHY: DINSHAW BILLIMORIA
ART: SUDHENDU ROY
CHOREOGRAPHY: SURYA KUMAR / VINOD CHOPRA / SATYANARAYAN
CAST: SOHRAB MODI / DILIP KUMAR / MEENA KUMARI / NIGAR SULTANA / NAZIR HUSSAIN / ANWAR HUSSAIN / TIWARI / MURAD / INDIRA / BIKRAM KAPOOR / BABY NAAZ / ROMY / MUNSHI / HELAN / CUKKOO / KAMLA LAXMAN (GUEST ARTISTES)

Veteran Bombay Talkies team member Savak B. Vacha launched a new banner called Bombay Films with an ambitions film based on Agha Hashr Kashmiri's celebrated play *Yahudi Ki Ladki.* The film was *Yahudi* starring Dilip Kumar, Meena Kumari and Sohrab Modi. Directed by Bimal Roy, the film was yet another glowing example of the perfect director–actor tuning that existed between Bimal *Da* and Dilip Saheb. Savak Vacha, after the closure of Bombay Talkies, had fallen on hard times and Dilip Kumar, with a view to help him out, agreed to do the film and roped in Bimal *Da* to direct the venture. Bimal Roy put his stamp of directorial excellence on this charming movie and Dilip Kumar's was a disarmingly captivating portrayal of a Roman prince in love with a Jewish girl.

Sohrab Modi was at his dramatic best with Meena Kumari imparting her role with great charm. It was a treat to watch Dilip's natural act pitted against Sohrab Modi's theatrical rendition. Dilip and Meena's engagingly refreshing romantic interludes allured filmgoers. The film was a success at the box office and quite popular in re-runs as well. Even to date, it is available in sparkling DVD prints and is well patronised.

Dilip as Marcus

Savak Vacha wanted to make a spectacular production to recoup his losses and Bimal *Da* suggested basing the film on the famous theatrical play. *Yahudi* was a costume drama set against a very unusual background–Rome in the immediate post-Caesar days when the tyrannical Brutus (Nazir Hussain) was ruling the empire. The film's background required Dilip Kumar to wear the Roman toga and blonde wig and the actor carried it off with great élan. The story of the film opened with a victory march of the emperor during which some pebbles are thrown at Brutus. The culprit is discovered to be a little Jewish boy–he is at once ordered to be served as a meal to the lions. The boy's father–an old Jew (Sohrab Modi), is insulted by the Romans. As revenge, a Jew slave kidnaps Brutus's daughter Hannah (Meena Kumari). She grows up in the Jewish home, ignorant about her past. The Roman Prince Marcus (Dilip Kumar) falls in love with Hannah and frequents their home disguised as a Jew. An intensely emotional drama ensues with a tremendous display of powerful histrionics. Hannah is sentenced to be boiled alive in an oil cauldron but before the sentence is executed, the Jew reveals the secret that she is the daughter of Brutus. In the meantime, Marcus, who is unable to rescue Hannah, blinds himself not knowing that she would be let off being the daughter of Brutus. Hannah chooses to be the life partner of the blind Prince Marcus.

EP Disc of 'Yahudi'

Yahudi had another spellbinding score by Shankar–Jaikishan (SJ). Composer Shankar, resting on his bed at home, got a tune idea and Shailendra, in a jiffy, wrote the words on it to create the magnificent Mukesh classic *Yeh mera deewanapan hai ya mohabbat ka suroor.* According to us, this is one of best songs of Mukesh. But, grapevine has it that it took a lot of convincing on the part of SJ to make Dilip Saheb (who wanted Talat Mahmood to render the exquisite number) relent to retaining their choice of singer, that is, Mukesh. The leitmotif of this dream SJ score was Lata's rendition of a bunch of everlasting melodies such as *Meri jaan meri jaan pyar kisi se ho hi gaya hai* (a Binaca topper for weeks), *Aate jaate pehloo mein aaya koi* with mesmerising *Aalaps* and Mandolin interludes, *Dil mein pyar ka toofan na samjhe koi nadaan* with a rare Mediterranean flavour, and the plaintive *Aansoo ki aag leke teri yaad aayi.* Then, of course, the exuberant melody of a rare Lata–Geeta duet *in Bachain dil khoyi si nazar* was also unforgettable. This was SJ's third and last score for a Dilip Kumar starrer, the other two being *Daag* (1952) and *Shikast* (1953). SJ had composed with rare verve for the films of the thespian–usually a Naushad bastion.

SJ with Dilip / Raj

Premier of 'Yahudi'

LP Disc of 'Yahudi'

PAIGHAM

DATE / YEAR OF RELEASE: 1959
BANNER / PRODUCER: GEMINI / S.S. VASAN
DIRECTION: S.S. VASAN
MUSIC: C. RAMCHANDRA
LYRICS: KAVI PRADEEP
PLAYBACK: MOHD. RAFI / ASHA BHOSLE / CHITALKAR / SUMAN KALYANPUR / MANNA DEY
STORY / SCREENPLAY: GEMINI STORY DEPARTMENT
DIALOGUE: RAMANAND SAGAR
CINEMATOGRAPHY: P. ELLAPPA
EDITING: M. UMANATH
AUDIOGRAPHY: C.E. BIGGS / S.C. GANDHI
ART: M.S. JANAKI RAM
CHOREOGRAPHY: GOPI KRISHNA
CAST: DILIP KUMAR / VYJAYANTIMALA / RAJKUMAR / MOTILAL / B. SAROJA DEVI / PANDHARI BAI / JOHNNY WALKER / MEENU MUMTAJ / VASUNDHARA DEVI / PROTIMA DEVI / S.N. BANERJI / SHIVRAJ / ISHWARLAL / PUSHPMALA / MUKHERJI / MASTER GOPI / AMAR / KARUPAYA / RADHA / MADHVAN / KAMAL KRISHN

During the filming of *Insaniyat,* Dilip Kumar and the boss of Gemini Studios, S.S. Vasan, liked each other and became friends. Dilip found Vasan to be a genial and unassuming gentleman with a thorough grasp of motion picture production. It was, therefore but natural, that the two friends came together again for another film. That film was of Gemini Studio's *Paigham,* based on the topical subject of management and workmen relationship with strong undercurrents of Nehruvian socialism. The doyen cast the hit pair of *Naya Daur* and *Madhumati,* Dilip Kumar and Vyjayantimala in the main leads with a star studded supporting casts comprising Raaj Kumar, Motilal, B. Saroja Devi, Pandhari Bai, Meenu Mumtaz and of course Johnny Walker. The film propagated the ideal *Mill Malik–Mazdoor* partnership in manufacturing business. It was made as a

Dilip in "Paigham"

bi-lingual with the Tamil version titled *Iron Curtain* starring Sivaji Ganesan. Both the films were superduper hits at the box office.

The story of the movie centred around two brothers, Ram (Raaj Kumar) and Ratan (Dilip Kumar), who work in Sarvanand Mills. Things get complicated between them when Ram tries to support the mill owner Sevakram (Motilal) who defrauds all the employees and treats them badly. In the backdrop of conflict of principles, the narrative had the triangular love story of Ratan with the illegitimate daughter (Vyjayantimala) as well as the legitimate daughter (B. Saroja Devi) of the mill owner, the filial emotional conflict between the brothers, the sad travails of the spurned first wife (Pandhari Bai) of Sevakram and the revenge sought by the illegitimate daughter, etc. Dilip Kumar brilliantly interpreted and performed the role of the trade union leader with zealous aplomb. Vyjayantimala, once again, was an apt histrionic foil to Dilip. Raaj Kumar and Motilal performed naturally and with gusto. Johnny Walker (playing the servant of Sevakram) brought the house down with his impeccable comic timing.

Apart from the many socialist and emotional conflict, the pièce de résistance of the film were the captivating romantic scenes between Dilip and Vyjayanti which became the film's highlight. The scenes were beautifully written, deftly directed and superbly enacted and to date are a treat to watch. Ramanand Sagar was credited as the dialogue writer of the film, but the fact remains that Dilip Kumar himself had written many of these and had even penned the dialogue. There is an interesting anecdote regarding these splendid scenes. It so happened that Vasan and Dilip were travelling together by train in a coupe to Madurai. During the journey, the producer-director narrated a love scene to be shot in Channai upon their return. Vasan mentioned that he was unsure about the development of the scene to be shot and had been applying his mind to create a humorous situation but it was just not happening. Dilip Kumar suggested to do the scene a bit differently and narrated his own visualisation of it. Vasan was completely bowled over and Dilip wrote the whole scene during the train journey. Dilip Kumar later said: '**I think Vasan Saheb couldn't contain his happiness and excitement about the way the scene turned out. That day and for many days after that he was bursting with delight and sure enough, the scene turned out to be one of the highlights in the film.**' Ramanand Sagar received the Filmfare Award as Best Dialogue Writer in 1959.

Dilip and Vyjayanti in Paigham

Another major highlight of the film was the scenes of ideological confrontations between Dilip Kumar and Raaj Kumar which were a treat for the film lovers. Motilal was a natural in the role of the mill owner and his individual as well as collective scenes with Dilip, Raaj

Scenes from Paigham

Kumar and Vyjayantimala were superbly enacted. Dilip Kumar and Raaj Kumar never worked together in any film after *Paigham* for a long time until *Saudagar* (1991).

Around this time, Lata Mangeshkar parted ways with composer C. Ramchandra who was doing the music for *Paighaam.* Grapevine has it that Lata tried to persuade S.S. Vasan to replace C. Ramchandra with any other composer he may like, but the Gemini boss refused point blank. Anyway *Paigham* created box-office history by becoming a huge hit, but its music was not up to the composer's standard. The notable tracks of the film includes the dance number *Main kyun na nachoon aaj* (Asha), the Rafi-Asha duet *Jawani mein akelepan ki* and the title track by Manna Dey *Insaan ka insaan se ho bhaichara yahi paigham hamara.* One reason may be that rest of the songs were all situational numbers. Poet Pradeep had penned the lyrics.

The Ever Popular Dilip and Vyjayanti Romantic Banter

Dilip Kumar and Raaj Kumar's Histrionic Confrontation

Dilip Kumar by now had become a maestro not only in front of the camera but also behind it–accomplished in script and dialogue writing, conceptualisation of scenes and even direction. The time was ripe for him to make a magnum opus on his own. But, there was still some time.

LP Disc of Paigham

CHAPTER 3.3

THE MEGA-STAR PHASE–THE SERENADES OF THE SIXTIES

KOHINOOR

DATE / YEAR OF RELEASE: 1960
BANNER / PRODUCER: REPUBLIC FILMS CORPORATION / Dr V. N. SINHA
DIRECTION: S.U. SUNNY
MUSIC: NAUSHAD
LYRICS: SHAKEEL BADAYUNI
PLAYBACK: MOHD. RAFI / LATA MANGESHKAR / ASHA BHOSLE
STORY / SCREENPLAY: RAMANAND SAGAR / WAJAHAT MIRZA
DIALOGUE: WAJAHAT MIRZA
EDITING: MOOSA MANSOOR
ART: V. JADHAV
CHOREOGRAPHY: SITARA DEVI / B. HIRALAL / SATYANARAYAN / CHIMAN SETH
CAST: DILIP KUMAR / KAMINI KAUSHAL / GOPE / CUCKOO / AARIF / PREM DHAWAN / SHASHIKALA / SEETA BOSE / NEELAM KHAN / GAJJOO / CHANDABAI / ZAIDDI / RAM SHASTRI /HAMEED / KAMLAKAR

S.U. Sunny has the distinction of directing Dilip in four films–*Mela, Babul, Uran Khatola* and *Kohinoor*–a privilege not shared by any other director. Notably, all Dilip Kumar films directed by Sunny were huge successes with Naushad's music being the other common factor. *Kohinoor,* produced by V.N. Sinha's Republic Film Corporation, had Dilip Kumar and Meena Kumari in the lead roles. It was not only a jubilee hit but became a cult film in the times to come. The film stood out for the brilliant performances of the lead pair (with the 'Tragedy King' and 'Tragedy Queen' combining effortlessly to create a boisterous comedy) and Naushad's lilting musical score. *Kohinoor* brought Dilip Kumar his fifth Filmfare Award for Best Actor for a smooth and natural portrayal of a prince with a devil-may-care attitude. Dilip brought the house down with his truly hilarious comedy interludes, ably supported by Meena Kumari. Kumkum had the role of a lifetime as the supporting actress (also performing memorable dances in two spectacular numbers) with Jeevan displaying his stylised villainy and Mukri mirthfully essaying the role of Dilip's sidekick.

Scenes from Kohinoor

The story of the film revolved between two kingdoms (Rajgarh and Kailash Nagar) and the love story of their Prince Devendra (Dilip Kumar) and Princess Chandramukhi (Meena Kumari) respectively. A third angle to the love story was the selfless love of the Rajnartakee Rajyalakshmi (Kumkum) of Rajgarh. The palace intrigues and deceptions of S. Nazir and Jeevan were the evil elements in the plot. Prince Devendra survives an attempt on his life by the wily senapati (who wants his own son to be the king but the son is very loyal to the prince). The prince renounces the kingdom and meets Chandramukhi (who is enroute the kingdom of the prince), with whom he has to be shortly betrothed. Chandramukhi is kidnapped from her camp. Prince Devendra rescues Princess Chandramukhi and they escape only to be caught by the rebellious senapati's soldiers. Prince Devendra gets severely injured but is rescued by Rajnartakee Rajyalakshmi and nursed back to health. Meanwhile, the senapati has held Princess Chandramukhi captive in a well-guarded fortress but she steadfastly spurns his advances and refuses to marry him. Prince Devendra, disguised as Kohinoor Babaand accompanied by his lackey (Mukri), goes to the fortress, charms the senapati promising that he would be able to win over the princess to accept him. His actual purpose is to plan the princess' rescue. A number of twist and turns in the tale eventually lead to a happy ending with good triumphing over evil.

The Lead Pair

As has been noted earlier, comedy and action films (*Aan, Azaad, Insaniyat, Kohinoor, Leader, Ram Aur Shyam*) were an escape route for Dilip Kumar to obviate overtly tragic roles. Dilip Saheb himself told us that while doing such light films, each day was full of fun, pranks and laughter. These films contained class entertainment without so much as a smidgen of vulgarity or obscenity. *Kohinoor* is replete with comedy and a prime example of Dilip Kumar brand of comic relief which was humorous yet effortless. Dilip's natural brilliance enabled him to strike a rapport with his fans from the very first reel. While singing *Zara man ki kiwadiya khol* disguised as Kohinoor Baba, he could make the audience roar, clap and whistle. Moreover, in the marvellously crafted and enacted scenes, Dilip Kumar and Meena Kumari effortlessly sparked more comedy than those who hang upside down from trees, dive and roll in muddy puddles and slip on banana skin to evoke laughter. Also, the iconic mirror scene, which was incredibly comic, which Jeevan and Dilip enacted with deft timing and great aplomb. In the scene, a drunk senapati barges into the chamber where the prince and a captive princess are together, interrupting their romantic interlude. Dilip hides behind a mirror which slips down from the dressing table, revealing Dilip crouching behind the table. On being exposed, Dilip duplicates the villain's gesture, guttural sounds and squeaks as though he were Jeevan's exact mirror image. The scene was a laugh riot. There was pinpoint precision as the great actor imitated his adversary's reactions, irritation and exasperation. He countered the villain's every yelp, guffaw and flaying of hands. Here was unadulterated wit and mirth. We have seen the scene copied by other filmmakers so many times that we have lost count. Some later day examples are Amitabh Bachchan's cameos in films like *Kasme Vaade, Amar Akbar Anthony* and *Mard.*

The Famous Mirror Scene

The banters of Dilip–Meena pair imbued *Kohinoor* with a timeless quality which made the film super hit and highly successful even in numerous re-runs. The fun-filled adventure is still very popular on the DVD circuit and its well-framed romantic songs continue to sell.

Dilip Kumar and Meena Kumari in Kohinoor: A Scintillating Comedy

Dilip's immaculate dedication to his craft came to the fore in the film as Dilip was required to play the sitar while emoting the evergreen Naushad classic *Madhuban me radhika naache re.* Naushad spoke about this to *Cine Blitz* in December 1992 issue: "**Dilip was upset, he said that it was a very difficult piece and how would he mime it? I told him not to worry–Ustad Abdul Haleem Zafar Khan (who had recorded the piece of sitar music) would do the close-up of his hand movements. Dilip did not agree and actually learnt the sitar from the Ustad and only when we felt he had mastered it reasonably well did he shoot for the film**". Dilip Saheb had this to say: '**It was a difficult**

task to learn the sitar for *Kohinoor*, it meant a regime of five to six hours for some weeks. The sitar is still with me though I don't play it any more. Perhaps I could still return to it.' There were other sitar-based songs like *Jaadugar qatil hazir hai mera dil* (Kumkum's dance) and *Dhal chuki shaam-e-gham* (at the film's climax) where Dilip Kumar actually played the sitar during the shooting. The great actor had meticulously acquired considerable prowess in playing the sitar to perform those classical beauties in the film.

Dilip Playing Sitar in Kohinoor

Composer S.D. Burman in *Vividh Bharti's Fauzi Jawan* programme had remarked that presentation of a difficult raga like Hameer in a lighter vein is a tall order, which only a composer of the prowess of Naushad can achieve. His reference, of course, was to Rafi's perennial favourite *Madhuban mein Radhika naache re,* which has truly stood the test of time. Replete with numerous hit songs, *Kohinoor*'s music was one of Naushad's most popular–with songs like *Do sitaron ka zameen par* (Lata-Rafi), *Koi pyar ki dekhe jadoogari* (Rafi-Lata), *Dil mein bajin pyar ki* (Lata), *Zara man ki kiwadiya khol* (Rafi), *Dhal chuki shaam-e-gham* (Rafi) and *Jadoogar qatil haazir hai* (Asha).

Naushad on Sitar

Dilip Saheb himself is quite fond of his association with S.U. Sunny and the experience of creating the super hit movie *Kohinoor.* He has mentioned in his autobiography:

'*Kohinoor* will remain etched in my mind for the efforts I made to learn to play the sitar. It was another chance for me to test my flair for the comedy genre in acting. I was very confident after *Azaad's* success and I had a fine rapport with S.U. Sunny, who understood me and my tenacity to get as close to perfection as is possible in everything I did. He gave me ample freedom and time to take lessons before I did a scene. I enjoyed the making of *Kohinoor* also for the camaraderie that grew between me and Meena Kumari after *Azaad* as we, who were known for our forte with emotional drama and tragedy, came together for another light-hearted film.'[1] Dilip Kumar had an interesting but eerie experience while location hunting for *Kohinoor* with S.U. Sunny. The wife of S.U. Sunny was a mysterious lady interested in the supernatural and probably practised black magic. But, more about that later.

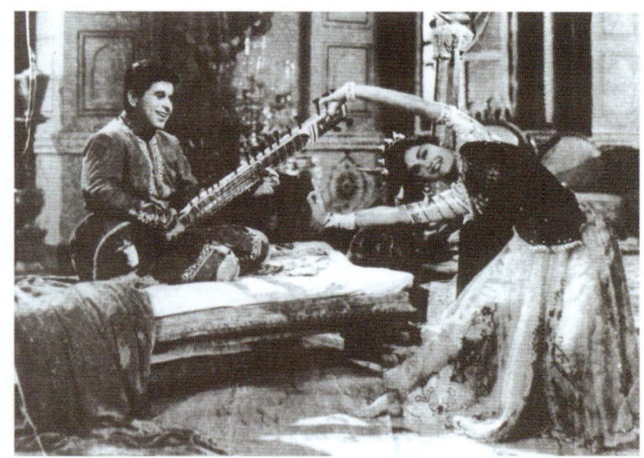

Dilip and Kumkum in Kohinoor

10" LP Disc

S.U. Sunny and Dilip

24" LP Disc

Posters of Kohinoor

[1] Dilip Kumar, Dilip Kumar: The Substance and the Shadow - An Autobiography (Hay House, Inc, 2014)

DATE / YEAR OF RELEASE: 05 AUGUST 1960
BANNER / PRODUCER: STERLING INVESTMENT CORPORATION (P.) LTD.
DIRECTION: K. ASIF
MUSIC: NAUSHAD
LYRICS: SHAKEEL BADAYUNI
PLAYBACK: BADE GHULAM ALI KHAN / SHAMSHAD BEGUM / MOHD. RAFI / LATA MANGESHKAR / MUBARAK BEGUM
STORY / SCREENPLAY: K. ASIF / AMAN
DIALOGUE: WAJAHAT MIRZA / KAMAL AMROHI / AMAAN / EHSAAN RIZVI
CINEMATOGRAPHY: R.D. MATHUR
EDITING: DHARMVEER
AUDIOGRAPHY: ROBIN CHATTERJI / KAUSHIK / B.N. SHARMA
CHOREOGRAPHY: LACHCHU MAHARAJ
ART: M.K. SYED (SHEESH MAHAL GLASS WORK–AGHA SHIRAZI)
CAST: PRITHVIRAJ KAPOOR / DILIP KUMAR / MADHUBALA / NIGAR SULTANA / AJIT / DURGA KHOTE / KUMAR / SHEELA DAYALA / MURAD / ZILLO BAI / VIJAYLAKSHMI / S. NAZIR / KHURSHID KHAN / KHWAJA SABIR / SHAHGUL / MAHGUL / JAGO / PAUL SHARMA / SAYYAD HUSSAIN / GHULAM SABIR / KHANNA / SURENDRA / JOHNY WALKER / GOPI KRISHN / JALAL AGHA & TABBASUM (GUEST ARTISTES)

In the annals of Indian motion pictures, 5 August 1960 is considered a red letter day. The date saw the theatrical release of K. Asif's magnum opus and timeless classic *Mughal-E-Azam* which remains one of the finest movies ever made in the country. K. Asif had inspired its entire cast to put their best foot forward which reflected in truly outstanding and flawless performances of Prithviraj Kapoor (as Badshah Akbar), Dilip Kumar (as Prince Salim), Madhubala (as Anarkali), Ajeet (as Durjan Singh), Murad (as Raja Man Singh), Nigar Sultana (as Bahar), Durga Khote (as Jodha Bai) and Kumar as (Sangtarash–the sculptor). Madhubala deserved the Filmfare Award for Best Actress, which she was unjustly denied. The grandeur and magnificence of the film was highlighted by Naushad's epic musical score (he too was very unjustly denied a Filmfare Award for his music). K. Asif and Naushad could even persuade Ustad Bade Ghulam Ali Khan to render two numbers supposedly sung onscreen by Sangeet Samrat Tansen. Four Lata solos and two delectable qawwalis shall remain evergreen hits. The fabulous script of *Mughal-E-Azam* could even be prescribed as an Urdu textbook in linguistic classes. K. Asif and Aman etched the memorable screenplay, while Aman, Kamal Amrohi, Ehsan Rizvi and Wajahat Mirza collectively wrote the unforgettable dialogue. The dialogue is like pieces culled from period literature; the lines reverberate in the mind of the viewer long after the seasons have changed and other merchandise has been placed on exhibition at the cinema halls. This colossal motion picture made in that era at a cost of ₹1 crore (when any star-studded film cost less than ₹10 lakh) over eight years went on to became a stupendous hit all over, reaping extremely rich dividends for its producers.

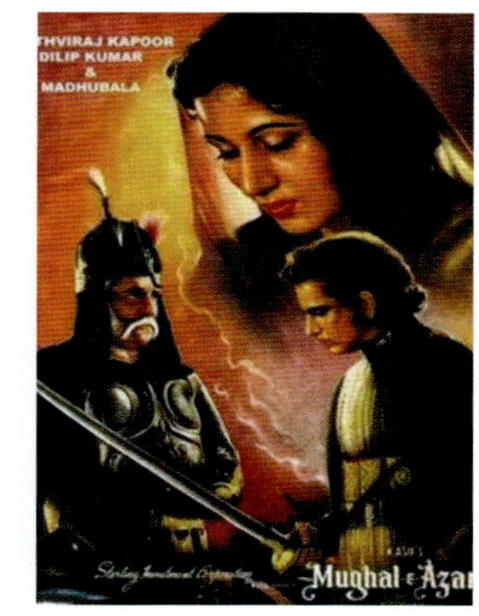

The saga of the maverick dreamer K. Asif and the making of his cinematic extravaganza *Mughal-E-Azam* is a great story in itself. An Urdu scholar-dramatist Imtiyaz Ali Taj came across an old and long-untended grave on which was inscribed 'Anarkali' in 1920, which stirred his imagination to a write a stage play titled 'Anarkali'. The play was staged with great success and became extremely popular which prompted many filmmakers to attempt celluloid versions of the play. The first movie on it was made by the Great Eastern Corporation of India in the silent era titled *The Loves of a Mughal Prince* starring Sita Devi–Swarna Singh under the direction of Praful Kumar Ray. It was a huge success. Another version of the play, starring Sulochana (Ruby Myers–the big star of those times) and D. Billimoria under the direction of R.S. Choudhury came soon after but was a box-office disaster. Then came with the talkie version in 1935 under Ardeshir Irani's banner Imperial Film Company which was again directed by R.S. Choudhury, with music by Anna Saheb Mayenkar, which was a great box-office success.

K. Asif then was a cocky, domineering young man with an overwhelming ambition to make it big in films. He was the nephew of the then famous actor S. Nazir, who was not eager to be used as his nephew's conduit into the film world. He, however, knew of Asif's ambitions through actors Jeevan, the famous villain, and Prem Adib, a well-known mythological hero who owned a restaurant at Khodadad Circle (Dadar East) which was frequented by film aspirants including Asif. There, Asif used to boast with great confidence of making it big in films. Nazir set-up a tailoring shop in the area for Asif and arranged very modest dwellings near Khodadad Circle. Asif at times shared his shop as living quarters with Naushad–who knew at that point in time as to what these legends-to-be would do together in future? Nazir soon found out that Asif, who had put up a signboard at his shop declaring himself a 'ladies tailor', was more interested in flirting with his lady customers and in making time with a neighbouring tailor's daughter. He was hardly interested in stitching clothes for the impatient clients he then

K. Asif

had. Fearing for his own good reputation, Uncle Nazir hastily hushed up the matter, shut the tailoring shop and ushered his nephew as a directorial assistant into the film world–a world in which, ironically, the act of seduction is treated more casually than in tailoring. Within a few years (by 1944), the same cocky, overconfident youth had risen from the ranks of assistant to become a full-fledged director of *Phool* (1945).

The producer who gave Asif his important directorial break was Shiraz Ali Hakim, joint owner, along with his brother-in-law K. Abdullah, of Famous Cine Laboratories and Studios at Mahalaxmi. Such was Shiraz Ali's confidence in the young director that he cast a whole series of superstars in *Phool* including Prithviraj Kapoor, Veena, Suraiya, Sitara Devi, Yakub, Wasti, Durga Khote, Mazhar Khan, Dixit, Agha and Jillo Bai, et al. *Phool* was mounted on a lavish scale with Asif's opulence very evident, and a popular musical score by legendary composer Master Ghulam Haider. The film had a bumper opening at the box office but did not fare too well in the long run. However, Asif's direction won all-round praise. An extremely impressed Shiraz Ali Hakim announced his next film *Heer Ranjha* starring Veena (opposite a newcomer Ramesh Saigal, who later went on to become a famous director). However, Veena wanted her brother (later day famous character actor Iftekhar) as director and therefore, Asif was deprived of the directorial assignment. Undeterred K. Asif also bowled Shiraz Ali over with his narration of the grand concept of *Mughal-E-Azam* which excited Shiraz Ali and he jumped at it. Asif wanted Dilip Kumar to be cast as Prince Salim but, at that time, Shiraz Ali thought that the legend-to-be was too skinny for the role. Eventually, *Mughal-E-Azam* was launched with the famous Chandra Mohan as Emperor Akbar, Nargis as Anarkali, Sapru as Prince Salim, famous Kathak dancer Sitara Devi (by that time she had become the second wife of Asif) as Bahar, Himalayawala as Durjan Singh and Durga Khote as Jodha Bai. Shooting started in 1946, but then came the partition of India when a large majority of Indian Muslims deciding to migrate to Pakistan without any delay. In this mass exodus, one of the earliest Muslims to leave for Pakistan, after selling his assets including the Famous Studios to J.B. Rungta, was Shiraz Ali Hakim and in the intervening period the famous Chandra Mohan also committed suicide. Grapevine also has it that the canned reels of the movie were burnt in the partition riots. No wonder the iconic film had to be was temporarily aborted.

The die-hard optimist in K. Asif took this setback in his stride. In between, he had developed a friendship with Dilip Kumar which continued to grow over years; his Kathak danseuse wife Sitara Devi also had a brother–sister relationship with Yusuf Saheb. Asif decided to graduate from director to producer and announced a film titled *Jaanwar* starring Suraiya and Dilip Kumar. Some shooting of the movie progressed but the film was shelved due to major differences that cropped up between the lead pair. Asif already

Mahurat of the Original Mughal-E-Azam

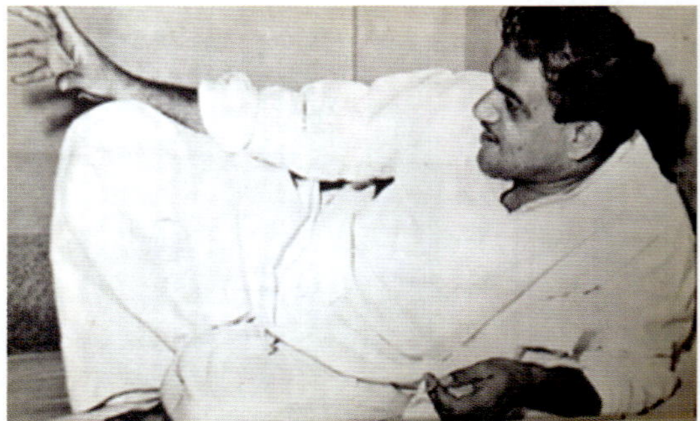
K. Asif

had a friendship with Nargis who was the leading lady of the original *Mughal-E-Azam* as well as the backing of Dilip Kumar. K. Asif launched a star-studded *Hulchul* featuring Dilip Kumar, Nargis, Sitara Devi, Balraj Sahani, K.N. Singh, Geeta Nizami, Faizee and Cuckoo. Launched in 1948, the film was released in 1951 to become a moderate success at the box office. During the film's making, Dilip Kumar and Nargis fell out with each other and Nargis vowed never to work with Dilip and Asif.

Prithviraj as Akbar

However, K. Asif had continued to dream of making a magnificent epic picture on the life and times of the Mughal Emperor Akbar and those days, he lived with the concept day in and day out. The folklore legend of *Anarkali* (in all probability, an unreal figment of a writer's imagination) and the associated conflict between Emperor Akbar and Prince Salim catalysed by the dancer *Anarkali* continued to fascinate Asif. He revived *Mughal-E-Azam* and signed the famous actor Prithviraj Kapoor (also a theatre legend with a rich baritone voice) to play the title role of Emperor Akbar. Construction magnate and multi-millionaires Seth Shapoorji Mistry and Seth Pallonji Mistry were avid theatre enthusiasts and fans of Prithviraj Kapoor. Prithviraj*ji* strongly recommended them to finance the grandiose *Mughal-E-Azam* and the Seths, quite fascinated by the subject, accepted. With the moneyed Shapoorji–Pallonji bankrolling the project, its finance no longer remained a problem.

Dilip and Seth Shapoorji

K. Asif was very keen on Dilip Kumar playing Prince Salim and had taken the acceptance of his dear friend for granted. He was very surprised when Dilip showed his reluctance and expressed some trepidation on doing the role. Dilip Kumar thought that Prince Salim's role may fall short of the expectations of his huge fan following since Prince Salim's character was somewhat passive rather than active in the overall scheme of the narrative. He also felt that the real conflict was between King Akbar and Anarkali with Akbar being an overtly domineering factor. Added to that, no songs were to be picturised on the leading man as per the screenplay of the film. With all this in mind, Dilip initially said 'no' to Asif. But, we all know Asif by now–what Asif wanted, he got. And the impassioned manner in which he narrated the story, and the style and flamboyance with which he, as the director, had visualised he would present Prince Salim on screen, eventually led to a 'yes' from his friend. But the fact remains that Prince Salim was a total departure from any role essayed by Dilip Kumar before. A character in the genre of the classical historical drama had not been attempted by any of his contemporaries, neither has it been attempted with as much success by any of the present generation of actors.

Dilip as Salim

Durga Khote (the original choice) was retained to play the role of Empress Jodha Bai. Actor Ajeet, whose career as a leading man was on the wane, was cast in the important role of Durjan Singh, with character actor-producer-director Kumar Mijjan as the maverick sculptor Sangtarash. Murad was given the role of Raja Man Singh. The coveted role of Bahar went to actress Nigar Sultana who was to be the third wife of K. Asif in the time to come. By now, Asif had hired two sound stages in Mohan Studios at Andheri (which eventually became the K. Asif Studio) and construction of the huge sets, artefacts and paraphernalia for *Mughal-E-Azam* began. Asif also worked very hard on polishing the final script in association with his team of writers, all Urdu-language literary heavyweights–Kamaal Amrohi, Ehsaan Rizvi, Wajahat Mirza, Amanullah Khan (father of later day actress Zeenat Aman) and their associates. The screenplay, scenic progression and the dialogue were meticulously crafted to perfection. Asif's highly competent senior production manager S.T. Zaidi had a major contribution in the perfect

Nigar and K. Asif

Durga Khote

Ajeet

Kumar and Nigar

preparation and launch of the grand motion picture. Initially, a 50-day shooting schedule was completed in which important scenes (those not featuring Anarkali*)* were filmed. Singularly, the most major problem that remained was the selection of the leading lady to play Anarkali. The most suitable actress for Anarkali, that is, Nargis had already refused to play the role.

Asif placed an advertisement in India's trade weekly *Screen* on 8 February 1952, inviting girls between the ages of 16 and 22 to apply for the role of *Anarkali.* Five young girls respectively from Delhi, Lucknow and Hyderabad were shortlisted and screen tested but none of them fit the bill. Nutan who by then was riding high on the success of her debut film (*Nagina*) was offered the role and *Screen* magazine of 2 May 1952 announced her as the leading lady. But, she backed out commenting that only Nargis or Madhubala could do full justice to the role. Due to the delay in selection of the heroine, shooting came to a standstill and the rumour spread that the film had been shelved. Father-son duo of Makhanlal Jain and Rajendra Jain, owners of the M&T Studios and Filmkar Production Concern (who had earlier produced the highly successful *Deedar)* quickly announced their own 'Anarkali' and signed Kamaal Amrohi as the writer and Anil Biswas as the music director. The mahurat of the film was held with Anil *Da* recording a sonorous Lata Mangeshkar number *Allah bhi hai mallah bhi hai, kashti hai ki doobi jaati hai* (later used in the film *Maan).* At that point in time, Filmkar was also producing a Dilip Kumar–Nutan starrer *Shikwa,* with music by Anil Biswas, under the direction of Ramesh Saigal and the film was 95 per cent complete. Dilip Kumar and K. Asif weaned Kamal Amrohi away leading to a serious row with the Jains. As a result, the nearly complete *Shikwa* as well as the announced 'Anarkali' got shelved and the shooting of *Mughal-E-Azam* resumed with Dilip Kumar's favourite co-star Madhubala as Anarkali. They were already doing *Tarana* and *Sangdil* together and she was highly recommended by Dilip Saheb himself. Madhubala lived the role of Anarkali and the rest is history.

Madhubala as Anarkali

In the meantime, another severe jolt was on the way from Filmistan Studios (under the leadership of one of Dilip's earliest mentors S. Mukerji) which also announced *Anarkali* with Nandlal Jaswantlal as the director, C. Ramchandra as the music director, Bina Rai as

Dilip Kumar, Madhubala and K. Asif

Anarkali and Pradeep Kumar as Prince Salim, which went into production immediately. Obviously, the question of Dilip Kumar doing anything against Filmistan's *Anarkali*, other than looking the other way, just did not arise. Also the astute S. Mukerji, had not signed even a single person working in *Mughal-E-Azam* for Filmistan's Anarkali! The film was completed in less than one year and became a super hit, mainly due to its magnificent musical score. K. Asif's laconic comment was, 'The film on Anarkali has been released and is a hit. My film is on Akbar-e-Azam with a very different treatment and would be a bigger hit.' An unfazed Asif continued to shoot his *Mughal-E-Azam* with renewed vigour.

From the word go, money flowed and was spent like water in the production of the film. However, there came a stage when the financers too got jittery and the fund flow dropped to a trickle. Naushad suggested to Asif to obtain some additional finance and took him to a well-known financer who was willing to help out. During the meeting, a deal was quickly finalised and as the celebration began, the financer poured whisky using a peg measure. Asif frowned, brusquely got up and left with Naushad bidding goodbye to the financer. Asif explained to a bewildered Naushad that '*Jo aadmi naap ke sharab pilata hai woh* Asif *ko kya* finance *karega, mujhe aise shaks ka paisa nahin chahiye*.' (How will someone who offers a measured drink finance Asif?) Such were the guts of Asif. He never compromised and made the film on his terms.

Naushad and Asif

The authentic battle scenes of the movie were a major highlight and Asif spared no efforts in ensuring that the depiction recreated the fierce remorselessness of the hard fought wars of the Mughal era. He sought and got the full co-operation of the Indian Army with trained horses, horse riders, canons, trained elephants, and battle wear. Real explosives were used in showing the canons being fired. Asif himself narrowly escaped being seriously hurt on many occasions. Battle scenes with such authenticity were never before (and never after) seen on silver screen. These key battle sequences were shot in the hot deserts of Jodhpur. The splendid support of the Indian Army was duly acknowledged in the titles of the film.

The Regal K. Asif

Another highlight and captivating feature of the film was the sheer romantic intensity of Dilip Kumar and Madhubala in their love scenes on the silver screen. Perhaps, it was their

Battle Scenes of Mughal-E-Azam

real love and intimate chemistry enhancing the reel love displayed by Salim and Anarkali on the celluloid. Particularly memorable were the song sequence *Prem jogan ban jaaoon* and *Yeh dil ki lagi kam kya hogi* and the famous candle-light first meeting of the lead pair when Salim visits Anarkali in her home. These love scenes truly became immortal.

Since Asif was taking his own time to complete *Mughal-E-Azam,* a rumour went around

The Unforgettable Love Scenes Enacted by Dilip and Madhubala

The Remarkable Chemistry Between the Lead Pair

the industry that the director was taking his financier (Sterling Investment Corporation) for a royal ride. Shapoorji pushed the panic button and was on the brink of stopping further investments. Dilip Kumar getting wind of this development rushed to Shapoorji and offered not to take any remuneration till the film was complete and implored Shapoorji not to pull out at a crucial juncture. A very touched Shapoorji agreed to continue and became very fond of Dilip Kumar. But more shocks were in the offing and as the film was nearing completion in the later half of 1950s, the era of colour films (*Aan, Jhansi Ki Rani, Jhanak Jhanak Payal Baje,* etc.) had already dawned. Asif therefore picturised three of the key song sequences (*Pyar kiya to darna kya, Jab raat hai itni matwali* and *Khuda nigahban ho tumhara)* in Technicolor. Encouraged by the successful picturisation of the songs and their sweeping impact, Asif thought of scrapping the entire black and white reels already canned and remake them in colour. He went and proposed this to Shapoorji –Pallonji who blew their top at Asif and with great difficulty, well-wishers persuaded the maverick director to drop the idea. The final print of the colossal film therefore was only partly in Technicolor.

The movie also had technical difficulties during filming, which were overcome with great ingenuity by cinematographer R.D. Mathur. For the song sequence *Pyar kiya to darna kya,* Asif designed and art director M.K. Syed erected a very special set of a *Sheesh Mahal* with complete mirror glass work (painstakingly created by Agha Shirazi) so that images of the dancing Anarkali could be shown all over with her reflections in the mirrors. The set became so famous that dignitaries from all over the world visited India to see the unique creation including King Saud Bin Abdul Aziz of Saudi Arabia, King Zahour Shah of Afghanistan, King Mahendra of Nepal, noted filmmaker Rossiline, and famous director David Lean, etc. However, when shooting on the set was to commence,

Asif was flabbergasted to hear from R.D. Mathur that it was virtually impossible to light the set because of the reflections from the numerous mirrors installed. The set had cost a whopping sum of ₹10 lakh and was to feature in the most dramatic scene of the film. The genius that R.D. Mathur was, he astutely devised a method of indirect lighting in which light was appropriately bounced through strategically placed reflectors. The experimental technique worked and became a landmark innovation in filmmaking. Most interestingly, after the shooting on the set was completed, it was thrown open to public who thronged the studio to visit the marvel. Also, an exhibition of the artefacts used in the movie was held at the Jehangir Art Gallery which was very well patronised. A major contribution to the eventual shaping-up of *Mughal-E-Azam* was made by the crisp editing of Dharmveer which enhanced and enriched the overall presentation of the story.

The Sheesh Mahal Set

The gigantic magnum opus *Mughal-E-Azam* strode across the silver screens all over the country on 5 August 1960 with the simultaneous release of 150 prints (a record for that era) at premiere theatres all over, which met with a rousing reception with huge enthusiastic crowds thronging the cinemas like never before. Miles long queues were seen at the box offices of the theatres all over India from advance booking stage itself and the landmark motion picture became a stupendous hit celebrating golden jubilees at numerous centres. The most memorable premiere was held at Maratha Mandir Cinema of Mumbai attended by the who's who of film industry. A beaming K. Asif welcomed the guests–the only notable absentees were Dilip Kumar and Madhubala, the estranged lovers.

Cinematographer R.D. Mathur

The Mughal-E-Azam Exhibition

Dharmveer and K. Asif

Movie Ticket

The magnum opus opens in style using a map of India as the *Sutradhar* (narrator) with

The Mumbai Premiere

A Promotional Advertisement

Huge Crowds

the background narration commencing with the catchy line '*Main Hindustan Hoon*' (I am Hindustan) and also ends with the map of the undivided India eulogising the nobility of Emperor Akbar, heralding him as the Mughal-E-Azam. There is a beautiful note in the beginning portion of the titles aptly summing-up the focal point of the grandiose motion picture.

Mughal-E-Azam became and has perennially remained a timeless classic. The pulse of the Mughal era had been touched with astounding acumen. The splendour of the bygone era has never been recreated with such eye-filling sumptuousness and that too, largely in black and white. Madhubala literally lived her role, captivating all with her seamless charm and the delicate rendering of the character of the tormented *kaneez* (bestowed with the title of Anarkali) so hopelessly in love with Prince Salim. She had umpteen brilliantly rendered scenes; the most memorable being the parting shot to Emperor Akbar after being condemned to death: *'Kaneez Jalaluddin Mohammad Akbar ko apna khoon maaf karti hai.'* Her rendition of the following moving lines (while emoting the qawwali competition with Bahar) are truly heart tugging for the viewers: *'Mohabbat humne maana zindagi barbad karti hai, yeh kya kam hai ki mar jane pe duniya yaad karti hai.'*

Madhubala and Prithviraj

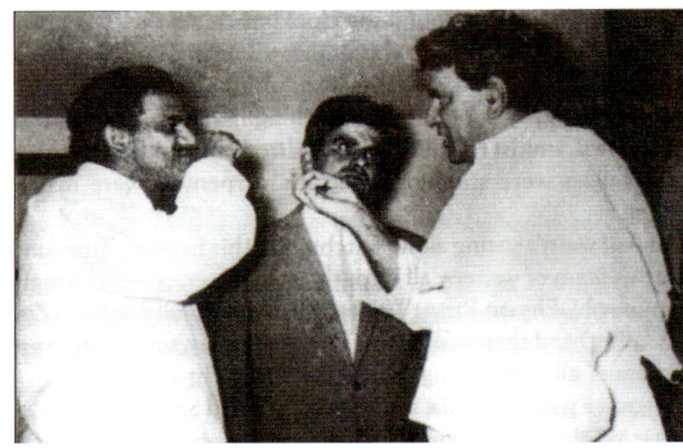

Asif, Dilip and Prithviraj

Dilip Kumar turned in a rare depiction, cast almost as it were in a Shakespearean mould. He rendered his dialogue with a crystalline diction and majesty. It was evident, right from the first to the closing frames, that he owned the character. An exercise outside the ambit of his personality, his performance in *Mughal-E-Azam* should rank with the best that he or for that matter anyone else has tried in the realm of the historical sagas in Indian cinema. We will never forget the scene where Jodha Bai wants to set eyes on her son Salim who has come home after years of separation as he has been courting battles to expand his father's empire. That scene will always be quoted by historians of our cinema for Salim's regal walk towards Jodha Bai, the way he kneels with respect and looks at his mother. Here is a man of steel with the softness of silk in his eyes. Similarly, it is impossible to forget the look in Dilip Kumar's eyes when he first steals a look at the life-size statue of Anarkali, the statue that will be unveiled to all the next morning. In a tight close-up, his eyes light up, and he smiles because he has liked what he has seen. These are merely two examples of the marvellous display of pristine histrionics by Dilip Kumar as Prince Salim–the film is replete with such memorable scenes.

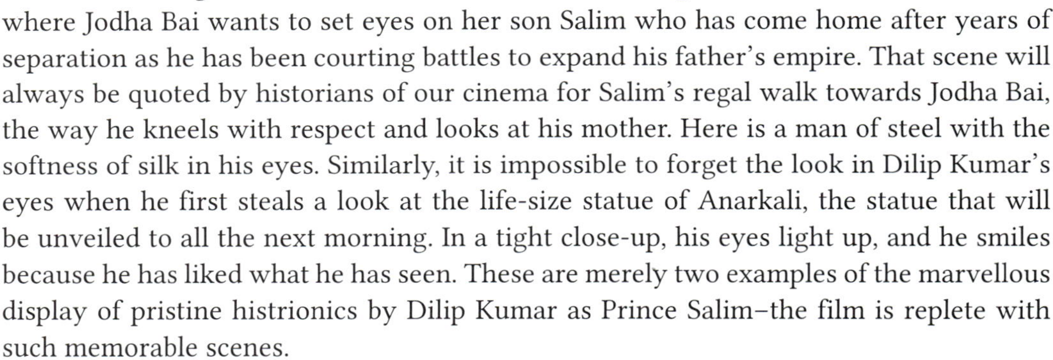

Prithviraj

Prithviraj Kapoor truly rendered a towering performance as the righteous Emperor Akbar torn between the love for his son and his principle of maintaining the sanctity of royal lineage. Durga Khote's performance as Jodha Bai matched the theatre doyen Prithviraj's overpowering histrionic splendour scene by scene and excelled in the highly dramatic scene of handing her husband the sword to kill her own son. Ajeet as the trusted lieutenant (Durjan Singh) of the prince was superb as were the veterans Kumar (Sculptor) and Murad (Maan Singh). The vampish Bahar was splendidly portrayed by Nigar Sultana and even Sheela Dalaya in her brief cameo of Suraiya (sister of Anarkali) left a lasting impression.
Quite expectedly, *Mughal-E-Azam* received rave reviews and universal accolades from scribes and film historians. We reproduce an excerpt review of the movie as published in

Durga Khote

Filmfare Magazine dated 26 August 1960 which had the headline, 'Asif's *Mughal-E-Azam* Adds a New Dimension to the Screen':

'Few films make history and one such history making film is producer-director K. Asif's *Mughal-E-Azam*, made under the banner of the Sterling Investment Corporation. It is the work of a team of creative artists drawn from different spheres of the art world. K. Asif has utilised the best available talent to give the Indian screen one of its most memorable and spectacular films.

Prithviraj Kapoor portrays Akbar the Great and his performance is the finest in the film. His majestic personality dominates the entire picture. Dilip Kumar as the rebellious Prince Salim, who stakes his honour because of his love for Anarkali, puts over an outstanding performance. His gestures, his apt facial expressions and the delivery of his lines of dialogues once again proclaim him as a top-flight actor. Madhubala as the beautiful Anarkali gives the finest performance of her career. Torn between her love for Prince Salim and her duty as a subject of Akbar, she has ample opportunity to display her histrionic talent. Nigar Sultana, as Anarkali's rival, is excellent and looks as exotic as her role demands. Durga Khote as Jodhabai, Ajit as Durjan Singh the Rajpur warrior who lays down his life for Prince Salim and Kumar as a sculptor are also impressive. Sheela Dalaya, Jillobai and Vijayalakshmi acquit themselves creditably. *Mughal-E-Azam* is a tribute to the imagination, hard work and lavishness of its maker, K. Asif. For its grandeur, its beauty, and the performances of the artistes it should be a landmark in Indian films.'

Asif with Naushad

Naushad was now in the third decade of his career as a music director which saw him retain his midas' touch in no small measure, as he hit the most coveted milestone of his musical journey in the shape and form of the all-time mega blockbuster *Mughal-E-Azam.* In the period when Naushad was composing the music of *Uran Khatola,* his 'tailor' friend of Dadar days (K. Asif) came to *Ashiana* (Naushad's Carter Road residence) to inform that he was reviving his pet Project *Mughal-E-Azam* and that Naushad had to compose the music. As the composer politely declined on the grounds of being over occupied, Asif flung a sheaf of currency notes on the harmonium and said, 'How will you not do the film? Only you will do it.' Naushad's rejoinder was that everything cannot be bought by money. At that very moment a window swung open to fill the room with sea breeze making the currency notes fly all around. Naushad's wife came in at that point in time and with the help of a maid started gathering the scattered currency. She stressed *'Ghar aayi daulat ko thukrana waajib nahin'* (It's not wise to disregard the monet that has come to you on its own). Asif's parting shot was, 'Naushad Saheb, keep the money as advance. Let us work together to show to the world, what kind of a magnum opus India is capable of producing.' That is precisely what happened and Naushad became a key member of the *Mughal-E-Azam* team.

The question of the choice of the playback artist for Tansen (played by Surendra, a singer himself, whose voice was considered inadequate for intricate classical rendition) cropped up. *'Aaj ke Tansen ki hi aawaz lee jaaye'* (Let's take the voice of today's Tansen only), suggested Naushad, hinting at Ustad Bade Ghulam Ali Khan. Asif loved the idea and insisted on Khan Saheb singing for Tansen but the latter refused point blank to sing for a film. Asif kept on insisting, *'Khan Saheb gaana to aap hi gayenge.'* (Khan Saheb, only you will sing the song) Khan Saheb's temper rose but Asif would not budge. A perplexed Ustad Bade Ghulam Ali Khan took Naushad aside to inquire, 'What should I do to get rid of this *museebat* (trouble)?' Naushad suggested that the maestro may quote an unaffordable, astronomical price. The Ustad told Asif that he would sing for a price of ₹25,000 (a huge sum considering that top singers like Rafi and Lata charged a meagre ₹5000 per song those days) and to Bade Ghulam Ali's surprise, K. Asif accepted without batting an eyelid. Such were the majestic ways of the royal persona of K. Asif. Naushad quickly arranged a recording session at Mehboob Studios, and the Ustad started singing in his usual classical style in *Raag Sohani (Prem jogan ban jaoon).* Naushad had to politely request the maestro to impart a softer tone to the rendering to match the mood of the scene. Ustad Bade Ghulam Ali Khan lost his cool and thundered, '*Recording band karo. Mujhe film mein nahin gaana, Chale jao*' (Stop the recording. I don't want to sing for films. Get lost). Asif quickly intervened and arranged for the love scene featuring Dilip Kumar and Madhubala (this song was in the background) to be projected in the studio itself, requesting the maestro to sing in a tone matching the picturisation. Grapevine has it that Ustad Saheb was so besotted by the beauty of the 'Venus of Indian Screen' Madhubala that he sang with rare sensitivity more than adequately fulfilling the tonal requirements. Since the love scene, as scripted, spans the entire night to end at dawn (*Raag Sohani* is a night Raga), Naushad mixed some *Anya Swar* to create the dawn effect. The Ustad refused to sing an impure composition. Naushad had to use all his persuasive powers in explaining the demands of the scene, before Ustad Bade Ghulam Ali Khan relented. The Ustad sang another song *Shubh din aayo (Raag Rageshri)* during the welcome sequence of Prince Salim during the film.

Naushad and Bade Ghulam Ali

Prem Jogan ban jaoon

Mughal-E-Azam is the last film in which the great Shamshad Begum sang for Naushad. She exited Naushad's musical realm in great style, singing one of the finest Hindi film qawwalis ever, *Teri mehfil mein kismet aazma ke...* with Lata Mangeshkar. Besides this qawwali, the rest of the album had Lata Mangeshkar numbers numbers – *Mohe panghat pe Nandlal (Raag Gaara), Mohabbat ki jhoothi kahani pe (Raag Darbari), Bekas pe karam kijiye sarkar-e-madina* (An immortal *Naat* in *Raag Kedar*)*, Yeh dil ki lagi kam kya (Raag Jayjaywanti), Humein kaash tumse mohabbat (Raag Bilawal), Khuda nigahbaan ho tumhara (Raag Yaman), Aye ishq yeh sab duniyawale (Raag Bilawal),* and, of course, the biggest hit song in the film *Pyar kiya to darna kya (Raag Darbari Kanhda* and a number of ragas). *Mohe panghat pe Nandlal* was recorded in many voices/styles until Asif settled for Lata's version. Naushad

Shamshad and Naushad

Mohe Panghat pe

Teri mehfil mein kismat

Aye ishq yeh sab duniyawale

Mohabbat ki jhooti kahani

Hame kash tumse

Mohabbat Zindabad

Bekas pe karam kijiye

Jab raat hai aisi

and Shakeel Badayuni were huddled up in the composer's music room for a full night and wrote hundreds of versions before finalising the lyrics based on a U.P. *lok geet* [folk song] *Prem kiya kya chori kari* to create *Pyar kiya to darna kya.* Naushad originally selected a tune in pure *Raag Darbari Kanhda* for the song, but later, considering the wide sweep of this *Darbari* sequence, he seamlessly interwove shades of ragas such as *Kaafi, Shaahna, Megh, Sarang, Pilu* and *Bahar* in the interludes–a great musical feat. The best in the business vocalists Ustad Niyaz Ahmad Khan, Hafiz Ahmad Khan, Faiyyaz Ahmad Khan (the song opens with their classical *alaaps*), Ustad Abdul Haleem Jafar Khan (on sitar), Pt Ramdas (on Pakhawaj), Pt. Ramnarayan (on Sarangi) were specially invited to sing/play in the song. The episode with the song, however, did not end with the recording completion. The film was partly in colour and when the Technicolor prints of the *Sheesh Mahal* sequence containing the song arrived, K. Asif desired that the song be further enlivened. It was a truly onerous task, but Naushad rose to the occasion. Summoning Lata, he recorded the passage *Chaaro taraf hai unka Nazara*—which accompanies the portion when the dancers' images are seen in the mirrors of the court dome—four times without musical accompaniment. Her voice was recorded on four different sound tracks with multiple effects. The four distinctly located sounds were then transferred on to the original voice track of the song. The result was terrific–a hauntingly magical effect had been created. As the songs started playing on the radio hit parades, everyone thought that *Pyar kiya to darna kya* was sung by Lata and chorus and marveled at Naushad's creative genius, upon learning that it was a Lata solo. Mohd. Rafi had just one song *(Mohabbat Zindabaad)* with a chorus in the film. *Mughal-E-Azam* became an immortal diamond jubilee hit, with major contributory factors being its performances, dialogue and music. The evergreen popularity of the music can be gauged from the fact that twenty years after its initial release, HMV issued a twin LP album of the songs and dialogue of *Mughal-E-Azam* which sold like hot cakes. A number of other songs and musical tracks (in addition to the published music) were recorded for the film but remained unused. Like there were two more songs–*Husn ki baraat chali* and *Mujh par hi chale kyoon teer-e-nazar* sung by Mubarak Begum but they have been irretrievably lost.

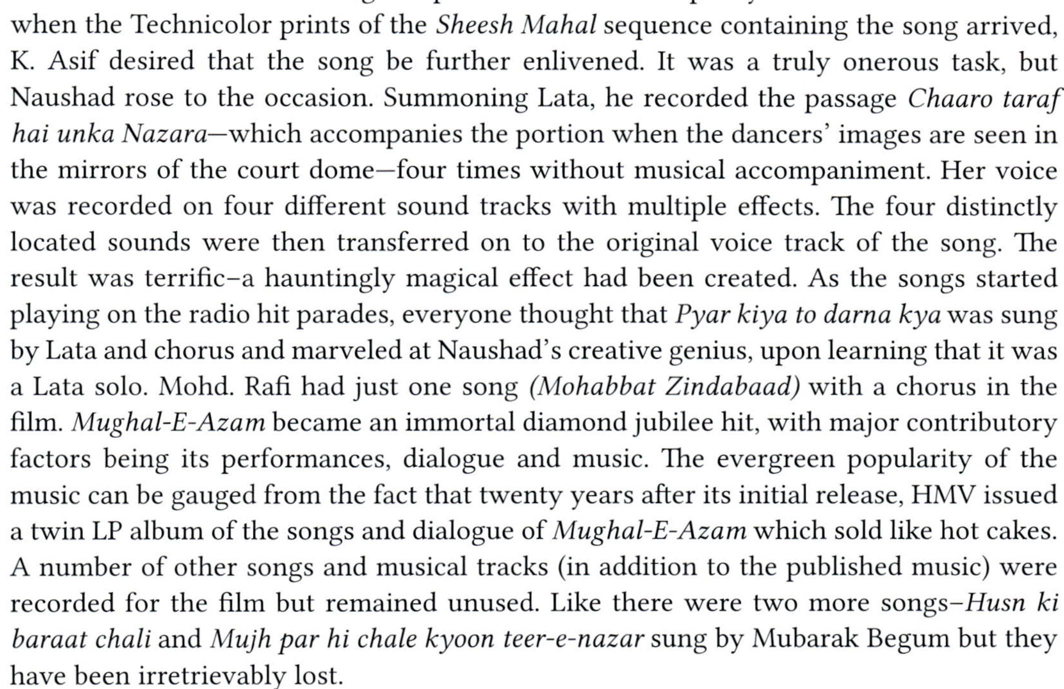

Pyar kiya to darna kya

Twin LP Album

LP Disc

After forty years, the producers Shapoorji–Pallonji along with K. Asif's son Akbar Asif got the film digitally re-mastered and fully coloured. Naushad meticulously re-recorded the entire score (songs plus background) in digital format without changing a single note–what a brilliant achievement! The fully-coloured digital version got a nation-wide release again and history repeated itself. The four decades plus old film once again stormed the box office recreating history. Such was the lasting power of the epic–that it could captivate viewers even in an era when audience tastes have hit an all-time low.

Mughal-E-Azam was to K. Asif what *Gone with the Wind* was to author Margaret Mitchell. Whereas other well-known filmmakers have had to build a body of work comprising several films to achieve immortality, K. Asif did so through just this one film, much as Margaret Mitchell did through her one book. *Mughal-E-Azam* stands out among Indian films and the fact that it has retained its popularity over many decades since its 1960 release, confirms the certainty of its survival for posterity. The story of the conception and making of *Mughal-E-Azam* and the life of its great maker K. Asif is a fable to be cherished forever. The grandeur and magnificence of *Mughal-E-Azam* has remained unrivalled over sixty-four years and shall perennially remain so. What a man and what a film!

GUNGA JUMNA

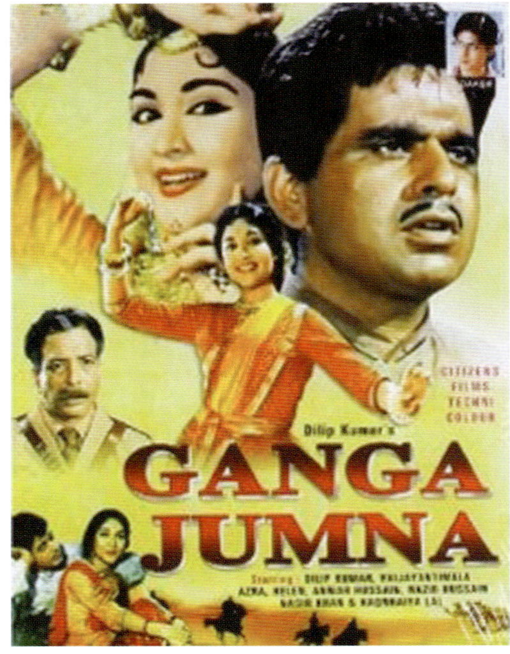

DATE / YEAR OF RELEASE: 1 DECEMBER 1961
BANNER / PRODUCER: CITIZENS FILMS / DILIP KUMAR
DIRECTION: NITIN BOSE
MUSIC: NAUSHAD
LYRICS: SHAKEEL BADAYUNI
PLAYBACK: MOHD. RAFI / LATA MANGESHKAR / ASHA BHOSLE / HEMANT KUMAR / SHANTI MATHUR
STORY / SCREENPLAY: DILIP KUMAR
DIALOGUE: WAJAHAT MIRZA
CINEMATOGRAPHY: V. BABA Saheb
EDITING: HRISHIKESH MUKHERJEE / DAS DHAIMADE
AUDIOGRAPHY: M.I. DHARMSEY / KAUSHIK
ART: SUDHENDU ROY
CHOREOGRAPHY: B. HIRALAL
CAST: DILIP KUMAR / VYJAYANTIMALA / NASIR KHAN / AZRA / KANHAIYALAL / S. NAZIR / LEELA CHITNIS / NAZIR HUSAIN / PRAVIN PAUL / ANWAR HUSAIN / HELEN / HUSN BANO / RANJIT SOOD / KHWAJA SABIR / AMAR / BIHARI / NARBADA SHANKAR / FAZLOO / RAMKUMAR / AKASH DEEP / BABY ARUNA IRANI / BABY NAAZ

Dilip Kumar's (arguably) the best performance and (probably) his greatest film was his next release after the magnum opus *Mughal-E-Azam.* This landmark film was the timeless classic *Gunga Jumna* which released on 1 December 1961. Made in opulent Technicolor under the actor's own banner Citizens Films, the film turned out to be Dilip Saheb's most successful hit, loved equally by his fans. This jewel of a film and the actor's immortal performance has truly stood the test of time. Dilip Saheb's work in this trendsetting motion picture is a textbook in acting. Each scene in the film speaks eloquently of the infectious vitality and sheer true to life credibility. Besides very strong performances–particularly from the lead pair of Dilip Kumar and Vyjayantimala–and Naushad's lilting music, the USP of the film was its narrative that combined hard-hitting realism and strong storytelling within the popular format. The film went on to become a golden jubilee hit and a cult classic, and came to be heralded as one of the finest films ever.

There are fascinating anecdotes about how this classic film came about and the launch of Dilip Kumar's own film production banner. After *Amar,* Mehboob Khan announced his next project as 'Habba Khatoon', based on the life of the legendary Kashmiri poetess Habba Khatoon, in which Dilip was to play Habba's husband Yousuf Shah Chak. A complete script was worked out but due to some reasons (best known to Mehboob Saheb), he did not proceed with the film and instead announced *Mother India.* Mehboob offered Birju's role to Dilip Kumar (later played by Sunil Dutt), but the actor felt very uncomfortable with it–how could he play the son of Nargis, his heroine in seven films? Dilip Kumar eventually turned down the role. At the same time, Dilip had also recommended Mehboob to cast his brother Nasir Khan (who was re-establishing himself in Mumbai after a disastrous stint in Pakistani films) in the elder brother's role (done by Rajendra Kumar) in *Mother India.* But Mehboob Khan rejected the idea and their relationship took a beating. Even before this fracas, the megastar had been toying with the idea of making his own film and the story of *Gunga Jumna* had already taken shape in his mind. Of course, Dilip Saheb wanted Nasir Khan to be featured in it in a plum role. He wrote the complete screenplay of film which featured the story of star-crossed lovers flung in the backdrop of a dacoit drama with rebellious revenge. In one of our meetings with the thespian, Dilip Saheb candidly told us that he had drawn inspiration for *Gunga Jumna* from an old Wallace Beery western about a sheriff in the Wild West, who was duty bound to uphold the law at all costs and the conflict that emanates out of his son becoming an outlaw. In the end, the father is compelled to shoot his own son. In *Gunga Jumna*, the father and son were substituted by younger brother and elder brother with Nasir Khan (Jumna) playing the police inspector (the good) and his elder brother Dilip Kumar (Gunga) playing the outlaw (the bad). Grapevine has it that this was Dilip Kumar's answer to Mehboob Khan's *Mother India.* Yet another factor that encouraged Dilip Saheb to launch his own venture was his wonderful relationship with business magnates Shapoorji Mistry and Pallonji Mistry, who happily offered unlimited finances for the movie to Dilip. That is another story in itself.

Dilip Writing Gunga Jumna

When after due consideration, Dilip decided to launch his own production, he got a chance to mention the same to Shapoorji. He narrated his story to Shapoorji, also mentioning that he had no idea on how to go about seeking finance to make this film. Shapoorji loved the subject and its treatment sketched out by the megastar and he instantly proposed to finance the movie. When asked about the budget of the film, Dilip Kumar said that he had no idea but he wanted to make the film on a grand scale and in Technicolor. Completely trustful of Dilip Saheb, Shapoorji had no hesitation in loosening the purse strings for *Gunga Jumna.* The elderly Parsi magnate handed two cheque books to Dilip Kumar, saying, 'Take these–one is for your cost of production; it is for

your use in making the film. And the other one here is for your personal remuneration. Fill in whatever figures you want. They're all blank and signed cheques.' This gesture was not merely magnanimous, it was also very touching. And, though Dilip didn't make any promises then, he decided immediately in his own mind how to repay that generous gesture with an equally charitable one! Dilip Saheb himself told us this story as to how the iconic film was financed, adding in the end: '**Shapoorji shook his hands with the first cheque held in between our hands so that the ink got imprinted on my palm–a Parsi ritual for good luck. Shapoorji was a towering giant in the construction business and he commanded instant respect from the authorities because of his untainted reputation. He was a man of small build and of medium height, his intrinsic goodness being reflected in the radiance on his gentle face. He visited the location whenever he found time and, at other times, he dropped in at my new house I had bought on Pali Hill.**' After the film was released and became a super hit, Dilip Kumar returned the two cheque books to Shapoorji partly using only the first one (for production expenses) and leaving the second one (for his personal remuneration) untouched. This gesture deeply touched Shapoorji who fondly embraced Dilip Saheb.

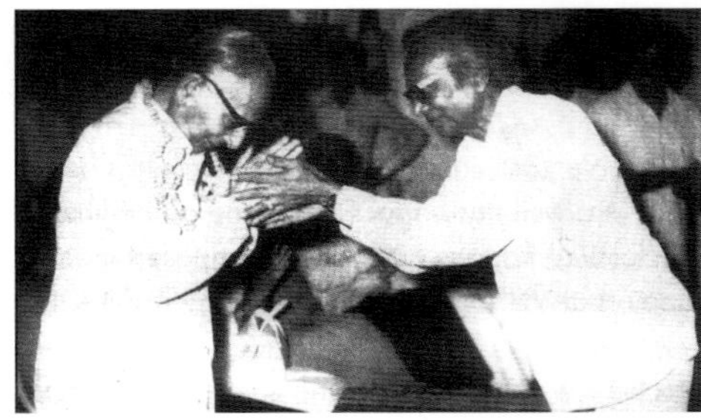

Naushad Facilitating Gunga Jumna's Director Nitin Bose

Dilip Kumar assembled a splendid cast and crew for making his epic home production, led by his mentor–veteran director Nitin Bose, who had earlier directed him in his first success *Milan* (1946) and the super-duper hit *Deedar* (1951), and his favourite music director Naushad. Nitin Bose also greatly contributed to the development of the brilliant screenplay crafted by Dilip Kumar. On his experience of directing the film, Nitin *Da* said: '**Dilip and I got together once again for his own production *Gunga Jumna* and here I must correct a misconception that has somehow arisen. I believe there is a strong rumour that Dilip took over the direction from me. This is absolutely wrong. Not only is Dilip a very disciplined actor but also a very warm human being. We used to discuss the next day's scenes threadbare every night before. So when I wanted small changes in the script, Dilip would come up with suggestions readily. I had noticed this ability even earlier and had encouraged it myself! *Gunga Jumna* was an action-packed, emotional film. During the shooting of a skirmish between the jawans and the dacoits, one of the junior artists all the time kept closing the wrong eye, while aiming his gun filled with blanks. My assistant director Jawad Hussain got very upset and catching hold of the gun barrel, shouted: "This way man, not the way you are holding it!" The artist's finger was on the trigger and by mistake, the gun went off; the blank piercing his chest, Jawad fell dead on the spot. Everything happened so suddenly and so inexplicably that for a moment I could not comprehend what had happened and when I did–I went to pieces. During this time, when I was emotionally unable to work in any coherent manner, I asked Dilip to take over. And only then did he come into the picture as anything other than an actor. I have not come across a man who is as cultured and warm-hearted as him.**'

To handle the ambitious production, Dilip Kumar roped in Bimal Roy's Controller of Productions, Premji, whom he had grown close to him during the making of *Devdas* and *Madhumati*. 'Dilip Kumar never forgets his friends and masters,' recalled Premji. As mentioned, Dilip's mentor and guru Nitin Bose was brought back from Kolkata to make a major directorial contribution to the movie. Audiographer M.I. Dharamsey (ex-Bombay Talkies and producer of *Yahudi*) was brought in as a sound recordist. Cinematographer

V. Baba Saheb with whom Dilip Kumar had worked in *Daag* was signed though he had never worked on a colour film and the better-known cameramen like Jal Mistry and Fali Mistry were available. Dilip Saheb also roped in his trusted college friend Ved Puri to oversee the production. Besides this, there were at least twenty artists who had fallen on bad days and were involved by Dilip Kumar in the film in recognition of their having worked with him in the past.

The choice of the music director automatically fell on Naushad. The script of *Gunga Jumna* was set in the Gangetic belt of Uttar Pradesh. Naushad suggested to Dilip Kumar that in order to impart a unique authenticity to the powerful narrative, the dialogue should be in the *Poorabiya* dialect. Dilip readily agreed and writer Wajahat Mirza wrote some brilliant pithy dialogues which were delivered with incredible ease by Gunga (Dilip Kumar) and Dhanno (Vyjayantimala). Dilip Saheb told us that he had taken the cue for conversing in the *Poorabiya*/Bhojpuri dialect from his Bihari gardener and his wife during the period he lived in Deolali. Dilip Saheb remembered that the couple constantly chattered, quarrelled and then made up with each other. Their conversational dialect was truly colourful and fascinated the thespian. Several of the memorable Dilip–Vyjayanti banter episodes in *Gunga Jumna* had shades of the gardener couple quarrels. Dilip Saheb first mooted the idea of having the new dialect in the film to Mehboob Khan, K. Asif and the distributors; they outright rejected the idea saying that it would be 'suicidal'. Only S. Mukherji, Bimal Roy, good friend Hiten Chaudhary, Naushad (who hailed from Lucknow in U.P.) and Wajahat Mirza (who belongs to Sitapur in U.P.) supported the idea. In his quest for blazing a new trail, Dilip Saheb decided to go for the dialect and the rest is history. Legendary character artist Kanhaiyalal, who hailed from Varanasi in U.P. and had a pivotal role in the movie, was a big help in training the artists to speak the dialect with the right diction. Poet Pt. Rammurti Chaturvedi too personally coached the lead artists in the use of *Poorabiya* dialect. The result was that even Vyjayantimala, who generally wrote down her dialogue in the Roman script, spoke the folk language with consummate ease and facile conviction for her character of Dhanno. Becoming tone-perfect and as accent-perfect as an original UP-ite in the dialect was a challenge squarely met by her. Vyjayantimala, aware that this was a new dimension to be added to her histrionic repertoire, worked night and day to become a *Poorabiya*/Bhojpuri-speaking girl of U.P. She rapidly submerged her real-life personality, her sophistication into the persona of the village belle. Vyjayantimala deservedly won the Filmfare Award as Best Actress for *Gunga Jumna*. It goes without saying that Dilip Kumar had completely mastered the dialect and fully comprehended the nuances of his character to deliver a stunning performance. The Dilip–Vyjayanti lead pair lit up the silver screen with their sparkling chemistry and remarkable histrionics.

Kanhaiyalal

Selection of an appropriate locale to serve as the backdrop for unfolding the story was a key requirement of the script and it took Dilip Saheb a month to zero in on a location called *Surya Mahal* in a village named Jawar and some areas around Kasara Ghat near Igatpuri, 120 km from Mumbai. He came across these locations just by chance while being on an excursion with dear friend and comedian Johnny Walker. The locations had virgin beauty and unexplored ruggedness of craggy hills and a valley besides a flowing river skirted by sloping land covered with tall trees and bushes with a dense forest looming large in the not-too-distant skyline. Nitin Bose and V. Baba Saheb were delighted with the location and foresaw that it would provide the right backdrop for the village, dacoits' hideout and a scenic setting for picturisation of the songs. Little did Dilip know that the location he had discovered would be repeated in numerous films in the future. A temporary structure authentically replicating a Zamindar's haveli was constructed on location. Some of the indoor shooting was done at Mehboob and Filmalaya Studios.

The Igatpuri Locations

The shooting of *Gunga Jumna* commenced with an outdoor schedule at Igatpuri. At that point in time, Dilip Saheb was completing his work in Bimal Roy's *Madhumati* and K. Asif's unending saga *Mughal-E-Azam.* Just then, he received a word from the S.S. Vasan of Gemini Studios (with whom Dilip had developed an extraordinary rapport during the making of *Insaniyat*), who wanted Dilip to give him continuous dates for his forthcoming film *Paigham.* Vasan wanted to recover the heavy losses he incurred on two of his previous failures and was in a financial trouble. Dilip did not hesitate for a second and committed himself to the film. This delayed the production of *Gunga Jumna.* Only a Dilip Kumar could have been so considerate and grant such an out-of-the-way favour in putting his own picture on hold to help a producer friend.

What makes an honest and law-abiding man forsake the very things he cherishes and take to violence is a sensitive question which had not been tackled on the screen prior to this great film. It is to the credit of Dilip Kumar that he tackled the bold and sensitive subject so effectively in *Gunga Jumna.* It was his first and only foray as a producer-writer and the thespian kept the narrative remarkably close to life. In a world of make-believes and pretences, truth is at times a dangerous commodity and yet this film dared to tell the truth without reservations. The result was explosive entertainment. The story depicted the trials and tribulations of an impoverished peasant (Gunga) and his intense love for his younger brother (Jumna). Inextricably interwoven with Gunga's quest was his romantic and supportive relationship with childhood sweetheart (Dhanno). The

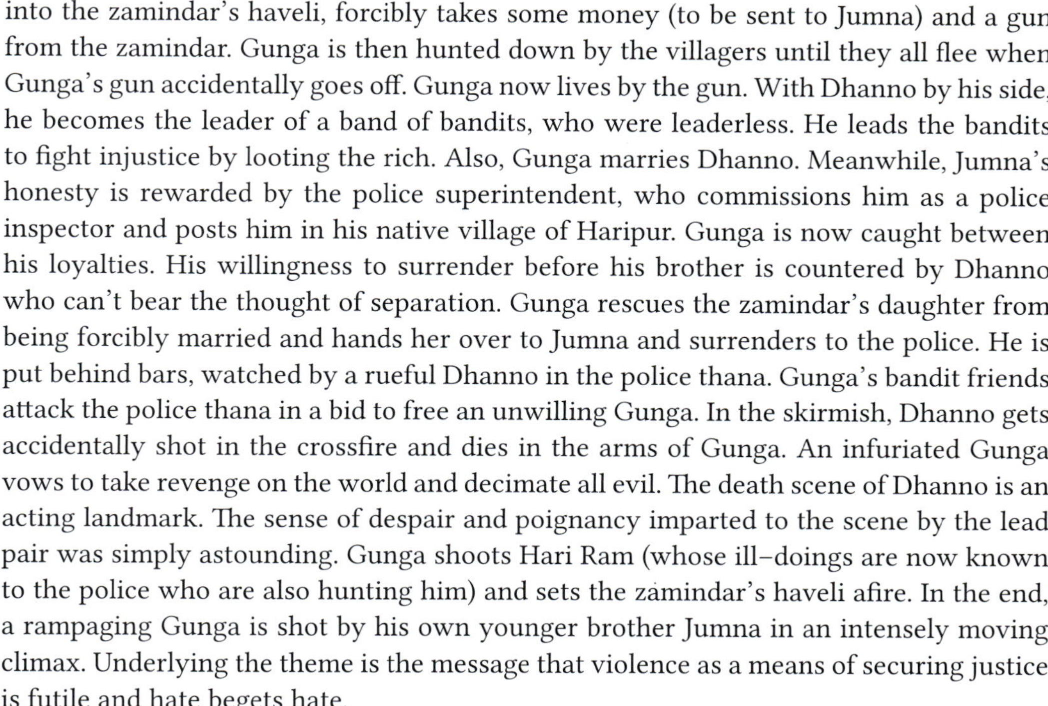

sombre Jumna, meanwhile, is in love with the zamindar's to-be-married daughter (played by Azra). Gunga's struggle to educate his brother against great odds and the machinations of a tyrannical brother-in-law (Hari Ram) of a kind landlord (who remarried and later died) formed the film's earlier part. The picture took a dramatic turn when Gunga foiled Hari Ram's nefarious attempt to molest Dhanno and gave the evil man a sound thrashing. This was a wonderfully enacted scene in which Gunga consoles an enraged Dhanno with the famous words *'Na ro Dhanno na ro'.* A vengeful Hari Ram falsely implicates the innocent Gunga in a case of theft–a crime he had never committed. After he is released from jail, Gunga is grief-stricken to learn about Jumna's predicaments (whom he had sent to the city for studies which could not be paid for) and plight from Dhanno. An enraged Gunga storms into the zamindar's haveli, forcibly takes some money (to be sent to Jumna) and a gun from the zamindar. Gunga is then hunted down by the villagers until they all flee when Gunga's gun accidentally goes off. Gunga now lives by the gun. With Dhanno by his side, he becomes the leader of a band of bandits, who were leaderless. He leads the bandits to fight injustice by looting the rich. Also, Gunga marries Dhanno. Meanwhile, Jumna's honesty is rewarded by the police superintendent, who commissions him as a police inspector and posts him in his native village of Haripur. Gunga is now caught between his loyalties. His willingness to surrender before his brother is countered by Dhanno who can't bear the thought of separation. Gunga rescues the zamindar's daughter from being forcibly married and hands her over to Jumna and surrenders to the police. He is put behind bars, watched by a rueful Dhanno in the police thana. Gunga's bandit friends attack the police thana in a bid to free an unwilling Gunga. In the skirmish, Dhanno gets accidentally shot in the crossfire and dies in the arms of Gunga. An infuriated Gunga vows to take revenge on the world and decimate all evil. The death scene of Dhanno is an acting landmark. The sense of despair and poignancy imparted to the scene by the lead pair was simply astounding. Gunga shoots Hari Ram (whose ill–doings are now known to the police who are also hunting him) and sets the zamindar's haveli afire. In the end, a rampaging Gunga is shot by his own younger brother Jumna in an intensely moving climax. Underlying the theme is the message that violence as a means of securing justice is futile and hate begets hate.

The Na ro Dhanno scene

Bride Dhanno

The Dramatic Police Thana Scene

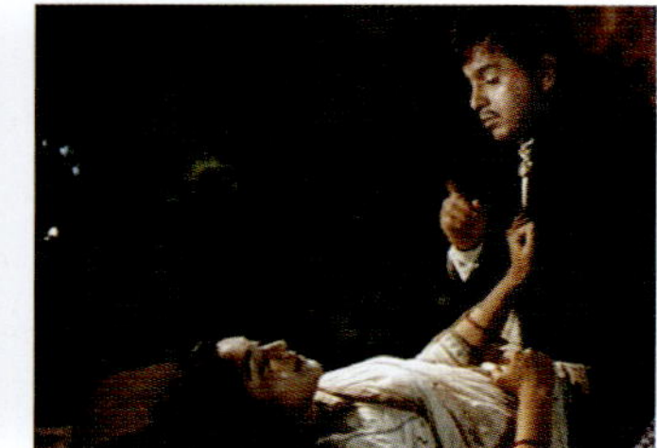

Dhanno's Death Scene

The Na ro Dhanno scene

Interwoven with this drama of a peasant's struggle for justice is the beautiful love story of two star-crossed lovers enacted brilliantly by Dilip Kumar and Vyjayantimala. In fact, out of all the conundrums of human relationships that *Gunga Jumna* explores, the most appealing is the one between Gunga and Dhanno—an extraordinary romantic saga between two ordinary people, handled with great thought and charm. The profusely engaging and captivating histrionic *jugalbandi* between the lead pair in the film was a treat to watch and over decades has continued to bewitch the viewers. They endearingly complimented each other in romantic *nok jhonk,* playful banters, intensely dramatic scenes and pathos-laden parts in equal measure. Their bewildering chemistry is evident in dialogues delivered with perfect timing and telling effect, such as: '*Dekha Dhanno main apne Munna ke liye Fontem laya hoon*', '*Arey susri main to tera jigra dekh raha tha*', '*Nahin to daihon ek lappad aur giriho dusre gaon mein*', '*Maar Ganga maar, yeh paapi hamri izzat loote chahat raha*', '*Arey na ro Dhanno na ro*', '*Yeh ladki to ek dum gaiya ho gayi hai*', etc. The readers may revisit the film and as one more illustrative point pay attention to the scene where Gunga is shot by the police and a nervous Dhanno struggles to extricate the bullet. Gunga in great pain hits Dhanno in a reflex action and a hurt Dhanno runs off into the forest only to be chased by the injured Gunga to be cajoled into forgiving her husband, '*Maan ja Dhanno maan ja*', A pacified Dhanno enticingly sings, '*Na manoo na manoo re*', What a scene! The characterisations ran really deep to extract magnetic performances from two supreme artists.

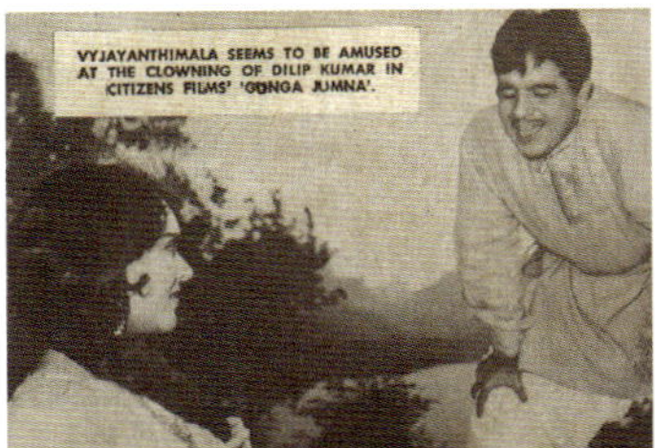

The High-power histrionics of Dilip Kumar and Vyjayantimala

The Wonderful Chemistry of the Lead Pair

Besides the lead pair, other actors too delivered truly believable performances. Kanhaiyalal was simply marvellous as Kallu Chacha. His scenes with Dilip Kumar are lessons in natural acting. Then, there were interesting cameos by Pravin Paul (zamindarni), S. Nazir (Beni Pandit), Nazir Hussain (police superintendent), Anwar Husain (Hari Ram) and Leela Chitnis (the mother). Somehow, Nasir Khan failed to impress in the meaty role of Jumna, but Azra excelled in her understated role.

Gunga and Kallu Chacha

Kanhaiyalal, Leela, S. Nazir

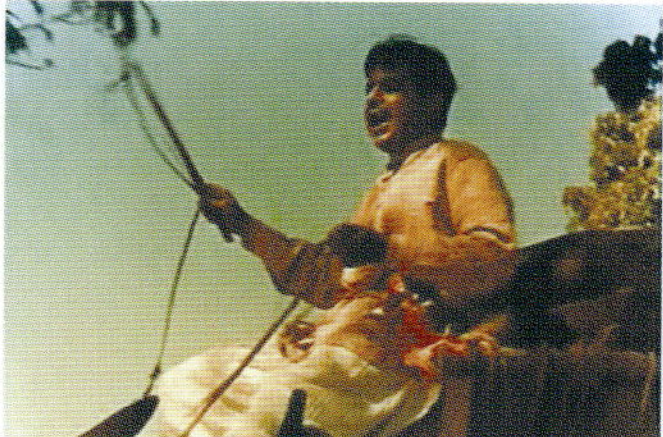
Baillan ki judian

Vyjayanti, Nasir and Dilip

Kanhaiyalal and Anwar Husain

Anwar, Dilip, Vyjayanti

Azra and Dilip

Nasir Khan

Nazir Husain, Anwar Husain

Director Nitin Bose, a former cinematographer himself, framed some terrific shots while keeping a tight rein on the narrative. In the harrowing chase wherein Gunga is hunted down by the entire village and a panting Gunga bends to drink water from a pond and sees his pursuers therein, was a stunning shot. Another amazing shot was of him single-handedly chasing the village crowd after the gun accidentally goes off as Dhanno crosses the fleeing crowd in the opposite direction towards Gunga. The train loot scenes were also brilliantly shot with the camera tied underneath the engine carriage. Moreover, Nitin Bose had a tight grip on storytelling maintaining a never-a-dull-moment tempo throughout the film. He never let go of the emotional jugular. Ace cinematographer V. Baba Saheb effectively teamed with the director to lend this Technicolor opus the opulent look that it deserved and highlighted the film with the beautiful vignettes of the rural scenes with colourful bazaars, *mela*s and sports. As mentioned, V. Baba Saheb was particularly brilliant in capturing the exciting chase and train hold-up sequences. The Technicolor processing of the movie was carried out at the Pinewood Studios in London.

Brilliant Lensing

The Opulent Look of Gunga Jumna

Among numerous highlights of this magnificent movie was the festive kabaddi sequence in which Dhanno dares Gunga to win against the rival team. She challenges him saying, *'Main na kahoon iss baar bhi Tanakpurwale jeetenge... dekho na kaise kaise gabroo jawan aaye hain!'* (I am saying this time around too people from Tanakapur will win... see the hunk players they have got!). To this Gunga's classic rejoinder is '*Toh ja besharam pakad le kisi ka haath...*' (So, chose any one of them as your life partner, O shameless). The sequence has an incredible graph, building up, as a piece of music does, to a crescendo. We still hold our breath as the competition starts, as we see Gunga's despondency when his team is on the verge of losing, as we keep pace with Gunga single-handedly gaining ground. And finally, there is the thrilling victory, followed by the exuberant scenes of celebration by the villagers in which a surprised Gunga watches Dhanno dancing with delight.

The Opulent Look of Gunga Jumna

Gunga's Tragic Homecoming

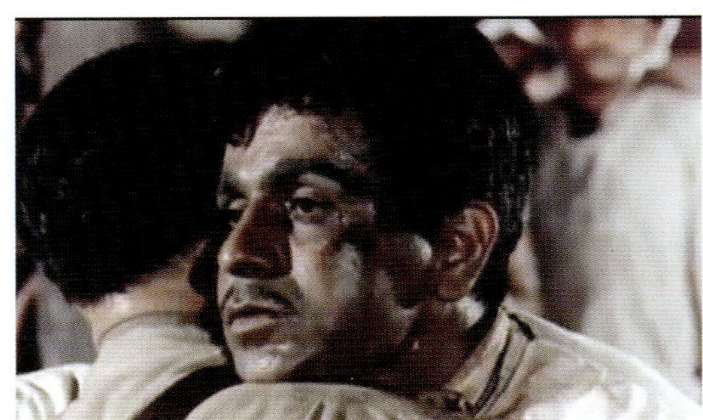

'Hum ghar aai gaye Munna!'

The film's shattering climax is as bitter as poignant. Driven by his sense of duty, Jumna is compelled to shoot down Gunga and the death scene is heart-wrenching. Dilip Kumar scaled new heights with this moment, tugging at the hearts of the audience and leaving them in a daze before the lights came on in the auditorium. However, there is an interesting anecdote to the final construction of the climatic portion of the film. As the film was nearing completion, Mehboob Saheb came unannounced to the mini theatre of his studio where the rushes were being viewed. He saw the sequence in which Jumna shoots Gunga, quietly went out without giving any reaction and called Dilip Saheb to his office to express his opinion–'**Yusuf, you have taken the shot quite correctly but, I feel, it does not have the proper impact. In my opinion, the shot must have much more life in it. People are bound to make comparisons of other similar shots in *Mother India* where the heroine shoots her son if you want to avoid the similarity, you'll have to make changes. Think it over. Yusuf, it's not very difficult. Let the shot remain as it is but add some more footage to it. Let the injured Gunga come staggering back to his house; let other characters of the film follow him–including his brother Jumna. Gunga knows his death has come and he being a Hindu character, let him go to the God's idol in the house and die at its feet. In his final moments, let somebody offer him holy *Gangajal* and let the others chant prayers for him so that he may die peacefully.**' This idea gelled immediately with both Dilip Saheb and Nitin *Da* and the new scenes were incorporated into the climax. Dilip Kumar also added his own touch by showing that after being hit by a bullet fired by his own brother Gunga wanders into his cherished house where he was born and collapses in the arms of his brother uttering '*Hum ghar aai gaye Munna*!' (I am home, Munna!) Also, Dilip Kumar added that vital utterance of '*Hey Ram!*' as Gunga dies. It was a very well-meaning advice given by Mehboob Saheb which made the climax immortal. That death sequence lingers in the minds of cinegoers to this day. Dilip Saheb has recorded his reminiscences of shooting the immortal death scene as: '**This scene was filmed on the sets at a studio at dusk. I took the cameraman, V. Baba Saheb, into confidence and told him to keep everything ready as there would not be a rehearsal or a second take. I stressed the point that the synchronisation between the action and the running camera would have to be perfect.**

He understood and was absolutely ready. The other unit members had no clue what I was going to do. What I did was my own idea. I took several rounds of the studio's premises, jogging at first and then running. When I felt breathless and I thought that I would just collapse, I entered the sets where Baba Saheb was ready with the camera running to perfection. The scene of Gunga's collapse in his house at the feet of the deity whom his mother worshipped devoutly could not have been achieved in any other way. It was a victory for the law when Gunga succumbs to his bullet wounds but I wanted to tell the audience that it was Gunga who has achieved a bigger triumph – the mortal victory God has given him by fulfilling his objective or establishing his poor mother's innocence and restoring her reputation in the village.'

Dilip and Naushad

Naushad successfully experimented with folk tunes to come up with a super hit score. Lata's solos *Dhoondo dhoondo re sajna* (*Raag Nat Bhairav*), *Do hanson ka joda* (*Raag Bhairavi*), *Na manoo na manoo dagabaaz tori batiyan* (*Raag Pilu*) and *Jhanan ghunghar baaje* are unforgettable alongside Rafi's chartbuster *Nain lad jaihein to manwa mein* and the Rafi-Asha duet *Oh chhalia re chhalia.* Asha's *mujra 'Tora man bada paapi sanwaria* (*Raag Pahadi*) and Hemant Kumar's *Insaaf ki dagar par bachchon* too were hits. Then there were some specially recorded short pieces in the voices of Mohd. Rafi (*Bailan ki judiyan jaane man ki sab batiyan*), Lata-Rafi *(Aaj hua re gori hamra gavanva)* and Shanti Mathur (*Jal mein chamke jal ki machhariya*), etc. These very aptly contributed to creating the village atmosphere in which the narrative was set. This was the tenth film of Naushad and Dilip Kumar together and the composer gave his best for his favourite star and friend's home production.

LP Disc

Nain lad jaihein to manwa ma

Dhoondo dhoondo re sajana

Oh chhalia re chhalia

Do hanson ka joda

Jhanan ghunghar baje

The Splendorous Music of Gunga Jumna

Tora man bada papi

Post completion in early 1961, the great day came when the first 'married print' (the fully re-recorded print which would actually be screened in the theatres) of *Gunga Jumna* emerged from the laboratory. The entire glitterati of the film industry saw the film and went ga-ga over it, declaring in unison that a classic had been made which would decidedly be a super-duper hit. But the film ran into rough weather from the least expected quarters to the utter surprise and shock of everyone. The board of film certification initially banned *Gunga Jumna* and later recommended 250 cuts on grounds of vulgarity and violence. This was the era of the late Dr B.V. Keskar, who was then the

EP Disc

minister for information and broadcasting, Government of India. Keskar hated films and had gone to the extent of banning film songs from being played on All India Radio (AIR), resulting in the huge popularity of Radio Ceylon which broadcast Indian film music. For six months, Dilip Saheb ran from pillar to post to get his dream project cleared and even submitted a memorandum, running into 120 pages, but to no avail. The censor board did not even look at the exhaustive document calling it too lengthy. The minister and censor board did not budge from their stand. Dilip Kumar had no option but to try to approach the then Prime Minister Pt Jawaharlal Nehru. The meeting with Pt. Nehru was arranged by Nehru's daughter Indira Gandhi (later day Prime Minister herself), and it was supposed to be only for fifteen minutes. Dilip Kumar very ably articulated his cause and Nehru*ji* listened to him with rapt attention for more than two hours. Subsequently, Pt Nehru passed the film and Dr B.V. Keskar was dropped from the ministry. However, grapevine has it that due to some secret machinations, the certification of the movie was purposely delayed so that Raj Kapoor's *Jis Desh Mein Ganga Behti Hai* (also based on the dacoit scene) could be released without competition from a bigger box-office bonanza!

Pt Nehru and Dilip Kumar

For the record, it must be pointed out that in that year Dilip Kumar did not get the Best Actor Award for *Gunga Jumna*. Instead, Raj Kapoor got it for *Jis Desh Mein Ganga Behti Hai*. *Gunga Jumna* did not get the Best Picture of the Year Award either; that also went to Raj Kapoor's film. *Gunga Jumna* won only three Filmfare Awards that year–Best Actress (Vyjayantimala), Best Dialogue (Wajahat Mirza) and Best Cinematography (V. Baba Saheb). Many scribes were very critical of the coveted award being denied to Dilip Kumar and *Gunga Jumna*. However, it was extremely sporting on part of Dilip to personally handover the Best Actor Award to Raj Kapoor for *Jis Desh Mein Ganga Behti Hai* at the Filmfare Awards function. When *Gunga Jumna* was screened at Karlovy Vary Festival in Czechoslovakia, Boston and Cairo, Dilip Kumar was besieged by film critics, who appreciated the movie and were intrigued by his acting, the meticulous research made for the film and the daring linguistic deviation attempted. Dilip Kumar was bestowed with an honorary diploma for his memorable performance in *Gunga Jumna* at the international film festival at Karlovy Vary in 1962. *Gunga Jumna* also went on to win the Silver Bowl at Boston in 1963.

The film was premiered at Lamington (Mumbai) and Regal (New Delhi) on 10 November 1961 and Midland (Chennai) on 1 December 1961. There was a tumultuous response to the film across the country, making *Gunga Jumna* one of the stupendous hits of all time. The fans went crazy praising the movie, its performances and music. It became a cult classic and a sort of textbook on filmmaking. *Gunga Jumna* is the only film which has achieved jubilees in repeat runs down the years. Film critics in unison applauded the film as a timeless classic and praised the matchless performances. The *Filmfare* in its review congratulated Dilip Kumar for his rare art of motion picture production.

Dilip Saheb himself considers *Gunga Jumna* to be a monumental achievement of his career, and is on record stating: **'I knew that my script of *Gunga Jumna* had merits for me as an actor. Since the character was on the wrong side of the law, it was important** for me to acquaint the viewer with the reasons for his taking to a lawless way of life and I had to make him pay the penalty for taking to that life, however right he may have been under the circumstances he was caught in. Gunga, I decided, should get no reprieve from the law when he tries to explain that he was the victim of a trap set by the zamindar and that he could fight the powerful feudal system only by becoming an outlaw. *Gunga Jumna's* enduring achievement is the inspiration it provided to writers to give the hero a flaw or what you call a negative shade. I had done 'anti-hero' roles earlier too. For instance, the character I had played in Mehboob Khan's *Amar* (1954) did commit an outrage. Therefore, this character was flawed and was not the conventional blemish-free hero. The character I played in Zia Sarhadi's *Foot Path* (1953) was a black marketeer and so he was also a tarnished hero. However, those films were not as successful as *Gunga Jumna*. In the case of *Gunga Jumna*, the hero was on the wrong side of the law but he had the audience sympathy with him and the conflict in the story is not so much between the brothers as it is between the law of the country and the moral freedom of a human being to fight injustice and corruption and take the world forward. The most wonderful thing about playing Gunga was that it was not difficult at all for me to understand the emotional current of the story, especially the feeling of adoration and protection for the younger brother,' said the thespian.

Well said and very succinctly put Dilip Saheb! The ultimate fact is that in *Gunga Jumna*, Dilip Kumar exhibited the glorious range a good actor can traverse, and the infinite shades he can inject into such a characterisation.

What a film *Gunga Jumna* was–a masterpiece!

The Mumbai premiere

The Kolkata premiere

Delhi Airport Welcome

The Delhi premiere

LEADER

DATE / YEAR OF RELEASE: 1964
BANNER / PRODUCER: S. MUKERJI FILM SYNDICATE PVT. LTD.
DIRECTION: RAM MUKERJI
MUSIC: NAUSHAD
LYRICS: SHAKEEL BADAYUNI
PLAYBACK: MOHD. RAFI / LATA MANGESHKAR / ASHA BHOSLE
STORY: DILIP KUMAR
SCREENPLAY: RAM MUKERJI
DIALOGUE: WAJAHAT MIRZA / HARISH MEHRA
CINEMATOGRAPHY: V. BABA Saheb
EDITING: J.S. DIWADKAR
AUDIOGRAPHY: ISHAN GHOSH
ART: SOUREN SEN
CAST: DILIP KUMAR / VYJAYANTIMALA / MOTILAL / JAYANT / LEELA MISHRA / NAZIR HUSSAIN / SAPRU / JAGDISH SETHI / HEERALAL / P. KAILASH / JANKIDAS / AMAR / CHAMAN PURI / RAJAN HAKSAR / MIRZA MUSHARRAF / INDIRA BANSAL / KUSUM THAKUR / MONI CHATTERJI / B.K. MUKERJI / MASTER NISSAR / SHARMA / RAJ RANI / SHAHGUL / AYUB / KABULI / DATTU DESAI / AJIT BENGALI / BAZID KHAN / RAM KUMAR / POLSON / MADHUMATI / MARLYN

Doyen filmmaker S. Mukerji whom Dilip Kumar held in highest esteem as one of his mentors was riding high after having successfully created his own exclusive banner and studio, Filmalaya. It was therefore but natural for him to launched an ambitious Technicolor film like *Leader,* with top stars Dilip Kumar and Vyjayantimala, under his another banner, S. Mukerji Syndicate India (SSI). Based on a story by Dilip Kumar himself, the film was a cinemascope extravaganza styled as a breezy entertainer full of mirthful episodes. The story had a socio-political base around which this romantic crime thriller was deftly woven. Initially, the film may not have been a roaring hit but numerous successful re-runs over decades testified its undiminished popularity among cinema lovers. Mukerji Saheb entrusted the direction of the magnum opus to his nephew Ram Mukerji (father of later day actress Rani Mukerji) with V. Baba Saheb again handling the cinematography. Dilip's natural alluring performance won him his sixth Filmfare Award for Best Actor. His comical banters with a brilliant Vyjayantimala were again utterly hilarious and effortlessly succeeded in evoking desired laughter. The Dilip-Vyjayanti pair simply floored the fans with delightfully timed light-hearted acting. Motilal put across his character of political leader Acharya*ji* with sheer dignity and conviction. Jayant's villainy was suave and polished.

Receiving his Sixth Filmfare Award

The advent of 1960s witnessed a continuation of the happy-go-lucky narratives in motion pictures combining exuberant romance, overstated emotions and liberal dose of mirthful comic episodes reflecting the mood of a young and confident post-independence India practising Nehruvian socialism. *Leader* was Dilip Kumar's subtle effort to adapt to the emerging trends of the time while keeping his cinematic excellence intact. Cinemagoers saw their favourite star in a sort of new avatar performing effortless comedy and serenading his leading lady in many novel ways. The film had a unique freshness and ting of modernity about it and exuded great charm in terms of presenting a new style of breezy romanticism. As mentioned, Dilip Kumar and Vyjayantimala excellently performed their romantic scenes in the first half of the film and dramatic scenes in the second half of the film. The performances won rave reviews and the *Filmfare* commented: **'Dilip Kumar undoubtedly brings to the Indian screen a new concept of graceful comedy. At no stage in the film does he stoop to raise a laugh or two from the groundings. Restrained and natural, subtle and subdued, Dilip's performance is easily his best in the comic genre. Vyjayantimala looks pretty and is very impressive. She wears pastel colour saris with grace and dances with her twinkle-toed aplomb. Jayant's capitalist, Hiralal's "goonda", Amar's fire-fighter, Nazir Hussain's professor are convincing but Leela Misra, as Vijay's mother, appears briefly to give an interesting and one of the finest performances in the film.'**

Dilip and Vyjayanti

Political Undertones in an Entertainer

Leader was the story of Vijay Khanna (Dilip Kumar), a law student (a son of a law professor–played by Nazir Husain) who also publishes a newspaper to make people aware of the evils in society. He takes the help of young boys (who are his die-hard fans) to distribute his modest publication. As an ardent follower of a popular national leader Acharya*ji* (Motilal), he also disrupts political meetings and harangues corrupt opposition politicians and their followers on what true patriotism is. It is election time and Acharya*ji* is contesting against Anupamrao Ghatak of Janata Sevak Sangh, who is supported by a group of unscrupulous businessmen led by Dewan Mahendra Nath (Jayant) and his henchman Karga (Hiralal), an assassin. Vijay Khanna regularly attends the political meetings of Acharya*ji*, which are also attended by Princess Sunita (Vyjayantimala) of Shyamgarh Estate who stays in Mumbai with her younger brother to familiarise herself with the way of life of commoners at the behest of her father His Highness Shyamgarh (Sapru). The younger brother (Akashdeep) is also a member of the Vijay Khanna gang. Vijay Khanna runs away from home to escape his marriage arranged by his father (Nazir Husain), mother (Leela Misra) and elder brother (Amar). His young friends also accompany him. Fun and mirthful episodes follow as the parents of the young children along with Princess Sunita give chase. Vijay Khanna masquerades as a righteous political supporter and astrologer to woo Princess Sunita. The romance between Vijay and Sunita blossoms amid several highly hilarious light-hearted quarrels which are great fun to watch. The film takes a dramatic turn as Karga assassinates Acharya*ji* and Vijay Khanna is wrongly accused of the murder. Sunita is aware of Vijay's innocence and helps him. In the second half of the film, Vijay is chased by the police as well as the goons but escapes both along with Sunita to eventually expose the real culprits behind Acharya*ji*'s murder. The movie had a light escapist undercurrent throughout and Dilip Kumar imparted amazing sophistication to the slapstick and remarkable panache to the farcical.

Dilip in Leader

The Breezy Mirthful Look of the Movie

As *Leader* thundered across the wide screen in quest of visual glory, with the pen flamboyantly playing to the gallery, it progressively gives up logic and common sense albeit in a subtle manner to provide full freedom to the accomplished artists to perform uninhibitedly. From frame to frame, the colour, splendour and majesty of production values lend a fascinating look to the motion picture. When the movie ends, Dilip Kumar, the actor emerges dominant–by virtue of his intrinsic histrionic genius and by uniquely sketching a new romantic and socially aware character which stands out. *Leader* was obviously intended to depict class struggle, the evil influence of one class over others in general and society in particular; it is all about democracy and Pt. Jawaharlal Nehru's

Scenes from Leader

socialism and the manner in which it is being sabotaged. Interestingly, the film exuded nationalistic recreation, not in-your-face patriotism, in which we heard clarion calls to come out and fight, '*Apni azadi ko hum harghiz mita sakte nahin, sar kata sakte hain lekin sar jhuka sakte nahin*'.

Naushad created some really modernised (including western orchestration) tunes to match the mood of the extravaganza, creating a super hit score with chartbusters like *Mujhe duniyawalon sharabi na samjho* (Rafi), *Tere husn ki kya tareef* (Lata-Rafi), *Humeen is mohabbat humeen se* (Rafi), *Ek Shahenshah ne banwa ke* (Rafi-Lata), *Aaj kal shauq-e-deedar hai* (Rafi-Asha), *Daiya re daiya laaj mohe* (Asha), *Aaj hai pyar ka faisla aye sanam* (Lata), et al. With this album, he proved that he could successfully compose for a film of any genre. The title music of the film featured Naushad's interpretation of *Vande Matram* sung by a chorus which he had recorded way back in 1948 at the behest of the Government of India for a nationwide competition.

Leader, over the years, has acquired the status of a cult movie and enjoyed highly successful repeat runs. It is still popular in current times with its sparkling DVDs selling regularly.

Sar kata sakte hain

Aaj kal shauq-e-deedar

Tere husn ki kya

Ek shahenshah ne

Humeen se mohabbat

Aaj hai pyar ka

Daiyya re daiyya

Mujhe duniyawalon

DATE / YEAR OF RELEASE: 1966
BANNER / PRODUCER: KAY PRODUCTIONS (AKHTAR SULTANA KARDAR PRESENTATION)
DIRECTION: A.R. KARDAR
MUSIC: NAUSHAD
LYRICS: SHAKEEL BADAYUNI
PLAYBACK: MOHD. RAFI / LATA MANGESHKAR / ASHA BHOSLE
STORY / DIALOGUE: KAUSHAL BHARTI
CINEMATOGRAPHY: DWARKA DIVECHA
EDITING: M.S. HAJI
AUDIOGRAPHY: YASHWANT MITKAR / KAUSHIK
ART: DESH MUKHERJI
CHOREOGRAPHY: SATYANARAYAN
CAST: DILIP KUMAR / WAHEEDA REHMAN / SHYAMA / REHMAN / PRAN / RANI / S. NAZIR / JOHNY WALKER / TUN-TUN / MURAD / SAPRU / AMAR / SAJJAN / DULARI / SHAH AGHA / PARASRAM / ISMAIL / BAZEED KHAN / RAJA / KABULI / KHURSHID KHAN / AJEET BANGALI / BIHARI / AMIR / ABRAR / YUSUF / BABY FARIDA / MASTER ANWAR / MASTER AZIZ / PRAKASH BAGALA / BABY RUKHSANA / MASTER SHAHID

Dilip Kumar's next release was veteran producer-director Abdul Rashid Kardar's *Dil Diya Dard Liya* in which Dilip Kumar starred for the first time opposite the consummate actress Waheeda Rehman. They eventually did four films together. We have, over the years, seen this interesting film many times and are at a loss to understand as to why the movie failed to click despite terrific performances, tightly-knit narrative and a hit musical score. I, Trinetra Bajpai saw the film at the Chitra Cinema (Varanasi) upon its release in 1966 and was floored. The Bajpai clan has had many repeat viewings of the picture particularly to savour the amazing histrionics of Dilip Kumar in a complex role but the film's box-office failure, after a bumper opening, has remained a mystery. Some critics may have panned the film but for us, it has always remained a memorable watch. It is unfortunate that a first and last union of A.R. Kardar and Dilip Kumar did not exactly set the box-office on fire.

A.R. Kardar initially wanted to make a biographical film on Omar Khayyam and he even gave Dilip Kumar a signing amount of ₹2 lakh for it. However, during discussions Dilip Saheb pointed out the pitfalls in the film's script and convinced Kardar to drop the idea. The producer-director then opted for a 'safe' project and presented a leather-bound script based on Emily Brontë's novel *Wuthering Heights* to the megastar. However, Kardar was not sure whether Dilip, who had already played Heathcliff-inspired roles before in *Mela, Aarzoo* and *Hulchul,* would accept to play a character-based on Heathcliff again. Kardar originally had considered casting his *Dastan (1950)* hero, Raj Kapoor, but thought that Dilip Kumar was better suited for the role. Heathcliff is a character that seems to have fascinated Dilip Kumar, for apart from playing it in three films, he has used shades of the character in several other films like *Aadmi.* In the novel, Heathcliff is a man on the edge–spiteful, mad, insecure and thirsting for revenge. In his interpretation, Dilip Kumar added the dimension of the tormented lover who has been denied his rightful love and hence seeks to avenge his mental trauma. Apparently, Dilip Saheb did this to tone down and partly remove the stark negativity of the role and maintain audience's sympathy. Interestingly, the first Hollywood adaptation of *Wuthering Heights*, produced by Samuel Goldwyn and directed by the great William Wyler in 1939, had a very formidable star cast with Sir Laurence Olivier, Merle Oberon and David Niven playing the principal characters. Anshula, the co-author of this book, personally asked Dilip Saheb about his fascination for repeatedly portraying the character and the thespian flatly denied that he entertained any fondness for playing Heathcliff and insisted that 'the remakes just happened'. He candidly said: **'It has really never crossed my mind that I have been in four versions of the novel. Earlier, Jaimini Dewan's *Rattan* (1944) was inspired by *Wuthering Heights*. Then S.U. Sunny narrated the story of *Mela* to me which I didn't quite understand but agreed to do it because I fell in love the lyrics of its song, *Gaye ja geet milan ke tu apni lagan ke*. After that Shahid Latif derived some inspiration from Mela and made Arzoo and K. Asif and S.K. Ojha followed suit in *Hulchul*. Later, there was A.R. Kardar's *Dil Diya Dard Liya*. I didn't insist on the remakes, they just happened.'**

In *Wuthering Heights,* the only novel by its celebrated author, both the main protagonists are villainous/vampish characters. Obviously, in the Hindi film adaptation, the negative traits in the leading man Shankar (Dilip Kumar) were heavily toned down and virtually eliminated from the character of the leading lady, Roopa (Waheeda Rehman). The simplification made *Dil Diya Dard Liya,* a story of a young man's untold suffering and consequent determination to make himself eligible to win the hand of his beloved, his disillusionment in love and vow to avenge the injustice and humiliation meted out to him. Ample justification for the vengeful attitude of Shankar was incorporated in the script. The love story part was converted into a love quadrilateral with childhood friends of the lead pair, Satish (Rehman) and his sister Mala (Shyama) thrown in. The only starkly villainous character that remained was Ramesh (Pran), the tyrannical brother of Roopa who ill-treats Shankar and resents his proximity to Roopa. Ramesh gets Shankar beaten up by his goons and thrown in the sea. Shankar is presumed dead but survives to discover that he is the lone surviving heir to the throne of the State of Belapur and is crowned by a loyal wazir (S. Nazir) as the monarch of the estate after Shankar has saved wazir from

Roopa and Shankar

his evil sons. In the meantime, Ramesh is seduced by a nautch girl (Rani), succumbs to her charms and is defrauded and ruined by her as he has bequeathed his ancestral haveli to her. Roopa unable to bear humiliations heaped on her and her family gets betrothed to Satish. Shankar returns as the monarch of the state of Belapur and buys back the haveli from Rani. He now plots revenge and craftily punishes Ramesh. He also buys the nautch girl just to humiliate Ramesh. Coming to know of Roopa's engagement, Shankar also humiliates her. Ramesh kills Rani and eventually shoots himself. After quite a few dramatic turns, the movie ends on a happy note as the lovers unite.

Pran, Johnny and Rani

S. Nazir with Dilip

Rehman, Shyama and Waheeda

Dilip Kumar and Pran

The pièce de résistance of *Dil Diya Dard Liya* was the towering performance of Dilip Kumar as Shankar. He lived the role giving amazing depth to the character, excellently depicting interplay of his conflicting emotions. The scenes in which he deals with Pran extracting revenge and the scenes of heaping humiliation on Waheeda, Rehman and Shyama are a treat to watch. Waheeda's Roopa was credibly etched by the fine actress and Pran delivered a terrific performance as Ramesh. In our opinion, veterans Rehman and Shyama gave polished performances but did not look their parts being over-age in looks. Johny Walker was his usual entertaining self and S. Nazir, Sajjan and Rani (she was the surprise package in the film and had two songs filmed on her) did justice to their roles. Sapru and Murad exuded their usual majesty in short cameos. Kaushal Bharti wrote some brilliant dialogue pieces such as '*Dil ne bahut dhokhe diye hain aaj kal dimaag se kaam leta hoon*', '*Tum jis chhat ke neeche saans loge main us chhat ko jala ke raakh kar doonga*', et al. Dwarka Divecha's cinematography lent an opulent look to the movie.

Grapevine has it that Dilip Kumar actually ghost directed the film as director Kardar's technique had become outdated and the veteran was painfully slow in canning scenes.

Dilip Kumar Emoting Different Shades of the Lead Role

Dilip Kumar and Waheeda Rehman in Dil Diya Dard Liya

Ostensibly, it was done in the interest of the film. However, critics of the time gave it an unsavoury twist saying that Dilip Kumar was interfering in every department of filmmaking. The truth was quite different though. The iconic producer-director, late Yash Chopra, had once clarified that A.R. Kardar was only too happy to let Dilip Saheb direct the picture. In any case, the lukewarm response to the film caused losses to Kardar who made only one more movie (a non-star cast Muslim social) after *Dil Diya Dard Liya* which too flopped, leading to the closure of his production house. That, however, was unfortunate. At one time, he was considered Mumbai's biggest movie tycoon but his decline had started when six to seven of his films failed at the box-office. His craftsmanship did have class but he would often try to cut corners and finish a picture on a shoestring budget. He overlooked the advancement of film technology and the market demands and was, therefore, sadly left behind.

Naushad's music, the songs and the background music both were once again well received. The *Raag Kalavati*-based *Koi sagar dil ko behlata nahin* (Rafi) was an outstanding composition, with other Rafi beauties including *Guzre hain aaj ishq mein* (*Raag Darbari*) and *Dilruba maine tere pyar mein* (*Raag* Yaman) being equally captivating. Lata's *Raag Jhinjhoti*-based *Phir teri kahani yaad aayi* is also an evergreen melody. However, the best song of the film was the delectable classical duet *Sawan aaye ya na aaye* (*Raag Sarang*) by Rafi and Asha. Surprisingly, Naushad made Lata Mangeshkar sing a completely western orchestration based fast number *Kya rang-e-mehfil hai dildaram* which became quite popular. Asha Bhosle rendered two typical Naushadian *mujra* songs – *Haye haye rasiya tu bada bedardi* and *Dil haarnewale aur bhi hain*. Shakeel Badayuni again wrote the well-meaning lyrics, matching the thematic requirements.

Dil Diya Dard Liya may not have been a box-office bonanza like other Dilipian films, but it is remembered for Dilip Kumar's terrific histrionic range and music maestro Naushad's timeless music which exuded his class and is still popular–about fifty-two years after the movie hit the screens.

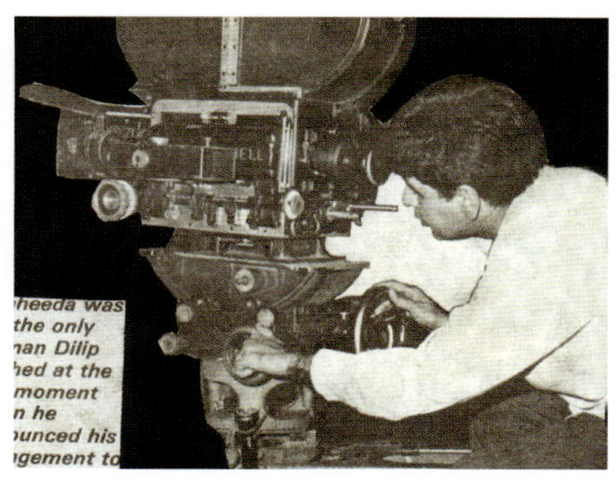

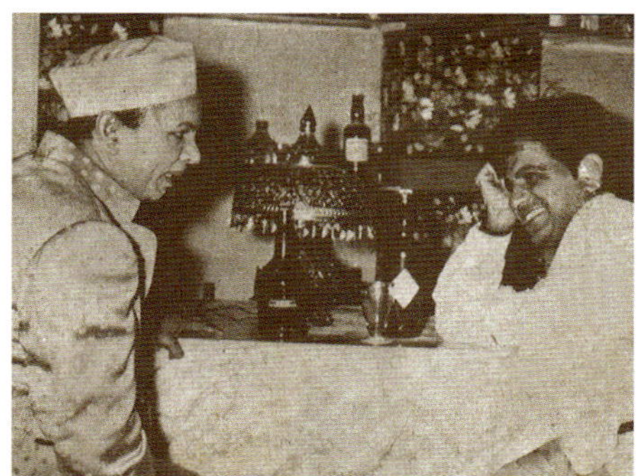

Ghost Direction by Dilip Kumar

Dilruba maine tere pyar mein

Kya rang-e-mehfil hai dildaram

Haye haye rasiya tu bada

Sawan aaye ya na aaye

Phir teri kahani yaad aayi

Guzre hain aaj tshq mein

Dil haarnewale aur bhi hain

Koi sagar dil ko behlata nahin

DATE / YEAR OF RELEASE: 1967
BANNER / PRODUCER: R.J. VAZIRANI PRESENTATION / VAZIRANI MOVIES / NEW INDIA PICTURES (PRONOTI GHOSH)
DIRECTION: JAGANNATH CHATTOPADHYAY
MUSIC: SALIL CHOWDHURY
LYRICS: HANIF / JACKIE
STORY: JARASANDH
DIALOGUE: CHANDRAKANT
ART: BOTU SEN
CINEMATOGRAPHY: BIBHUTI CHAKRABARTY
AUDIOGRAPHY: RAJ / SOPAN / MANGESH DESAI
EDITING: AJIT DAS
TECHNICAL DIRECTOR: SADANAND DESAI (HINDI VERSION)
CAST: DILIP KUMAR (SPECIAL APPEARANCE) / DHARMENDRA / PRONOTI / ABHI BHATTACHARYA / DILIP RAY / KESHTO MUKHERJI / NRIPATI CHATTOPADHYAY / BIKASH RAY / SATYA BANDYOPADHYAY / PADMA DEVI / RENUKA RAY / BIDYA ROY / SHILA PAL

Dilip Kumar made a special appearance in a Bengali movie titled *Paari*, which featured Pronoti Ghosh, wife of veteran Bangla actor Abhi Bhattacharya, in the female lead, opposite Dharmendra. Dilip did this guest role for Abhi, an old friend whom he affectionately addressed as Gobindo. Dilip and Abhi Bhattacharya had commenced their careers virtually together in the Hindi and Bengali versions of Nitin Bose's *Milan* (1946). Directed by Jagannath Chattopadhyay, *Paari* had Pronoti and Dharmendra playing the roles of convicts lodged in an island prison of which Dilip Kumar is the jailor. This black-and-white film was also dubbed in Hindi and released under the title *Anokha Milan.* Dilip Saheb's special appearance was a crowd-puller for this serious film.

Pronoti Ghosh with Dilip Kumar in Paari

Nothing much is available regarding the movie but the dubbed Hindi version *Anokha Milan* is available on the DVD circuit.

Composer Salil Chowdhury scored the music of the film with two folk tunes-based numbers, the dubbed versions of which are *Man na more sata yeh mohe bata piya gaye kahan* and *Bandhu re, hey...yeh man dole bole kya re.*

It is indeed unfortunate that Dharmendra could never work with Dilip Saheb whom he idolised. He was the original choice for *Aadmi* (1968) but could not do the film due to date problems and the role eventually went to Manoj Kumar.

Stills from Paari

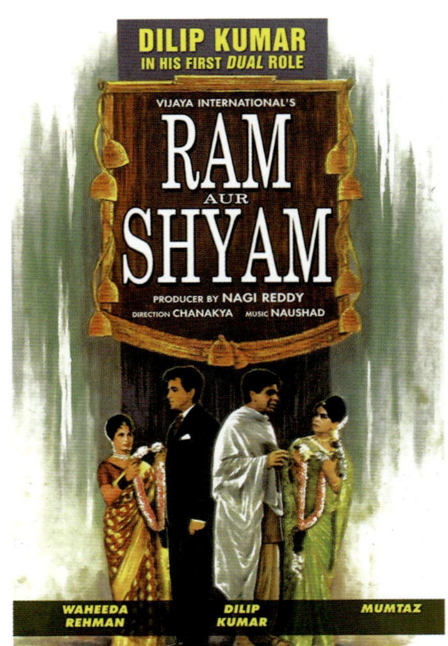

DATE / YEAR OF RELEASE: 19 OCTOBER 1967
BANNER / PRODUCER: VIJAYA INTERNATIONAL / DR B. NAGI REDDY / CHAKRAPANI
DIRECTION: TAPI CHANAKYA
MUSIC: NAUSHAD
LYRICS: SHAKEEL BADAYUNI
PLAYBACK: MOHD. RAFI / LATA MANGESHKAR / ASHA BHOSLE / MAHENDRA KAPOOR
STORY / SCREENPLAY: D.V. NARSARAJU
DIALOGUE: KAUSHAL BHARTI
CINEMATOGRAPHY: MARCUS BARTLEY
EDITING: C.P. JAMBULINGAM
AUDIOGRAPHY: V.B.C. MENON
ART: S. KRISHNA RAO
CHOREOGRAPHY: CHINNI AND SAMPATH
CAST: DILIP KUMAR / WAHEEDA REHMAN / MUMTAZ / PRAN / NIRUPA ROY / BABY FARIDA / NAZIR HUSSAIN / MUKRI / KANHAIYALAL / SAJJAN / LEELA MISHRA / ZEBBUNNISSA / LAKSHMI CHHAYA / AMAR

Dilip hits a six in Ram Aur Shyam—screamed the headlines in a few movie tabloids featuring reviews of Dilip Kumar's next release, *Ram Aur Shyam*. This golden jubilee hit marked Dilip's powerful comeback after *Dil Diya Dard Liya* proved a damp squib at the box office. Produced by B. Nagi Reddi's Vijay Vahuni Studios, it was an out-and-out Dilip Kumar film. His terrific double role as Ram and Shyam, opposite Waheeda Rehman and Mumtaz respectively, became immortal and fetched him his seventh Filmfare trophy for Best Actor. It was a hugely entertaining movie based on a dream script with not a single dull moment, which offered a vast scope to its leading man to display his all-round acting prowess. Waheeda Rehman was aptly cast and she rendered a delightful performance. Mumtaz too performed commendably and soon after broke into the big league of A-grade heroines of the Hindi cinema. Director Chanakya made his Hindi debut, a language he was not quite unfamiliar with.

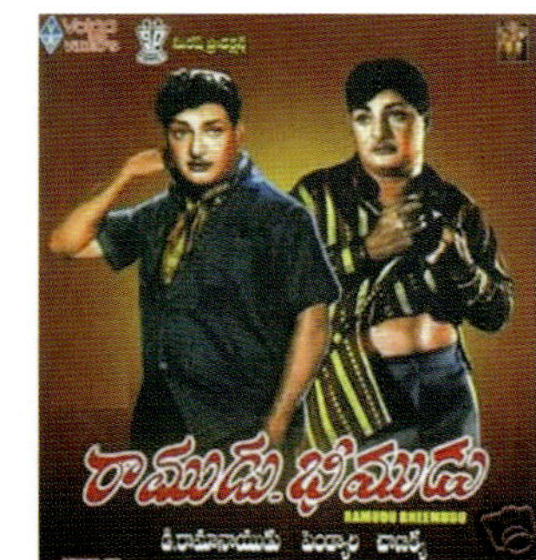

The making of this cult hit is nothing sort of a film story. Technically, it is a Hindi remake of the Telugu film *Ramudu Bheemudu* (1964), starring N.T. Rama Rao and Jamuna, which was produced by D. Rama Naidu and directed by Tapi Chanakya. The film was also adapted in Tamil as the super hit *Enga Veettu Pillai* (1965), starring M.G. Ramchandran and B. Saroja Devi. It was perhaps natural for B. Nagi Reddy to remake of those hit Telugu/Tamil films in Hindi as *Ram Aur Shyam*, and Dilip Kumar was a natural choice to play the dual roles in it. But, *Ram Aur Shyam* excelled the original Telugu/Tamil versions and was a slick entertainer. Unlike the then prevalent trend among Southern films, there wasn't an ounce of melodrama or crude comedy in the fabulous Hindi version, which became a timeless classic. Dilip Kumar and Waheeda's banters in Kodaikanal, Dilip's scenes with Leela Misra (particularly the 'My tractor is out of order' scene), Mumtaz, Mukri and his confrontations with Pran are histrionic landmarks. The movie is replete with rivetingly engaging comic and emotional scenes from beginning to the end offering unforgettable entertainment. Dilipian fans were utterly delighted and the film became one of their hot favourites of all times.

It was by chance that the famous producer–studio owner B. Nagi Reddy came about making the Hindi version. The whole incident is lucidly recorded by the doyen in an interview to the *Picture Post* magazine: '**But for the fire that threatened to destroy my studio, I would not have been able perhaps to make *Ram Aur Shyam*. It indeed proved a blessing in disguise. It all happened when the Tamil film from which *Ram Aur Shyam* had been made was still on the floors. A spacious set depicting a marketplace, was erected on the newly-added stage (one of the largest in Asia) in our Vijaya Vauhini Studios. Incidentally, Dilip Kumar, who was in Madras then, had come to pay a courtesy visit to me. After the shooting was packed up for the day, I persuaded the star to stay on for some time and we settled down for a friendly chat on the verdant lawns of the studio. As Dilip expressed a word or two of praise for the set he had witnessed that day and surmised that the subject too must be very interesting, I suddenly hit upon the idea of transforming the film on the Hindi screen. Mentioning it to Dilip Kumar, I said that we could go ahead with the scheme only if he agreed to play the dual role of the hero in the film and inquired whether he would or not. Dilip asked me to put off the matter for six months, as his hands were already tied up and told me that he would then be in a better position to give a correct reply. As we were still immersed in our discussions, one of the studio hands came sprinting to where we were seated and informed that a fire had broken out on the new floor of the studio where the set was erected. On hearing the news Dilip agitatedly got up from his seat, only to be cooled down by me even without rising up from my chair saying: Don't be so worried. I am sure the necessary steps must have been taken by my people and besides, the damage has been done. Why should we spoil our evening on that count? Well, it indeed required nerve on my part to say this and Dilip who was more unnerved by my nerve than by the fire itself was just not prepared to believe what he heard! Meanwhile, M.G. Ramachandran (the hero of the original Tamil**

B. Nagi Reddy and his Studios

version and later day celebrated Politician and Chief Minister of Tamil Nadu) appeared. On receiving the news about the accident, he had hurriedly returned to the studio and had participated in the daring efforts of Venu, one of my sons, to extinguish the fire. When I introduced him to Dilip Kumar, M.G.R. said: "Sir, I do not want to intrude upon you people, I only came to tell you that the fire has been put out. The damage to the set is negligible. We shall be able to continue with the shooting tomorrow as per the schedule." Apparently, Dilip Kumar must have been deeply impressed by the discipline and management of the studio and immediately said: "It would indeed be my pleasure and privilege to work with you Sir and do the proposed film on top priority." Thus Ram Aur Shyam was launched, completed in less than eleven months and released to become an all-time super-duper hit.'

Once Dilip Saheb gave his nod, Reddy quickly assembled the rest of the cast including Vyjayantimala for the main female lead, Anjana (the role was eventually was performed by Waheeda Rehman), and shooting of the film commenced in right earnest at Vijaya Vauhini. After a few days of work, there reportedly was a spat between Vyjayntimala and B. Nagi Reddy owing to some tantrum on the sets related to the earrings and saree to be worn by the leading lady and mistakenly given to the side heroine by an assistant of the director. This peeved Reddy and he replaced Vyjayantimala with Waheeda Rehman. Unfortunately, Vyjayantimala misconstrued that she was being replaced because Dilip (with whom she worked in six films) wanted to bring in Waheeda (who was paired with him in *Dil Diya Dard Liya* and *Aadmi).* Vyjayanti stopped speaking to Dilip and they remained aloof during the making of under-production *Sunghursh,* their seventh and last film together.For the role of the other heroine Shanta, there was intense lobbying by many leading actresses of those times including Saira Banu (future wife of the megastar). Comedian Mehmood lobbied for Mumtaz showing several reels from her films to the thespian. Dilip Saheb thought that Saira Banu was too delicate and innocent for Shanta's character which demanded a buxom appearance and seductive appeal. He, therefore, went by the sincere and persistent recommendation of Mehmood and opted for the vivacious Mumtaz.

The 'double role' was a special weapon exclusive to cinema, something that no stage play could logically employ due to obvious reasons. The earliest authors focused on twin brothers of opposite temperaments, dramatically separated from each other and thrust into diametrically opposite environments–the subject held great fascination for the viewers. The celebrated classic *The Corsican Brothers* (1941) provided inspiration for India's first double role film, that is, Gemini's *Nishan* (starring the swashbuckling hero Ranjan opposite Bhanumathi) in 1949. In a similar vein, the terrific screenplay of *Ram Aur Shyam*'s–based on D.V. Narasa Raju's story–was brilliantly crafted to provide unbridled entertainment with the ideal mix of comedy and emotions. The script did not have a single loose end or dull moment. Ram and Shyam (Dilip Kumar) were the twin sons of a mill owner with Shyam getting separated from the family due to a quirk of fate and raised by his adopted mother (Leela Misra) to become an intrepid youth handling his agricultural farm. Ram on the other hand becomes an introverted and timid young man who is pathologically terrified of his brother-in-law Gajendra Babu (Pran) from childhood. Gajendra who is married to Sulakshana (Nirupa Roy, the sister of Ram and Shyam) manages the family business after the death of Ram's parents and plans to finally usurp the property and then bump off Ram. Gajendra even plots to get Ram married off to Anjana (Waheeda Rehman), the daughter of a tycoon (Nazir Husain), an heiress, to

Dilip's Seventh Filmfare Award

get her property too. But the modern and educated girl Anjana rejects the timid man. In a chance encounter, Shyam, who is the exact antithesis of Ram–bold, tough, jolly and extrovert–rescues her from some hoodlums. Shyam is visiting the city and Anjana feels that she has been mistaken in assessing Ram's nature. She falls in love with him, even asking him to accompany her dad and her to their Kodaikanal resort, which Shyam does taking the whole episode as a joke. While in Kodaikanal, he makes futile attempts to tell Anjana that she has mistaken him for someone else, but gets closer to Anjana as they have a rollicking time in the salubrious locale. In the meantime, Ram comes to know that he will be forced to sign a document giving his brother-in-law full control of his vast properties and then killed. He runs away to join the disciples of Swami Shivanand who are touring around. Ram then lands up in Kagal (Shyam's village) where he is naturally mistaken for Shyam. Shyam's childhood friend Shanta (Mumtaz) is pleasantly surprised to see that Shyam has sobered down. Meanwhile, Anjana's dad informs Gajendra that Ram (actually Shyam) was staying with them for a while. Enraged at Ram's daring, Gajendra comes to Kodaikanal to take him home to find a completely different Ram openly defying and confronting him. Shyam accompanies Gajendra to his home and instinctively realises that something is amiss there. Shyam meets Sulakshana and her daughter Munni (Baby Farida) and seeing their miserable plight vows not to leave till he has taught an appropriate and adequate lesson to Gajendra and his Munim (Kanhaiyalal in a brilliant cameo). Shyam turns the tables on Gajendra, whips him when Gajendra tries his usual tactics on him and even grants the workers of the mills they own a much-needed bonus. The rest of the highly-entertaining film deals with the desperate Gajendra tracing the mystery behind Ram's sudden boldness and later framing Shyam for Ram's 'murder' after keeping Ram and Shanta locked up. Meanwhile, Anjana and her father discover that Shyam is none other than Ram's long-lost twin brother who was found abandoned by his foster-mother. Shyam thwarts Gajendra's nefarious intentions and the long-lost twins are reunited and also get their respective girls.

The Double Role

Dilip as the Docile Ram

Dilip as the Ebullient/Intrepid Shyam

Dilip Kumar delineated the diverse characters of Ram and Shyam accentuating their diverse disposition with ease. He gave the twins their own little quirks and responses. Dilp Kumar played the roles with compelling conviction lacing humour with laconic underplay and emotional dramatics with rare sensitivity. He was the crusader, the nemesis of evildoers and the vulnerable underdog in the same breath for the twin characters. Waheeda Rehman's Anjana was played with the right assurance of a modern city-bred girl effortlessly exuding sophisticated charm and practicality of purpose. Mumtaz looked every inch the village belle she portrayed and effectively conveyed the change of approach while dealing with the ebullient Shyam and the subdued Shyam. Pran's menacing villainy, Nirupa Roy's concerned helplessness, Leela Misra's brilliant rustic mother, Nazir Husain's Rao Saheb, Mukri's sidekick of Shyam and last but not least Kanhaiyalal's utterly natural Munim were all very good indeed.

Scenes of Ram in the film

Shyam in the Movie

The Delightful Kodaikanal Sequences

Key Dramatic Scenes of Ram Aur Shyam

Expectations went sky high among the cinemagoers as the release of *Ram Aur Shyam* approached. Advance bookings opened on the 11 October 1967 and the first week went House Full (meaning 'sold out') within hours. Huge unprecedented crowds queued up at the theatres across the country. Such crowds thronging every theatre were reminiscent of the *Mughal-E-Azam* days. To ease the theatre rush, the tickets were sold at petrol pumps and other outlets. The gala Mumbai premiere held at the Apsara Theatre on 19 October 1967 was a glittering affair with the who's who of the political world, the film industry and the glitterati attending. Needless to add that the movie had a nation-wide bumper opening to become a megahit. The film had jubilees at Regal and Novelty (Delhi), Novelty (Lucknow), Prakash (Varanasi), Sangeet (Kanpur), Pushpraj (Allahabad), Krishna (Gorakhpur), Nishat (Meerut), Novelty (Saharanpur) and scores of other theatres apart from Mumbai, of course. The 1967 film was such a superhit all over the country that a legend has it that the film was running to full theatres just a corner away from a riot-hit, curfew-laden town in Madhya Pradesh.

The movie happened to be yet another hit of Naushad and Shakeel Badayuni combination. Naushad's music may not have been of his past excellent standards, his song *Aaj ki raat mere dil ki salaami le le* endures to this day (with Shakeel's superb lyrics). The songs like *Main hoon saqi too hai Sharaabi* (Rafi-Lata), *Aayee hain baharein mite* (Rafi), *Balam tere pyar ki thandi chhaon* (Rafi-Asha) and *Aaj Sakhi ri mere* (Asha) also became hits. Shakeel Badyuni penned the lyrics at a time his health was beginning to decline. The musical score also had a captivating number *Maine kab tumse kaha tha ki mujhe pyar karo* (Lata) which was unfortunately deleted from the film due to the compulsions of reducing the overall length of the movie.

EP Disc

Gala Premiere at Apsara (Mumbai) on 19 October 1967

LP Disc

Film Opening at Apsara (Mumbai)

Main hoonsaaqi

Aaj sakhi re mere

Balam tere pyar mein

Aayi hain baharein

Aaj ki raat mere dil ki

Zara dheere dheere bol

The great popularity of the film '*Ram Aur Shyam*' has remained undiminished over years and there have been a number of rehashes ('*Seeta Aur Geeta*' and '*Chaalbaaz*') over years. Yours truly (T. Bajpai) during a recent trip to Iran was pleasantly surprised to see DVDs of the film selling even in current times in Tehran and Isfahan. The movie is also popular in Egypt, Turkey, several Russian States, Bangladesh, Pakistan and Afghanistan.

Russian Poster

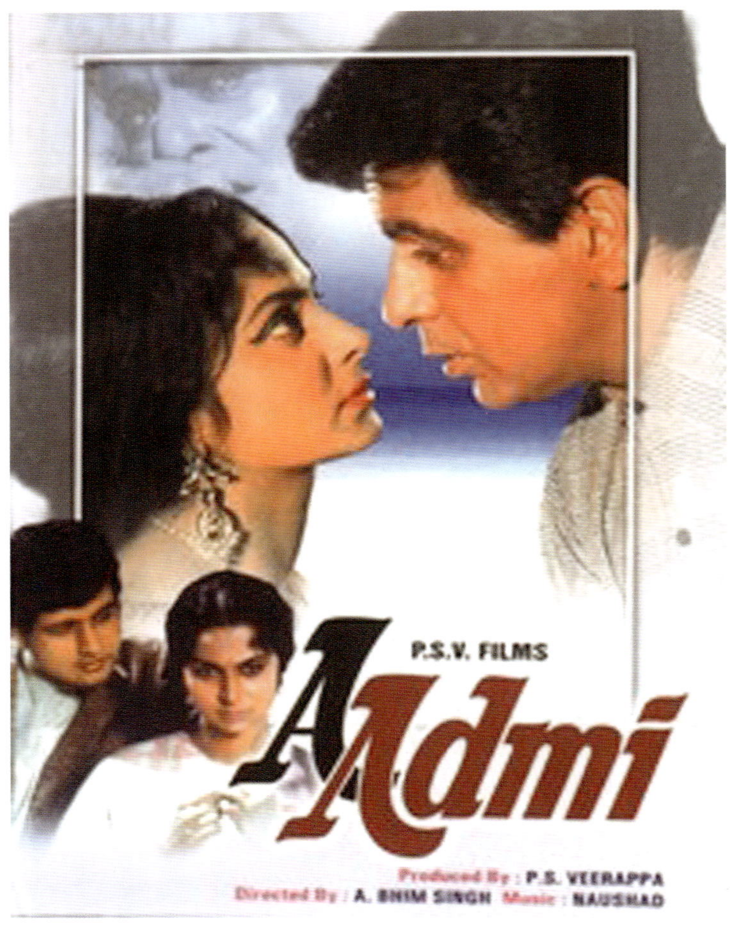

DATE / YEAR OF RELEASE: 1968
BANNER / PRODUCER: P.S.V. FILMS / P.S. VEERAPPA
DIRECTION: A. BHIM SINGH
MUSIC: NAUSHAD
LYRICS: SHAKEEL BADAYUNI
PLAYBACK: MOHD. RAFI / LATA MANGESHKAR / TALAT MAHMOOD / MAHENDRA KAPOOR
STORY: JAWAR N. SITARAMAN / G. BALASUBRAMANIAN
DIALOGUE: AKHTAR-UL-IMAN / KAUSHAL BHARATI
CINEMATOGRAPHY: FAREDOON IRANI
EDITING: A. PAUL DORAISINGHAM
AUDIOGRAPHY: MANGESH DESAI
ART: SUDHENDU ROY / DESH MUKHERJEE
CHOREOGRAPHY: CHINNI SAMPATH
CAST: DILIP KUMAR / WAHEEDA REHMAN / MANOJ KUMAR / SIMI / PRAN / SULOCHANA LATKAR / PADMA CHAVAN / AGHA / SHIVRAJ / MOHAN CHOTI / ULHAS / NATARAJAZIZ / PRAKASH BAGALA / BABY RUKHSANA / MASTER SHAHID

Dilip Kumar's towering performance presenting a complex character in all its veritable shades was the hallmark of this A. Bhim Singh directed hit, *Aadmi.* Waheeda Rehman, Manoj Kumar, Simi, Pran and Agha ably complimented Dilip in the movie. Dilip's famous '*Teen Ka Dibba*' banter with Waheeda, his *'Mat samjho tum ek insaan ho'* battle with conscience and the scenes where he shows streaks of jealousy and mistrust for Manoj were a showcase of the ultimate in histrionic brilliance.

It would indeed be prudent to put in perspective Dilip's a masterful performance of an obsessed man who is consumed with pangs of jealousy which he tries hard to overcome. An elaboration from us on how he performed with tremendous control and finesse, underplaying his role to perfection would perhaps make an interesting reading. The perplexing complexities of the role of Raja Rajesh Chandra doubtlessly presented a daunting and rousing challenge to any actor worth his salt. To effectivelytranslate the psychological turmoil, behavioural inconsistency and inner contradictions in Rajesh's character by precise comprehension of the driving force that made a compassionate human being get overwhelmed by the devilish desires of his alter ego on screen could only be handled by an actor of the mettle and polish of Dilip Kumar. Conveying numerous shades of Rajesh's emotions–disturbed by his guilt and shocked by erroneous judgement of a betrayal that was not there—is one of the greatest histrionic triumphs of the megastar. Take a look at the film and you would agree that no other actor could have so convincingly handled such complexities. Hats off to Dilip Saheb for such an engagingly delineation of an extremely complex role. Dilip Kumar has placed on record his own perception of how he performed this challenging role:

'As an actor, I was struck by the promise that the character I played in *Aadmi* held. I had to bring out the protagonist's cerebral struggle to leave his past behind and move on. The basic conflict in the story, which had the external appearance of a common love triangle, was unusual in the sense that it was not so much a conflict between two men over one woman as is common in film stories. The friction was in the minds of the characters. The character I played was to be explored from a psychological angle and that intrigued me. From my experience and understanding, I concluded that the film had to have a mood and an ambience that would go with the vicissitudes in the protagonist's life and the Freudian thought processes he gets into. So I got involved in two vital aspects of its making, besides the writing. I took a keen interest in the camera movements and lighting and also in the selection of shots on the editing table.'

Dilip Kumar in the Title Role of Aadmi

The *Picture Post* magazine very aptly published a collage of Dilip Saheb's moods in the film showing glimpses of the great performance which is recapitulated:

We were such good friends.

We were inseparable.

He was selfless and restored my prestige.

We never differed in anything.

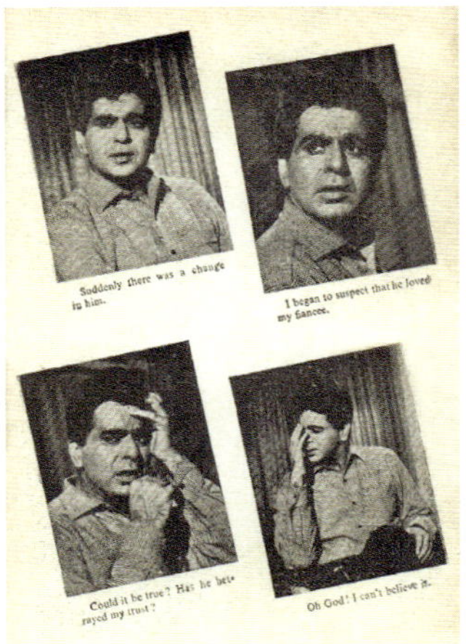
Suddenly there was a change in him.

I began to suspect that he loved my fiancee.

Could it be true? Has he betrayed my trust?

Oh God! I can't believe it.

Finally I came to a decision.

I found no other alternative.

He was a good friend but he must go.

He must die for his sin.

102

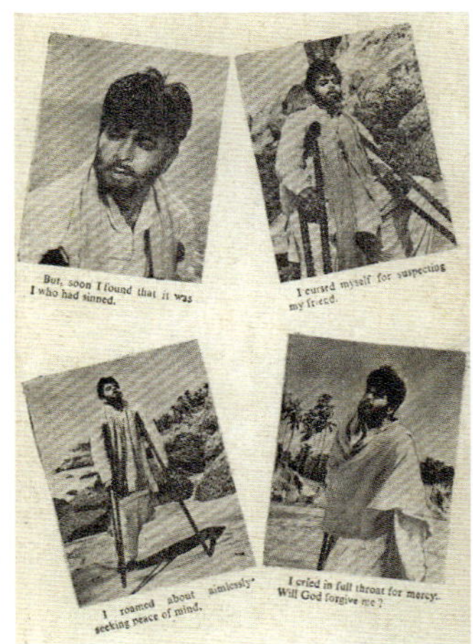
But, soon I found that it was I who had sinned.

I cursed myself for suspecting my friend.

I roamed about aimlessly seeking peace of mind.

I cried in full throat for mercy. Will God forgive me?

Dilip Kumar in Aadmi

The movie in fact was a remake of sorts of the Tamil hit *Aalayamani* (meaning temple bells) directed by K. Shankar with Sivaji Ganesan, B. Saroja Devi, S.S. Rajendran, C.R. Vijaya Kumari and M.R. Radha in the main roles with music by Vishwanath Ramanurthy. Produced by P.S. Veerappa, the film was released on 23 November 1962. It was also remade in Telugu as well in 1964 as *Gudi Gantalu* and in Malayalam as *Oru Raagam Pala Thaala* in 1979. But none of those films had the sophistication and finesse of *Aadmi* and the natural performances of its star cast comprising of Dilip Kumar, Waheeda Rehman, Manoj Kumar, Simi and Pran. Originally, Raaj Kumar was approached for the role the other male lead (Shekhar) but wanted Dilip Kumar himself to request him and was hence dropped. Dharmendra was the next choice but had to opt out due to date problems. Eventually, the Manoj Kumar played the role. Waheeda Rehman was already working with Dilip Saheb in *Dil Diya Dard Liya* and was a natural choice for the leading lady (Meena).The side heroine's role was assigned to the then upcoming actress Simi (she impressed Manoj in *Do Badan*) whereas Pran was the archetypal villain. A. Bhim Singh who was considered to have a better grip on the Hindi milieu was assigned the direction—he later developed an excellent rapport with Dilip Kumar and directed him in *Gopi* (1970). The Naushad–Shakeel Badayuni combo was again an automatic choice for the music department.

Filming of *Aadmi* commenced before *Ram Aur Shyam* but Veerappa was not a moneyed producer and finance came to him in fits and starts. The progress of the movie was therefore impeded and it was released some nine months after the super-duper hit

Dilip Kumar in the Title Role of Aadmi

Ram Aur Shyam and was quite a success. Dilip Kumar gave P.S. Veerappa the rights to remake his megahit *Gunga Jumna* in Tamil free of charge to ease the producer's financial pressures. Veerappa remade *Gunga Jumna* as *Iru Thuruvam* starring Sivaji Ganesan and Padmini under the direction of S. Ramnathan.

Aadmi was based on a story in which the main protagonist Rajesh (Dilip Kumar) undergoes a serious psychological turmoil owing to some shockingly unsavoury happenings in his childhood. Rajesh belongs to a very wealthy and noble family and though orphaned at a very young age, he has preserved his inheritance and expanded the family businesses including the Vijay Industries empire and a vast number of estates. As a child, he had loved a girl named Meena, and when she tragically passes away, Rajesh substituted her with a doll. He became extremely insecure and possessive about the doll (named Meena), almost to the point of an obsession. When his friend Babu, innocently starts playing with the doll, the kid Rajesh is enraged and ends up accidentally killing him. Rajesh now suffers from a huge guilt complex and the guilt pangs of accidentally killing his friend relentlessly haunt him. Years later, Rajesh has grown up, but still has carefully preserved the Meena doll in his closet. Rajesh is a very popular employer and philanthropist adroitly running a huge business empire which also includes some spice gardens and estates. Rajesh has patronised the education of a friend Shekhar (Manoj Kumar) to make him a doctor and is very fond of him. Girdharilal (Shivraj) is the manager of Rajesh's vast estate and has two daughters, the younger one being Meena (Waheeda Rehman). The elder daughter Parvati (Padma Chavan) falls in love with the son Prem (Agha) of Rajesh's wily munim and money lender Mayadas (Pran). On the other hand, Shekhar and Meena fall in love with each other. A classmate of Shekhar, Aarti (Simi) of Shekhar is also in love with him. After hearing about the plight of Girdhari during a visit to the estate, Rajesh gives him some money so that he can get Parvati married to Prem. Also during the same visit Rajesh meets Meena (the film has some delightful chemistry between Dilip and Waheeda) and develops great fondness for her. In fact, Rajesh falls in love with Meena and proposes to marry her. Girdharilal gratefully accepts the proposal. Shekhar sacrifices his love for Meena, for the sake of his friendship with Rajesh and Rajesh's huge obligations to him. Rajesh and Meena get engaged but as they are returning from an excursion, Mayadas removes the brakes of their car resulting in an accident, in which Rajesh becomes paralysed and is confined to a wheelchair. Meena dutifully nurses Rajesh and Dr Shekhar regularly visits him. Rajesh suspects that Meena and Dr Shekhar are having an affair blissfully unaware of their past affection. Jealousy now consumes him and he tries to cope with freshly re-ignited negative emotions. The old murderous and possessive hatred that Rajesh had managed to suppress and conceal surfaces again – and this time, like Babu, it becomes Shekhar's turn. Rajesh takes Meena and Dr Shekhar on a picnic after which he pushes Shekhar of a cliff attempting to kill him. Dr Shekhar, precariously hanging from the cliff, convinces Rajesh of his innocence and once again guilt-struck Rajesh (on a wheel chair) wheels himself off the cliff after saving Shekhar. The interesting psychological drama after an intriguing climax ends on a happy note with Rajesh and Dr Shekhar respectively getting married to Meena and Aarti, and Rajesh getting rid of his guilt pangs.

Dilip and Waheeda in Aadmi

In a stunning sequence expounding the split personality syndrome and underlining the fine distinction between the benevolent loving Rajesh and his devilish alter ego, the later appears as a tall larger-than-life monstrous figure, dwarfing the wheelchair-ridden compassionate Rajesh, egging him on to seek revenge for the suspected infidelity. The alter ego yells oozing sheer hatred, *'Mat samjho ki tum Aadmi ho samjho ki tum insaan nahin janwar ho ek khoonkhar wahshi darinde ho.'* The chilling impact of the astounding performance of the one and only Dilip Kumar leaves the audience in a daze. If there ever was complete figurative audience participation in a scene it was this one–we still remember the awestruck faces of the audience totally surrendering to the incredible histrionics of the megastar! Then, there were those light-hearted Dilip-Waheeda banters performed with rare polish and finesse which contributed to the repeat value of the hit film in no small measure. Movie buffs loved these well-written and brilliantly-performed sequences, and clamoured for more. Truly fascinating!

The Alter Ego

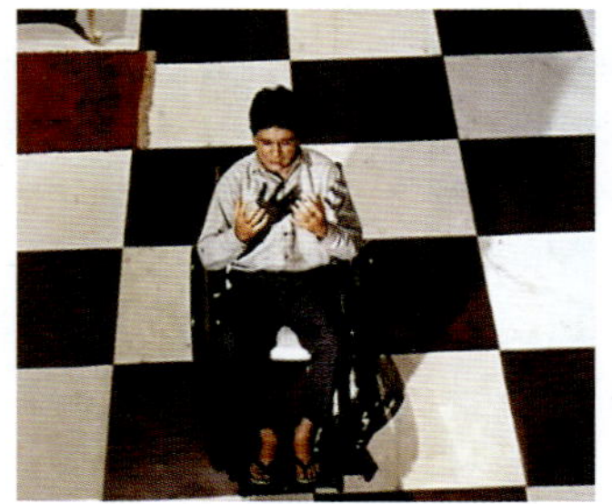

The Stunning Alter Ego Sequence

The Famous 'Teen ka dibba' Banter of the Lead Pair

Dilip and Waheeda Banter on the Lakeside

Additionally, there supposedly was a very interesting sequence in the film showing Dilip Kumar playing golf and having an enjoyable banter with Waheeda Rehman on the golf course. The publicity of the film and the lobby cards displayed in movie theatres showed scenes from this sequence. One of the covers of the then extremely popular *Filmfare* magazine also contained a picture of Dilip Saheb in full golf gear. Inexplicably, the sequence did not appear in the film and for unknown reasons was deleted.

The Climax

Naushad churned out some brilliant Mohd. Rafi numbers – *Aaj purani raahon se koi mujhe awaaz na de*" (*Raag Bhimpalasi*), *Na Aadmi ka koi bharosa* and *Main tooti huyi ek naiya*, which fit the story like a glove and matched the mood set by the actor's powerful histrionics. The film also had a Rafi–Talat duet (*Kaisi haseen aaj baharon ki raat hai*), with the Talat's playback being shot on Manoj Kumar. Regretfully, despite HMV discs already been issued, Talat's voice was changed to that of Mahendra Kapoor in the film, reportedly at the behest of Manoj Kumar. Yet another raw deal was meted out to Talat in a Naushad film after *Palki* (the 1966 Rajendra Kumar–Waheeda Rehman starrer in which the number *Kal raat zindagi se mulaqat ho gayi* was first recorded in the voice of Talat Mahmood, but was later changed in the voice of Mohd. Rafi, reportedly at the behest of the hero). *Kari badariya mare nazariya* and *Kal ke sapne aaj bhi aana* were the two lilting Lata numbers picturised on Waheeda. Shakeel Badayuni once again wrote the songs. The film had a fairly good run at the box office and its music was popular too.

The Golf Sequence

Aadmi was another major landmark in the illustrious career and histrionic graph of Dilip Kumar. The film and the performance of the megastar in it continue to be loved by Dilip fans and the film keeps on circulating on the DVD circuit.

EP Disc

LP Disc

Kari badariya mare nazariya

Kal ke sapne aaj bhi aana

Kaisi haseen aaj

Main tooti huyi ek naiya

Na aadmi ka koi bharosa

Aaj purani rahon se

DATE / YEAR OF RELEASE: 1968
BANNER / PRODUCER: RAHUL THEATERS / HARNAM SINGH RAWAIL
DIRECTION: H.S. RAWAIL
MUSIC: NAUSHAD
LYRICS: SHAKEEL BADAYUNI
PLAYBACK: MOHD. RAFI / LATA MANGESHKAR / ASHA BHOSLE / MAHENDRA KAPOOR
STORY: MAHASHWETA DEVI (BASED ON THE NOVEL LAYALI AASMANER AINA)
SCREEN ADAPTATION: ANJANA RAWAIL
SCREENPLAY: H.S. RAWAIL
DIALOGUE: ABRAR ALVI / GULZAR
CINEMATOGRAPHY: GOPI KRISHNA
ART: SUDHENDU ROY
EDITING: KRISHNA SACHDEV
AUDIOGRAPHY: Y.M. WAGLE / KAUSHIK / MINOO KATRAK / MANGESH DESAI
CAST: DILIP KUMAR / VYJAYANTIMALA / BALRAJ SAHANI / SANJEEV KUMAR / JAYANT / ULHAS / SAPRU / IFTEKHAR / DURGA KHOTE / SULOCHANA / PADMA KHANNA / MUMTAZ BEGUM / URMILA / DEVEN VERMA / JAGDISH RAJ / RAM MOHAN / PARO / SADHU SINGH / LATA SINHA / ANJU MAHENDROO / DILIP DHAWAN / MUNSHI / PRINCE ARJUN / RANI / KAMALDEEP / SNEHLATA / RAJESH KUMAR / DEVDATT / MASTER LEVI / MEHMOOD JUNIOR / MASTER ARUN / MASTER AZIZ

Riding high on the huge box-office success of his super-duper hit *Mere Mehboob* (1963), producer-director Harnam Singh (H.S.) Rawail aimed higher and announced a magnum opus titled *Sunghursh* with the top drawer cast led by the reigning megastar Dilip Kumar and his *Mere Mehboob* star, the petite Sadhana. The film's lead cast was considered a casting coup. A grand mahurat of the film was held at Mehboob Studio with the lead pair participating. However, sadly at that point in time Sadhana developed a terrible eye ailment and opted out of the coveted film. The popular pair of Dilip–Vyjayanti, thus, once again came together for the movie which regrettably turned out to be their last film with each other.

Roopa and Shankar

The story set in the 19th century Banaras (Varanasi) focused on the generations-old enmity between two well-off families headed by a businessman Naubatlal (Sapru) and Bhavani Prasad (Jayant), an ardent worshipper of Kaali Mata and a blood thirsty thug. Bhavani Prasad dupes a rich businessman and his family and murders them upon their refusal to submit to his astronomical demands. Naubatlal gets wind of this heinous crime and exposes the misdeed of Bhavani Prasad in front of his wife (Durga Khote) and daughter-in-law (Sulochana Latkar). In retribution, Bhavani Prasad gets Naubatlal killed setting off a bloody feud between the families. Bhavani Prasad's son (Iftekhar) is totally against violence and comes to take away his son Kundan from the grandfather Bhavani Prasad when the latter wants Kundan to be his successor. Bhavani Prasad kills his own son and vows to groom Kundan as his true successor. The wife and daughter-in-law of Bhavani leave him to live in a different village with his brother-in-law and other children. A grown-up Kundan (Dilip Kumar) has developed into a fine intrepid lad who does not subscribe to the beliefs and ideology of Bhavani Prasad. He has a childhood crush on an orphaned girl who has been picked up by a brothel keeper Madame (Manorama) and groomed to be a nautch dancer Munni (Vyjayantimala) who has been conferred the title of *'Laila-E-Asmaan'* by Nawab Wajid Ali Shah himself. Ganeshi Prasad (Balraj Sahani) and Dwarka (Sanjeev Kumar) grow up harbouring the bloody grudge and vow to decimate Kundan and Bhavani Prasad. Kundan successfully wards off the attempts on his life by the feuding counterparts and is aided by the long-time trusted henchman of Bhavani, the redoubtable Bhim Kaka (Ulhas). The wedding of Kundan's sister (Anju Mahendroo) is arranged to which Kundan and all relatives including the feuding family are invited with the exception of Bhavani Prasad. Ganeshi Prasad deputes Dwarka to join the wedding celebrations with dubious intent of killing Kundan perfidiously and has hired Munni to accompany him and help in poisoning the adversary. Munni remembers Kundan and goes with the intention of protecting Kundan, and craftily makes Dwarka take poisoned wine meant for Kundan. But, Dwarka is saved. Later, Dwarka makes another attempt on Kundan's life who thwarts him but in the fracas Bhim Kaka kills Dwarka. Now Ganeshi Prasad wants to wage an all-out war on his adversaries whereas Kundan wants to practise non-violence and end the generations old feud. In the meantime, Bhavani Shankar dies of old age but not before his daughter-in-law confronts him with the brutal truth that Bhavani Prasad had killed his own son before becoming a devout. Kundan is shocked and appalled to realise that his father was killed by his grandfather. Against the backdrop of this grim tale of bloody vendetta, the film has the utterly fascinating love story of Kundan and Munni with Ganeshi Prasad being an extraneous angle. The gripping drama ends on a happy note with Ganeshi and Kundan embracing each others as brothers to bury the hatchet as Kundan saves Ganeshi by killing his own trusted henchman Bhim Kaka. Kundan and Munni happily live ever after.

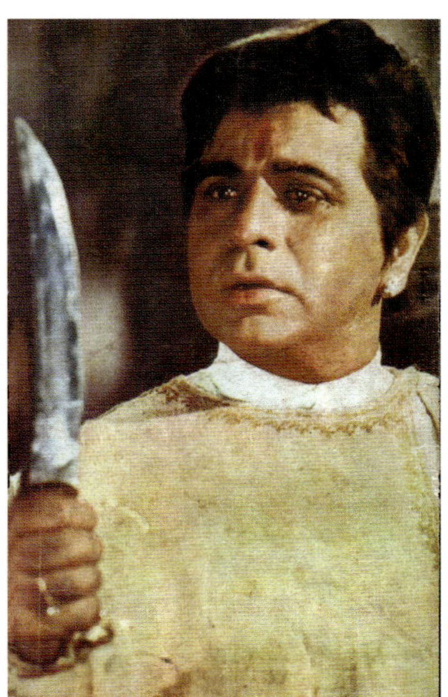

Dilip in Sunghursh

The major highlight of the classic film was the intriguing love-hate chemistry with the associated interplay of emotions and conflict of convictions between the lead pair. It was indeed incredible that inspite of not being on speaking terms for a major portion of filming, Dilip and Vyjayanti rendered such tour de force performances with their well-acknowledged consummate artistry. The histrionic jugalbandi of Dilip Kumar and Vyjayantimala was a sheer treat to watch as always which made *Sunghursh* eminently watchable and special. Meanwhile, Dilip Kumar's scenes like the '*Jiyo Dwarka kya cheez pilayi hai*' sequence performed with marvellous finesse simply floored the viewers as did the '*Koi tuk hai koi dhang hai*' scene and the '*Snake-Mongoose*' fight sequence et al. Dilip–Vyjayanti at their best always provided explosive entertainment and it is indeed sad that *Sunghursh* was their last histrionic hurrah together.

Dilip Kumar and Vyjayantimala at their Best in Sunghursh

Not to be outdone, the entire supporting cast too performed with facile aplomb. Jayant with his towering carriage and imposing personality brought out the menacing character of Bhavani Prasad in its full splendour with Ulhas as Bhim Kaka being an apt foil. The '*Jai Bhavani*' rant of Jayant was truly spine chilling. Balraj Sahani as Ganeshi Prasad was the polished aristocratic businessman to the core, Sanjeev Kumar as Dwarka was very convincing and the actor stood up to his legendary colleagues. Durga Khote, Sulochana, Iftekhar, Sunder, Deven Verma, et al too lived their roles. The chess sequence and Dwarka's death sequence between Dilip Kumar and Sanjeev Kumar along with the fascinating repartees among Dilip, Vyjayanti, and Balraj Sahani were simply captivating and deserve special mention.

Jayant / Ulhas

Dilip and Vyjayanti

Dilip and Balraj Sahani

Dilip and Sanjeev Kumar

Naushad's music did justice to the complex subject and its majestic sweep and many of the songs were hits, such as *Mere pairon mein ghungroo bandha de* (Rafi), *Chhedo na dil ki baat* (Lata), *Jab dil se dil takrata hai* (Rafi), *Mere paas aao nazar to milao* (Lata), *Ishq diwana husn bhi ghayal* (Rafi), *Agar yeh husn mera* (Lata) and *Tasveer-e-mohabbat thi jisme* (Asha). Sadly, this was the last time Shakeel Badayuni wrote for Naushad, as he succumbed to his illness soon after. Dilip Kumar's memorable onscreen rendition of *Mere pairon main ghunghroo bandha de* has remained a cinematic masterpiece as has the film. Vyjayantimala's twinkle-toed dances on the songs *Agar yeh husn mera* and *Tasveer-e-mohabbat thi jisme* were truly memorable.

Naushad and Lata

Sunghursh is an outstanding film by any standards with a powerful and author-backed script and a great cast of outstanding performers. It shall be remembered for the powerful performances of its star-studded cast and fascinating storytelling.

LP Disc

Agar yeh husn mera

Jab dil se dil takrata hai

Mere pairon mein ghungroo

Chhedo na dil ki baat

Ishq deewana husn bhi ghayal

Mere paas aao nazar to milao

Tasveer-e-mohabbat thi jisme

CHAPTER 3.4

THE ROMANTIC TWILIGHT– THE SWINGING SEVENTIES

GOPI

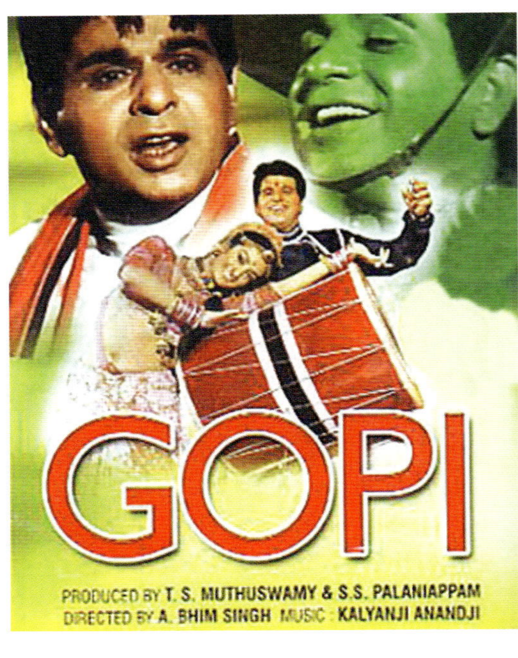

DATE / YEAR OF RELEASE: 1970
BANNER / PRODUCER: PROSPERITY PICTURES / T.S. MUTHUSWAMI / S.S. PALANIAPPAL
DIRECTION: A. BHIM SINGH
MUSIC: KALYANJI–ANANDJI
LYRICS: RAJENDRA KRISHNA
PLAYBACK: MOHD. RAFI / LATA MANGESHKAR / MAHENDRA KAPOOR
STORY / SCREENPLAY: SAILAJANAND MUKHERJI / RAJENDRA KRISHAN
DIALOGUE: RAJENDRA KRISHNA
CINEMATOGRAPHY: FAREDOON IRANI
CHOREOGRAPHY: S. SOHANLAL / ROSHAN KUMARI
EDITING: A. PAUL DORAISINGHAM
ART: S. KRISHNA ROA
CHOREOGRAPHY: S. SOHANLAL / ROSHAN KUMARI
CAST: DILIP KUMAR / SAIRA BANU / PRAN / NIRUPA ROY / OM PRAKASH / LALITA PAWAR / DURGA KHOTE / SOODESH KUMAR / FARIDA JALAL / TIWARI / MUKRI / ARUNA ROY / SHYAMLAL / JOHNY WALKER

After their much-talked about wedding, the film lovers' clamour for seeing the celebrity couple Dilip Kumar–Saira Banu together on silver screen reached a crescendo. At the time of his marriage on 11 October 1966, Dilip Saheb was busy doing *Ram Aur Shyam, Aadmi* and *Sunghursh* and it was impossible for the thespian to take up the challenge of embarking on a new project and that too co-starring his wife. Therefore, the first Dilip–Saira starrer *Gopi* could only be launched in 1969. The film was released in 1970 to a tremendous public response. It was again a south Indian production under the banner of Prosperity Pictures (P.S. Muthuswami and S.S. Palaniappan) and was directed by A. Bhim Singh, with whom Dilip Saheb had developed a special rapport during the making of *Aadmi.* Dilip Saheb brought in the veteran lyricist-writer Rajinder Krishan (they had done the super-duper hit *Azaad* together and besides he was a favourite of south Indian film producers) to pen the screenplay, dialogue and lyrics of the film based on the story of Sailajanand Mukherji. Veteran Faredoon Irani shot the picture and the star cast included many Dilip Kumar regulars such as Pran, Johnny Walker, Mukri and other dependable performers like Nirupa Roy, Durga Khote, Lalita Pawar, Om Prakash, Farida Jalal, Soodesh Kumar, Tiwari, et al. Music director duo Kalyanji–Anandji, who were gaining ground as hit music directors those days, were the surprise choice as composers, drawing curtains on the legendary actor-music director association of Dilip Kumar-Naushad which spanned fifteen classic films. *Gopi* was a silver jubilee hit with the 'Tragedy King' and 'Beauty Queen' pair performing some boisterous comedy to charm the viewers and bring the house down. Such was the sway and grasp of the megastar over his audience that the movie's first-week collections resulted in a revenue around ₹10 lakh from the Delhi-U.P. territory alone. I remember that on the opening show of *Gopi* at Prakash Theater (Varanasi), the huge crowds were so uncontrollable that the then District Magistrate of the town Ayodhya Prasad Dikshit had to himself supervise crowd control and distribution of tickets. A Mumbai scribe witnessing the film's premiere at the Apsara Theater wrote that 'Last night, 'Gopi' Dilip Kumar was responsible for the damage to many a fin-tailed Impalas as surging crowds were just unmanageable.'

The film was advertised as 'Gopi–a good man, a man's man, and a God's man' and was an out-and-out Dilip Kumar film in which the thespian got ample opportunity to showcase his incredible depth as a method actor by masterfully displaying his histrionic skills to the hilt. From spontaneous comic timing to serious emoting to presenting the veritable shades of the inner being of the character to convincing action sequences—everything was there to gladden and madden his fans. He played to the gallery at will and with relish drawing thunderous applause.

Besides Dilip Kumar, the success of *Gopi* can also be attributed to its story, written by Sailajanand Mukherji, which draws heavily from the great Indian tradition of a loving family, set in a fictional idyllic village. The film revolved around the central character of Gopi Ram, a paragon of virtue. There is bonhomie and respect for elders, there is love and sacrifice—even between step siblings (Om Prakash and Dilip Kumar)–and there is penance and reconciliation.

The large-hearted, good-for-nothing prankster–Gopi (Dilip Kumar), who is spoilt silly by his elder step-brother Girdharilal (Om Prakash) and his dutiful wife Parvati (Nirupa Roy), is loved by the villagers. Every evening, he soulfully sings *bhajans* at the village *Chaupal* (congregation), plays Lord Hanuman in *Ram Leela;* and wants to be a *Brahmchari* [celibate] but is the favourite of the village lasses. While Gopi fools around the village, his younger sister Nandini (Farida Jalal) too is a very decent girl and is liked by the villagers. The kitchen fire is kept burning by the meagre income generated through the sales of clay idols (mostly of Gods and Goddesses) made by Girdhari, which he sells to the village merchant Lala (Pran) at a pittance—something that Gopi resents. To add to Girdhari's woes, Parvati's relatives, Seema (Saira Banu) and Lilavati (Lalita Pawar) come to stay with them. Predictably, love blossoms in the heart of Seema for Gopi and she subtly woos him aided by Nandini (there was that charming scene in which Nandini hiding behind Lord Hanuman's idol commands Gopi to marry Seema to his utter consternation). Gopi and the city-bred nephew of Lala, Ramu (Johnny Walker), expose the misdeeds of Lala including hoarding of food grains, etc. However, matters come to a head when Girdhari goes to Lala to take the money saved for Nandini's wedding, to be mercilessly spurned. An infuriated Gopi forcibly extracts the money, for which he is branded a thief. A seething Girdhari is not able to bear the infamy and throws Gopi out of the house. Gopi heads for the city in search of a job, which he gets in a maharani's (Durga Khote's) house. Thereafter, misfortune befalls Girdhari and Parvati, who are also forced to head for the city in search of their beloved Gopi. The maharani is deeply impressed by Gopi's genial demeanour, respectful behaviour and honesty in dealing and becomes very fond of him taking him under her fold. The separated siblings reunite as Nandini ties the knot with maharani's son (Soodesh Kumar) and after the bad men have been taken care of, Gopi gets Seema.

One can only marvel at the immense depth of talent available in the then Mumbai film industry whereby actors like Pran, Om Prakash, Nirupa Roy, Lalita Pawar and Johnny Walker can hold their own performing cameos against the formidable Dilip Kumar. But, Johnny Walker was somewhat wasted in a half-baked role that didn't do justice to his calibre. Even Om Prakash is made to go over the top in certain scenes (the southern style of tear jerking) despite his otherwise compelling portrayal of the respectable, albeit poor idol maker. Pran, true to his prowess, is truly mean as the Machiavellian Lala. There also were attempts to nostalgically rehash some earlier ever popular Dilipian scenes albeit in a new garb with Gopi going on a tonga to receive Leelavati and Seema at the railway station in the typical *Naya Daur* style. The comical banters performed by Dilip Kumar with sheer gusto and captivating elan were the pièce de résistanceof the movie.

Gopi is perhaps one of the last films that had dialogues and lyrics (by Rajinder Krishan) highlighting social evils of the time, something that filmmakers like Raj Kapoor, B.R. Chopra and Bimal Roy never failed to incorporate in their works. There were several references to black money being siphoned off by people with black hearts, as also wily hoarding of food grains that was endemic in India of the late 1960s. The joyous *bhajan, Ram Chandra kah gaye Siya se,* performed charmingly by Dilip had large doses of the social and treacherous malaise of the fabric of the society in a most entertaining manner with lines like, *'Dharm bhi hoga, karm bhi hoga, lekin sharm nahin hogi...'* There was another hilarious nostalgic dig in a song *Ek padosan peechhey pad gayi* Jungli *jiska naam, Pyar mohabbat kya samjayein isko* Ram Aur Shyam, which contained the names of Dilip Kumar and Saira Banu films and was performed with tongue-in-cheek sauciness by the Dilip–Saira pair. Even the boisterously loud *'Gentleman Gentleman'* sequence was imparted subtle polish by Dilip Saheb.

Dilip and Saira with Kalyanji–Anandji

The music of Kalyanji-Anandji matched the mood of the film with most of the songs such as *Akeli hi akele chala hai (Lata), Ramchandra kah gaye* (Mahendra Kapoor), *Gentleman Getleman* (Lata-Mahendra Kapoor), *Ek Padosan* (Lata/Mahendra Kapoor)–all hitting the charts. In a surprise choice, the composer duo used the voice of Mahendra Kapoor as playback for Dilip Kumar in most of the songs. But it was the sole Mohd. Rafi number *Sukh ke sab saathi dukh mein na koy* performed with captivating feeling by Dilip Saheb that stole the show.

LP Disc

Ram Chandra keh gaye

Akele hi akele chala hai

Akele hi akele chala hai

Sukh ke sab saathi

Ek padosan peechhe

Musical Team of Gopi

EP Disc

DATE / YEAR OF RELEASE: 1971
BANNER / PRODUCER: RUPA SREE INTERNATIONAL / J.K. KAPUR
DIRECTION: TAPAN SINHA
MUSIC: TAPAN SINHA
PLAYBACK: ANUP GHOSHAL / AARTI MUKHERJEE
STORY / SCREENPLAY: RUPADARSHI / TAPAN SINHA
CINEMATOGRAPHY: BIMAL MUKHERJEE
EDITING: SUBODH ROY
ART: SUNITI MITRA
CAST: DILIP KUMAR / SAIRA BANU / SUMITA SANYAL / ANIL CHATERJI / SWAROOP DATT / CHINMAY ROY / BHANU BANERJI / RAJNI GUPTA / KALYAN CHATERJI / ALOK CHAUDHRY / NANI GANGULY / SATI MAJUMDAR / MODI KOHEN / ABE KOHEN / T.A. LIDDAL / PANNA KAPOOR / AJIT / SHANTIMAY CHATERJI / SHYAM KUMAR / RASRAZ CHAKRAVARTI

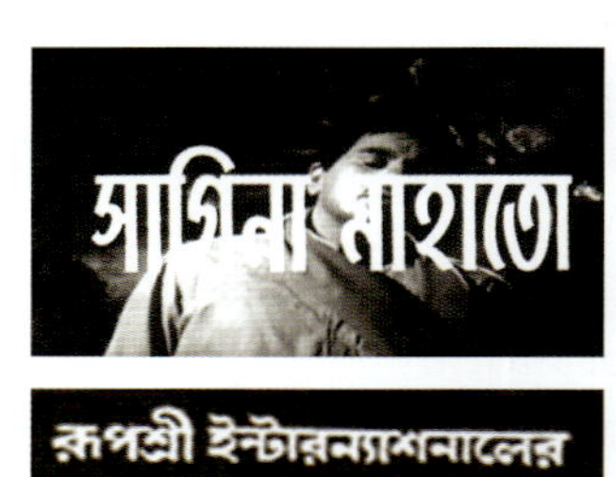

Dilip Kumar's all-encompassing fan club included some iconic filmmakers of Tollygunj (the Bengali filmdom) such as Satyajit Ray and Tapan Sinha. Dilip Kumar had been fascinated by some of the works of Tapan *Babu* (*Kshudit Pashan*, 1960, being one) and so when the legendary director broached the idea of a film on how healthy and objective trade unionism could be practised, the thespian immediately accepted it. The subject in question was Gour Kishor Ghosh's story *Sagina Mahato* published as a short story in the 25:12 issue of the *Desh* magazine on 18 January 1958 and later converted into a novel. Dilip Kumar's close friends industrialist-hotelier J.K. Kapur and Hemen Ganguly offered to produce the movie and that's how *Sagina Mahato*, the actor's first and last full-fledged foray into the Bengali cinema, happened. Once again, the celebrity couple Dilip-Saira were paired as the lead actors of the film which had music by the director Tapan Sinha himself. The film, which was made in black and white and shot in the salubrious locations of Kurseong (near Darjeeling), turned out to be a golden jubilee hit with Dilip Kumar again rendering an impeccable performance as the trade union leader of a factory in the pre-independence era (1943–44) fighting for the rights of labourers against the British management. It was another feather in the cap of the great actor and one of his most memorable performances. The supporting cast of Bengali actors and actresses, handpicked by the veteran director Tapan Sinha, included Sumita Sanyal, Anil Chatterji, Swaroop Dutt, Chinmoy Roy, Bhanu Banerji, Rajni Gupta, et al and all of them acted quite creditably.

On Sagina Mahato Sets

The Golden Jubilee Celebrations of Sagina Mahato

The story revolved around the main protagonist Sagina Mahato, the naive simpleton but steely-willed factory worker and later trade union leader, resolutely espousing the cause of the workers. Mahato is manipulated by the British factory owners to further their own devious interests by exploiting his popularity among his fellow workers. The true story of the labour movement of that era was told through fictional characters. Sagina Mahato fights for the rights of the workers combating the tyranny of the British bosses. He is helped in his fight by Amal (Swaroop Dutt) who comes to the place at the behest of the union leaders of Kolkata. But many of these communist union leaders have the penchant to indulge in dirty, petty politics. Amal, though an outsider, becomes fond of the honest intentions of Sagina and backs him up to the hilt. Sagina is enamoured by a destitute girl Seema (Saira Banu) and protects her from the evil eyes of the locals. Sagina becomes the unquestionable leader of the labour force rising in their esteem due to his stout defiance of the British managers in the interests of the workers. On one hand, the Kolkata-based union leaders led by Aniruddha (Anil Chatterjee) become jealous of Sagina's stature, while on the other hand, the British bosses play a master stroke by elevating Sagina to the position of the labour officer. The devious move alienates Sagina from the masses. In a memorable scene, Sagina comes to the labour colony to show off, high on both–his new status–and alcohol, and looking lika a caricature of his former self in goofy western clothes. Due to the joint machinations of the caucus of trade unionists and the British management (Aniruddha plays a double game in cahoots with the British boss Cunnigham), Sagina is cleverly sent to Kolkata to apparently further the cause of the union. He is helped to some extent by a member of the trade union Vishakha (Sumita Sanyal), who is actually the daughter of a wealthy tycoon but believes in upholding the rights of the poor workmen. Meanwhile, in the absence of Sagina, the British management unleashes its tyranny on the workers. Sagina, subsequently, realises that he has been used as a pawn and trapped by his own actions. Sagina is court-

martialled by the Kolkata trade union caucus (several members of which led by Aniruddha have become terrorists), but he successfully fights them and the British bosses to emerge triumphant. The film ends on a positive and happy note, underlining the manner in which healthy trade unionism should be practised.

Dilip and Saira with Kalyanji-Anandji

The timing of the release of the film was rather propitious since the infamous Naxalite movement in Bengal had just been successfully quelled by Indira Gandhi*ji*'s government. The theme of effectively tackling the problems of vulgar vanguardism from a radical humanist standpoint gelled with Bengali masses. The revered Bengal Film Journalist Association (BFJA) deservingly awarded the Best Actor Award to Dilip Kumar in 1971 for his brilliant portrayal of Sagina Mahato.

As discussed, the music of the film was composed by the director himself who excelled in creating situational melodies, matching the mood of the film, and were ably sung by

Scenes from Sagina Mahato

Anup Ghoshal and Aarti Mukherjee. Anup Ghoshal won the BFJA Award as the Best Playback Singer for that year. The prestigious BFJA Awards for that year also deservingly went to Tapan Sinha (Best Music), Anil Chatterjee (Best Actor in a Supporting Role) and Suniti Mitra (Best Art Direction).

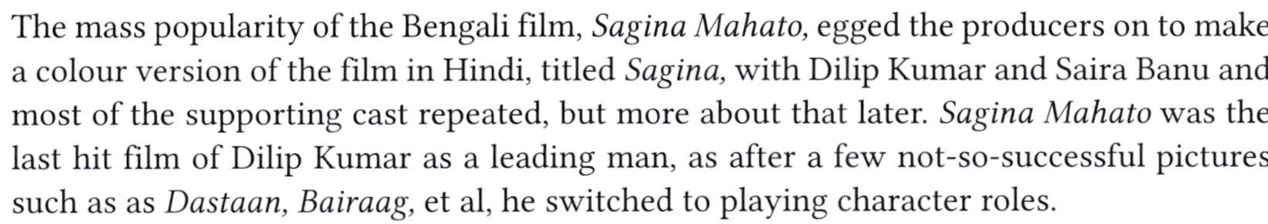

The mass popularity of the Bengali film, *Sagina Mahato,* egged the producers on to make a colour version of the film in Hindi, titled *Sagina,* with Dilip Kumar and Saira Banu and most of the supporting cast repeated, but more about that later. *Sagina Mahato* was the last hit film of Dilip Kumar as a leading man, as after a few not-so-successful pictures such as as *Dastaan, Bairaag,* et al, he switched to playing character roles.

Sagina was India's official entry to the Seventh Moscow International Film Festival held in October 1971. The Indian delegation comprised Dilip Kumar, Saira Banu and Dharma Vir Sinha (the then Deputy Minister of Information & Broadcasting, India) and the movie won universal acclaim and a certificate of merit at the festival.

The Seventh Moscow International Film Festival

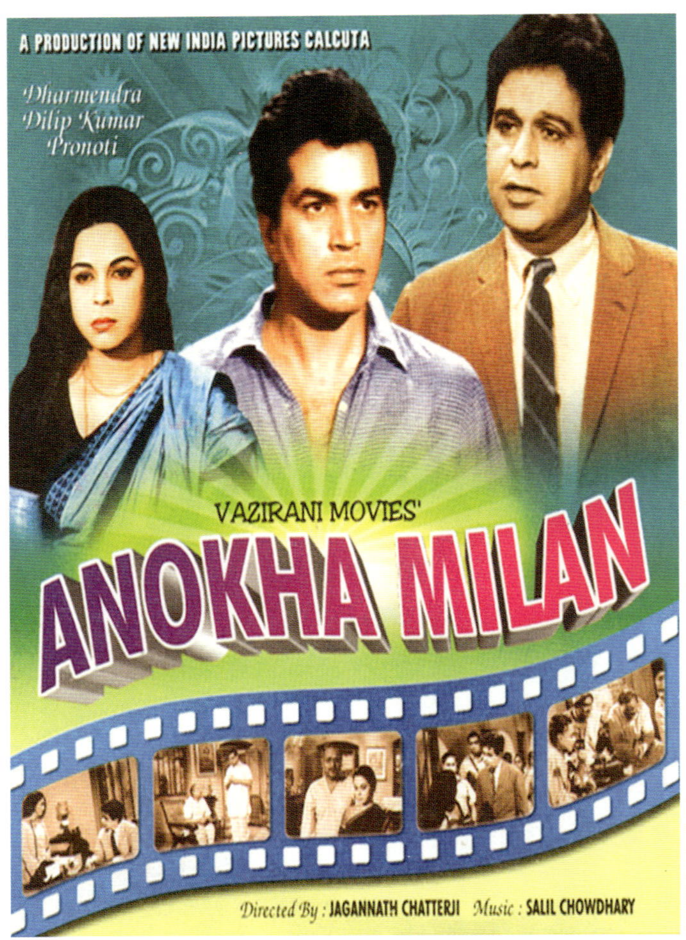

(Paari dubbed in Hindi – with Dilip Kumar in special appearance)

DATE / YEAR OF RELEASE: 1972
BANNER / PRODUCER: VAZIRANI MOVIES / R.J. VAZIRANI
DIRECTION: JAGANNATH CHATOPPADHYAY
MUSIC: SALIL CHOWDHURY
STORY / SCREENPLAY: JARASANDH
DIALOGUE: CHANDRAKANT
EDITING: AJIT DAS
AUDIOGRAPHY: RAJ / SOPAN
ART: BOTU SEN
CAST: DILIP KUMAR (SPECIAL APPEARANCE) / DHARMENDRA / PRONOTI / ABHI BHATTACHARYA / DILIP ROY / KESHTO MUKHERJI

Pronoti Ghosh's *Paari* (Bengali, 1966), starring herself and Dharmendra and Dilip Kumar in a special appearance, was dubbed in Hindi and re-released as *Anokha Milan* (1972) with Salil Chaudhury's music also being dubbed and republished. Two traditional songs, *Tora sundari saami paabi* (Sabita) and *Yeh man dole bole kya re* (Manna Dey) were classy.

DASTAAN

DATE / YEAR OF RELEASE: 1972
BANNER / PRODUCER: B.R. FILMS / B.R. CHOPRA
DIRECTION: B.R. CHOPRA
MUSIC: LAXMIKANT–PYARELAL
LYRICS: SAHIR LUDHIANVI
PLAYBACK: MOHD. RAFI / ASHA BHOSLE / MAHENDRA KAPOOR
STORY / SCREENPLAY: I.S. JOHAR / B.R. FILMS STORY DEPT.
DIALOGUE: AKHTAR-UL-IMAN
CINEMATOGRAPHY: DHARAM CHOPRA
EDITING: PRAN MEHRA
AUDIOGRAPHY: M.A. SHAIKH
ART: SANT SINGH
CHOREOGRAPHY: GOPI KRISHNA / SOHAN LAL
CAST: DILIP KUMAR / SHARMILA TAGORE / BINDU / PREM CHOPRA / PADMA KHANNA / I.S. JOHAR / MANMOHAN KRISHAN / IFTEKHAR / NANA PALSIKAR / BADRI PRASAD / KESHAV RANA / JANKIDAS / JAGDISH RAJ / SABINA / S.K. PREM / MASTER SACHIN / MASTER SHAHID / PREM SAGAR / PRAVIN KUMAR / PRATAP PAWAR / NARBADA SHANKAR / UMA DATT / C.L. SHAH / NAZIR KASHMIRI / MUNSHI MUNAKKA / DEEPAK / LALA NAZIR / GOPI KRISHN / MADAN PURI / JAYASHRI T. (GUEST ARTISTES)

Legendary director-producer Baldev Raj (B.R.) Chopra's first successful directorial venture in Mumbai film industry–after a disastrous debut with *Karwat* starring Geeta Nizami and Satish in 1949–was *Afsana* (1951). The film starred Ashok Kumar, Veena, Kuldeep Kaur and Pran in lead roles and had music by Husnlal Bhagatram. The film had Ashok Kumar playing a double role based on a story by comedian-director-writer I.S. Johar. Naturally, Chopra Saheb was very fond of *Afsana* since it was his first commercial success. He decided to remake the subject in colour with Dilip Kumar essaying the popular double role. The subject was narrated by B.R. Chopra to the megastar who liked it and said, '*Ajeeb baat hai is dastaan mein ki ek insaan marne ke baad dekh raha hai ki uske saath ke logon ki asli fitrat kaisi hai*' (It's strange that a man after his death gets to see the true colours of people close to him). Dilip Saheb accepted the role and the movie was launched with much fanfare with Sharmila Tagore, Bindu, Prem Chopra, I.S. Johar co-starring the thespian. Inexplicably, Chopra Saheb assigned the music direction to Laxmikant–Pyarelal in preference to his regular and highly successful composer Ravi. The movie proved to be a damp squib at the box office for a variety of reasons.

Vishnu Sahay

Dilip Kumar played the dual roles of Judge Vishnu Sahay and theatre owner, actor and playboy Dewan Anil Kumar to perfection delineating the characters with facile lucidity. He was simply outstanding as the judge and sporting a beard, his stance and personality looked completely different from Anil Kumar. The impact of the flawless portrayals was mind blowing. Sharmila Tagore looked petite whereas Bindu made a convincing vamp. Prem Chopra and I.S. Johar just passed muster.

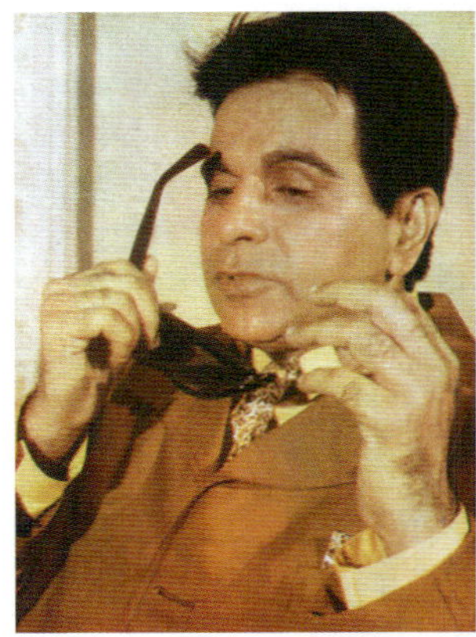

Anil Kumar

Dastaan was virtually a scene-by-scene remake of *Afsana* with the storyline and the treatment remaining unaltered. The movie was flaunted as a 'Page torn from life's storybook, whose author is Fate'. The story was about twin look-alike sons, named Sunil and Anil, born in a rich family. They have a neighbouring girl Meena, who later grows to be beautiful lass–a role played by Sharmila Tagore). Meena has a childhood crush on Sunil. The twins get separated in childhood in a deadly storm while returning from a fair. Sunil is rescued by a benevolent orphanage owner and Anil survives to be with his rich family. Meena misses Sunil and longs for his return one day. Sunil is renamed Vishnu Sahay and grows up to become a highly-respected judge in the town of Gorakhpur. Anil runs his theatre business in Delhi and is a well-known actor. Vishnu Sahay is married to a pretty woman Mala (Bindu) and has a friend Rajan (Prem Chopra) whom he implicitly trusts. Anil is a happy-go-lucky play-boyish character and tries to woo Meena apart from having a roving eye for his starlets including the heroine (Padma Khanna). Meena spurns the romantic advances of Anil and is lamenting for Sunil hoping for his return one day. A financer Dhanraj (Jankidas) also has an eye on the heroine and gets killed during an altercation with Anil Kumar. Judge Vishnu Sahay goes on a trip to Mussoorie in connection with a legal matter. A panicky Anil shocked at the death of Dhanraj also drives off to Mussoorie. Vishnu Sahay and Anil meet in the restaurant of their hotel in Mussoorie and share a table (a brilliantly written and performed scene) to strike a sort of friendship and goes to Sahay's room to have coffee together. Anil drugs Vishnu's coffee and as the latter passes out shaves off his beard and substitutes his belongings with his own. Anil wears a false beard, impersonates Vishnu and leaves the hotel in the judge's car, only to meet with a fatal road accident and die. In the morning, Vishnu Sahay gets a shock of his life when he is arrested as Anil Kumar on the charge of murder. Being a judge, Vishnu defends himself in court and is exonerated as it turns out that Dhanraj actually died of a heart attack. Vishnu runs off to Gorakhpur to surprise Mala and Rajan with glad tidings of him being alive. Another shock awaits Vishnu as he sees his wife Mala and trusted friend Rajan in each other's arms. While resting on a bench at the railway station, the devastated and heartbroken Vishnu

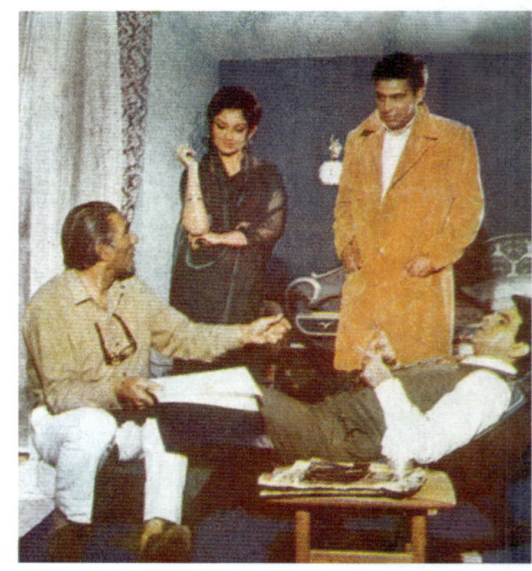

On the Sets of "Dastaan"

(enacted touching on the Rafi number *Na tu zamaan ke liye hai na asmaan ke liye*) meets Anil Kumar's assistant Johar, who convinces him to return to his palatial abode in Delhi, which he does to solve the intriguing riddle. He meets Meena who recognises him to be actually Sunil by noticing a birth mark on his neck. Later, Meena takes Vishnu/Sunil to the same fair where Sunil had got separated from his family. Memories come flooding back to Sunil as he recalls his childhood. Acting as Anil Kumar, Sunil unleashes revenge on Rajan and financially ruins him by clever stock market manipulations. After some dramatic twists and turns, the film ends with Mala committing suicide and Sunil and Meena coming together.

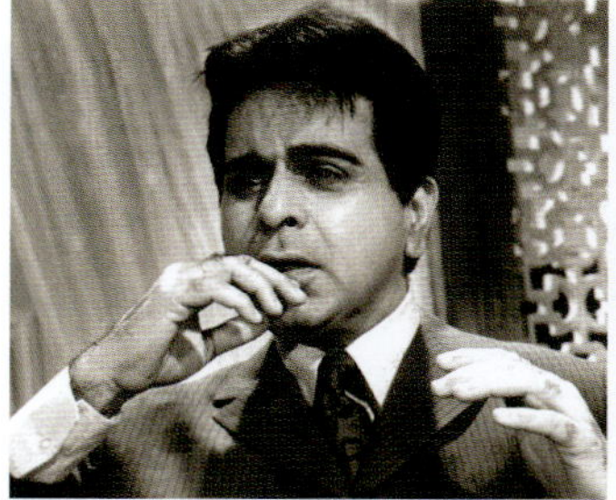

Stills from Dastaan

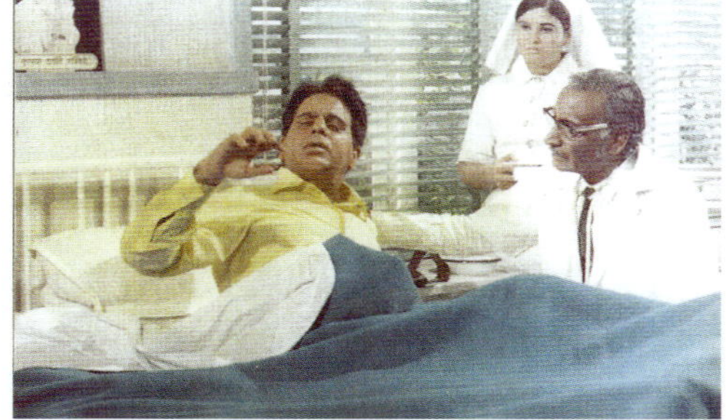

Afsana

Dastaan

The debate as to why *Afsana* clicked in a big way while *Dastaan* failed at the box office was a favourite topic of film industry gossip in those days. A variety of opinions were flaunted, but in our opinion the main reasons were the dated subject, slow-paced narrative and disappointing music.

As far as the performances go, Dilip Kumar had done more than justice to the complex double role with Dilip imparting an extra edge to the simple yet endearing Vishnu Sahay and a laconic Dewan Anil Kumar's characters. Pran's Rajan and Kuldeep Kaur's Mala were several notches above Prem Chopra and Bindu respectively. Sharmila's Meena was more charming than a brooding Veena as Meena. Sharmila Tagore's comment, 'It is a pleasure to work with Rajesh Khanna but it is a pleasure and a challenge to work with Dilip Kumar' caused quite a flutter in filmi circles those days. Both Sharmila Tagore and Prem Chopra fulfilled their lifetime ambition of working with Dilip Kumar in *Dastaan.*

Stills from Dastaan

Composer duo Laxmikant–Pyarelal combining for the first time with lyricist Sahir Ludhianvi joined the select band of music directors who worked with the 'Big Three' – Dilip Kumar, Raj Kapoor and Dev Anand. It was an opportunity of a lifetime but LP, with the exception of the above mentioned classic Mohd. Rafi number, failed to live upto the musical standards of B.R. Films. Songs such as *Koi aaya lachak gayi kaya, Haay main ki karan,* (Lata), *Maria my sweetheart, Mela jagwala* (Mahendra Kapoor) were disappointing and could not hit the charts. Comparisons are odious but just one song of composers Husnlal Bhagatram *Abhi to main jawan hoon* (Lata) in the original score of *Afsana* beats the entire score of *Dastaan* hollow. A flash of the timeless Lata, the classic was very nostalgically used by B.R.Chopra in a key sequence of *Dastaan.*

Sadly, the opulent *Dastaan* with superlative performances failed to click causing heavy losses to B.R. Films and proving a disappointment for the thespian.

PHIR KAB MILOGI (SPECIAL APPEARANCE)

DATE / YEAR OF RELEASE: 1974
BANNER / PRODUCER: SHIVALAY FILMS / HARI MEHRA
DIRECTION: HRISHIKESH MUKHERJEE
MUSIC: R.D. BURMAN
LYRICS: MAJROOH SULTANPURI
PLAYBACK: LATA MANGESHKAR / KISHORE KUMAR / MUK
STORY / SCREENPLAY: D.N. MUKHERJI / BIMAL DUTT
DIALOGUE: RAJINDER SINGH BEDI
CINEMATOGRAPHY: JAYWANT R. PATHARE
EDITING: DAS DHAIMADE
AUDIOGRAPHY: GEORGE D'CRUZ
ART: AJIT BANERJI
CAST: DILIP KUMAR (SPECIAL APPEARANCE) / MALA SINHA / BISWAJEET / DEVEN VARMA / BIPIN GUPTA / DAVID / ABHI BHATTACHARYA / VIJAY CHAUDHERY / SUJATA / BISHAN KHANNA / NILIMA / PRAVEEN PAUL / UMA DUTT / BEENA BHALLA / RAM MURTI CHATURVEDI / NANDU BABU / KAMLESH PUROHIT / VIKRAM / SHRIDHAR

Producer Hari Mehra announced this movie under the banner of Shivalaya Films, with Mala Sinha and Biswajit in the leads under the direction of the veteran Hrishikesh Mukherjee and with music by R.D. Burman in the early 1970s. At that point in time, the 'Angry Young Man' era of Amitabh Bachchan and fast-paced multi-starrers had already dawned and the lead pair selected was not much of a box-office draw. To bolster the saleability of the project, Hrishi *Da* requested his long-time friend Dilip Kumar to revive the sinking project by agreeing to make a featured special appearance in the movie. A special role of 'Teja Singh' was created for Dilip Saheb which he agreed to play. Mala Sinha fulfilled her lifetime ambition of working with Dilip Kumar.

The story centred around a business tycoon Sapna (Mala Sinha) and her romance with an employee Rajesh (Biswajit). She masquerades as a village belle Paro in a scenic Himachal village to woo Rajesh. They fall in love but Rajesh, on knowing that Sapna and Paro are the same girl, gets very upset and returns to his village in a huff. He once again encounters Sapna in the village but she is now betrothed to a wealthy local contractor Dewan Sailesh (Sailesh Kumar). The Dewan has a roving eye and seduces a local girl Amba (Naaz) who happens to be the sister of the dreaded local dacoit Teja Singh (Dilip Kumar). Amba goes missing and even the police inspector (Abhi Bhattacharya) fails to find her. An enraged Teja Singh roughens Sailesh up and kidnaps Sapna to seek revenge for his sister. After some twists and turns the movie ends on a happy note. Though Dilip Kumar's towering presence did help embellish the film, its slow paced and rather trite narrative proved its undoing at the box office. R.D. Burman's music was passable.

Dilip as Teja Singh

After *Paari* and its Hindi-dubbed version *Anokha Milan,* this was Dilip Saheb's second special appearance for a friend.

Posters of the Film

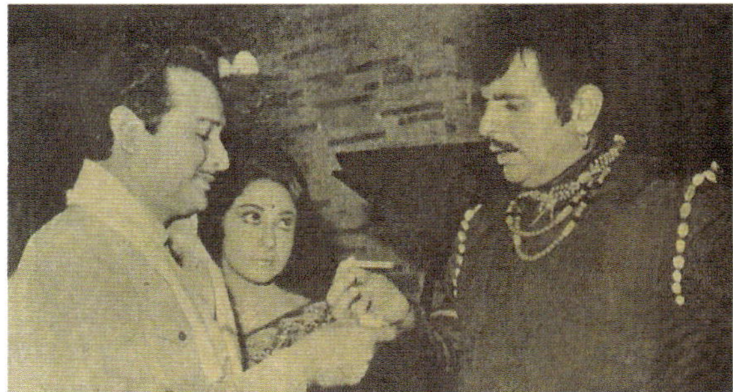

On the Sets of Phir Kab Milogi

DATE / YEAR OF RELEASE: 1974
BANNER / PRODUCER: RUPA SREE INTERNATIONAL / J.K. KAPUR (MINNI KAPUR AND RUMA GANGULY PRESENTATION)
DIRECTION: TAPAN SINHA
MUSIC: S.D. BURMAN
LYRICS: MAJROOH SULTANPURI
PLAYBACK: KISHORE KUMAR / LATA MANGESHKAR / ASHA BHOSLE / PANKAJ MITRA
STORY: RUPADARSHI
SCREENPLAY: TAPAN SINHA
DIALOGUE: DR RAHI MASOOM RAZA
CINEMATOGRAPHY: BIMAL MUKHERJI
EDITING: SUBODH ROY
AUDIOGRAPHY: J.M. BAROT / DABESH GHOSH / D.O. BHANSALI / MANGESH DESAI
CHOREOGRAPHY: P.L. RAJ
CAST: DILIP KUMAR / SAIRA BANU / APARNA SEN / ANIL CHATTERJI / SWAROOP DUTT / CHINMOY ROY / RAJNI GUPTA / KALYAN CHATTERJI / BHANU BANERJI / QADAR KHAN/ T.A.LIDDLE / MODI COHEN / ABE COHEN / ALOK CHOUDHARY / PANNA KAPUR/RASORAJ CHAKRAVORTY / NANI GANGULY / SATU MANUMDAR / AJIT BENGALI / CHANDU/ PARDESI / SHYAM KUMAR / SHANTIMOY CHATTERJI / MUSTAFA/SAYED / NAQI / AZIZ/ PUTAN & K.N.SINGH WITH OMPRAKASH

In the wake of the magnificent commercial and critical success of the Bengali film *Sagina Mahato*, its producer (J.K. Kapur; Heman Ganguly had, by that time, died), director Tapan Sinha and Dilip Saheb deemed it prudent to replicate the success at an all-India level. So, they decided to remake the hit film in Hindi, titled *Sagina,* with virtually the same set-up. There were some alterations necessitated due to dates issues and few structural changes.

Aparna Sen played the role assigned to Sumita Sanyal in the Bengali original, the veteran actor Om Prakash essayed the important role of Sagina's trusted associate, and Kader Khan. Then the veteran character actor K.N. Singh was brought-in to portray the newly-created role of a Kolkata-based government official. The music was composed by the great S.D. Burman (Tapan Sinha himself had scored the music in the Bengali original) with the viewpoint of incorporating popular Hindi numbers. The lyrics were penned by Majrooh Sultanpuri. The movie was shot at the same picturesque location of Kurseong (Darjeeling) where the original Bengali film was shot. The film once again had a truly spectacular performance by Dilip Kumar. *Sagina* by himself is a wonderful character and Dilip takes him to great heights. Unforgettable are the scenes where he gives a speech in the mountains in the workers' own language, when he speaks of his childhood, when he fights injustice physically but becomes helpless near bureaucracy and the sequence in which he compels the British officer to let him make a telephone call to unionist Anil Biswas in Kolkata. But, somehow, despite being a well-made film with all the trappings of an entertainer, *Sagina* did not succeed at the box office.

Dilip Kumar as Sagina

Dilip Kumar as Sagina

The story of *Sagina* basically followed the narrative pattern of the original Bengali movie except for the Kolkata sojourn portion of the protagonist which was shortened to some extent. The underlying theme that the working class is exploited by two kinds of people–the capitalists to fill their coffers and the radicals to obtain power—remained potently unaltered. As has been mentioned earlier (in the Bengali version) the story is set in the early 1940s. Sagina Mahato (Dilip Kumar) is a worker in a British factory. Its employees seem content with their work. Sagina rescues a married girl Lalita (Saira Banu) whose husband attempts to sell her to a concupiscent British officer Smith (Cohen) of the same British factory where Sagina is employed. Discontent begins to simmer only when Smith tries to rape one of the local girls who is newly-married to one of Sagina's follower worker Badal. Partly through coincidence, but more because of temperament, Sagina finds himself in open defiance of the authority. When this defiance goes unpunished, his co-workers lionise him and a labour movement is born. News of Sagina's success reaches the metropolis where a group of trade unionists led by Anupam Dutt (Kader Khan) propose to induct him and his followers into their movement by making them members of their party. The main functionaries of the trade union outfit are Anirudha (Anil Chatterji), a dubious character, Amal Banerjee (Swaroop Dutt), an honest unionist, and Vishakha (Aparna Sen), who is the daughter of an industrialist tycoon (K.N. Singh) but supports unionists against her father. Amal Banerjee is deputed to go and meet Sagina and his cohorts and bring them under the union fold. Amal becomes extremely fond of Sagina. Or at least so it appears, till we hear the leader Anirudha say to a confidant, 'I hate people like Sagina.' What he hates is not merely Sagina's superficial crudities, but his attitude to work, 'This factory is like a mother to me because it gives me life.' As Anirudha sees it, Sagina's loyalty is to the factory (and so in effect its management) rather than to the movement (and the workers). A struggle within a struggle develops with the unionist pitted in insidious combat with Sagina. He seems to have lost at first when he is suddenly catapulted to the position of Welfare Officer. He wears the officer's suit awkwardly and lives in a grand house, without realising that he has been duped with the purpose of alienating him from his mass base. The extremist elements want to blow up the factory as they see it as an instrument of repression. Anirudha's logic is that, with their livelihood gone, the workers will join the radicals. His movement needs desperate men. But such evil designs are successfully thwarted by a resurgent Sagina who saves his people from the brink in the ultimate confrontation. Interwoven with this proletariat conflict is the love story between Sagina and Lalita. Based on a weighty story set against the backdrop of the British as rulers and employers, *Sagina* had some important points to convey about the exploitation of the working class, the trade union movement, the dirty political games of the so-called leaders and revolutionaries.

Sagina, as per us, had the making of an avant-garde film but it failed at the box office. Perhaps Dilip fans who gave the film its bumper opening went to the theatres expecting a no-holds-barred fast-paced entertainer and could not come to terms with the film for the discerning. All said and done, *Sagina* was a beautiful film and definitely yet another histrionic triumph for Dilip Kumar. A special feature of the movie was that it opened with a brilliantly-delivered voice over of Dilip Kumar himself introducing the narrative.

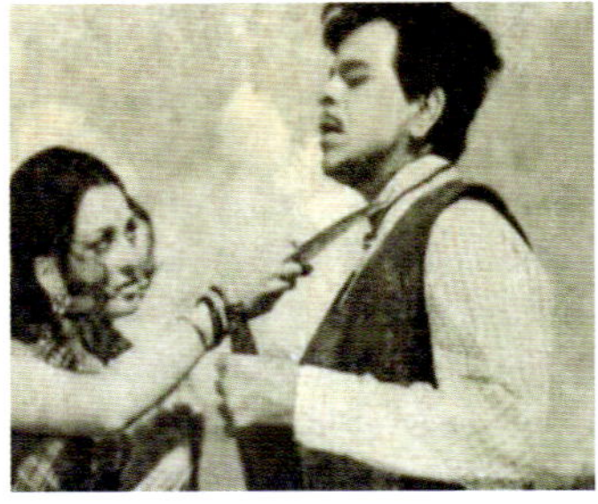

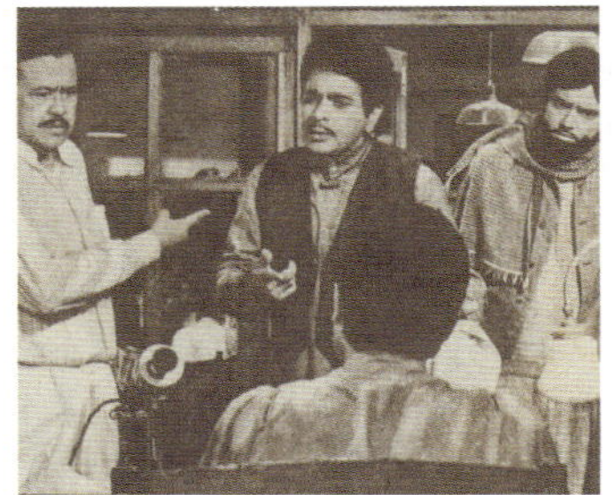

Scenes from Sagina

Composer S.D. Burman also belonged to that select band of music directors, who had the privilege of scoring music for the legendary trio of Dilip Kumar, Dev Anand and Raj Kapoor. Of course, Dada Burman's friend and favourite Dev Anand had the highest number of films (twenty-six) with his music, whereas Dilip Kumar and Raj Kapoor had three each. *Sagina* was S.D. Burman's last film with Dilip Kumar (after *Shabnam* and *Devdas*) in which the veteran composer afforded his protégé Kishore Kumar the opportunity of giving playback for the thespian for the first and last time. It was quite a commendable sprightly score with some enchanting melodies like *Tumhare sang to rain bitayi* (Lata-Kishore), *Ooparwala dukhiyon ki naahin sunta re* (Kishore-Dilip Kumar), *Ghazab chamke bindiya tohar* (Kishore-Asha) and the album's most number, *Saala main to Saheb ban gaya* (Kishore-Pankaj Mitra).

Dilip and Dada Burman

Uparwala dukhiyon ki

Gajab chamke bindiyaa

Tumhare sang to rain bitayi

Sala main to Saheb ban gaya

EP Disc

Kishore's playback for Dilip

A Sagina Song Recording

LP Disc

DATE / YEAR OF RELEASE: 22 OCTOBER 1976
BANNER / PRODUCER: M.R. PRODUCTIONS / MUSHIR ALAM / MOHAMMED RIAZ
DIRECTION: ASIT SEN
MUSIC: KALYANJI–ANANDJI
LYRICS: ANAND BAKSHI
PLAYBACK: MOHD. RAFI / LATA MANGESHKAR / MAHENDRA KAPOOR / ASHA BHOSLE
STORY / SCREENPLAY: S. KHALIL
DIALOGUE: ABRAR ALVI / Dr RAHI MASOOM RAZA
CINEMATOGRAPHY: KAMAL BOSE
EDITING: TARUN DUTT
AUDIOGRAPHY: P. HARIKISHEN / KAUSHIK / D.O. BHANSALI
CHOREOGRAPHY: P.L. RAJ / M. NAIDU
ART: SUDENDU ROY
CAST: DILIP KUMAR / SAIRA BANU / LEENA CHANDAVARKAR / PREM CHOPRA / NASIR KHAN / MADAN PURI / RUMA GUHA THAKURTA / SACHIN / JAIRAJ / NAAZ

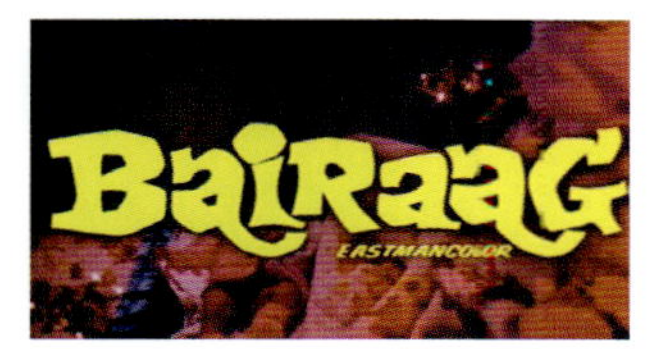

Bairaag was Dilip Kumar's last film as a romantic hero, which featured the thespian in a triple role of a father and his two sons. After the box-office failure of *Dastaan,* Dilip Saheb wanted to come up with a blockbuster magnum opus and designed *Bairaag* on those lines. It was produced by Mushir Alam and Mohammad Riaz (of Mushir–Riaz Productions which had also produced Rajesh Khanna starrer *Safar,* 1970*)* and directed by Asit Sen who had earlier directed films like *Mamta* (1966), *Anokhi Raat* (1968), *Sharafat* (1970), et al. The film's story-screenplay was written by S. Khalil and dialogue by Abrar Alvi and Dr Rahi Masoom Raza. However, the grapevine has it that Dilip Kumar himself ghost-directed the film, which took around three–four years to complete with the city version of the narrative undergoing numerous changes with a view to make the movie a sure-fire hit. However, the movie could only be a moderate success at the box office. Dilip Kumar worked arduously to define the three roles and enacted them distinctively to once again come up with a bravura performance. But, age was not on his side now and after *Bairaag*, the actor decided to accept meaty central character roles only.

Dilip Kumar and Saira Banu in Bairaag

Dilip Kumar and Leena Chandavarkar in Bairaag

The story of the movie centred around three characters—the tycoon Kailash Nath; Sanjay, his happy-go-lucky and philandering son; and Bhola, his renounced son–all played by Dilip Kumar. The romantic foils opposites Sanjay and Bhola were Sonia (Leena Chandavarkar) and Tara (Saira Banu) respectively. The film begins brilliantly with Kailash Nath soulfully humming a *Raag Malkauns*-based *Mukh mod mod muskaat jaat* while shaving in the morning, blissfully unaware that it is his wedding anniversary until his wife Pushpa (Ruma Guha Thakurta) and doctor friend (Nasir Khan) greet him. Kailash Nath is very busy in looking after his business empire and multiplying his wealth paying scant regard to his health (he has an eye problem), despite warnings from the doctor friend. Kailash Nath soon becomes blind. He prays for having children and the prayers are answered as Pushpa delivers twins, one of whom is born blind. Having seen the terrible handicap of blindness, Kailash requests his doctor to get rid of the blind son. The doctor instead leaves the blind son at the doorsteps of an ashram. A temple priest (Nazir Husain) picks up the blind son and takes him to his village where he looks after a temple owned by a zamindar (Jairaj). The blind son is christened Bhola and is employed by the zamindar after he grows up. Bhola is very loyal to his employers and looks after his sprawling zamindari despite his handicap. On the other hand, Sanjay is brought up with all comforts provided by his tycoon father and turns out to be a playboy. Sanjay is engaged to Sonia, the cousin of Prince Kunwar (Prem Chopra), and also serenades a dancer Lucy (Helen). In the village, Tara (whom Bhola addresses as Chhoti Malkin) is in love with Bhola. Tara declares her love for Bhola and her intentions to marry him. Bhola is blissfuly unaware of this. The zamindar wants Kunwar to marry Tara despite her refusal. On pretext of marrying Tara, Kunwar demands a large sum of money to marry Tara, Bhola arranges the amount out of the savings he has ensured regardless of zamindar's expensive way of life. He takes Kunwar to the underground vault where his master's money is safely stashed. Kunwar is attacked by the family's protector snake but succeeds in running away with the fortune. The snake licks the eyes of Bhola and the blind man recovers his eyesight. Bhola follows Kunwar to the city to recover his master's money. On the other hand in the city, Crasto (Madan Puri), the owner of a gambling den, is duped of some money by Kunwar and the dancer Lucy. Sanjay meets Lucy overnight in a hotel and the dancer is later killed. Kunwar implicates Sanjay in the murder of Lucy and Bhola due to his resemblance with Sanjay is arrested by the police for the murder of Lucy. Bhola discovers that Sanjay is his own brother and takes the murder rap on himself to save Sanjay. On learning that Bhola is his twin, Sanjay also gives himself to the police and diverts the murder rap from Bhola. The two brothers meet at the police station, baffling the police as to who the real murderer is? Eventually the climax of the movie leads to the real murderer getting apprehended and the film ends on a happy note with Bhola getting Tara and Sanjay marrying Sonia.

Bairaag took longer than usual time in production, due to an overzealous effort to re-shoot and re-edit some parts of the films particularly related to the city–based parts. As a result, several very interesting scenes were deleted from the film due to alterations in the original narrative. However, the movie aroused great expectations in filmgoers and tremendous hype was built around its release. The film was released at Ganga Theatre and other venues in Mumbai and had a spectacular opening, going housefull for several weeks. I, Trinetra Bajpai saw the film twice at Basant Theatre (Chembur, Mumbai) and Lalita Cinema (Varanasi, U.P.) in housefull shows. However, the collections petered-out after a few weeks. In Mumbai, the film was shifted to Swastik Cinema after a 15-week (100 days) run at Ganga Theatre.

Dilip Kumar in a Triple Role

By now, the composer duo Kalyanji–Anandji had developed a special rapport with Dilip Saheb and were assigned the musical score of *Bairaag*. They came up with several popular numbers including *Sare shahar mein aapsa koi nahin* (Rafi-Asha), *Peete peete kabhi kabhi* (Rafi-Asha), *Main bairaagi nachoon gaoon* (Rafi-Lata) and *Chhoti si umar mein lag gaya rog* (Lata).

Main bairagi nachoon gaoon

Chhoti si umar mein

O Shankar mere

Sare shahar mein aapsa

Peete peete kabhi kabhi

EP Disc

LP Disc

Second LP Disc

CHAPTER 3.5

LEAD CHARACTER TO THE FORE–THE INTRIGUING EIGHTIES

KRANTI

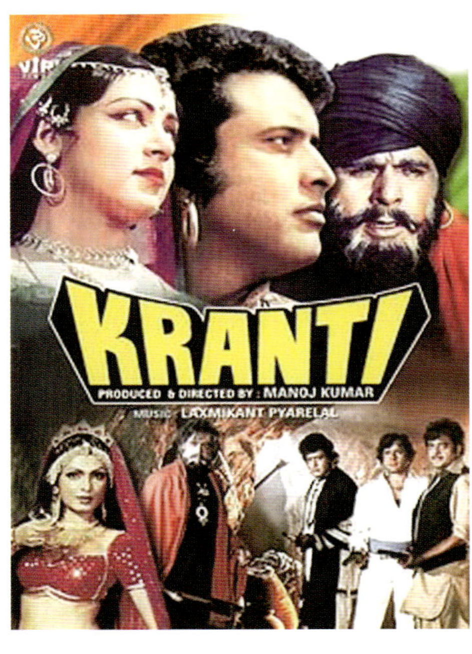

DATE / YEAR OF RELEASE: 27 FEBRUARY 1981
BANNER / PRODUCER: V.I.P. FILMS / MANOJ KUMAR
DIRECTION: MANOJ KUMAR
MUSIC: LAXMIKANT–PYARELAL
LYRICS: SANTOSH ANAND / MANOJ KUMAR
PLAYBACK: MOHD. RAFI / LATA MANGESHKAR / KISHORE KUMAR / MAHENDRA KAPOOR / MANNA DEY / MINOO PURSHOTTAM / NITIN MUKESH / SHAILENDER SINGH
STORY / SCREENPLAY: SALIM–JAVED
DIALOGUE: MANOJ KUMAR
CINEMATOGRAPHY: JOE D'SOUZA
EDITING: MANOJ KUMAR
AUDIOGRAPHY: VENKAT CHENNUBOTLA
CAST: DILIP KUMAR / MANOJ KUMAR / SHASHI KAPOOR / SHATRUGHAN SINHA / HEMA MALINI / PARVEEN BABI / SARIKA / PRADEEP KUMAR / JAIRAJ / NIRUPA ROY / AGHA / MADAN PURI / BHAGWAN / SHASHIKALA / PREM CHOPRA / DHEERAJ KUMAR / MASTER KUNAL / MASTER ADITYA / SULOCHANA

After his much talked about triple role in *Bairaag* (1976), Dilip Saheb voluntarily took a sabbatical from films. But in 1980, actor-director-producer-writer Manoj Kumar managed to persuade and sign the thespian to play the pivotal role in his multi-starrer saga of freedom struggle *Kranti.* Manoj Kumar had been an ardent admirer of Dilip Kumar since he, as a teenager, saw the latter's blockbuster *Shaheed* (1948). Even his acting style was fashioned on the histrionics of Dilip Saheb. The two had earlier worked together in *Aadmi* (1968). Therefore, Dilip Kumar had to accept Manoj's offer and fulfil his lifelong ambition to direct the thespian. After a string of highly successful home productions like *Upkar* (1967), *Purab Aur Pachhim* (1970), *Shor* (1972) and *Roti Kapada Aur Makaan* (1974), *Kranti* was Manoj Kumar's most ambitious cinematic adventure which paid rich dividends at the box office.

Dilip Kumar in Kranti

Manoj Kumar's *Kranti* was inspired by the legendary historical figure Kanhoji Angre, the first-ever Indian admiral who ruled the seas. He drafted the then superhit writer duo Salim–Javed to write the screenplay with Manoj himself penning the dialogue. Flaunted and heralded as the 'Greatest spectacle of the century', the mega movie had a magnificent star cast featuring Dilip Kumar, Manoj Kumar, Shashi Kapoor, Hema Malini, Shatrughan Sinha, Parveen Babi, Dara Singh, Prem Chopra, Sarika, Pradeep Kumar, Jairaj, Agha, Shashikala, Dheeraj Kumar, Madan Puri, etc. *Kranti* went on to become a stupendous success all over the country.

Kranti marked the start of the third phase in Dilip Saheb's career during which he played some meaty character roles. There were huge expectations and speculation as to how the marvellous actor would make the transition and how would his legion of fans react, as he was striding across the celluloid after a hiatus of four years. Dilip Kumar gave a power-packed performance as the central character of *Sanga,* once again emphatically proving his peerless histrionic mettle to the utter delight of his fans. The usually difficult career transition was made effortlessly.

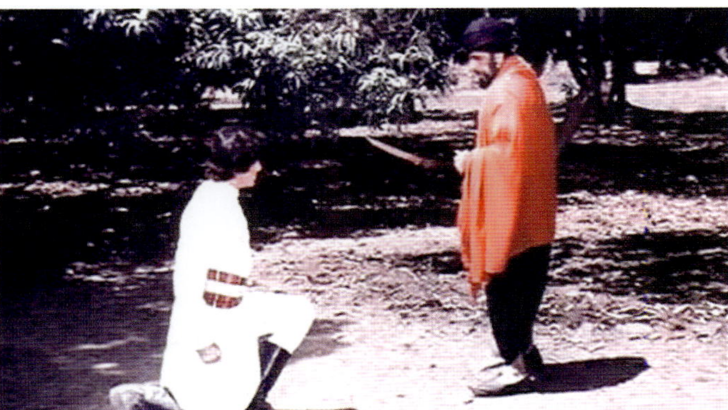

Scenes from Kranti

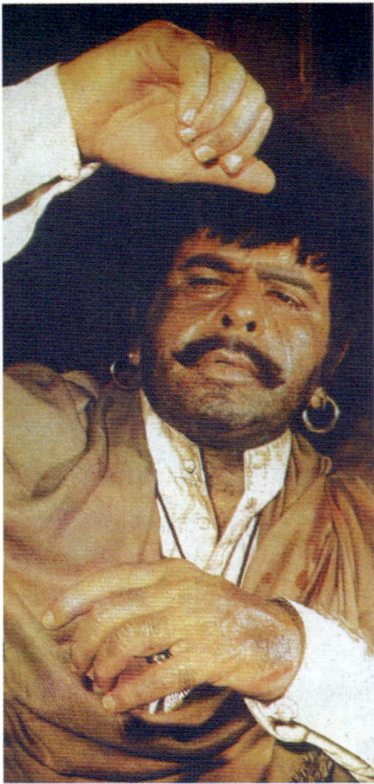

Dilip as Sanga

The film's story spanned a period of forty years of the long freedom struggle of Indians against the British rule, beginning in 1825. The film was dedicated to an anonymous revolutionary farmer who struggled to free the motherland and lit the torch of *kranti* (meaning revolution). The action began in the state of Ramgarh, ruled by Maharaj Lakshman Singh (Jairaj), annexation of which was vital for the British. The Maharaj gets betrayed by his brother Kunwar Shamsher Singh (Pradeep Kumar) who was ill-advised by his brother-in-law Shambhu Singh (Prem Chopra), who himself proclaims: '*Shambhu ka dimaag dodhari talwar hai*' (Shambhu's mind is a double-edged sword).At the behest of Shamsher, Lakshman Singh permits the British to use his marine ports for one year on the condition that the ships shall not bring any explosives. Sanga (Dilip Kumar) is a trusted confidant of the Maharaj who is a farmer living with his wife (Nirupa Roy) and a son named Bharat (Manoj Kumar). The British in defiance of Maharaj import explosives which Sanga discovers. Shamsher and Shambhu kill Maharaj Lakshman Singh, and implicate Sanga in the murder and imprison him. While fighting Shambhu, Sanga amputates the traitor's right arm, and escapes. Sanga launches the revolutionary outfit 'Kranti' to fight the British. Meanwhile, Sanga's wife and son also somehow escape. The Maharaj's sister Charumati (Shashikala), who had suffered several abortions, is given Sanga's newly-born son when she delivers yet another still-born child. Sanga, aided by his tiller followers, raises the battle cry, '*Humein Hindustan ke khoon ki qasam hai, hum iss khoon se aasmaan par Inquilab likh denge... Kranti likh denge*' (We swear by our motherland Hindustan that we will write revolution in the sky with our blood... we will write Kranti), and he captures a British ship. Sanga is now known as Kranti. With passage of time, Kranti's crusade continues and his son Bharat, raised by villagers, grows up and also becomes a revolutionary. Bharat eulogies Kranti unaware that he is latter's son. He saves an erstwhile cannon expert of Queen of Jhansi, Karim Khan (Shatrughan Sinha), aided by the villagers and Sureeli (Parveen Babi), and the daughter of a priest Sheetal (Sarika), who all are members of a gang of revolutionaries. Sureeli is secretly in love with Bharat. The new-born son of Sanga has grown up as the son of Charumati and is now Shakti Singh (Shashi Kapoor), the commander-in-chief of Ramgarh.

Bharat's gang of revolutionaries waylay and loot British sympathisers for the cause of their freedom struggle. A beautiful princes of the mighty Shivpur state Meenaxi (Hema Malini) enroute Ramgarh is intercepted by Bharat. She becomes furious but gradually understands the cause of the revolutionaries and falls in love with Bharat. Later, Shakti Singh also joins the revolutionary cause. Sanga and Bharat and all others together take on the British and their sycophants, but in a bloody battle Bharat, Shakti, Kareem Khan, et al perish. Sanga and Meenaxi (she had married Bharat) survive and Sanga carries the cause of *Kranti* through Bharat's son (Kunal Goswami).

Dilip and Hema Malini

Key Sequences from Kranti

The movie took around a year to complete and was shot in ten schedules. Manoj himself edited the magnum opus. Compared to the last hit of Manoj Kumar, *Roti Kapada aur Makaan,* and even the greatest hit of all-time, *Sholay,* which sold for ₹18 lakh and ₹22 lakh per territory respectively, *Kranti* commanded a whopping ₹65 lakh per territory! The magnum opus was released all over India on 13 February 1981 to a thunderous public response. Patriotic fervour, splendid performances, a racy script and good music were the USP of the blockbuster *Kranti* and the film remains popular to this day. The 21-reels magnum opus celebrated golden jubilees at many centres, netting around ₹10 crore against a total production cost of ₹1.5 crore.

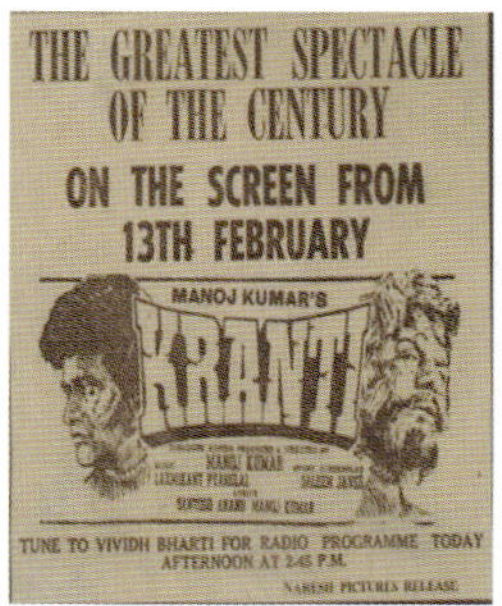

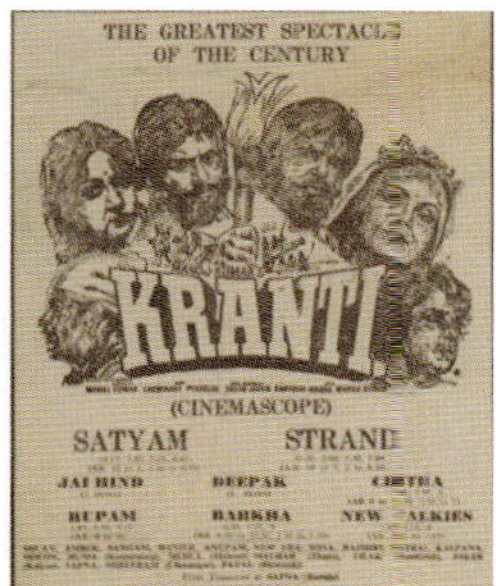

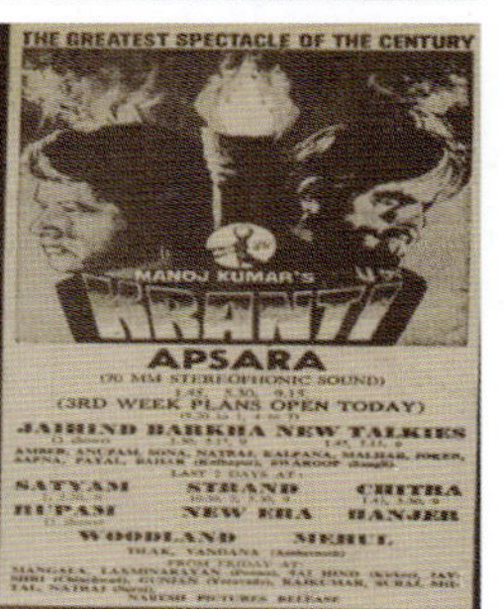

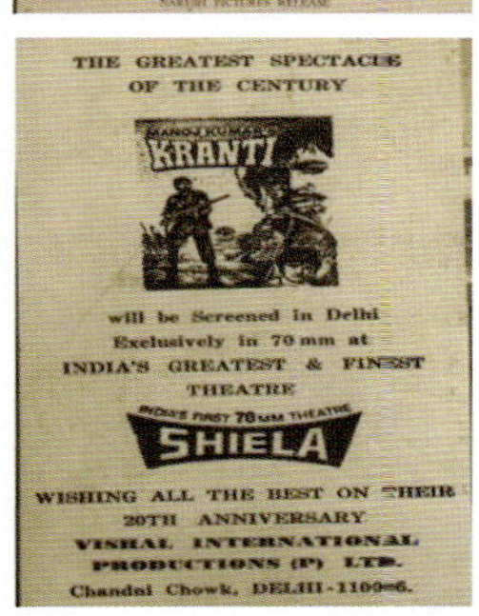

Newspaper advertisements of 'Kranti' for Film release

Music directors Laxmikant–Pyarelal composed a hit musical score to the lyrics of Santosh Anand and Manoj Kumar himself. The entire bouquet of melodies including popular numbers such as *Dilwale dilwale tera naam kya hai–Kranti* (Lata Mangeshkar, Manna Dey, Nitin Mukesh, Shailendra Singh, Mahendra Kapoor), *Chana jor garam* (Kishore Kumar, Lata Mangeshkar, Nitin Mukesh, Mohammed Rafi), *Zindagi ki na toote ladi* (Lata Mangeshkar, Nitin Mukesh), *Ab ke baras* (Mahendra Kapoor), *Durga hai meri maa* (Mahendra Kapoor, Minoo Purushottam), *Mara thumka* (Lata Mangeshkar) and *Looie shama sha* (Lata Mangeshkar, Nitin Mukesh). After the disappointing music of *Dastaan,* the composer duo came up with a foot tapping score for a Dilip Kumar film. It was their second musical score post *Shor* for a Manoj Kumar production and they did not let him down.

Laxmikant–Pyarelal

Kranti is best known for Dilip Kumar's maiden celluloid foray in to character roles, and a highly successful one at that.

LP Disc Jacket of Kranti

SHAKTI

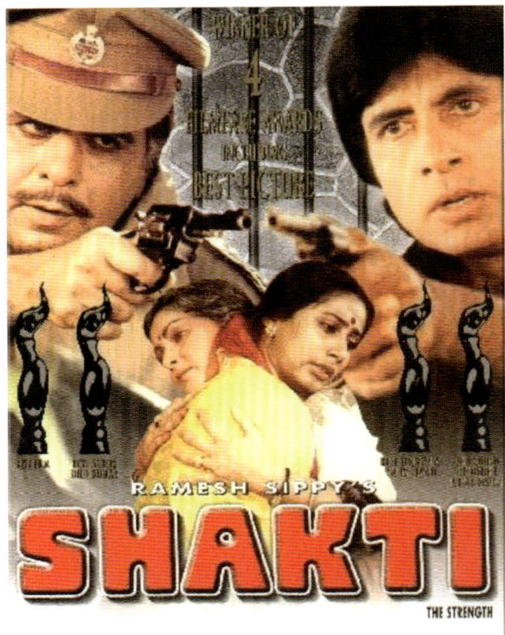

DATE / YEAR OF RELEASE: 30 SEPTEMBER 1982
BANNER / PRODUCER: M.R. PRODUCTIONS / MUSHIR–RIAZ
DIRECTION: RAMESH SIPPY
MUSIC: R.D. BURMAN
LYRICS: ANAND BAKSHI
PLAYBACK: LATA MANGESHKAR / KISHORE KUMAR / ASHA BHOSLE / MAHENDRA KAPOOR
STORY / SCREENPLAY: SALIM–JAVED
DIALOGUE: SALIM–JAVED
CINEMATOGRAPHY: S.M. ANWAR
CHOREOGRAPHY: P.L. RAJ
EDITING: M.S. SHINDE
ART: SUDHENDU ROY
AUDIOGRAPHY: P. HARIKISHAN / MANGESH DESAI / KAUSHIK
CAST: DILIP KUMAR / AMITABH BACHCHAN / RAKHEE / SMITA PATIL / ANIL KAPOOR / AMRISH PURI / KULBHUSHAN KHARBANDA / GOGA KAPOOR / VIKAS ANAND / JAGDISH RAJ / CHANDRASHEKHAR / MURLI / NIRAJ / SHARAT SAXENA / MASTER RAVI / DILIP TAHIL / ARUN DESAI / SUDHIR PANDEY / ASHOK / SATISH & ASHOK KUMAR (GUEST ARTISTES)

The producer duo Mushir–Riaz, who had made *Bairaag* (1976) with Dilip Kumar, was keen on making a mega successful film. They requisitioned Salim–Javed, the top-notch writer duo of the time, to come up with a script befitting their concept of a mega film. Salim–Javed suggested a script based on an epic father-son conflict. They also recommended that Mushir–Riaz sign up Ramesh Sippy, the upcoming hit director–son of the veteran producer G.P. Sippy. They asked the producers to persuade Ramesh

Sippy—who had a strings of hit films like *Andaz* (1971), *Seeta Aur Geeta* (1972), *Sholay* (1975), *Shaan* (1980) to his credit—to do a film outside his home banner, Sippy Films. Sippy agreed to direct the film on the condition that the meaty roles of the father and son should be portrayed by none other than the megastar Dilip Kumar pitted against the reigning super star Amitabh Bachchan supported by a team of the best in the business performers. Such a great histrionic clash of titans would make cinematic history and match the ambitious project concept of the producers, agreed Salim–Javed. At that point in time, Dilip Kumar attended the premiere of *Sholay*, where Amitabh Bachchan was also present. Dilip was deeply impressed with the directorial acumen of Ramesh Sippy and the work of his team in the super-duper hit movie. The two superstars were narrated the project and they loved the well-rounded script which had a fascinating delineation of two powerful characters of a father and his son caught in a conflict of emotions. A spectacular mahurat was held at Juhu beach with the main protagonists arriving in helicopter and the film was royally launched. Ramesh Sippy too was said to be thrilled to direct the formidable star cast of the film–Dilip Kumar, Rakhee, Amitabh Bachchan and Smita Patil–and in a subject which he was truly fascinated with. The result was a truly remarkable film, *Shakti,* which can easily make it to the list of timeless classic Hindi films of epic dimensions in the annals of the moviedom. While the coming together of the two of the superstars was the biggest highlight of the film, it splendidly exploited sustained play of emotions between the two lead characters in one of the well-scripted tales of upholding morality. The movie went on to become a silver jubilee hit. It is one of the finest human dramas made in our country featuring memorable performances.

Mahurat of Shakti

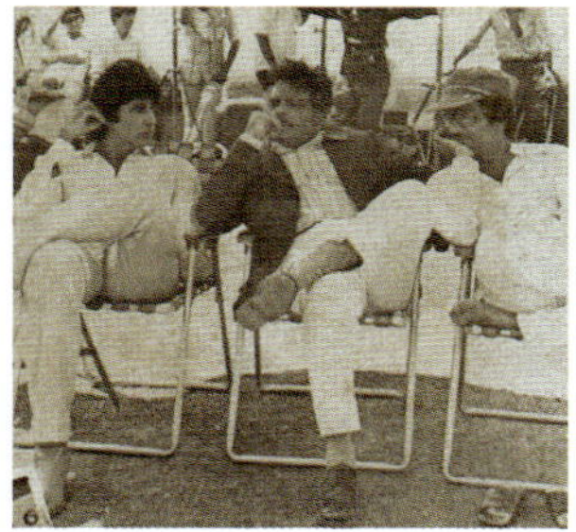
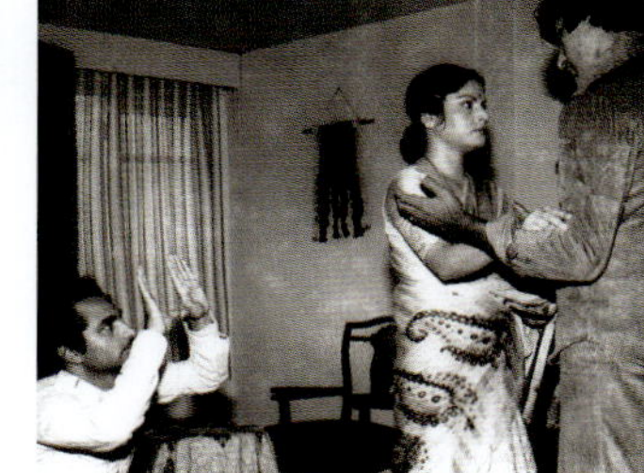

On the Sets of Shakti

Dilip Kumar, stole the thunder as the irksome yet righteous Dy. Commissioner of Police (D.C.P.) Ashwini Kumar, who would stop at nothing to nab the lawbreakers. The great actor outbid himself to unveil a brilliant play of emotions through mind-blowing expressions. Dilip Kumar with his measured tones of mesmerising intonations in dialogue delivery and engaging expressive demeanour once again lived his role and bagged the top acting honours. Amitabh Bachchan exuded the brooding intensity demanded by his character Vijay, of the son the D.C.P, while keeping his usual penchant for 'playing to the gallery' at a minimal. Amitabh portrayed the detached personality of Vijay superbly, bringing out that curious mix of cynicism and sentimentality. Not to be outshone in any way, Rakhee played the pivotal character of Sheetal, the DCP's wife, giving a heart-warming performance displaying warmth, despair and tragedy. As Vijay's wife Roma, Smita Patil gave an utterly natural performance and made her mark in a not-so-elaborate role. Other actors like Kulbhushan Kharbanda, Amrish Puri, et al filled the bill. Veteran pioneer super actor Ashok Kumar made a special appearance in the movie as the boss of the D.C.P. and that one Ashok Kumar–Dilip Kumar scene evoked great nostalgia among their fans.

Dilip as DCP Ashvini

Scenes from Shakti

Dilip and Amitabh in Shakti

The histrionic *jugalbandi* between the indomitable Dilip Kumar and the irrepressible Amitabh Bachchan generated a lot of curiosity among the filmgoers who were eager to witness the professional duel between the great actors. It was more of a challenge for Amitabh since he came face-to-face with an actor whom he truly admired and drew inspiration from. The credit of establishing a fine balance in the characters of Ashwini Kumar and Vijay Kumar goes to director Ramesh Sippy who subtly stressed on the different acting styles of Dilip and Amitabh. Moreover, the expert handling of all the four main characters in the film by the director lifted the film to a different level. In those days, a lot of people compared Amitabh's acting style with that of Dilip Kumar's. Undoubtedly Amitabh was influenced by Dilip, but is it not natural to draw inspiration from the best? The difference is subtly discernible. Amitabh's hallmark is his ability to create a 'presence' through his personality, his baritone voice and calculated body movements. On the other hand, Dilip Kumar's style is his power of effortless expression with a highly mobile face, subtle gestures–and his expressive voice disseminates a gamut of emotions through intonation. Dilip Saheb has an uncanny ability to temper his performance to match the temperature of the scene being emoted. The similarity in acting becomes evident when the influences of the 'Dilip Kumar school of histrionics' appear loud and clear on Amitabh when he conveys intensity of characterisation through mannerisms and gesticulations.

The film's story centred around DCP Ashwini Kumar (Dilip) and his son Vijay Kumar (Amitabh). The DCP is staunchly honest and obsessed about upholding the highest traditions of morality. His obsession to duty at times is bereft of logic. Vijay, over the years, has built up a wall within himself against his father since the incident when he was kidnapped as a child and his father refused to negotiate with his kidnappers (who were demanding release of one of their key men). Vijay grows up with an utter contempt for his father and his profession, as he nurtures a hurt that the only person who had every power to save him was his father who refused to negotiate with the kidnapers to save him. Vijay, apparently, is never told about his father's clamping down on the kidnappers, minutes after he himself had escaped from their hold. The

Dilip Kumar and Amitabh Bachchan: The Historical Histrionic Jugalbandi

alienated parties thus established, Ramesh Sippy uses their confrontation scenes with superb calculation, aiming at the total emotional involvement of the audience in them. The awestruck cinemagoers watch the father-son duo strike dramatic postures, hear their taut and spiteful exchanges and sense their despair at their inability to reach out to each other. Meanwhile, Sheetal, DCP Ashwini's wife and Vijay's mother, trying to lubricate the father-son friction with her ever moist eyes, underlines the deep–seated conflict and its causative factors. Vijay takes up a job in a hotel and as coincidences go, it is owned by a smuggler. Expectedly, DCP Ashwini orders Vijay to leave the job or leave home. Vijay, with his hatred for the law, leaves with only one comment, 'Name one profession in this country, where there is no corruption, including your own, and I'll take it.' DCP Ashwini's classic rejoinder to Vijay is the famous dialogue, *'Mujhe is baat ka afsos nahin ki tumne badtameezi ki, dukh to is baat ka hai ki tumhare khayalat kitne wahiyat aur ghatiya hain'* (I don't rue that you misbehaved, but the fact that your thinking is so useless and rotten). The final rupture comes when Vijay is hauled up in a murder frame-up in spite of him pleading not guilty before his father. When the same smuggler bails him out, the father gets hurt watching his son slip away. A defeated, tearful DCP Ashwini tells his wife, 'I saw my son being bought away like he was a piece in an auction sale.' The film is randomly punctuated with action of the finest technique, and superb camera work. A sample is the scene in which Vijay escapes from the police jeep and does a split second crossing in front of a speeding train. Later Vijay chases the villain (Amrish Puri), his mother's killer, and shoots him down at point–blank range in one of the most thrilling climatic action sequences of the film, only to be shot by his own father and die in his arms.

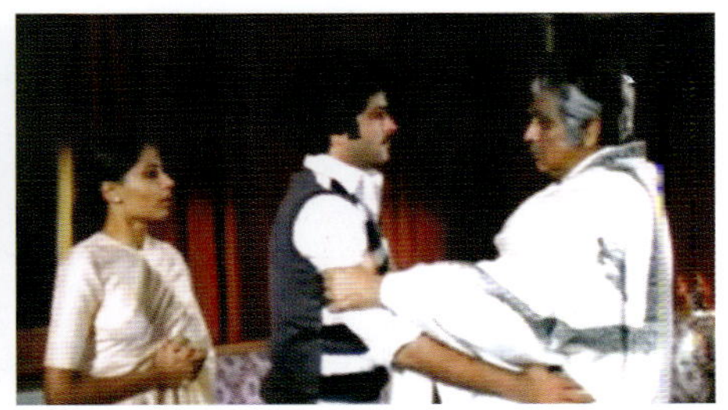

Stills from Shakti

The movie had a tremendous public response from all over India and a record opening at Minerva Theatre (Bombay). A major event was that the Indian Academy of Motion Picture Arts and Sciences organised a premiere of the film at the Minerva on 30 September 1982. Virtually the entire film industry attended the gala premiere and the guests were welcomed by G.P. Sippy, F.C. Mehra (who owned Minerva) and producers Mushir–Riaz. Dilip Kumar's close friend, contemporary and arch rival (as a leading man in cinema), Raj Kapoor also attended the premiere and was deeply impressed with the movie and the performance of Dilip Saheb. He sent a large bouquet of flowers to Dilip Saheb with a note 'Once a king always a king'. Dilip Kumar was very touched. The movie celebrated a housefull silver jubilee at the Minerva.

Premiere and Posters of Shakti

With *Shakti*, its music director R.D. Burman, after having scored music for numerous Dev Anand films and a couple of Raj Kapoor films (*Dharam Karam* and *Naukari*), joined the elite club of composers—S.D. Burman, Shankar–Jaikishan, C. Ramchandra, Salil Chowdhury, O.P. Nayyar, Kalyanji–Anandji and Laxmikant-Pyarelal—who had composed music for the movies of 'The Trinity' of Dilip Kumar, Dev Anand and Raj Kapoor). R.D. came up with some interesting songs such as *Humne sanam kokhat likha* (Lata), *Maangi thi ek dua jo qabool ho gayi* (Mahendra Kapoor) and *Jaane kaise kab kahan* (Lata–Kishore). *Shakti* is a landmark in the illustrious career of thespian Dilip Kumar.

DATE / YEAR OF RELEASE: 03 DECEMBER 1982
BANNER / PRODUCER: TRIMURTI FILMS / GULSHAN RAI
DIRECTION: SUBHASH GHAI
MUSIC: KALYANJI–ANANDJI
LYRICS: ANAND BAKSHI
PLAYBACK: LATA MANGESHKAR / KISHORE KUMAR / ASHA BHOSLE / ANURADHA PAUDWAL / SURESH WADKAR / ANWAR / SADHANA SARGAM / HEMLATA / ALKA YAGNIK / KANCHAN / PADMINI KOLHAPURE / SHIVANGI KOLHAPURE
STORY / SCREENPLAY: MUKTA GHAI / SACHIN BHOWMIK
DIALOGUE: KADER KHAN
CINEMATOGRAPHY: KAMLAKAR RAO
EDITING: WAMAN GURU
AUDIOGRAPHY: AKKI SURESHCHANNDRA / KAUSHIK / MANGESH DESAI
CHOREOGRAPHY: SATYANARAYAN
ART: S.S. SAMEL
CAST: DILIP KUMAR / SHAMMI KAPOOR / SANJEEV KUMAR / SANJAY DUTT / PADMINI KOLHAPURE / SARIKA / MADAN PURI / AMRISH PURI / SUDHA SHIV PURI / DR SHRI RAM LAGOO / MADHU MALHOTRA / SURESH OBEROI / TOM ALTER / MANMOUJI / BIRBAL / VIJU KHOTE / JAGDEEP / MUKRI

The year 1982 witnessed a rare feat of two films starring Dilip Kumar in the third phase of his career getting released almost back-to-back. Trimurti Films' *Vidhaata* followed *Shakti* with both the movies hitting the jackpot, the former proving to be a blockbuster. Veteran film financer-distributor Gulshan Rai had funded Ramesh Saigal's Dilip Kumar and Nalini Jaywant starrer *Shikast* way back in 1953 and lost heavily as the film had flopped. Now, a successful producer with films like *Johny Mera Naam* (1970), *Joshila* (1973), *Deewaar* (1975), *Trishul* (1978) under his belt, Gulshan Rai launched an ambitious multi-starrer *Vidhaata*, with Dilip Kumar in the pivotal central role with Shammi Kapoor, Sanjeev Kumar, Sanjay Dutt, Padmini Kolhapure, Amrish Puri, Madan Puri, etc. Director Yash Chopra, who until then was a common feature of Trimurti Films, surprisingly was not directing this big-budget extravaganza and Subhash Ghai helmed the film. Another surprise was the fact that the script was not penned by Salim–Javed, Trimurti Films, regulars, but Sachin Bhowmik. The narrative was loosely inspired by the iconic *Godfather.* Dilip Kumar rendered a towering performance lending suave sophistication and rare human credibility to the character of Shobhraj, the underworld don. It was a mesmerisingly underplayed exposition of cold-blooded ruthlessness. On the other hand, the thespian was at his best in portraying the tormented grandfather overtly concerned about his grandson. Another notable feature of *Vidhaata* was its casting—the 'Rebel Star' Shammi Kapoor fulfilled his lifetime ambition of working with Dilip Kumar whereas Sanjeev Kumar got yet another chance to cross histrionic swords with the thespian. Shammi Kapoor and Sanjeev Kumar were brilliant in their roles too. Padmini Kolhapure was vivacious and exuded the desired oomph demanded by her role. Sanjay Dutt, then at the threshold of his career, got the opportunity to be exposed to some high power histrionics.

Dilip in Vidhaata

Scenes from Vidhaata

The story was about Shamsher Singh (Dilip Kumar), a locomotive driver whose life centred around family, work and dear friend and co-driver (Shammi Kapoor). His son (Suresh Oberoi), a police inspector, is killed by a smuggler don (Amrish Puri) while his daughter-in-law (Seema Dev) dies after giving birth to a son. Shamsher protects his grandson Kunal (Sanjay Dutt) at all costs and gives him a life of comfort. He saves a mafia don (Dr Shriram Lagoo) from his hunters and the grateful don takes him under his wings. In due course, Shamsher inherits the mafia empire of his benefactor don, and becomes very wealthy. To avoid Kunal growing up in an environment of crime, Shamsher (now known as Shobhraj) places him in the care of a close confidant, Abu Baba (Sanjeev Kumar). As Kunal grows up, he falls in love with a poor village belle

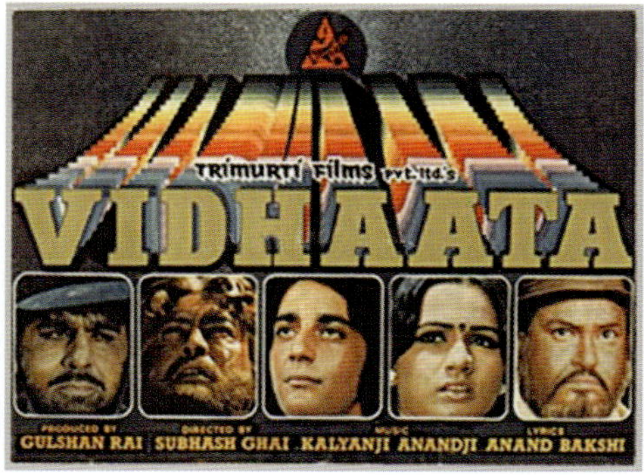

(Padmini Kolhapure) who Shobhraj does not approve of. The ensuing confrontation between the grandfather and the grandson forms the crux of the narrative leading to a spectacular climax. Confrontational scenes between Dilip Kumar and Amrish Puri, the utterly fascinating Dilip Kumar–Shammi Kapoor banters and the scenes of conflicting principles between Dilip Kumar and Sanjeev Kumar were a treat to watch. The movie was completed in a record time of thirteen months and went on to become a super-duper hit, celebrating jubilee runs at the Roxy Cinema (Mumbai) and many centres all over India. Shammi Kapoor won the Filmfare Award for Best Supporting Actor for his performance in the film.

Dilip Kumar's emerging favourites Kalyanji–Anandji, who are also involved with some of the most successful Gulshan Rai films like *Johnny Mera Naam, Tridev,* etc., were entrusted with the music of the film and the duo did conjure up a hit musical score. There were many songs which became chartbusters in those times including *Saat saheliyan khadi khadi* (Kishore Kumar-Alka Yagnik-Sadhana Sargam-Anuradha Paudwal-Hemlata-Kanchan) with seductive impish under tones, *Haathon ki band lakeeron ka* (Suresh Wadkar-Anwar), *Udi baba udi baba* (Asha Bhosle), *Pyar ka imtihaan* (Asha Bhosle) and *O saathiya* (Lata Mangeshkar). Anand Bakshi penned the lyrics for the film.

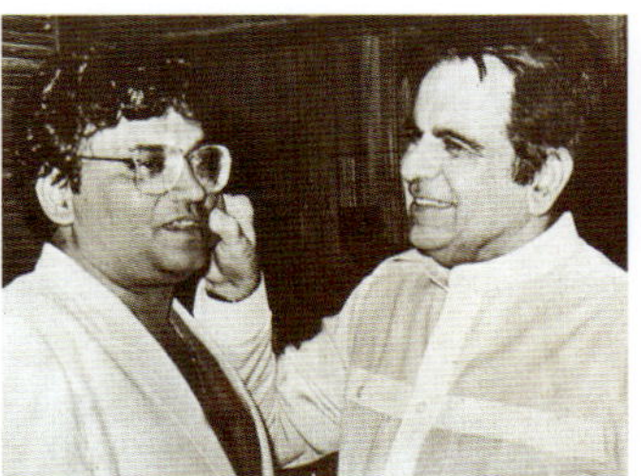

On the Sets of Vidhaata

DATE / YEAR OF RELEASE: 1983
BANNER / PRODUCER: B.R. FILMS / B.R. CHOPRA
DIRECTION: RAVI CHOPRA
MUSIC: R.D. BURMAN
LYRICS: HASAN KAMAAL
PLAYBACK: ASHA BHOSLE / MAHENDRA KAPOOR / CHANDRASHEKHAR GADGIL / HARIHARAN / SALMA AGHA
STORY / SCREENPLAY: SATISH BHATNAGAR / C.J. PAVRI
DIALOGUE: SATISH BHATNAGAR / HASAN KAMAAL
CINEMATOGRAPHY: DHARAM CHOPRA
EDITING: S.B. MANE
ART: SHANTI DAS
CAST: DILIP KUMAR / NANDA / RAJ BABBAR / PADMINI KOLHAPURE / RATI AGNIHOTRI / RAJ KIRAN / SURESH OBEROI / MADAN PURI / JOHNY WALKER / YUNUS PARVEZ / IFTEKHAR / NAZIR HUSSAIN / AMAR / JAGDISH RAJ / SUNIL DHAWAN / R.S. CHOPRA / RAJESH PURI / ARUN BAKSHI / DINESH ANAND / HASAN KAMAAL

Veteran director-producer B.R. Chopra and thespian Dilip Kumar forged a lifelong friendship, as they worked together on *Naya Daur* (1957), *Dastaan* (1972) and later during the planning of shelved magnum opus 'Chanakya Chandragupta' and beyond. When Chopra Saheb's son Ravi Chopra began direction with films like *Zameer* and *The Burning Train*, the father was keen to have the son work with Dilip Kumar and recreate the magic of *Naya Daur*. Dilip Saheb readily agreed to the proposal. The B.R. Films' story department, led by Satish Bhatnagar and C.J. Pawari, worked out a script based on the concept that 'every mill/industrial worker has a right to share the fruits of his sweat

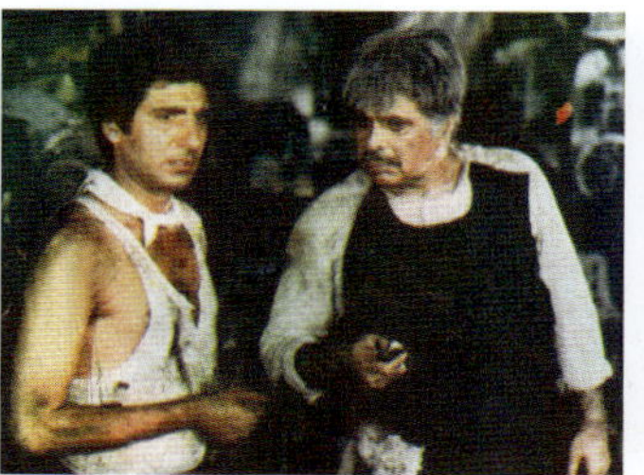

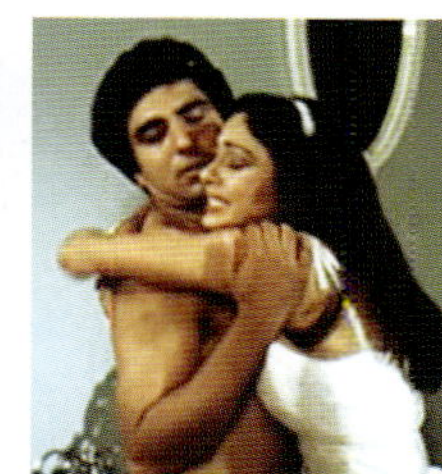

Scenes from Mazdoor

and blood and the wealth accrued there from' coupled with a family tussle which became the film, *Mazdoor* starring Dilip Kumar, Nanda, Raj Babbar, Rati Agnihotri, Padmini Kolhapure, et al. Consummate artist Nanda fulfilled her desire of working with Dilip which she coveted. But, the son could not create a compelling drama which his father was known for and the film proved to be a damp squib at the box office.

Dilip Kumar with Ravi Chopra

The story revolved around the mill worker Dinanath Saxena or Dinu Kaka (Dilip Kumar) and his family. The film tried to put together a rambling narrative of diverse threads such as emotional conflicts within the protagonist's family, unrest among millworkers, their dreams of a corporate utopia, and the subsequent labour-management conflict, etc. The film's central theme of the capitalists giving the workers their due rights somehow got lost in the maze of plots and sub-plots which crammed the screenplay. Dinanath has a devoted wife Radha (Nanda), a devoted daughter Meena (Padmini Kolhapure), an adopted protégé Ashok (Raj Babbar) and an idler son Ramesh (Raj Kiran) who is jealous of Ashok. The mill for which Dinu Kaka and his close friends Govinda (Johny Walker) and Yunus (Yunus Parvez) work is an epitome of perfect industrial relations due to the kind-hearted approach of its owner Seth Sinha (Nazir Husain). After Seth passes away, his son Hiralal Sinha (Suresh Oberoi) takes over. Foreign-educated Hiralal starts exploiting the workers and things come to a head when a worker dies on duty but the family is denied compensation. Dinu Kaka organises a protest and a strike in the mill and is dismissed by Hiralal. A philanthropist Kundan Lal Batra (Iftekhar), who is impressed by Dinanath's honesty and upright commitments, helps him set up his own business and in a short time Dinu Kaka's business (with the assistance of Ashok) flourishes. Batra's daughter Smita is in love with Ashok whereas Dinu's daughter Meena also is in love with Ashok. Indebted to Dinanath, Ashok marries Meena much to the chagrin of Smita. Seeking revenge Smita marries Dinu's son Ramesh and family melodrama ensues. Ramesh, envious of Ashok, joins hands with villainous Daulatram (Madan Puri) to sabotage his own father's business. After many twists and turns, the good triumphs over

Dilip Kumar as Dinu Kaka

evil and the conflicts are happily resolved. The film targeted emulating the grand success of *Naya Daur* and even borrowed some sequences and dialogue but the scattered script proved its undoing. Dilip Kumar towered over the film once again delivering a tour de force performance with able support from Nanda, Raj Babbar, Rati Agnihotri and Padmini Kolhapure. Reportedly, Dilip Saheb wanted to opt out of the film but B.R. Chopra persuaded him not to do so. The film was released at the Naaz Theatre in Mumbai with a bumper opening but could not sustain the initials.

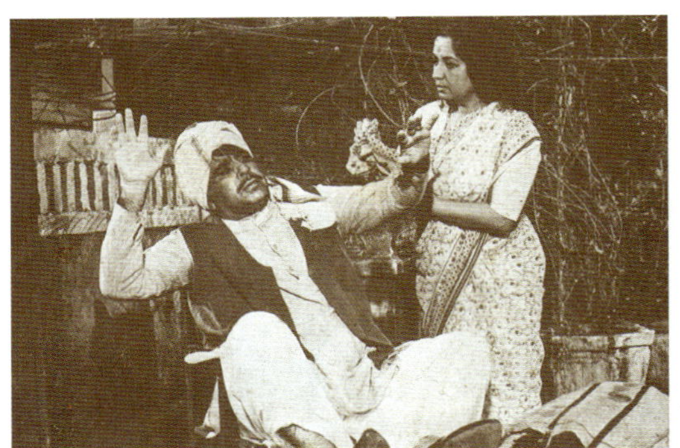

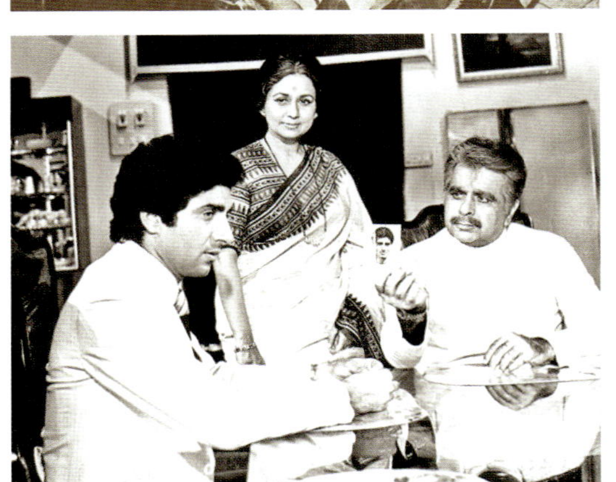

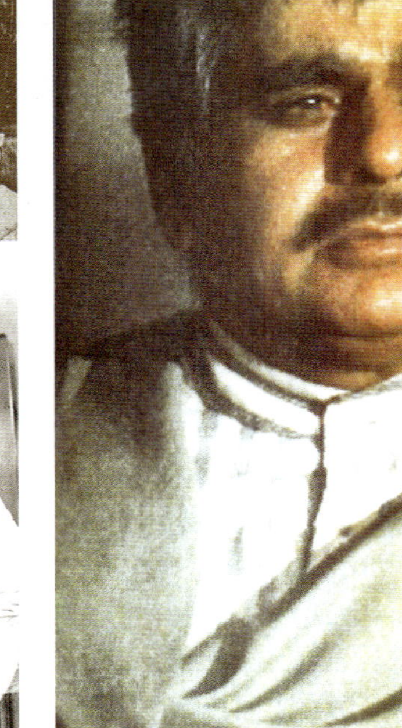

Stills from Mazdoor

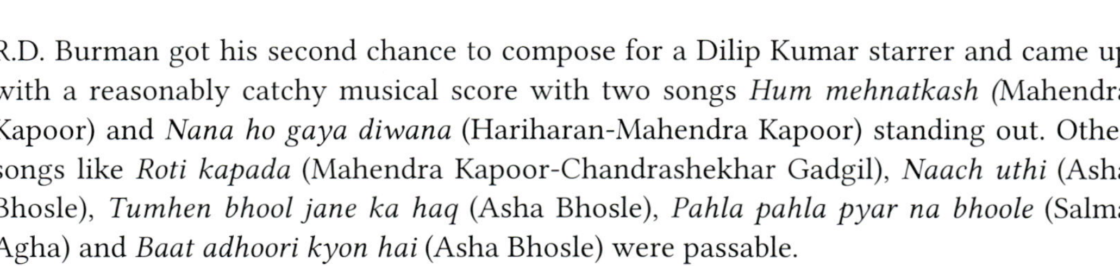

R.D. Burman got his second chance to compose for a Dilip Kumar starrer and came up with a reasonably catchy musical score with two songs *Hum mehnatkash* (Mahendra Kapoor) and *Nana ho gaya diwana* (Hariharan-Mahendra Kapoor) standing out. Other songs like *Roti kapada* (Mahendra Kapoor-Chandrashekhar Gadgil), *Naach uthi* (Asha Bhosle), *Tumhen bhool jane ka haq* (Asha Bhosle), *Pahla pahla pyar na bhoole* (Salma Agha) and *Baat adhoori kyon hai* (Asha Bhosle) were passable.

DATE / YEAR OF RELEASE: 09 FEBRUARY 1984
BANNER / PRODUCER: YASH RAJ FILMS / YASH CHOPRA
DIRECTION: YASH CHOPRA
MUSIC: HRUDAYNATH MANGESHKAR
LYRICS: JAVED AKHTAR
PLAYBACK: LATA MANGESHKAR / MAHENDRA KAPOOR / KISHORE KUMAR / SURESH WADKAR / ANOOP JALOTA / A. HARIHARAN / SHAILENDRA SINGH
STORY / SCREENPLAY: JAVED AKHTAR
DIALOGUE: JAVED AKHTAR
CINEMATOGRAPHY: KAY GEE
EDITING: KESHAV NAIDU
ACTION: RAVI DEWAN
ART: SUDHENDU ROY

CAST: DILIP KUMAR / WAHEEDA REHMAN / ANIL KAPOOR / RATI AGNIHOTRI / MADAN PURI / AMRISH PURI / SAEED JAFRI / MOHAN AGASHE / NILU PHULE / GULSHAN GROVAR

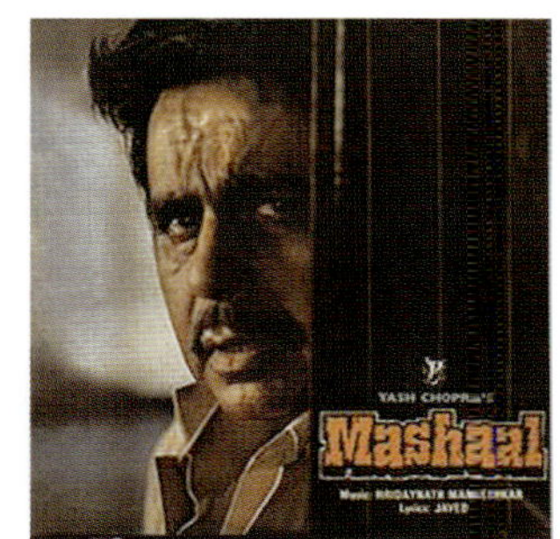

From the days of making of *Naya Daur,* renowned director-producer Yash Chopra struck a close friendship with Dilip Kumar. Yash Chopra was then assisting his brother B.R. Chopra in *Naya Daur,* and later himself directed big films like *Dhool Ka Phool* (1959), *Dharmputra* (1961), *Waqt* (1965), *Ittefaq* (1969), *Daag* (1973), *Kabhi Kabhie* (1976), *Trishul* (1978), *Kaala Patthar* (1979), *Silsila* (1981), et al. He, however, harboured a keen desire to direct the thespian in his own home production. The desire was fulfilled when Yash*ji* signed up Dilip Saheb to play the role of an honest journalist in *Mashaal.* It was a role of a fiery investigative journalist who discovers a network of crime on the part of a respectable industrialist. After publishing his report, he finds that his life is in danger and begins to live in a slum with an urchin whom he has reformed. Facing numerous trials and tribulations due to which he even loses his wife, the journalist seeks revenge by turning into a dreaded don. The role fascinated Dilip Saheb and he took ten days to study the bound script before giving the nod to Yash Chopra. Interestingly, Dilip Saheb's heroine of three earlier films, Waheeda Rehman, was cast as his wife. Then young and upcoming actor Anil Kapoor got the dream role of the urchin lad with Rati Agnihotri romantically paired with him. Javed Akhtar wrote the script and dialogues of the movie.

Dilip Kumar and Waheed Rehman in Mashaal

The theme of the well-made *Mashaal* was the moral rise and fall of a crusading journalist, Vinod Kumar Malhotra (Dilip Kumar). Resigning from a senior journalist's post because the editor (Nitin Sethi) wants him to change an article attacking the criminal, S.K. Vardhan (Amrish Puri), Malhotra is compelled to shift to a gang-haunted *basti* (settlement). This is a journey in the middle of life for Malhotra and his wife Sudha (Waheeda Rehman). They adjust to the new, ugly, dangerous surroundings, and start an investigative paper with the help of a friendly broker (Saeed Jaffrey) and an idealistic woman reporter, Geeta (Rati Agnihotri). At this point, the film changes track to tackle its second theme, that is, the reform of the goons led by Raja (Anil Kapoor). Malhotra tames the toughs and practically adopts Raja. The Raja–Geeta romantic affiliations also begin promisingly and Raja is sent to Bangalore for further studies. Meanwhile, Malhotra's fortunes take a tumble. Hurt by an attack in Malhotra's paper, Vardhan forecloses the mortgage on Malhotra's home and office, after having set fire to his press. Driven into the street with his possessions, Malhotra suffers a tragedy when Sudha dies on the street. Malhotra's desperate cries fetch no help. In the second half, the crusading journalist becomes an avenging angel. 'After interval, the teams change not only sides but goals,' says a bitter Malhotra. In an amazing transformation, he becomes a bigger 'Godfather' than Vardhan, and sets up his own gambling-bootlegging chain. Raja now returns from Bangalore, joins a communist paper and is stunned when Geeta tells him about the sea change in his 'Saheb'. 'Fight me, expose me,' says the unperturbed 'Saheb'. There is a kind of dialectic Monte Cristo fable in this story.

Mashaal: The Creative Team

Dilip Kumar, Anil Kapoor and Rati Agnihotri in Mashaal

The film and his performance won rave reviews across the board from the reviewers. Excerpts from Iqbal Masud's review in *The Indian Express* read: **'Yash Chopra's *Mashaal* is a brilliant, marvellously watchable, melodrama in the first half–the best thing Yash Chopra has ever done. If the film gradually disintegrates in the second half, it is not only because, Yash Chopra, perhaps suddenly apprehensive that the film is too "serious", plays to about half a dozen galleries at once... All the same, it remains a film to be seen. This is one of Dilip's great efforts–I would place it higher than *Shakti's* because of its wider dimension. There are interesting touches–Dilip shooting goal, playing with the gang et al–the old throw-away humour, the flashes of fury, are back. There is something new–helpless, beaten, vulnerable pleading–an unbearably poignant scene with Dilip, lost and desolate in the heart of Mumbai at night, fighting to save Waheeda's life. He repeats this later to Anil Kapoor ('when you expose me, write in this too') and it is fascinating to see this slightly off the groove repetition stand up in its own right. Waheeda is excellent as the wife who bears up–a decent performance. Rati comes on and off but I liked her for the first time after *Ayaash*. Amrish Puri remains a caricature villain–but he is exceedingly watchable here. A splendid debut (in a big role) by Anil Kapoor as the slums' lost kid is laudable. When he recounts his parents' death, he is just right. And he is the first actor to stand up to and match Dilip at his best.'**

On the Sets of Mashaal

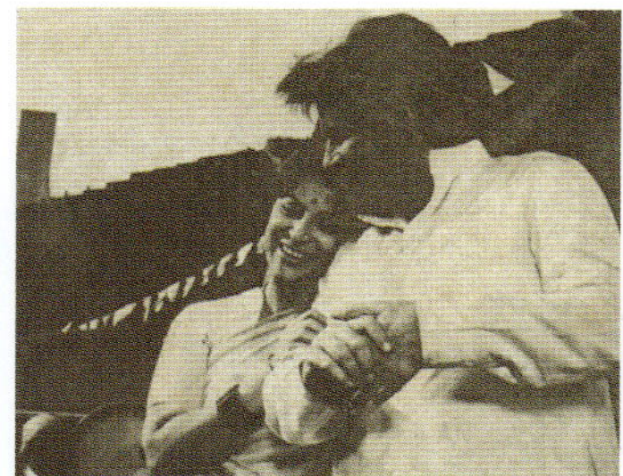

Stills from Mashaal

Dilip in Mashaal

Reviewer Khalid Mohammed in his praise for the film was also effusive and an excerpt from his review read: **'Dilip Kumar after *Shakti* is masterly: the very nakedness of acting. His journalist isn't a beaming hero but a battered veteran, stubborn and shambling. Caught in a corner, his voice is as tormented as the neigh of a battle-maddened charger. Truly, he's one of the few living actors who has shown us the mystery and power of which cinema is capable. All the grand unplayable part should be open to him after this: as long as you can see that great jaw sag, those lion eyes search for solace. Also Anil Kapoor's natural exuberance is consistently likeable.'**

Yash Chopra had said that Dilip Kumar's performance in *Mashaal* represents a textbook on acting with the high point being the awe-inspiring night scene on the South Mumbai streets when a desperate and helpless Dilip Kumar pleads with every passing car to take his dying wife to the hospital. *Mashaal* undoubtedly is another great milestone in Dilip Kumar's career. The movie raised tremendous public expectations and had a bumper opening with a gala premiere at the Metro Cinema in Mumbai on 9 February 1986. The film, however, was only a moderate box-office success. The reasons perhaps were the grim narrative and the screenplay not being able to sustain the tempo of one-third of the film towards the end.

The Awe-Inspiring Scene

Scenes from Mashaal

Mashaal: The creative team

There comes a time in the life of every genuine filmmaker (though their tribe is decreasing) when he looks within, takes stock of his situation, the work he has done, the work he still has to do. Then he looks out and around and finally takes a 'bold, brave and timely' step. Yash Chopra's that 'bold, brave and timely' step was *Mashaal* which told the story of an honest journalist who fights a one-man war against all wrong for change in a city corrupted to the core. Yash*ji* had called the film 'a major milestone' in his career. *Mashaal* had a theme that was as timely as it is today, and a talented cast that was much more than just being stars. Yash*ji*'s casting of Dilip Kumar, the actor who loved challenging roles, as 'the most daring and striking role of the intrepid journalist' was the tour de force of the movie.

The film was extensively shot (forty days uninterrupted shooting stint) on a grand set erected by art director Sudhendu Roy showing a sprawling slum colony in which major portion of the filming took place. One of the visitors struck by the realistic 'slum' was the noted American film director Robert Wise. He was so impressed by the set, which he first thought was an actual location that he insisted on going around. Another interesting aspect of *Mashaal* is that the film was shot in a start-to-finish schedule which is commendable as no producer had ever attempted such fast-track filming with stars like Dilip Kumar.

Visitors and Shooting on the Imposing Set Erected at the Rajkamal Studios

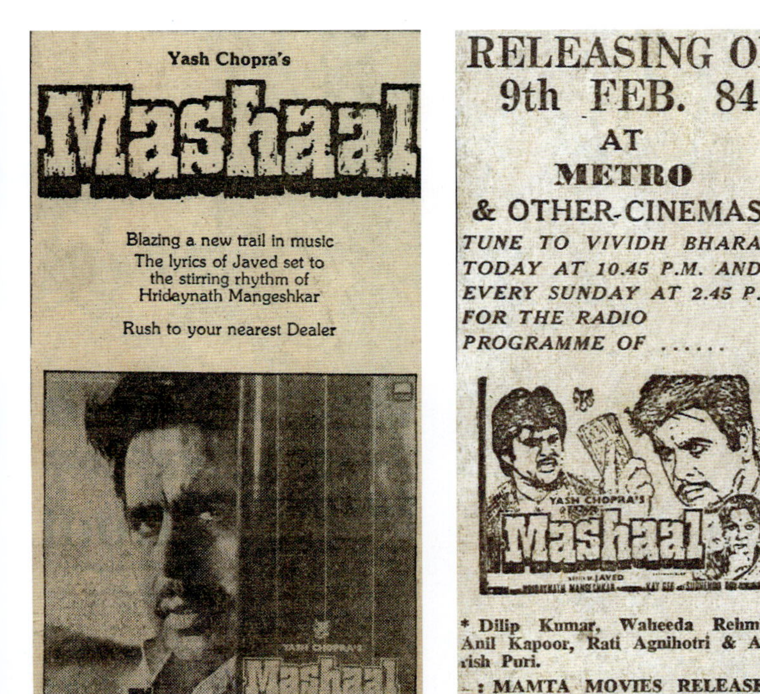

The Metro Premiere

Music Release of Mashaal

Dilip Kumar and Lata Mangeshkar always shared a brother–sister relationship, and it was on her recommendation that Dilip Saheb got her brother Hridaynath Mangeshkar to compose the music of *Mashaal.* His music could have been catchier, still it passed muster with songs like *Mujhe tum yaad karna* (Lata Mangeshkar-Kishore Kumar), *Foot-pathon ke hum* (Anup Jalota-Hariharan-Suresh Wadkar-Shailendra Singh), *Holi ayee re* (Lata Mangeshkar-Kishore Kumar-Mahendra Kapoor), *Om namah shivaye* (Lata Mangeshkar), *Zindagi aa raha hoon main* (Lata Mangeshkar-Kishore Kumar) and *Zindagi aa raha hoon main* (Kishore Kumar). But it was the *Holi ayee re* song inspired by an earlier Hridaynath composition *Jambhul piklya jhadakhali* from *Jait Re Jait* (1977) became most popular.

Mashaal would definitely figure among the landmark films of Dilip Kumar and is a delight to watch even in current times.

DUNIYA

DATE / YEAR OF RELEASE: 18 SEPTEMBER 1984
BANNER / PRODUCER: DHARMA PRODUCTIONS PVT. LTD. / YASH JOHAR
DIRECTION: RAMESH TALWAR
MUSIC: R.D. BURMAN
LYRICS: JAVED AKHTAR
PLAYBACK: LATA MANGESHKAR / KISHORE KUMAR / ASHA BHOSLE
STORY / SCREENPLAY: JAVED AKHTAR
DIALOGUE: JAVED AKHTAR
CINEMATOGRAPHY: JAL MISTRY / JEHANGIR CHOWDHURY
EDITING: WAMAN BHOSLE / GURUDUTT SHIRALI
ART: SUBHENDU ROY
AUDIOGRAPHY: JAGMOHAN ANAND
CAST: ASHOK KUMAR / DILIP KUMAR / RISHI KAPOOR / AMRITA SINGH / PREM CHOPRA / AMRISH PURI / PRAN / SAIRA BANU (SPECIAL APPEARANCE) / SULBHA DESHPANDE / SATYEN KAPPU / MAC MOHAN / JAVED KHAN / ARVIND DESHPANDE / DHUMAL / BABY PUJA / MASTER RINKU / PRADEEP KUMAR / KULBHUSHAN KHARBANDA / OM PURI (GUEST APPEARANCE)

Ace production controller Yash Johar, who had worked with stalwarts like Dev Anand, Sunil Dutt, etc., had branched off to float his own production house called Dharma Productions. Its maiden production was the super hit *Dostana*, starring Amitabh Bachchan, Shatrughan Sinha and Zeenat Aman. Currently the banner of Dharma Productions is one of the premiere production houses in the country managed by the director son of the founder, Karan Johar. Like others, Yash Johar too wanted to make a multi-starrer in the early 1980s with top-notch actors like Ashok Kumar, Dilip Kumar, etc. He fulfilled his ambition by launching *Duniya* (1984) with great performers Ashok Kumar, Dilip Kumar, Rishi Kapoor, Amrita Singh, Pran, Prem Chopra, Amrish Puri, Kulbhushan Kharbanda, et al. The film was based on the age-old storyline of *The Count of Monte Cristo* and was scripted by Javed Akhtar. Dilip Saheb was fascinated by the role and accepted to play it, greatly enthused that he would get yet another chance to work with the great Ashok Kumar. Saira Banu made a special appearance as Dilip Kumar's wife. The direction was assigned to Ramesh Talwar, a member of Indian People's Theatre Association, and director of films like *Doosra Aadmi* (1977), *Baseraa* (1981), etc. However, the screenplay and dialogue of Javed Akhtar lacked punch and novelty and the plot of the movie meandered pointlessly. It was a re-hash of rather stale material and the gamble did not work. The film did not do well at the box office.

Dilip Kumar's character in the film was of a man who believes in doing all that is right and truthful. His values make a gang of three work against him. He is wronged and harmed till he can bear no longer and fights back. Dilip Kumar played the role with his trademark measured approach to once again render captivatingly effective underplayed performance. Ashok Kumar was his usual effortless self but did not have much to do in the film, as was the case with the array of top villains in the movie. The romantic pair of Rishi Kapoor and Amrita Singh was charming.

Dilip Kumar in Duniya

The story begins when Mohan Kumar (Dilip Kumar) is released from jail after a 14-year sentence, recalling the happiness he lost when his good friend Pradeep Kumar hired him to look after his business affairs. Too honest for his own good, Mohan falls afoul of the three scoundrels who have been robbing their employer with the connivance of his evil brother-in-law (Satyen Kappoo). The roles of the three scoundrels were played by Pran (who fancies himself as a '*Haathi*', an elephant), Prem Chopra and Amrish Puri as his (as the two '*Machchars*', mosquitoes). The gang of scoundrels have killed Pradeep, and pinned the crime on Dilip and think they have got away with it. Brooding in prison, the victim plans to get even when he gets out, for the wrongs done to him—the false charge of murder, the death of his beloved wife (Saira Banu) and the separation from his small son. Old don Puri (Ashok Kumar), a fellow prisoner who owes his life to

Mohan's courage, is prepared to pay his debt at all costs and provides stout support to him. While Mohan hunts out his betrayers, his first link-up with the past comes when he is able to rescue the nubile daughter (Amrita Singh) of his dead friend, the man he was accused of killing. Out in the city, his young son Ravi (Rishi Kapoor) is brought up by a faithful domestic servant couple. He lives on his wits and makes a living by picking pockets and cardsharping. Ravi is hired by the scoundrel trios to keep an eye on Mohan, using his romantic affiliation with Roma (Amrita). The son spies on father and even tries to kill him, only to become beholden to the older man for saving his life. Reels and much skulduggery later, Mohan has the 'Haathi' on his knees begging for mercy, having managed to eliminate the two 'Machchars'. The film ends on a happy note with all the villains eliminated and Mohan's vendetta completed. This was a familiar theme previously used in Rajshri Productions' Dharmendra and Rakhee starrer *Jeevan Mrityu* (1970) directed by Satyen Bose, and a few other films. The writer's inability to infuse the picture with freshness and surprise elements proved to be its bane, regardless of the star value and competent performance. Even thespians of the stature of Ashok Kumar and Dilip Kumar were helpless in salvaging a pointless plot which was nothing better than a trite tale of clichés strung together like beads to make a briefly colourful bauble.

Dilip and the 'Scoundrels'

Stills from Duniya

R.D. Burman's third Dilip starrer musical score was passable. The songs penned by Javed Akhtar included *Tu chand nagar ki shehzadi* (Kishore Kumar), *Duniya bahut hi kamaal hai* (Kishore Kumar), *Gehre halke halke gehre* (Lata Mangeshkar-Kishore Kumar), *Teri meri zindagi pyar bhari zindagi* (Asha Bhosle) and *Jhoomti raat jawan* (Kishore Kumar-Asha Bhosle-Mahendra Kapoor). Staleness was perhaps beginning to creep in the music of the much-in-demand and over-worked R.D. Burman.

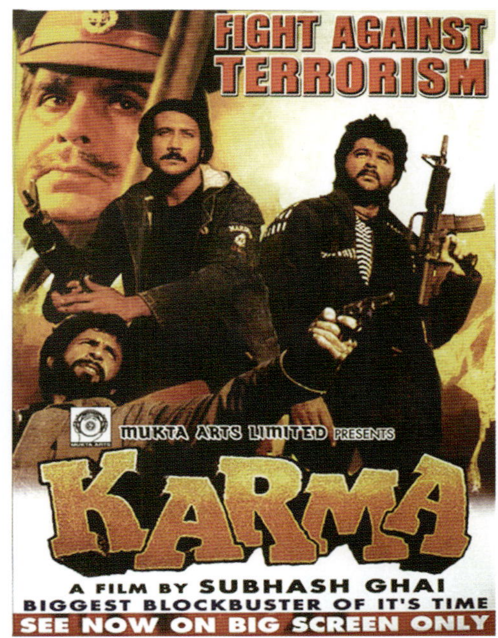

DATE / YEAR OF RELEASE: 8 AUGUST 1986
BANNER / PRODUCER: MUKTA ARTS PVT. LTD. / SUBHASH GHAI
DIRECTION: SUBHASH GHAI
MUSIC: LAKSHMIKANT–PYARELAL
LYRICS: ANAND BAKSHI
PLAYBACK: KISHORE KUMAR / KAVITA KRISHNAMURTHY / ANURADHA PAUDWAL / MOHD. AZIZ / MANHAR UDHAS / MAHENDRA KAPOOR / DILIP KUMAR
STORY: SUBHASH GHAI
SCREENPLAY: SACHIN BHOWMIK
DIALOGUE: KADER KHAN
CINEMATOGRAPHY: KAMALAKAR RAO
EDITING: WAMAN BHOSLE / GURUDUTT SHIRALI
ART: SUDHENDU ROY
CAST: DILIP KUMAR / NUTAN / SRIDEVI / DARA SINGH / JACKIE SHROFF / ANIL KAPOOR / ANUPAM KHER / NASEERUDDIN SHAH / POONAM DHILLON / SHAKTI KAPOOR / VINOD NAGPAL

Director-producer-writer Subhash Ghai had struck a good rapport with Dilip Saheb during the making of the superhit *Vidhaata* (1982) and was keen to cast the thespian in a multi-starrer magnum opus for his own production house, Mukta Arts. He succeeded in persuading Dilip Kumar to play a pivotal role in his star-studded box-office bonanza *Karma* (1986), in which actress Nutan got the opportunity to do a complete film with the thespian (their last film together 'Shikhwa' in 1953 remained only 98 per cent complete). The movie also had other big stars like Anil Kapoor, Jackie Shroff, Sridevi, Naseeruddin Shah, Poonam Dhillon, Dara Singh, Anupam Kher, etc. and was mounted on the typical lavish scale of Ghai. *Karma* went on to become a tremendous box-office success.

Dilip Kumar in Karma

Dilip Kumar and Nutan in Karma

The 70-mm extravaganza movie was launched with a spectacular mahurat on the auspicious day of Diwali on 24 October 1984 at Mehboob Studios. In keeping with the mammoth venture, the crowds thronged the studio. A voice on the walkie-talkie welcomed the guests–it was Subhash himself. Shammi Kapoor broke the coconut, Sunil Dutt gave the clap, Manmohan Desai switched on the camera and Ramesh Sippy directed the first shot. On the stage, the curtains parted to reveal the technicians involved in the project. Accompanied by the sounds of thunder and lightning, the background on the stage slid away to reveal the top star cast—Dilip Kumar, Naseeruddin Shah, Jackie Shroff, Anil Kapoor and Anupam Kher. They stood with bowed heads as the accompanying music reached a crescendo. The grand finale had the stars raising their hands in farewell, while they were enveloped in the smoke that filtered out from the jail in the background. This impressive affair was followed by a grand celebration at the then popular Sea Rock Hotel (now defunct and demolished).

Dilip with Subhash Ghai

The Spectacular Mahurat

The film's story revolved around the main protagonist Vishwa Pratap Singh (Dilip Kumar), an upright and stern jailor with an immaculate track record of honesty and efficiency. He had a wife (Nutan) and two grown up sons and grandchildren. The jailor though being a disciplinarian was also kind-hearted and caring, but did not brook any political or otherwise interference. The action starts when an international head of a dreaded terrorist network, Dr Dang (Anupam Kher), who is lodged in Singh's jail, misbehaves with the jailor and gets a resounding slap in return. No extra facilities are given to Dr Dang and the rogue plans his escape as well as revenge for the jailor's 'audacity'. One day when the jailor is away, terrorists descend on the jail premises and bomb the entire area, killing most of the inmates and the family of the jailor except his wife, who loses her voice becoming dumbfounded. The jailor and his right-hand man (Dara Singh) are shattered to see the massacre and vow to take revenge and wipe out the terrorist organisation. The jailor resigns from his job and with the help of his minister friend Tripathi*ji* (Vinod Nagpal) recruits three young condemned convicts from three different jails. He takes them to Kashmir and starts training them to assist him in busting the well-equipped terrorist gang. The jailor also assumes a new identity. Among the recruited convicts is Khairuddin Chishti (Naseeruddin Shah), who is a loner. He was tortured and his beloved was killed by the terrorists. Since then, he has been thirsting for their blood. The other two are young criminals who are fun-loving and constantly in a hurry to accomplish things. One is Baiju (Jackie Shroff), who falls in love with Radha (Sridevi), the daughter of Dr Dang's comic lackey who manages a large estate. Another recruit is Johnny (Anil Kapoor) who is chased and wooed by a simple village maiden (Poonam Dhillon) as she believes that he is the man, God has assigned to marry her. Understandably, some of the more enjoyable moments in the film are contributed by Johnny who is shown as a cheerful, rash, witty and sensitive youth and his romantic escapades are as comic as his encounter with the villains. The convicts who are recruited as soldiers for a spell of training to eventually annihilate the terrorist gang indulge in all sorts of frivolous activities and get into brawls and scuffles. The build-up leading to the climax has every *masala* known to Hindi cinema in it, as the former jailor brings the convicts in line to accomplish the onerous national cause of eliminating the terrorists. The film ends on a happy note with Dr Dang and his henchmen being killed, and Johnny and Baiju pardoned to marry their sweethearts. Rana Vishwa Pratap Singh gets his revenge and is lauded for his accomplishment.

Dilip Kumar as the jailor towered above everyone else as he rendered the most impressive performance. Nutan, as the dumbstruck wife, showed what an accomplished actress she was, effortlessly conveying her emotions through just signs and expressions. Anil Kapoor as Johnny gives a truly lovable portrayal making excellent use of the lively situations he is thrown in and the sparkling dialogue he is given to speak. Jackie Shroff as Baiju partners Johnny in most of the crazy situations they get into and seemed to be endowed with everything that a good-looking actor should have. Naseeruddin Shah, as the philosophical melancholy recruit, was quite impressive. The two leading ladies, Sridevi and Poonam Dhillon, were around only because the film has to have some feminine glamour and fill the bill. And who doesn't remember the dangerous Dr Dang (Dilip Saheb had a doctor friend named Dang in Dubai and the thespian himself gave the character's name)! The role, played by then a new actor Anupam Kher, was one of the most powerful villainous characters portrayed on the Indian screen, quite in the league of Gabbar Singh (*Sholay*) and Mogambo (*Mr India*). Dara Singh as Dilip's right-hand man and Shakti Kapoor as his treacherous brother played their roles with the right enthusiasm.

Karma was more than a dream-come-true for the new showman of Hindi film industry–Subhash Ghai. The film had four premieres on 6 August 1986 at Satyam Theatre, Maratha Mandir, New Excelsior and the Metro in Mumbai. Proceeds from the premiers—₹12 lakh—were presented in aid of the Chief Minister's Drought Relief Fund at a function organised by actor-politician Sunil Dutt, MLA Baldev Khosa, Dilip Kumar and Subhash Ghai among others. At the event, the then chief minister of Maharashtra S.B. Chavan thanked Subhash Ghai and his unit for the unique gesture.

Later in the evening, the cast of the film assembled at the Sea Rock Hotel and then a caravan (an air-conditioned bus) with the stars left for the various theatres. Their first stop was the Satyam Theatre at Worli where their entry took the audience by surprise as it was a big moment for them. The next stop was the iconic Maratha Mandir in Mumbai Central. Even as the theatre was full inside, a huge crowd waited for their favourite stars. Then the stars moved to the other two venues. Nutan and Dilip Kumar introduced the stars at all the four theatres.

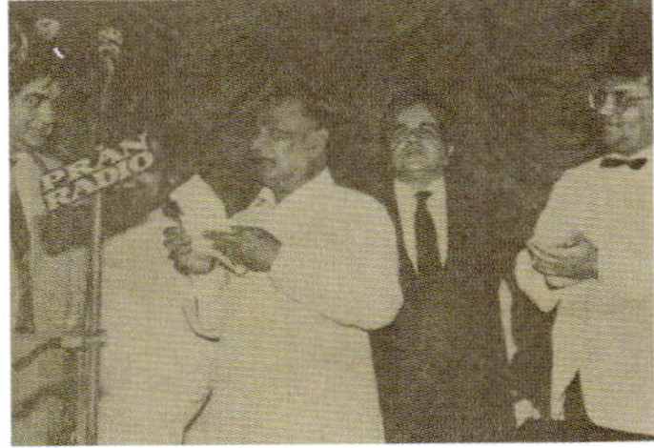

The Multi-theatre Premiere

This film was shot, in 70mm with six track stereophonic sound, at the locations such as Kashmir, Himachal Pradesh and Mumbai (Essel Studio) at a rapid pace in twenty-one reels. The film was a bigger challenge for Subhash Ghai as video piracy had become a menace leading to a drop in footfalls at cinema halls. But *Karma* got the audiences back to the theatres with 'Housefull' signs at most of the halls where it was showing. The movie was a huge success at the box office. The film's song *Aye watan tere liye* is still considered to be one of the most patriotic songs. The movie celebrated silver jubilees at multiple theatres all over India, including the iconic Maratha Mandir in Mumbai.

Music directors Laxmikant–Pyarelal and lyricist Anand Bakshi come up with a hit musical score for *Karma,* topped by the evergreen patriotic number *Dil diya hai jaan bhi denge, aye watan tere liye* (Mohammed Aziz-Kavita Krishnamurthy; and another version with Dilip Kumar's voice). The others popular songs included the title track *Mera karma too, mera dharma too* (Mohammed Aziz-Anuradha Paudwal), *De daru, de daru, o mere bhaiya de daru* (Kishore Kumar-Manhar Udhas-Mahendra Kapoor), *Maahi naa jaaiyo parades mein* (Anuradha Paudwal-Mohammed Aziz), *Aye muhabbat teri dastan ke liye* (Anuradha Paudwal-Mohammed Aziz), *Sajanaan ve, aa bhar de meri maang piyaa* (Anuradha Paudwal-Manhar Udhas), *Sajana ve sajana ve sajana* (Anuradha Paudwal). But it was Dilip Kumar's teaser *Poochhe meri biwi, do you love me?* for Nutan took the cake. However, except for the first and last named song, rest of the music did not have any lasting appeal.

The Music Team

Scenes from Karma

DATE / YEAR OF RELEASE: 1986
BANNER / PRODUCER: GOPI KRISHNA MOVIES
DIRECTION: K. RAGHAVENDRA RAO
MUSIC: BAPPI LAHIRI
LYRICS: INDIVAR / RAJENDRA KRISHNA
PLAYBACK: KISHORE KUMAR / ASHA BHOSLE / S. JANAKI / SHABBIR KUMAR / MOHD. AZIZ
STORY: PARUCHURI BROTHERS (BASED ON FILM "*BABBULI BRAHMANNA*")
SCREENPLAY: RAJENDRA KRISHNA
DIALOGUE: RAJENDRA KRISHNA
CINEMATOGRAPHY: K.S. PRAKASH
EDITING: D. VENKATRATNAM
ART: SUDHENDU ROY
CHOREOGRAPHY: SALEEM
CAST: DILIP KUMAR / JEETENDRA / SRIDEVI / PRAN / ROHINI HATTANGADI / ANURADHA PATEL / KADER KHAN / SHAKTI KAPOOR / ASRANI / PREETI SAPRU / MAYUR

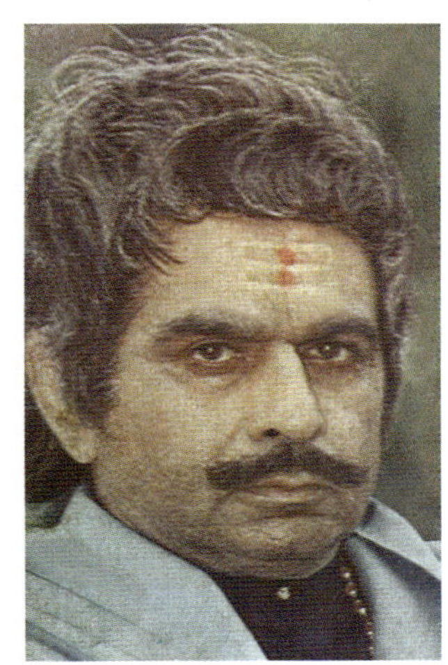

Dilip Kumar is well known for his obsessive selectivity vis-à-vis choice of his roles and the films. It shall, therefore, remain a mystery as to why he accepted a trite film like U.V. Surya Narayan Rao's *Dharm Adhikari,* a Hindi remake of a Telugu hit *Babbuli Brahmanna*–both directed by K. Raghvendra Rao. It was Dilip Saheb's seventh foray down south and perhaps it was the eminent lyricist-writer Rajinder Krishan, an old friend (who scripted the movie) who might have prevailed upon the thespian to act in this film. As such, it was a star-studded film featuring Dilip Kumar, Jeetendra, Sridevi, Pran, Kader Khan, Shakti Kapoor, etc. Theatre artist Rohini Hattangadi played Dilip Kumar's wife. The movie flopped at the box office and did not come anywhere near the lofty standards of Dilipian films. It was a mediocre film from which the thespian should have stayed away.

Scenes from Dharm Adhikari

It was the story of Dharmraj of Nandgaon village (Dilip Kumar), an upright and principled *Sarpanch* (village chief), and his younger brother Prakash (Jeetendra), and their ideological conflict. Sridevi as Priya was Jeetendra's romantic foil. Dilip Saheb rendered Sanskritised dialogues with facile ease and with great impact. He as usual lived his character.

But Dilip Kumar minced no words as he expressed his deep disappointment over the film in print: **'The film had Sanskritised dialogue and I made the effort to learn Sanskrit only for the role. When they started shooting the film, I was promised that it would not have any vulgar comedy. But they went back on their words. Other than my scenes, the picture had such obnoxious comedy.'**

Bappi Lahiri, composing for the first time for a Dilip Kumar starrer, could not come up with anything special. The songs *Ankhe do* (Kishore Kumar-S. Janaki), *Ek to kam zindgani* (Asha Bhosle-Shabbir Kumar), *Mamla gadbad hai* (Kishore Kumar-S. Janaki), *O patthar ke insaan* (Asha Bhosle-Mohammed Aziz) and *Suno suno amar kahani* (Asha Bhosle) did not hit the charts.

KANOON APNA APNA

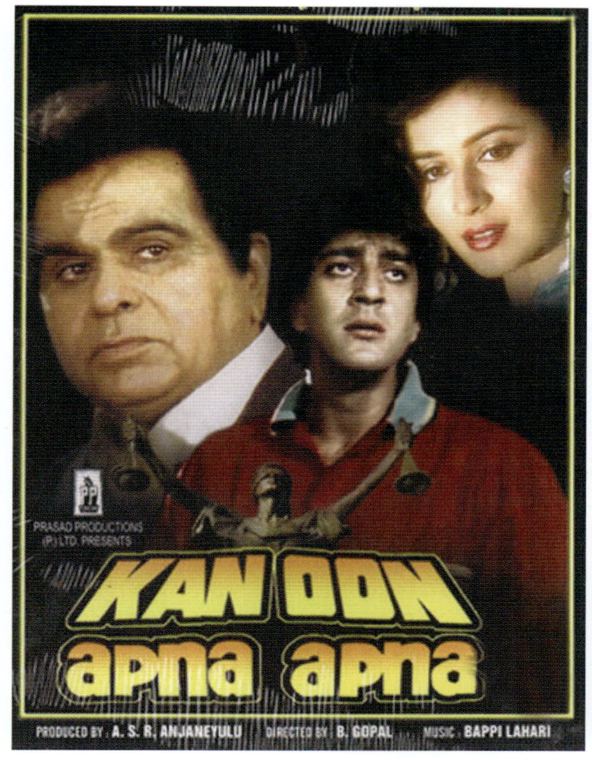

DATE / YEAR OF RELEASE: 27 OCTOBER 1989
BANNER / PRODUCER: MADHAVEE PRODUCTIONS / A.S.R. ANJANEYULU
DIRECTION: B. GOPAL
MUSIC: BAPPI LAHIRI
LYRICS: INDIVAR
PLAYBACK: ASHA BHOSLE / ALKA YAGNIK / S.P. BALASUBRAMANYAM
STORY: PUSHPANAND / K. GANAPATHY RAO
SCREENPLAY: SACHIN BHOWMIK
DIALOGUE: KADER KHAN
CINEMATOGRAPHY: S. GOPAL REDDY
EDITING: V.R. KOTAGIRI
ART: SUDHENDU ROY
CAST: DILIP KUMAR / NUTAN / SANJAY DUTT / MADHURI DIXIT / KADER KHAN / ANUPAM KHER / GULSHAN GROVAR / TEJ SAPRU / SATYEN KAPPU / MAYUR / JAYSHREE GADKAR / MEETHY / PINKY / ABHILASHA / DISCO SHANTI / VIJAYALAKSHMI

Madhavee Productions' *Kanoon Apna Apna,* which was directed by B. Gopal for producer A.S.R. Anjaneyulu, was the next film signed by Dilip Kumar in which Nutan once again essayed the role of his wife. The movie, which also starred Sanjay Dutt and Madhuri Dixit among others, was a purposeful entertainer with histrionic encounters as its highlights. The film managed to sustain interest from the beginning to the end and was a moderate success after being released as a Diwali attraction on 27 October 1989 all over India.

The film is based on the story of District Magistrate Jagat Pratap Singh (Dilip Kumar), who fights the criminal and politician combine of Kabza Kanhaiyalal (Anupam Kher) and Bhushannath Bhadbhole (Kader Khan). He has wife Lakshmi (Nutan), son Ravi (Sanjay Dutt) and two daughters as his family. But his peaceful and principled existence is soon tarnished by his own son who does not hesitate to take the law in his hands. Ravi is in love with Bharathi (Madhuri Dixit). Kanhaiyalal is the mafia lord of the town and Bhushannath is his aide. A crusading journalist Ramprasad (Satyen Kappu) and his son Satyen (Mayur) try to bring the criminals to task. Bhushannath contests the assembly elections and with Kanhaiyalal's support, he wins and also becomes a minister. Bhushannath tries to settle scores with Jagat Pratap, but the DM sticks to his guns. His belief is that as an IAS, he belongs to the permanent service and he need not succumb to a criminal-turned-minister whose tenure is temporary. Jagat Pratap faces one more confrontation and that is with his son Ravi, who is an angry young man and takes the law in his own hands to get justice. But, one day he leaves home and becomes a police inspector. Eventually, the father and son come together and fight the villains. The film had music by Bappi Lahiri. The other member of the cast included Gulshan Grover, Tej Sapru, Raza Murad, etc.

Nutan and Dilip Kumar

The film received reasonably good reviews and an excerpt from the review published in the *Screen* magazine is reproduced:

'The performances are generally good or very good. Dilip Kumar naturally dominates the scene by his stature. His typical nuance and style are difficult to equal. But Kader Khan is able to muster up interesting encounters with Dilip. The scene where Kader calls Dilip to the guest house after he becomes a minister will remain memorable. Anupam Kher brings in a distinctive and amusing style to his interpretation of the mafia lord. Sanjay's performance is more spirited than in his recent films. Madhuri Dixit, as Sanjay's sweetheart, does not have much of a role in the story as such. But she looks very charming and is an asset to the film by her mere presence. She adds to the entertainment value by her dances. B. Gopal's direction serves the purpose. Kader Khan's dialogue has the usual punch, and occasionally sounds sophisticated when Dilip speaks it. Bappi Lahiri's music is better than his recent films. It sounds good while one is seeing the movie, but the lyrics are not likely to be remembered as writing by Indivar does not rise above the routine level.'

CHAPTER 3.6

HISTRIONIC CURTAIN CALL–
THE CLIMATIC NINETIES INTO MILLENIUM

IZZATDAAR

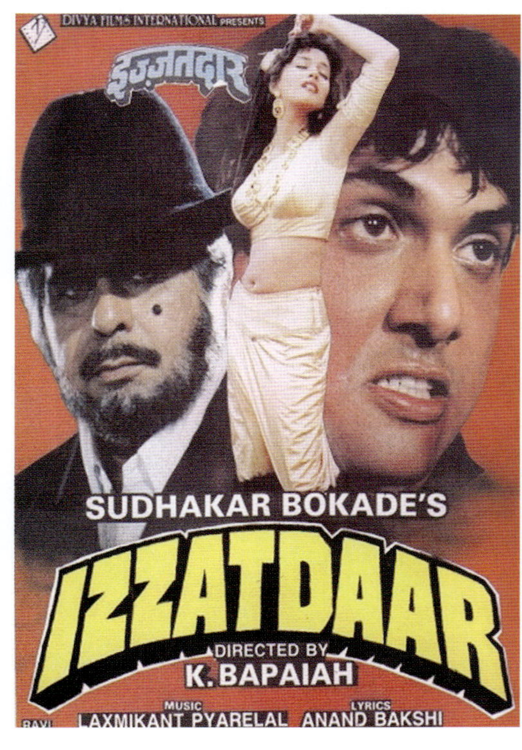

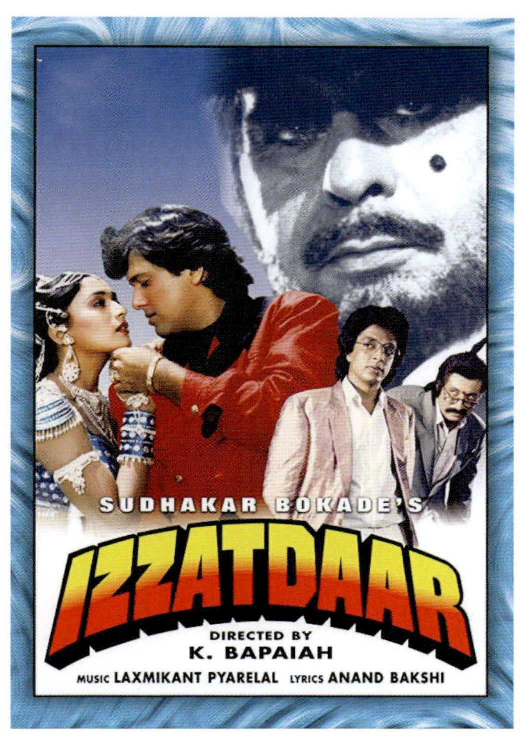

DATE / YEAR OF RELEASE: 16 MARCH 1990
BANNER / PRODUCER: DIVYA FILMS INTERNATIONAL / S.K. BOKADE
DIRECTION: K. BAPAIAH
MUSIC: LAKSHMIKANT–PYARELAL
LYRICS: ANAND BAKSHI
PLAYBACK: ALKA YAGNIK / AMIT KUMAR / MOHD. AZIZ / SUDESH BHOSLE
SCREENPLAY: SHAFIQ ANSARI
DIALOGUE: SHAFIQ ANSARI
CINEMATOGRAPHY: A. VENKATESH
EDITING: WAMAN BHONSLE
CAST: DILIP KUMAR / MADHURI DIXIT / GOVINDA / BHARATI / ANUPAM KHER / SHAKTI KAPOOR / SHAFI INAMDAR / RAKESH BEDI / RAGHUVARAN / DILIP DHAWAN

Dilip Kumar in Izzatdaar

After a number of hits under his belt, Dilip Saheb was getting somewhat disillusioned with the falling standards of films being made in the late 1980s. The legendary directors with whom Dilip Saheb had been associated, such as Amiya Chakrabarty, Nitin Bose, S.U. Sunny, Bimal Roy, S.S. Vasan, et al, had all departed the scene. Very few of the iconic makers from the past era were left. There was a vacuum of filmmakers who were capable of producing and directing movies at par with the lofty standards set in the Dilipian films of yore. Dilip Kumar was wedded to his craft and for some time did continue to accept some assignments while rejecting a plethora of them. One such film he accepted against his better judgement was *Izzatdaar,* a multi-starrer with Govinda, Madhuri Dixit, Anupam Kher, Shafi Inamdaar, Rakesh Bedi, Shakti Kapoor, Asrani, et al. Made under the direction of K. Bapaiah, the movie was a moderate box-office success, including a silver jubilee run.

Scenes of Izzatdaar

Posters of Izzatdaar

The story centred around Brahm Dutt (Dilip Kumar), a rich steel magnate who is falsely convicted for the murder of his best friend. In prison, he finds out that his son-in-law Indrajeet (Raghuvaran) has conspired against him and vows to avenge the betrayal. The motion picture was dominated by Dilip Kumar who stole the show. Govinda and Madhuri Dixit made a charming romantic pair.

Laxmikant–Pyarelal gave the music but the songs did not have much to write home about. The songs included *Yaad rakhiyo yeh akshar pyar ke* (Alka Yagnik-Mohd. Aziz), *Suno o mister ek taaza khabar* (Amit Kumar-Alka Yagnik), *Tumko dekh ke jhoom gaya* (Amit Kumar-Alka Yagnik) and *Kiss kiss ko main kiss karoon* (Sudesh Bhosle-Alka Yagnik).

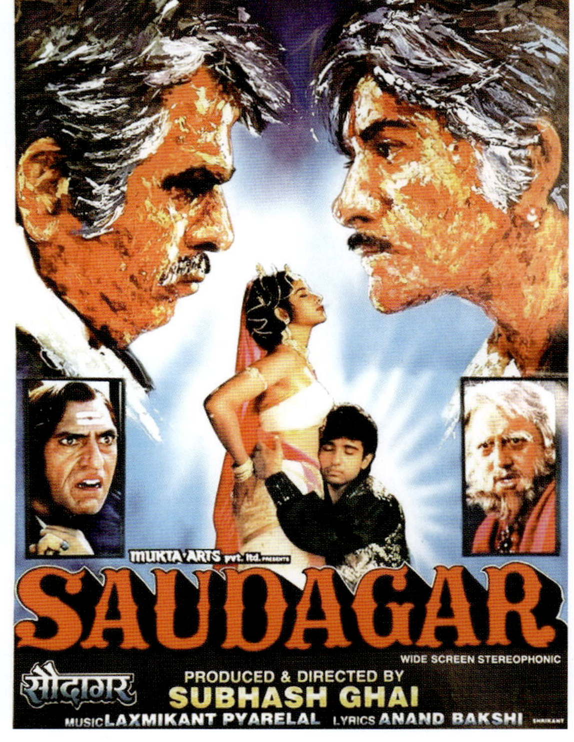

DATE / YEAR OF RELEASE: 1991
BANNER / PRODUCER: MUKTA ARTS PVT. LTD. / SUBHASH GHAI
DIRECTION: SUBHASH GHAI
MUSIC: LAKSHMIKANT–PYARELAL
LYRICS: ANAND BAKSHI
PLAYBACK: LATA MANGESHKAR / SURESH WADKAR / KAVITA KRISHNAMURTHY / ANURADHA PAUDWAL / MANHAR UDHAS / SUKHWINDER SINGH
STORY: SACHIN BHOWMICK / SUBHASH GHAI
SCREENPLAY: SACHIN BHOWMICK
DIALOGUE: KAMLESH PANDEY
CINEMATOGRAPHY: ASHOK MEHTA
EDITING: WAMAN BHOSLE / GURUDUTT SHIRALI
AUDIOGRAPHY: AKHILESH / HITENDRA GHOSH
CHOREOGRAPHY: SAROJ KHAN
ART: SAMEER CHANDA / MARUTI KALE
CAST: DILIP KUMAR / RAAJ KUMAR / MANISHA KOIRALA / VIVEK MUSHRAN / AMRISH PURI / ANUPAM KHER / DIPTI NAVAL / MUKESH KHANNA / DILIP TAHIL / GULSHAN GROVER / AKASH KHURANA / PALLAVI JOSHI / DINA PATHAK / ABHINAV CHATURVEDI / MALVIKA TIWARI / ANAND BALRAJ / PARVEZ KHAN / ARCHANA PURAN SINGH / SHUBHA KHOTE / SUCHITA VAJPEYI / CHANG / LEE / DENISE HALL / TARKESH CHOWHAN / ANIL YADAV / RUBINA / DEV MALHOTRA / MANOJ THAKKAR / BIPIN TRIVEDI / MASTER KRISHNA / NASIR SHAIKH / ASHISH CHATERJI / GOPI SHINDE / MANU RAJ / JAHEED MERCHANT / VED THAPAR & JACKIE SHROFF (GUEST APPEARANCE)

Director-producer and then a 'Showman' in the making, Subhash Ghai loved pulling surprises and raising audience's expectations sky-high from the very start of a film. After creating a casting coup of sorts in *Vidhaata* by bringing together three legends–Dilip Kumar, Shammi Kapoor and Sanjeev Kumar–he pulled another major casting surprise by bringing together Dilip Kumar and Raaj Kumar after thirty-two years in his next magnum opus *Saudagar* (1991). The two legends were last seen together onscreen in *Paigham* (1959). For the film's romantic leads, Ghai cast rank newcomers Manisha Koirala and Vivek Mushran, supported by an impressive pack of performers such as Anupam Kher, Amrish Puri, Deepti Naval, Mukesh Khanna, Gulshan Grover, et al. As the film approached its much awaited release date, the audiences' clamour reached a feverish pitch resulting in a spectacular opening for *Saudagar*, which went on to become a smash hit. The movie was nominated for thirteen Filmfare Awards and Subhash Ghai walked away with the Best Director trophy.

Posters of Saudagar

The two titans had interesting and meaty roles of bosom buddies-turned-foes in the film. Dilip Kumar played Veer Singh, a rustic chieftain of Sanatanpur village, and spoke in Haryanavi dialect. Raaj Kumar played Rajeshwar Singh, a well-read sophisticated zamindar of a nearby village called Palinagar, located across a rivulet. The histrionic confrontations between the thespians and their well-written repartees became the biggest crowd-pullers in the movie. The anecdotes related to Ghai pulling off the on-screen pairing of the legends make for an interesting reading. Subhash Ghai, having worked with Dilip Saheb in super-duper hits *Vidhaata* and *Karma,* had an excellent rapport with him. With the thespian liking the story/screenplay, getting his nod for a film was easy. Also when Ghai told Dilip Saheb that he had Raaj Kumar in mind for the other role, the thespian (to Ghai's surprise) had no objection and smilingly said, 'Raaj is a good actor and a nice person.' As the industry abounded with rumours of friction between Dilip Kumar and Raaj Kumar, Ghai approached the latter (who was also known for his eccentricities) with a lot of trepidation. Raaj too liked the script and pointedly asked as to who was playing the parallel role to which Ghai's tongue in cheek reply was, '*Aap ke dushman* Dilip Saheb' (The role is being played by your enemy Dilip Saheb). Raaj Kumar had a hearty laugh and said, '*Jaani wahi to ek actor hain jinhein main actor maanta hoon*' (He is the only actor whom I consider an actor). The deal was done and the rest is celluloid history. The film was launched with a spectacular mahurat, had a sensational opening and went on to become an all-time super-duper hit.

The Mahurat

THE HISTORIC DILIP–RAAJ PATCH-UP!

Joining the two veterans are youngsters Anil Kapoor and Farha who've also called truce to their constant bickering

Subhash Ghai's latest announcement, "Saudagar" has generated far greater interest than his earlier ventures. The main reason is that Ghai has accomplished a casting coup which no other director has been able to bring about for twenty-seven years. Namely, the co-starring of two veteran actors, Dilip Kumar and Raaj Kumar. The industry has already begun buzzing with anticipation and discussions about the feasibility of such a star cast.

The reason for all the doubts being expressed are the undercurrents and tension that have existed between the two screen giants ever since they worked together in the Gemini film "Paigham" in 1961. At that time, Raaj Kumar had walked off with all the accolades, despite his relatively minor role in the film. This naturally upset the 'master actor' Dilip Kumar and the two never

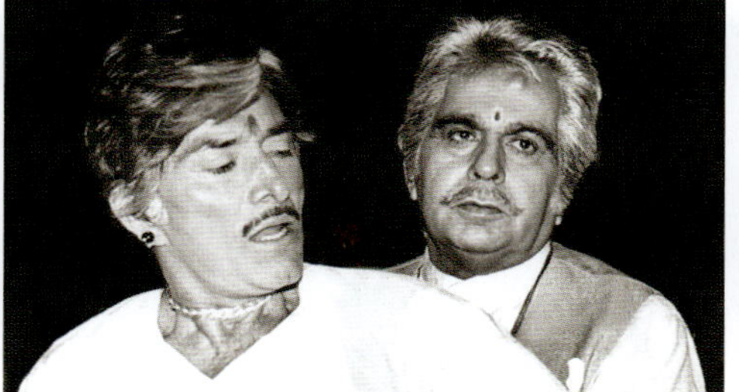

Dilip Kumar and Raaj Kumar in Saudagar

As hinted, *Saudagar* was the story of two close childhood friends, Veer Singh and Rajeshwar Singh, who became estranged and bitter enemies due to petty machinations and evil perfidious interests of people around them. The friends address each other as Veeru and Raju. Their only true friend and well-wisher was a hermit Mandhari (Anupam Kher). When a village scoundrel Bali Ram (Gulshan Grover) teases Biru's sister Raju beats Bali black and blue and the rascal losses an eye. As the two friends grow up, Raju gets married while his sister Palikanta is in love with Biru and the two are engaged to be married. But when Biru visits a nearby village, he end up compassionately marrying a girl who has been shunned by her would-be in-laws for dowry. On hearing this, Palikanta commits suicide. The brother of Raju's wife Chuniya (Amrish Puri) poisons the mind of Rajeshwar against Bir Singh. The friendship turns in to enmity. Then, Rajeshwar goes abroad and sets up a business. After twenty-five years, Rajeshwar's two sons Gajendra and Anand (Dalip Tahil and Anand Balraj) develop Palinagar and establish Pali industries. Biru becomes the chief of the village and his two sons Vishal and Gagan (Jackie Shroff and Mukesh Khanna) have a flourishing vegetables and fruits business. Vishal is married to Aarti (Deepti Naval) and has a son. Chuniya and Bali Ram plot to usurp the lands and kill Biru and Raju. Vishal gets wind of their plans and threatens to expose them in front of Rajeshwar. Bali Ram shoots Vishal during the latter's morning bath and puja ritual and all hell breaks loose as Bir Singh and his people unleash revenge. Bir Singh and his sister (Dina Pathak) send Vasudev, the kid son of Vishal, with Mandhari to the care of Acharya*ji* at his akhada. Rajeshwar returns to Sanatanpur to stem out the violence and goes to meet the collector V. Sinha at the appointed time but Sinha is killed by Chuniya and Bali Ram and Rajeshwar is falsely implicated in the murder and sentenced for fourteen years in jail. Chuniya again poisons Rajeshwar's mind by feeding false information that Bir Singh is behind the murder. Violence between Sanatanpur and Palinagar reaches such a peak that security forces had to build a check-post between the villages separately, demarcating the two villages with the boundary being the rivulet. The police force somehow maintains a very fragile peace. Gajendra's daughter and Rajeshwar's granddaughter Radha (Manisha Koirala) grows up and is educated in Delhi. Her brother (Abhinav Chaturvedi) is very fond of her and is in love with the Santanpur lass Amla (Pallavi Joshi). Chuniya plots for his son Monty (Anand Balraj) to be married to Radha. Chuniya also has a keep (Archana Puran Singh). A grown up Vasudev aka Vasu (Vivek Mushran) returns to Sanatanpur after fourteen years completing his education with Acharya*ji* on Janmashtami day. During the Janmastami puja, Radha wanders off to the border to be caught in the crossfire between the villages. Vasu rescues her unharmed. Sparks of love begin to fly between Vasu and Radha, and when the former wanders into the Palinagar area and gets injured,

Dilip Kumar and Raaj Kumar

she stealthily hides him and treats him. Love continues to blossom between the young couple. Rajeshwar returns to Sanatanpur after completing his jail term. Mandhari tries to end the enmity between Biru and Raju but they do not budge. Mandhari discovers that Radha and Vasu are in love and dances with joy. Amla becomes a mother and Biru (now known as Dada Bir) challenges Rajeshwar to have the child accepted and a new tussle gets underway. Egged on by Mandhari, Vasu and Radha cleverly switch sides and work in the households of Rajeshwar and Dada Bir respectively to endear themselves to the two patriarchs. Several twists and turns in the story lead to Dada Bir and Thakur Rajeshwar Singh burying their hatchet to revive their friendship on the occasion of Holi. Bali Ram tries to forcibly take the signatures of the Thakur to annex large chunks of land but is unsuccessful. The misunderstandings are all cleared. Biru and Raju join hands and defeat the Chuniya and Bali Ram caucus and their foreign collaborators but lose their lives in the process. Sanatanpur and Palinagar inmates become friends again and the lovers unite. It was quite a tortuous tale enlivened by the magnificent portrayals of the thespians and some inspired direction and editing.

Stills from Saudagar

Dilip Kumar's towering performance truly embellished the film, and it was a treat to watch the thespian render dialogue in impeccable Haryanvi and literally live the role of Dada Bir. Raaj Kumar too imparted the role of Rajeshwar with required dignity and polish. Anupam Kher's Mandhari was also laudable. The rest of the cast paled into insignificance compared to the towering portrayals of the legendary actors but most artists, including the debutants Vivek Mushran and Manish Koirala, performed competently.

Dilip Kumar as Dada Bir

The team of music directors Laxmikant–Pyarelal and lyricist Anand Bakshi did put forth a popular score with songs like *Imli ka boota beri ka ped* (Part 1: Mohd.Aziz-Sudesh Bhosle and Part 2: Sadhana Sargam-Mohd. Aziz), *Ilu ilu yeh ilu ilu kya hai* (Manhar Udhas-Kavita Krishnamurthy-Sukhwinder Singh), *Maine rab se tujhe* (Manhar Udhas-Anuradha Paudwal-Sukhwinder Singh), *Pyar karnewale* (Lata Mangehkar), *Radha naachegi* (Lata Mangeshkar-Mohd. Aziz), *Saudagar sauda kar* (Kavita Krishnamurthy-Manhar Udhas-Sukhwinder Singh), *Pyar karnewale* (Lata Mangeshkar-Suresh Wadkar) and *Mohabbat ki ki* (Suresh Wadkar-Kavita Krishnamurthy).

Raaj Kumar as Thakur Rajeshwar Singh

Saudagar is the last super-duper hit film of the great Dilip Kumar. The thespian later did only one film (*Qila*) and hung his boots, never to don the grease paint again.

DATE / YEAR OF RELEASE: 10 APRIL 1998
BANNER / PRODUCER: EAGLE FILMS / PARVESH C. MEHRA
DIRECTION: UMESH MEHRA
MUSIC: ANAND RAJ ANAND
LYRICS: DEV KOHLI
PLAYBACK: ANAND RAJ ANAND / SUSHMA SHRESTHA / PREETHI SINGH / SADHANA SARGAM / ALKA YAGNIK / UDIT NARAYAN
STORY: HUMAYUN MIRZA
SCREENPLAY: UMESH MISHRA / HUMAYUN MIRZA
DIALOGUE: HUMAYUN MIRZ
CINEMATOGRAPHY: S. PAPPU
CHOREOGRAPHY: CHINNI PRAKASH / SAROJ KHAN / JAY BORADE
EDITING: KAMAL SEHGAL
ART: N. SWAMI
AUDIOGRAPHY: KARNAIL SINGH / J.P. SEHGAL
CAST: DILIP KUMAR / REKHA / MAMTA KULKARNI / MUKUL DEV / SMITA JAYKAR / SATISH KAUSHIK / KUNIKA / MALAY CHAKRAVORTY / SHABAZ KHAN / AVTAR GILL / UMESH SHUKLA / PRAMOD MOUTHO / GULSHAN GROVER / RAJESHWARI SACHDEV

Producer Fakir Chand (F.C.) Mehra, owner of Eagle Films, was a close friend of Dilip Saheb. He had made films like *Mujrim* (1958), *Ujala* (1959), *Singapore* (1960), *Professor* (1962), *Amrapali* (1966), *Prince* (1969), *Manoranjan* (1974), *Alibaba Aur 40 Chor* (1980), *Sohni Mahiwal* (1984), et al. Like most of his contemporaries, F.C. Mehra too harboured the dream of producing a Dilip Kumar starrer. Mehra Saheb's dream came true close to

Scenes from Qila

the end of his cinematic journey with his son Umesh Mehra directing the thespian (playing a double role) in *Qila*. The film to date is the last released film of the megastar. Eminent writer Dr Rahi Masoom Raza had once laid a bet that Dilip Kumar will one day play a villainous character and he indeed did exactly that—one of Dilip Kumar's double roles in *Qila* had villainous traits. Legendary actress Rekha was cast opposite the megastar in the film.

Courtroom Drama

Dilip Kumar plays a double role of twin brothers who own a huge family inheritance including the family abode of a fort (Qila). One of the two brothers, Jagannath Singh is an evil landlord and treats his peers and family with disrespect. The other brother, Amarnath, is a good Samaritan and famous lawyer. Jagannath is a drunkard, a womaniser, a sadist, an abusive husband who constantly harasses his wife Suman (Smita Jaykar) before throwing her out of the house for good. She is forced to move into a slum area of the village with her son Amar (Mukul Dev). Amar becomes a poor truck driver and falls in love with his boss's daughter Neeta (Mamta Kulkarni). One night, Jagannath is murdered by a mysterious killer. Jagannath's twin brother Amarnath (Dilip Kumar) tries to unravel the mystery with the help of his beautiful daughter (Rajeshwari) and follows the trail of Jagannath's wrongdoings. The suspect of Jagannath's murder include the distressed classical dancer Yamini (Rekha), who was raped by the deceased man, her crippled brother, the other hurt woman Kunika, Suman and Amar. After the initial build up, the movie has a thrilling climax leading to revealing the identity of the killer. Dilip Kumar stole the show with his excellent rendition of the villainous role. A high point of the film was the song-dance *jugalbandi* of Dilip Kumar and Rekha filmed in the fort. Rekha was amazing in the dance sequences and pulled off a fine performance. Rajeshwari was natural and Mamta Kulkarni oozed her usual oomph.

The film had a musical score by Anand Raj Anand which was passable.

MUGHAL-E-AZAM (FULL COLOURED VERSION)

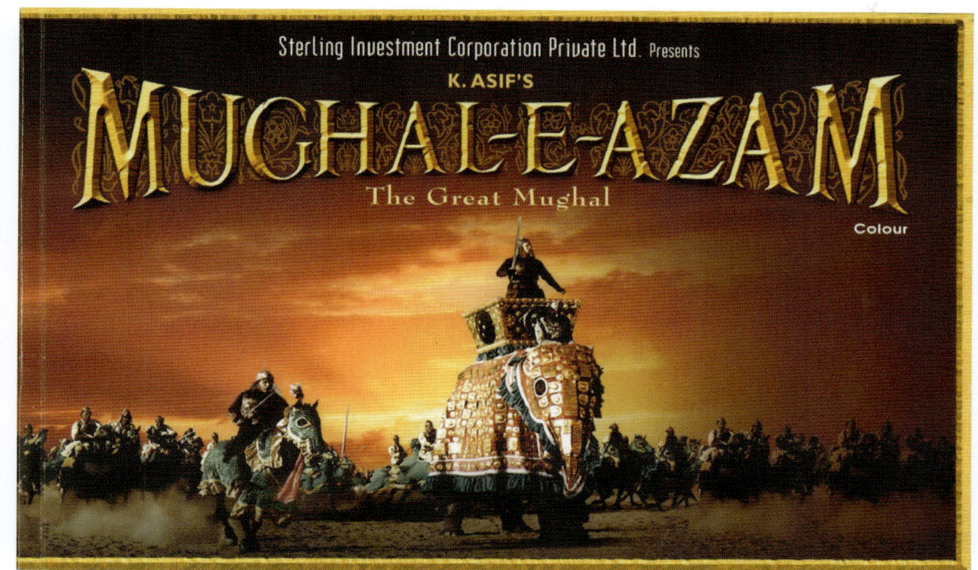

DATE / YEAR OF RELEASE: 10 NOVEMBER 2004 (COLOURED VERSION)
BANNER / PRODUCER: STERLING INVESTMENT CORPORATION (P.) LTD.
DIRECTION: K. ASIF
MUSIC: NAUSHAD
LYRICS: SHAKEEL BADAYUNI
PLAYBACK: BADE GHULAM ALI KHAN / SHAMSHAD BEGUM / MOHD. RAFI / LATA MANGESHKAR / MUBARAK BEGUM
STORY / SCREENPLAY: K. ASIF / AMAAN
DIALOGUE: WAJAHAT MIRZA / KAMAL AMROHI / AMAAN / EHSAAN RIZVI
CINEMATOGRAPHY: R.D. MATHUR
CHOREOGRAPHY: LACHCHU MAHARAJ
EDITING: DHARMVEER
ART: M.K. SYED (SHEESH MAHAL GLASS WORK–AGHA SHIRAZI)
AUDIOGRAPHY: ROBIN CHATTERJI / KAUSHIK / B.N. SHARMA
CAST: PRITHVIRAJ KAPOOR / DILIP KUMAR / MADHUBALA / NIGAR SULTANA / AJIT / DURGA KHOTE / KUMAR / SHEELA DAYALA / MURAD / ZILLO BAI / VIJAYLAKSHMI / S. NAZIR / KHURSHID KHAN / KHWAJA SABIR / SHAHGUL / MAHGUL / JAGO / PAUL SHARMA / SAYYAD HUSSAIN / GHULAM SABIR / KHANNA / SURENDRA / JOHNY WALKER / GOPI KRISHN / JALAL AGHA & TABBASUM (GUEST ARTISTES)

The magnum opus *Mughal-E-Azam* (partly coloured but mainly in black and white) was a super-duper hit of 1960, which soon became a timeless classic. Given its stupendous success at the box office, the full-colour version of the same seemed to be a well-thought-out decision by its producers Shapoorji Mistry and Pallonji Mistry (as Sterling Investment Corporation). The revised version of the film released with great fanfare in 2004.

Mughal-E-Azam (The Great Mughal) is a classic epic of Indian cinema which still remains the greatest film that India has ever produced. It would be prudent to recall the tortuous historical path that the grand *Mughal-E-Azam* took to stride across the silver screen with great pomp and splendour in the year 1960 to become an immortal classic:

1944: K. Asif wants to make the biggest film of Indian cinema and launches it with Shiraz Ali Hakim as its financier.
1946: The lead actor (Chandra Mohan playing Akbar) dies.
1947: Partition of India takes place and Shiraz Ali Hakim shifts to Pakistan leaving an incomplete film behind.
1951: K. Asif re-launches the ambitious film with new star cast and Shapoorji and Pallonji Mistry as its new financier. The film's shooting progresses on a grand scale.
1956: Technicolor arrives in India.
1958: K. Asif shoots one song in colour with fantastic results.
1959: Impressed by the results, Asif reshoots three more reels in colour.
1960: K. Asif wants to reshoot the whole film in colour. The producers lose patience. Asif is persuaded to release the film as shot (85 per cent in black and white, 15 per cent in colour) on 5 August 1960. After its release, the magnum opus soon turns out to be the biggest blockbuster of Indian cinema. K. Asif's dream of make *Mughal-E-Azam* fructifies. *Mughal-E-Azam* grosses huge returns even in re-runs of the film over the next decades.
1981-2001: Various people associated in some way with the film approached Shapoorji–Pallonji to colourise the film, to fulfil the last wish of K. Asif. Shapoorji–Pallonji refused, being of the opinion that the film was too big to be confined just to 35mm screen. Nevertheless, the era of 70mm had already dawned and the idea, did have some merit. In any case, it was an ambitious and audacious idea the realisation of which needed overflowing coffers. Restoration included digitalising the 3,00,000 frames of the film at 2K resolution with Gamma contrast, fungus correction, scratch and pinhole remover, digital stitching of torn frames and stabilisation work on the original negatives. 'It was too big a gamble to risk at that stage so we put the extravagant project on hold,' according to the later-appointed Project Manager Deepesh Salgia. At the turn of the millennium, the idea sprouted wings again when Dilip Kumar who played Prince Salim himself urged the original producers to approve Deepesh's plans. After eighteen months of intensive research, Sterling Investment Corporation of Shapoorji Mistry and Pallonji Mistry gave Deepesh the go-ahead to undertake the herculean task of colouring 3,00,000 frames, each containing 10 MB of data.
2002: The producers engaged Indian Academy of Arts and Animation to develop and execute colourisation technology of 35mm to suit the complexities of *Mughal-E-Azam.*
2003: Technology development was completed and execution commenced.
2004: Colourised version of the black and white classic film got ready to be released on big screen in colour, in wide-screen format, in Dolby-DTS surround sound—a first of its kind in the entire world. Asif's unfinished agenda is completed in style, exactly sixty years after he launched it. Six decades later, a dream challenged the technology in post-production to fill the extravagance with colours. Lo and behold, the legend was born again!

The crew involved in the restoration and colourisation of the grand magnum opus is listed below:

PROJECT DESIGN AND DIRECTION: DEEPESH SALGIA
COLOURISATION: INDIAN ACADEMY OF ARTS AND ANIMATION, MUMBAI
RESTORATION : IRIS INTERACTIVE, CHENNAI
COLOUR BALANCING AND NEGATIVE PREPARATION: RAJTARU VIDEOSONIC LTD., MUMBAI
MUSIC: NAUSHAD
MUSIC ASSISTANTS: UTTAM SINGH, RAJU NAUSHAD, GURMEET SINGH
MUSIC RECORDED BY: TANAY GAJJAR AT AVA STUDIO, MUMBAI
DOLBY MIXING: ALOK DE AT FIESTA STUDIOS, MUMBAI
SOUND RESTORATION: CHACE PROUDCTIONS (L.A)
MARKETING AND DISTRIBUTION: SANJAY BHANDARI
MERCHANDISE AND CO-PROMOTION: SATISH LAXMAN
CO-ORDINATION: SUNIL SURYAVANSHI, ARCHANA BANSAL
PUBLICITY AND WEBSITE DESIGN: INTERVENTION INDIA PVT. LTD.
ACKNOWLEDGEMENT & THANKS: RASKAVI RAGHUNATH BRAHMABHATT

While on the subject, it would be prudent to briefly describe the various processes involved in this momentous endeavours initiated and supervised by Deepesh Salgia.

The Process

Restoration: Restoration is an essential process of colourisation. Intense restoration was undertaken as the frames were in bad condition. The negative that was being scanned was actually a Dupe negative that was made in early 80s after the original negative had been used for more than twenty years. Restoration included digitizing the 300,000 frames of the film at 2K resolution, gamma correction, contrast correction, scratch removal, pinholes removal, digital stitching of torn frames, stabilization, fugus correction and various other digital restoration techniques. Each step involved processing 3000 GB of data. The work was done shot-by-shot or frame-by-frame depending on the condition of the negatives. All the above work was performed by a team of restoration specialists working at Iris Interactive, Chennai. These frames were then made ready for colourisation.

Colourisation: In the west, colourisation has been looked at as an artificial work or as an unethical attempt to touch an artist's creation. In this case, the purpose was to complete an unfulfilled dream of the creator. The taks was undertaken by the original production company, Sterling Investment Corporation Pvt. Ltd. The original music composer re-recorded the music in a digital environment and the original artists always supported the idea. Hence, there is no unethical attempt.

The software that was used has a very important feature that accepts only those colours that match the gray shades of the original input. This ensures that the final colours are as close as possible to the original. Since the kind of colourisation required for Mughal-E-Azam was never done before (Mughal-E-Azam has a rich use of exquisite jewelry, fine clothing, grand sets), a special software had to be written to incorporate such features and that too for a 35 mm release.

Since the film is an historical film, the colour scheme was regularly discussed with historians. History books of medieval times were referred in order to get the essence of the Mughal era. An in-depth research of 18 months was undertaken before the actual colourisation started in October 2002 at Indian Academy of Arts and Animation, Mumbai. The whole technology development and execution was undertaken in India.

Post Production: The whole film (frame-by-frame) was then given a finished product look through colour balancing and was digitally converted to Wide Screen format and then recorded to make a new negative at Rajtaru Videosonic, Mumbai.

The Music

Sound Restoration: The first part was cleaning the noise imbued within the old track with the assistance of Chace productions LA, a specialist in cleaning old tracks who have earlier worked on Hollywood classics like 'Gone with the wind', 'A bridge on the river Kwai', etc.

Separation of Voice Track from the Mixed Track: The second complicaed task was separation of the voice track from the mono mixed track. This was painstakingly undertaken at Ava Studio, Mumbai.

Re-recording: Then came the creative part of re-recording the original background score. At the then young age of 84 years, Naushad Sahab worked with his team along with 60 chorus singers and 120 musicians playing original Hindustani classical instruments. A special team of musicians was called from Chennai for the Strings section.

6.1 Mix: The last step comprised mixing the immortal voices of Ustad Bade Ghulam Ali Khan Sahab, Mohammed Rafi Sahab, Lata Mangeshkarji and Shamshad Begumji with the digitally re-recorded background music.

This recreation (Colourisation and Sound Enhancement) that took 30 months of hard work is the first of its kind in the history of world cinema and a proud moment for the Indian Film Industry.

Kudos to Deepesh Salgia and his team for successfully undertaking and completing this remarkable endeavour achieving outstanding quality.

With the re-furbished *Mughal-E-Azam* in wide screen and with digital sound being ready plans were made to release the full colour film on the same date as was the original black and white version. Exactly 44 years later, when the epic movie, was re-released on November 10 it was with the principal theatre being Eros in Mumbai instead of Maratha Mandir, which unfortunately was showing *Aitraaz*, an Abbas-Mustan flick featuring Akshay Kumar and Priyanka Chopra. History would have repeated itself had Maratha Mandir decided to premiere the refurbished *Mughal-E-Azam*. The iconic theatre missed its date with history.

With the full-colour print of *Mughal-E-Azam* for the wide screen ready with digital stereo sound, plans were made to release the new version of the film on the same date as the original. Exactly forty-four years later, the epic movie was re-released on 10

November 1960. Unfortunately, Maratha Mandir, the original venue of the premiere of the original *Mughal-E-Azam* was showing Abbas-Mustan's *Aitraaz.* The new version of the film was thus released at the Eros as the primary theatre. Had Maratha Mandir decided to premiere the new colour edition of *Mughal-E-Azam* also, history would have been made. The iconic theatre sadly missed its date with history.

A gala premiere was also held at the Eros theatre which was attended by the glitterati of Mumbai film industry led by Dilip Kumar himself. In an emotionally-charged speech, Dilip Saheb paid glowing tributes to Shapoorji Pallonji Mistry and standing in all humility asked God to make it divinely possible to send all those great people like K. Asif, Prithviraj Kapoor, Madhubala, Nigar, et al back to mother earth. The remastered film had a magnificent opening and a highly successful run all over India, re-writing history in a grand style.

Recently, Shapoorji Pallonji turned the magnificent movie *Mughal-E-Azam* into a play essentially keeping the scenario and dialogue of the original unaltered and entrusted the direction to the theatre director Feroz Khan. The play too was mounted on a lavish scale with live singing and music staged on very impressive sets, supervised again by Deepesh Salgia. The play has become a runaway success with every show (first staged at Tata Theatre of NCPA, Nariman Point, Mumbai) going house full across the country. Undoubtedly, the saga of the immortal *Mughal-E-Azam* shall outlive posterity.

UNRELEASED FILMS

AAG KA DARYA

DATE / YEAR OF RELEASE: UNRELEASED
BANNER / PRODUCER: PREMALAYA / R. VENKATRAMAN
DIRECTION: S.V. RAJENDRA SINGH
MUSIC: LAKSHMIKANT–PYARELAL
LYRICS: RAJENDRA KRISHNA
PLAYBACK: LATA MANGESHKAR / ASHA BHOSLE / ANURADHA PAUDWAL / SHABBIR KUMAR / KAVITA KRISHNAMURTHY
STORY: H.V. SUBBA RAO
SCREENPLAY: RAJENDRA KRISHNA
DIALOGUE: RAJENDRA KRISHNA
CINEMATOGRAPHY: P.S. PRAKASH
CAST: DILIP KUMAR / REKHA / PADMINI KOLHAPURE / AMRITA SINGH / RAJEEV KAPOOR / AMRISH PURI

Producer R. Venkatraman and Kannada director S.V. Rajendra Singh Babu created a sort of casting coup by pairing Dilip Kumar with Rekha for the first time in an ambitious film *Aag Ka Darya* in 1993–94. The movie co-starred Padmini Kolhapure, Amrita Singh, Rajeev Kapoor and Amrish Puri with music by Laxmikant–Pyarelal. The film was shot at a brisk pace at the Pakshiraj Studios (owned by the late S.M.S. Naidu who produced and directed Dilip Kumar's super-duper hit *Azaad* in 1955) in Coimbatore. Dilip Saheb shot at the Pakshiraj after thirty-eight years. Reportedly, Dilip Kumar was miffed with the over-bearing attitude of Naidu during the making of *Azaad* and had vowed never to work with him ever. S.M.S. Naidu on his part had decided that if he ever made a Hindi film it would be with Dilip Kumar. It was an interesting quirk of fate that Dilip Kumar eventually shot a film at the Pakshiraj Studios after more than three decades, but sadly after Naidu was gone. *Aag Ka Darya* was completed in good time and the 18-reel long film received a Censor certificate as a 'social' film on 12 October 1995 in Chennai. At that time, an announcement was made that the movie would be released on 26 January 1996. But sadly and strangely till date, the film has not been released for which many reasons have been given from time to time. One of the main reasons given was that the producer apparently had become bankrupt and left the film industry to be involved with hospitality industry. Recently, a word has got around that a well-preserved print is available with the Singapore distributor of the movie and the film may be released soon. We hope so and cross our fingers.

Scenes from Aag Ka Darya

Composers Laxmikant–Pyarelal teamed up with veteran lyricist-writer Rajendra Krishna to come up with a reasonably good score including songs like *Rishta yeh mohabbat ka* – happy version (Lata Mangeshkar-Shabbir Kumar), *Rishta yeh mohabbat ka* – sad version (Anuradha Paudwal), *Dilbar dilbar* (Asha Bhosle-Shabbir Kumar), *Tere har kadam pe* (Shabbir Kumar), *Dil hai lutne ko taiyyar* (Anuradha Paudwal-Kavita Krishnamurthy),and *Goriya uksi deewani jiski pocket garam garam* (Asha Bhosle). The mentioned song had become quite popular. An audio CD of the music was released by Venus and is still available.

DATE / YEAR OF RELEASE: UNRELEASED
BANNER / PRODUCER: DIVYA–CITIZEN COMBINE
DIRECTION: DILIP KUMAR
MUSIC: KALYANJI–ANANDJI
LYRICS: ANAND BAKSHI
CINEMATOGRAPHY: KAMAL BOSE
CAST: DILIP KUMAR / MEENAKSHI SHESHADRI / AMITOJ MANN / RAJ BABBAR / AMJAD KHAN / RAJ KIRAN / RADHA SETH

Dilip Kumar, after the release of his megahit *Karma,* was getting increasingly exasperated with the way films of the 1990s were shaping up and the quality of the end products of some of his own films like *Dharm Adhikari.* He went on record to state: '**Selectiveness has been my hallmark from the beginning and it is this that has enabled me to survive for so long. Today, you cannot choose between good and bad films. You have to choose between bad and horrible films. So, can you blame me for choosing the bad films? I cannot say that the new style of functioning suits my temperament. Our films are also becoming like fast food and this breakneck pace is taking us nowhere. There is no time to concentrate, no atmosphere to imbibe, absorb and deliver. Which is why I decided to give up acting again.**' The solution was to officially wield the megaphone himself and Dilip Kumar started thinking in that direction. Eventually, he was persuaded by producer Sudhakar Bokade to direct a film written by the thespian himself. Thus began *Kalinga,* which was launched with great fanfare. The film was produced under the banner of Divya-Citizen Combine (Citizen Films was Dilip Kumar's home production house under which he had produced the blockbuster *Gunga Jumna* and Divya Films International was Sudhakar Bokade's banner). The film was partially produced by Dilip Saheb who starred in the film too. The other star cast included Meenakshi Sheshadri, Amjad Khan, Raj Babbar and newcomer Amitoj Mann. Dilip Kumar had written the script of *Kalinga* and was directing the film as well. The film had music direction by Dilip Saheb's favourites Kalyanji–Anandji and cinematography by Bimal Roy's cameramen Kamal Bose.

The most inexplicable among Dilip Kumar's incomplete and/or unreleased films is producer Sudhakar Bokade's *Kalinga.* It is all the more baffling in view of the fact that Sudhakar Bokade had already produced a Dilip Kumar–Govinda starrer, Divya Films

International's *Izzatdaar,* co-starring Madhuri Dixit and Bharathi, which had been directed by K. Bapaiah. *Izzatdaar* was successfully released in 1990 and by that point in time, both the producer (who also produced the superhit *Saajan*) and Dilip Saheb had become very friendly. As a matter of fact, just before the shooting of a very major schedule of *Izzatdaar,* director K. Bapaiah had fallen ill, and at the frantic request of Bokade, Dilip Kumar took over as director for that particular schedule. In mid-1991, Sudhakar Bokade even went on record to say, 'I was totally mesmerised by his direction and more so by the way in which the other artists responded to his direction. After seeing Dilip Saheb wielding the megaphone, I decided that I must ask Dilip Saheb to direct a film all by himself.'

But by 1992, *Kalinga* went off the floors. Something went seriously wrong during the extended period of time when the film was under production. During the period, the relationship between the producer and the director soured enough to bring the project to a standstill. In 1996, after the behind-the-scenes efforts made by some well-wishers worked, both Dilip Saheb and Sudhakar Bokade said many positive things about each other and the film at a joint press conference. The media reacted very positively flashing the news that *Kalinga* would soon be restarted and released. In between, due to the deaths of cinematographer Kamal Bose and actor Amjad Khan, Meenakshi Sheshadri's marriage and retirement from acting, the disappearance of Raj Kiran, and other factors, *Kalinga* has remained unreleased and may never see the light of the day.

In *Kalinga,* Dilip Kumar played the role of a High Court judge and the subject dealt with the void between a father and son. He had two wives in the film, large chunks of which were shot in a desert and amid ruins. Those who have seen the movie speak very highly of the emotional impact of the film and its hair-raising scenes. Dilip Kumar was very enthusiastic in directing this picture and went on record to say, **'Directing has been a very different and not so different experience–yes and no. Yes, because I've mostly been on the other side of the fence. And no, because I have not only been directing but I've also been overseeing the production details which can be very tricky business. For instance, I may have prepared myself for a highly emotional scene and the production manager comes and tells me that because of unavoidable reasons, I'll have to picturise the action scene instead. I've also taken a lot of effort not only over the screenplay but also on things like reaching the outdoor location ten days in advance and searching for the right milieu. Apart from that, colour texturing for a film has always been important. In *Gunga Jumna*, I tried for very earthy colours, I used the forest and mountains to give the film a naturalistic look. In *Kalinga*, I have tried to ensure that colour should not dominate a scene but blend into the visuals like the scenes set in the desert and the ruins should be easy on the eyes. I am a perfectionist and believe in maintaining the tempo of the film through maintaining the right temperatures of individual scenes to create a cohesive whole by judicious amalgamation of accurate enactment of the narrative. I envy directors who can carry of 10 to 20 different details without creasing their brows. Think *Kalinga* will be an unusual film–depending, of course, on the extent that it holds the viewer's interest and how far he feels that it is worth his ticket money. This does bother me a bit but eventually whatever has to be will be.'**

Legions of Dilip Kumar admirers and fans deeply regret that their favourite star's labour of love *Kalinga* may never hit the celluloid.

DILIPIAN ASSISTANCE IN SOME FILMS

As has earlier been mentioned, Dilip Kumar helped many a friend by lending some sort of assistance in their movies and there are several examples of such endeavours.

Dilip Saheb lent his voice in a prologue of the film *Dayar-E-Habib* which was a small movie produced by Hari Pictures under the direction of Hira Singh with the cast comprising Nasima, Rajrani, Paul, Sudesh, Ravikant and Wazir Mohammed Khan. The names of the producer and the music director have been forgotten. But, a memorable feature of the film was that it had the poetry of Amir Khusro and lyrics by Bedam Warsi, Seemab Akbarabadi, Zia-Ul-Qadri and Anwar Sabri.

Producer Dev Anand and director Vijay 'Goldie' Anand in their 1960 super hit *Kala Bazar* included a sequence showing the premier of Mehboob Khan's legendary film *Mother India* (1957) at the Liberty Cinema, Mumbai. Dilip Kumar sportingly agreed for inclusion of a clip showing his arrival at the *Mother India* premier which became a highlight of *Kala Bazar.* Of course Dilip Kumar and Dev Anand shared a lifelong friendship with Dev Saheb openly acknowledging his competitor Dilip as a great actor and star of all time.

When ace comedian Mehmood produced the film *Sadhu Aur Shaitan,* directed by A. Bhim Singh and starring himself opposite actress Bharathi, he assembled a cast which comprised many guest artists including Dilip Kumar and Mumtaz. The film was shot in Chennai and around that time, Dilip Saheb's *Ram Aur Shyam* was under production. Mehmood grabbed the opportunity and created a highly amusing cameo for Dilip and Mumtaz which became a highlight of *Sadhu Aur Shaitan.*

Lyricist-writer-director Gulzar had impressed Dilip Kumar with his work and the thespian became quite fond of him. When Gulzar was producing and directing his avant-garde *Koshish* (1972), starring Sanjeev Kumar and Jaya Bhaduri, he persuaded Dilip Saheb to make a special appearance in a very interesting scene. The movie centred around the life of a deaf and dumb couple (background music by Madan Mohan) in which Sanjeev and Jaya curiously dial a telephone number and get connected to Dilip Kumar, who on not hearing any sound remarks, '*Aap to mujhse bhi dheema bolte hain*' (You speak even softer than me). The scene was a highlight of the film.

Producer N.P. Ali and director A. Bhim Singh had offered the lead role of their film *Naya Din Nai Raat* to Dilip Kumar which required nine different characters to be portrayed. Dilip Saheb did not accept the assignment and recommended Sanjeev Kumar instead. Eventually, the movie was made with Sanjeev Kumar and Jaya Bhaduri in the lead roles, with music by Laxmikant–Pyarelal and script and lyrics by Rajinder Krishan. Dilip Kumar still lent his voice to the background commentary of the movie.

CHAPTER 4

FILMS THAT WERE NOT TO BE

Dilip Kumar could slip into disparate personalities as easily as a hand slips into a glove. That is why, he is the actor we all love to love. His 59 completed films are testimony to his peerless histrionics. But, only a few would know that there were a number of ill-fated Dilipian films that were either partly canned or remained incomplete; there were also a couple which did not get a release even after completion for reasons best known to the thespian himself or the respective producers/directors. One can imagine as to what more captivating histrionic splendour was in store for Dilip fans had these films seen the light of the day. This chapter makes an effort in cataloguing such films based on research and available information.

The Post-*Amar* jinx with Mehboob Khan

In our several interactions with Dilip Saheb, he very fondly referred to a specific film titled 'Mere Watan', which according to him was based on a very good script but did not take-off. However, the thespian could not recall the cast and credits of the ill-fated film. Our best guess is that perhaps it was a film planned by the legendary Mehboob Khan after the failure of his *Son of India* (1963) with the title 'Hamara Watan'. It was to be mounted on the scale of a magnum opus with the cast including top names such as Dilip Kumar, Raaj Kumar, Rajendra Kumar and Saira Banu. Naushad and Sahir Ludhianvi were to be teamed for the first time in the venture. Sadly, this dream production probably died with Mehboob Khan's death in June 1964. However, post the critically acclaimed *Amar* (1954), some sort of a jinx seemed to have cast its shadow on the Mehboob–Dilip collaboration. First, Dilip Kumar declined to play the role of Birjoo, one of the two sons of Nargis, in the celebrated classic *Mother India* (which was eventually played Sunil Dutt). Second was a film called 'Habba Khatoon'. The legendary filmmaker Mehboob Khan was

very fond of the story of 16th-century Kashmiri poetess Habba Khatoon, also known as the Nightingale of Kashmir. He made the writing department of Mehboob Productions slog to evolve a perfect script on her life. Mehboob Saheb wanted to launch the film immediately after the super-duper success of *Mother India* (1957). In fact, some posters of *Mother India* carried the announcement of 'Habba Khatoon' starring Dilip Kumar as the next venture of Mehboob Productions. Apparently, Dilip Kumar was to play the role of Yousuf Shah Chak, a ruler of Kashmir and the husband of Habba Khatoon, with Nargis playing the legendary poetess. Perhaps, Dilip Saheb did not like the negative traits in the character of Chak or whatever be the reason, Mehboob Saheb shelved the film and a complete bound script of 'Habba Khatoon' is said to be languishing in the offices of Mehboob Productions. Meanwhile, the story of the poetess appears to be jinxed as many efforts to bring her life on screen have proved futile. For example, in 1988, Muzaffar Ali's Vinod Khanna–Dimple Kapadia starrer 'Zoonie', based on the poetess' story, was canned after ten reels and ten lovely songs had been recorded by Khayyam. Similarly, filmmaker Roshanlal Wadhera had announced a film on Habba Khatoon in 1983 starring Saira Banu and Sanjay Khan under the direction of legendary B.R. Chopra, with music by Naushad. But, for reasons unknown, the film did not progress beyond recording of a fabulous Mohammad Rafi song '*Jis Raat Ke Khwab Aaye, Woh Khwabon Ki Raat Aayi*', penned by Ali Sardar Jafri.

Probable *Mughal-E-Azams*?

Karimuddin Asif (or K. Asif), the legendary maker of *Mughal-E-Azam*, after his first multi-starrer film *Phool* (1946), launched an ambitious project titled 'Janwar', starring the then reigning singing star Suraiya and Dilip Kumar. A grand mahurat was held and shooting commenced to can three–four reels. Then, for mysterious reasons, the shooting halted and eventually the movie was shelved. Some say that there was a tiff between the lead pair while others say the perfectionist K. Asif did not like the script. The real reason shall remain shrouded in mystery! Down the years, K. Asif had also planned a film on the last Mughal emperor Bahadur Shah Zafar titled 'Aakhri Mughal' with Dilip Kumar in the lead role. The film remained a dream with the untimely demise of Asif. Meanwhile, K. Asif had also announced another film with Dilip Kumar titled 'Taj Mahal', which too never saw the light of the day.

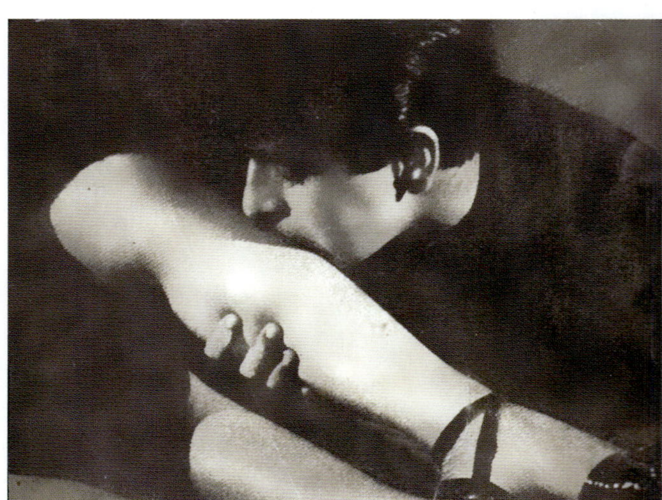

Stills from K. Asif's shelved 'Janwar'

Incomplete Dilip Kumar–Madhubala Starrers

Director-producer Mahesh Kaul had made a hit film *Gopinath*, starring Raj Kapoor and Tripti Mitra in 1948. He then wanted to make a romantic film titled 'Har Singaar' with the popular pair of Dilip Kumar and Madhubala as the protagonists. The movie was launched with high expectations under the banner of Allied Art Productions and its music direction was assigned to Anil Biswas. After completing six reels, the film was inexplicably shelved. Unfortunately, nobody has cared to retrieve the priceless footage of some enchanting Dilip Kumar–Madhubala scenes shot for the film, which must be languishing in cans in some musty godown.

Dr V.N. Sinha, the owner of Republic Films, which later produced the super hit Dilip Kumar–Meena Kumari starrer *Kohinoor*, had signed up the Dilip Kumar–Madhubala pair to star in his supposedly debut production titled 'Faasla'. The film was to be co-produced and directed by Zia Sarhady of *Foot Path* (1953, starring Dilip Kumar and Meena Kumari) and *Hum Log* (1951) fame. A mahurat of the film was held at Modern Studios in Dadar but the film did not proceed beyond that as Zia Sarhady opted to migrate to Pakistan. Yet another Dilip Kumar–Madhubala starrer titled 'Gohar' was planned by the veteran producer-director P.N. Arora, owner of All India Pictures. The film did not proceed beyond the announcement, reportedly, because of Dilip Saheb pointing too many pitfalls in the story's scenario. The film was eventually made in 1953 with actor Rehman as the leading man, with music by Ghulam Mohammad.

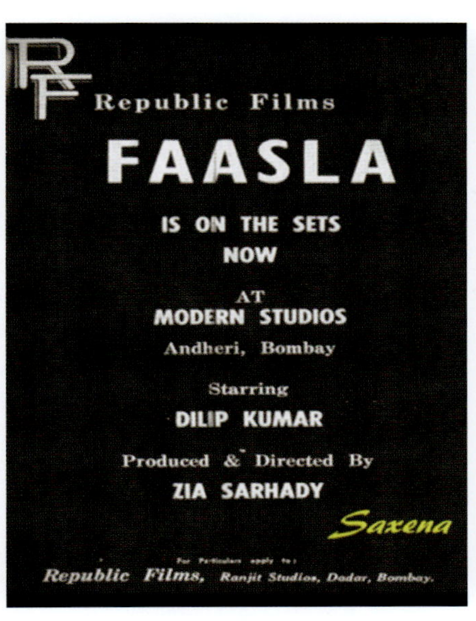

Jinxed Dilip Kumar–Madan Mohan Pairing

The association of Dilip Kumar and Melody King Madan Mohan was jinxed or so it seems. Whenever a Dilip Kumar starrer was announced to have a musical score by Madan Mohan, the film did not materialise. Producer-director R.C. Talwar, after the release of his Dilip Kumar–Madhubala starrer *Sangdil*, announced another film titled 'Bank Manager' with Dilip Kumar and Meena Kumari in the lead roles, with music by Madan Mohan. The film did not proceed beyond the announcement and Talwar instead went on to make *Rukhsana* (1955) with Meena Kumari and Kishore Kumar for unknown reasons. Director-producer Ramesh Saigal, who had worked with Dilip Kumar in films like *Shaheed* and *Shikast*, was to co-produce and direct 'Kala Aadmi' with Dilip Saheb's elder brother Ayub Khan. The music of the film was to be scored by Madan Mohan. The film was based on the life of coal miners and quite a lot of research and groundwork went into the scripting of the film; advance preparations for the shooting had also been made. Both Dilip and Ramesh even visited the coal mines in Dhanbad and Jharia in Jharkhand (then a part of unified Bihar). Ayub Khan, who had a failing health, passed away and the film was shelved, probably for this reason.

Posters of 'Bank Manager' and 'Kala Aadmi'

Dilip Kumar–Mithun Chakraborty: Another Jinx

Just like the earlier jinxed combo, there is another ill-fated pairing of Dilip Kumar and Mithun Chakraborty. Whenever they tried to come together on a project, it somehow did not materialise. First was a film by Ramanand Sagar titled 'Sanam', co-starring the two actors along with Rakhee, Reena Roy and Ranjeeta, which was launched with great fanfare under his banner, Sagar Arts. But, the film got shelved soon after its grand announcement when Sagar's magnum opus *Baghavat* (1982) bombed at the box office. Then, in July 1987, producers C.D. Mehta and Neeta Arora announced, under the banner of AGM International, an ambitious venture titled 'Raasta' starring Dilip Kumar, Mithun Chakraborty, Sridevi, Anupam Kher and others. Although some shooting of the film took place, the movie was eventually abandoned and shelved.

The Almost Complete Film: Shikwa

Seth Makhan Lal Jain and his son Rajinder Jain, who owned the Filmkar Production House, had produced the golden jubilee hit *Deedar* starring Ashok Kumar, Dilip Kumar, Nargis and Nimmi. Encouraged by the film's grand success, they decided to launch another Dilip Kumar starrer, co-starring Nutan, titled 'Shikwa'. The film was directed by Ramesh Saigal, who also played a role in it, and the music was to be composed by Anil Biswas. More than 99 per cent of the film was shot, canning around 100,000 feet of edited footage, but couldn't be completed. Based on a story by Khwaja Ahmad Abbas, it was an anti-war film which centred around an army officer Ram (Dilip Kumar), who criticises the martial instincts pervasive in the army, and his beloved, Indu (Nutan). Plunged in a war, Ram implores the warring soldiers of both the sides to not kill each other. Ram is caught in a crossfire in which he losses an arm and one eye. Ram is court-martialed for his anti-war act. Indu in a bid to save Ram from the gallows agrees to marry the commanding officer of the court martial (Saigal). Unaware that she has struck a deal to save his life, Ram is shocked and confronts her. Looking at the footage of the unreleased film available on the internet[1], one can easily say that it was another fine performance by Dilip Saheb, showcasing his sheer acting brilliance. A couple of scenes of the film were used in producer Shahab Ahmad's *Film Hi Film* (1983). Grapevine has it that the film remained incomplete owing to differences between the director and the producers. There are others who say it stalled because Filmkar launched another film titled 'Anarkali' when the production of *Mughal-E-Azam* had just been revived, which upset K. Asif and Dilip Kumar, subsequently leading to a court case. Apparently, another bone of contention was Kamaal Amrohi who wrote both the films.

Stills from 'Shikwa'

Halted at Start/After Initial Shooting

Samandar: The iconic Bombay Talkies Studios downed its shutters on 13 October 1953 with its premises being closed permanently. The studio's workmen floated a new concern in the name of Bombay Talkies Workers' Industrial Co-operative Society Limited to produce a classic motion picture *Baadbaan* (1954), directed by the famous Phani Majumdar with a formidable star cast including Ashok Kumar, Dev Anand, Meena Kumari, Usha Kiron, Jairaj, Shaikh Mukhtar, et al. The artistes reportedly worked free in the spirit of reviving the legendary banner. The film did reasonably well at the box office. Egged on by the successful experiment, the co-operative society launched an even bigger venture titled 'Samandar' with an even bigger cast, bringing together greats like Ashok Kumar, Dilip Kumar, Dev Anand, Meena Kumari, etc. But, their casting coup remained a pipe dream as the film never took off.

An untitled film with Shanta Apte: Dilip Kumar was also to star with Shanta Apte, a great actress of the 1940s whose super hit *Swayamsiddha* (1947) is remembered even to this date. Apte was to play his sister in the untitled film. Nothing much is known about the movie or the reason as to why it got shelved. All we are left with is a copy of the working still (placed alongside). It is rather unfortunate that the firebrand Shanta Apte and the endearingly suave Dilip Kumar could never be seen on screen and the cinegoers were denied the opportunity of witnessing the two acting greats together.

Dilip Kumar with Shanta Apte

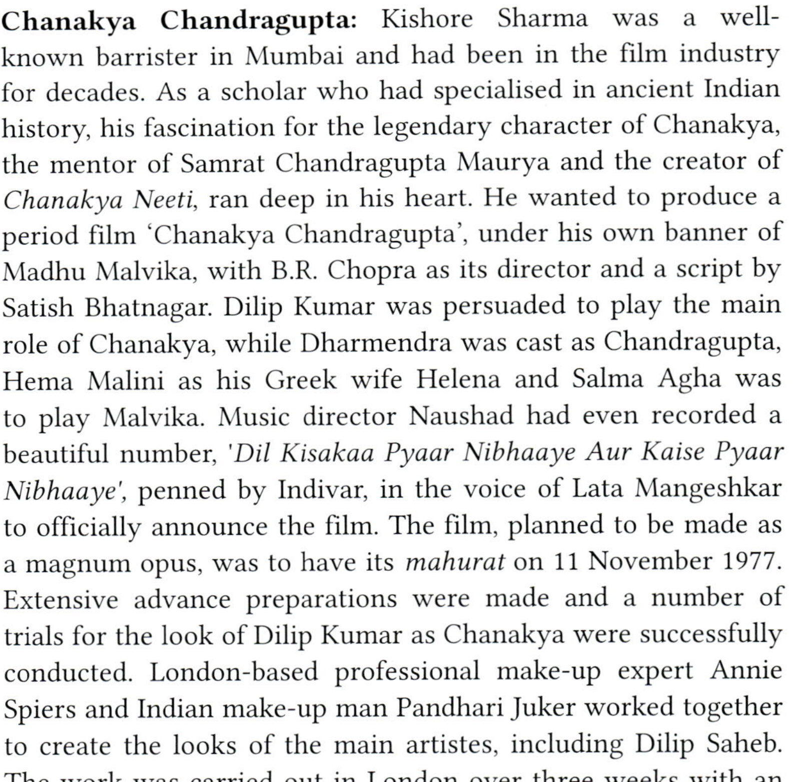

Chanakya Chandragupta: Kishore Sharma was a well-known barrister in Mumbai and had been in the film industry for decades. As a scholar who had specialised in ancient Indian history, his fascination for the legendary character of Chanakya, the mentor of Samrat Chandragupta Maurya and the creator of *Chanakya Neeti*, ran deep in his heart. He wanted to produce a period film 'Chanakya Chandragupta', under his own banner of Madhu Malvika, with B.R. Chopra as its director and a script by Satish Bhatnagar. Dilip Kumar was persuaded to play the main role of Chanakya, while Dharmendra was cast as Chandragupta, Hema Malini as his Greek wife Helena and Salma Agha was to play Malvika. Music director Naushad had even recorded a beautiful number, *'Dil Kisakaa Pyaar Nibhaaye Aur Kaise Pyaar Nibhaaye'*, penned by Indivar, in the voice of Lata Mangeshkar to officially announce the film. The film, planned to be made as a magnum opus, was to have its *mahurat* on 11 November 1977. Extensive advance preparations were made and a number of trials for the look of Dilip Kumar as Chanakya were successfully conducted. London-based professional make-up expert Annie Spiers and Indian make-up man Pandhari Juker worked together to create the looks of the main artistes, including Dilip Saheb. The work was carried out in London over three weeks with an active participation of Dilip Kumar, B.R. Chopra, Kishore Sharma, Pandhari Juker and Laxmikant Joshi, an expert on Chanakya. However, this ambitious venture could never reach the setsas Sharma suddenly passed away.

Dilip as Chanakya

The Unrealised Casting Coup

Sohrab Modi's magnum opus remake of *Pukar*: Veteran filmmaker and actor Sohrab Modi wanted to remake his super hit film *Pukar* (1939) in the early 1970s with a stellar star cast playing the roles from the original: Dilip Kumar as Emperor Jehangir, Raj Kapoor as washerman, Saira Banu as Empress Noor Jahan, Shashi Kapoor as Sangram Singh and Rakhee as washerwoman. Music director Naushad (Ali) had even recorded two songs for the filmfilm—'*Toree Nazaron Se Dhobaniyaa Laage Man Maa Kaantaa Re*', sung by Mukesh, and, '*Tore Kurte Se Toraa Badan Jhalake, Kaahe Dhoyaa Re Dhobaniyaa*', a duet in the voices of Mukesh and Asha Bhosle. The lyrics were penned by Jan Nisar Akhtar. Some scenes were also picturised on Dilip Kumar and Saira Banu but the magnum opus somehow got shelved.

Sunkavalli's untitled film: A producer from south Indian film industry, V.K.P. Sunkavalli announced an untitled Dilip Kumar–Saira Babu starrer to be directed by veteran K.S. Prakash Rao with music by Shankar–Jaikishan. A gala mahurat was held with much fanfare followed by an initial shooting stint in Chennai (then Madras). It was a light-hearted script based on the Telugu hit *Vichitra Kutumbam* (1969), with Dilip Saheb playing a lawyer and Saira Banu playing his wife. The film was reportedly financed by the political heavyweight Biju Patnaik from Odisha (then Orissa). Inexplicably, the film did not proceed beyond the initial shooting schedule and was shelved.

Mahurat and stills of Sunkavalli's film

Zabardast: Veteran producer-director Nasir Hussain launched his most ambitious venture titled 'Zabardast', starring Dilip Kumar, Asha Parekh, Sharda, Dharmendra, Zeenat Aman, Rishi Kapoor, Tina Munim, Amjad Khan, Kajal Kiran, etc. The film's other major credits included Sachin Bhowmick (script), R.D. Burman (music) and Majrooh Sultanpuri (lyrics). The shooting of the multi-starrer (in Cinemascope and stereophonic sound) commenced in right earnest at Filmalaya Studios but somewhere along the way Dilip Saheb and Nasir Saheb developed creative differences and the project was shelved. Asha Parekh till date deeply regrets missing the chance of working with Dilip Saheb.

Dilip Kumar with Asha Parekh

Discovery of India: During the emergency days (1975–1977), producer G.P. Sippy launched an ambitious project titled 'Discovery of India', based on Pt Jawahar Lal Nehru's famous book by the same title, with Dilip Kumar playing the main protagonist. It was to be directed by Ramesh Sippy (of *Sholay* fame) and written by writer duo Salim (Khan)–Javed (Akhtar). A grand *mahurat* was held in New Delhi which was attended by the then Information and Broadcasting Minister Vidya Charan Shukla. The film, however, did not proceed beyond the *mahurat*.

Masterji: Chandra Barot, who directed the Amitabh Bachchan–Zeenat Aman starrer *Don* (1978) which was produced by ace cinematographer Nariman Irani, launched his own film titled 'Masterji' based on George Bernard Shaw's celebrated play, *Pygmalion.* He signed up Dilip Kumar to play Professor Higgins and Saira Banu as Eliza Dolittle. An initial shooting schedule at Juhu Beach was completed but the film did not proceed beyond that.

Majnoon: Superstar Rajesh Khanna with great fanfare launched an ambitious production under his own banner of Aashirwad Films titled 'Majnoon', starring himself and Rakhi in the main leads, with music by Khayyam and lyrics by Naqsh Lyallpuri under the direction of Kamaal Amrohi. Full page advertisements were run in the *Screen* magazine pompously announcing a mega film with other co-stars being Ashok Kumar, Dilip Kumar and Raj Kapoor. A grand gala mahurat was held with the inaugural shot taken on Raj Kapoor. Two sonorous songs/title music of the film were recorded under the baton of Khayyam. However, Dilip Saheb ran counter advertisements in the *Screen* magazine denying that he had signed the film. In any case, the film got shelved after picturisation of the songs.

Asar: Producer Dinesh Gandhi, under the banner of Sonu Films, launched a film titled 'Asar' on 27 August 2001 starring Dilip Kumar, Ajay Devgn and Priyanka Chopra under the direction of Kuku Kohli. Dilip Saheb had sounded the clapper board, Aruna Irani switched on the camera, guest director Indra Kumar broke the auspicious coconut and Saira Banu called for 'action'. The film had music by Nadeem–Shravan, lyrics by Sameer, editing by Sanjay Jaiswal and cinematography by Baba Azmi. Shooting of the movie commenced at Royal Palm Club in Goregaon but the project was shelved after around four reels were canned.

Adaa: Producer-directors Tanvi Ahmed and JhamuS ugandh had pulled off a major casting coup by signing Dilip Kumar, Amitabh Bachchan and Aamir Khan for their film titled 'Adaa', based on a story spanning four generations. The music was assigned to A.R. Rahman but the film never took off.

Sahara's untitled film: Dilip Kumar and Manoj Bajpayee were signed for a film by Sahara One Motion Pictures to be directed by Tinnu Anand but this project also remained unrealised.

Subhash Ghai's 'Homeland': Producer-director Subhash Ghai, under his banner Mukta Arts, had launched a mega venture titled 'Homeland' and brought together three major stars Dilip Kumar, Amitabh Bachchan and Shah Rukh Khan to play the leads. But, this dream project also failed to take shape.

Film Ideas That Remained Just That

After the astounding success of his home production *Gunga Jumna,* Dilip Kumar was keen on working on a script titled 'Kaar Begaar'. It was based on the trials and tribulations of some cotton weavers who help a tycoon set up a factory in their hamlet, assuming that it will generate employment and change their lives for the better. But, they are met with disillusionment as the tycoon goes back on his words. The villagers then take up cudgels against the tycoon seeking justice. The film never got made. Saira*ji* told us that she was keen on playing the woman protagonist and regretted that the film was not made. Some other films that the megastar's own banner, Citizen Films, had announced were 'Kaali Sarson', 'Banmanas', and 'Satya'. 'Kaali Sarson' was a dark-skinned girl's story and was to star Saira Banu in the lead role.

Dilip Saheb had another dream project titled 'Oh Baba Jaan' for which he had crafted nine different versions of a script on schizophrenia and wanted the film to be directed by the well-known Marathi director Jabbar Patel. Baba Jaan was probably the name of a horse which the protagonist with split personality rides in the nights. The story had a riveting, suspense plot about a schizophrenic banker's diabolic bid to rob a bank. Dilip Saheb had several meetings with Jabbar Pater but somehow the film did not get off ground. The dream project sadly remained a dream. Another subject which remained on paper only was titled 'Kashmir Valley' or 'Song of the Valley' set against the backdrop of Kashmir and was specially written for Saira Banu before the couple had married.

Producer-director R.K. Nayyar had announced an ambitious film titled 'Bewafa' with an unusual star cast comprising his actress wife Sadhana, Dilip Kumar and Shammi Kapoor. The project did not move beyond the trade paper reports. Similarly, the ace producer-director Manmohan Desai had planned a film titled 'Hazaar Laakh Crore' starring Dilip Kumar in early 1960s but the project never took off.

The Roles Dilip Kumar Declined

Dilip Saheb's dear friend, contemporary and iconic actor-director-producer Raj Kapoor wanted to make a film titled 'Gharonda' starring Nargis, himself and Dilip Kumar with music by Shankar–Jaikishan on the same subject as his later day super hit film *Sangam* (1964). Raj Kapoor was extremely keen to have Dilip Kumar play the role which was eventually performed by Rajendra Kumar in *Sangam.* The late veteran director Lekh Tandon, then an assistant to Raj Kapoor (and a close family friend of the authors), was with Raj Kapoor when he broached the subject with Dilip Kumar. Lekh*ji* personally recounted the conversation which he said was in chaste Punjabi. Dilip Saheb's response to Raj Kapoor was, '*Subject vi twada, actor vi tu, director vi tu, hoar kainchi vi twade haath... ton saada ki hai?* He thus politely declined the offer.

Besides this, Dilip Saheb declined quite a few roles in films that later turned out to be classics. He had his own logic for turning down the lead roles in films like Vijay Bhatt's *Baiju Bawra* (1952), Guru Dutt's *Pyaasa* (1957) and *Sahib Bibi aur Ghulam* (1962), and Mehboob Khan's *Mother India.* We have already dwelled on his reasons for declining the role of Birju in *Mother India* in Chapter 3. Dilip Sahab, on his refusal to play the poet of *Pyaasa,*

said, 'I did not do Guru Dutt's *Pyaasa* which was offered to me since I saw no wisdom in doing it while I was playing a similar role in Bimal Roy's *Devdas* (1955). In both the pictures, I would have been heavily drinking, the characterisations were similar and any glimmer of repetition would have been unfair to both the directors.' Well, he seems to have a point there.

Guru Dutt with Dilip, Dev and Goldie

There was also an offer from the iconic Hollywood director David Lean, a friend of Dilip Kumar, to act in his landmark film *Lawrence of Arabia* (1962). But, for reasons best known to him, Dilip Saheb declined the offer. Similarly, the well-known British producer-director-distributor Sir Alexander Korda wanted to launch a magnum opus production titled 'Taj Mahal' but again Dilip Kumar politely declined. There also were rumours that the 'Master of Suspense' Alfred Hitchcock, during his visit to Mumbai, had considered making a thriller with Dilip Kumar. When we posed the question of working with Hitchcock to Dilip Saheb, he merely answered with his engaging smile. Despite our best efforts, we could not ascertain whether there was any truth in the said rumours.

Dilip and Hitchcock

In the 1960s, there were rumours of a possible collaboration between the legendary film director Satyajit Ray and Dilip Saheb to make a film. Apparently, the film was based on the famous sort by Munshi Premchand, *Kafan.* Ray and Dilip Saheb had a long friendship and the iconic director was very fond of the thespians, acting calibre and films. Dilip Kumar attended the Mumbai premier of Ray's *Abhijan* (1962) and that's where the possibility of such a film said to have been discussed. However, the Satyajit Ray–Dilip Kumar film did not materialise and that was a loss of Indian cinema.

Satyajit Ray and Dilip Kumar

CHAPTER 5

THE REEL ROMANTICISM: DILIP KUMAR'S LEADING LADIES

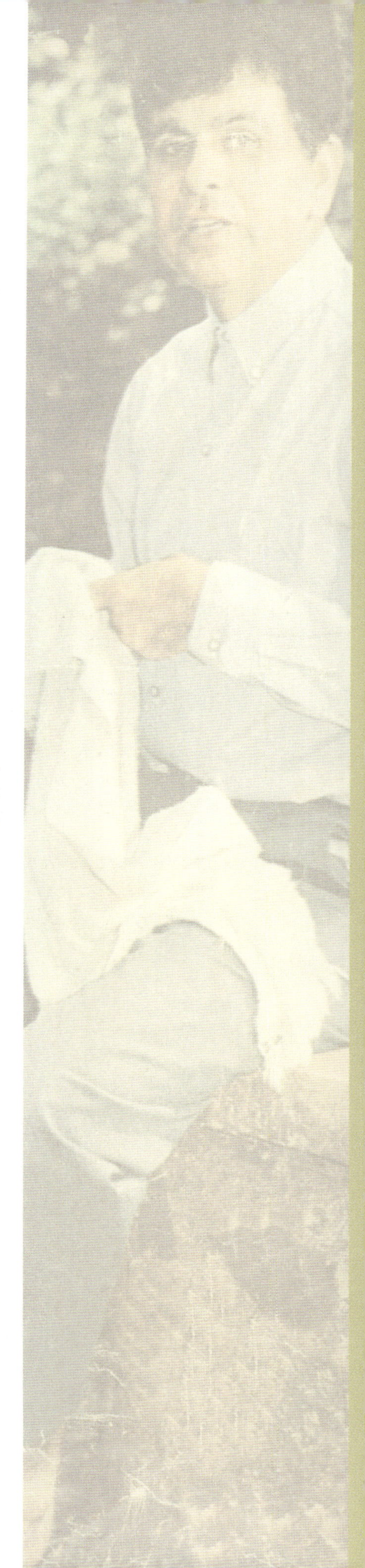

Top most leading ladies of Indian cinema, over the last half century or so, fell over each other to bag a role opposite Dilip Kumar in a film. Dilip Kumar's heroines were not only top names of their times, but were also endowed with rare charm and enormous histrionic abilities. To name a few:

Mridula (*Jwar Bhata*)
Swarnalata (*Pratima*)
Meera Misra and Ranjana (*Milan*)
Noor Jehan (*Jugnu*)
Kamini Kaushal (*Shaheed, Shabnam, Nadiya Ke Paar, Arzoo*)
Nargis (*Mela, Andaaz, Anokha Pyar, Babul, Deedar, Jogan, Hulchul*)
Nalini Jaywant (*Anokha Pyar, Shikast*)
Munawar Sultana (*Babul*)
Madhubala (*Tarana, Sangdil, Amar, Mughal-E-Azam*)
Nimmi (*Aan, Daag, Deedar, Amar, Uran Khatola*)
Meena Kumari (*Foot Path, Azaad, Yahudi, Kohinoor*)
Nutan (Shikwa (Incomplete), *Karma, Kanoon Apna Apna*)
Bina Rai (*Insaniyat*)
Surya Kumari (*Uran Khatola*)
Vyjayantimala (*Devdas, Naya Daur, Madhumati, Paigham, Gunga Jumna, Leader, Sunghursh*)
Suchitra Sen (*Devdas*)
Usha Kiron (*Musafir*)
Waheeda Rehman (*Dil Diya Dard Liya, Ram Aur Shyam, Aadmi, Mashaal*)
Mumtaz (*Ram Aur Shyam*)
Saira Banu (*Gopi, Sagina Mahato, Sagina, Bairaag, Duniya*)

Sharmila Tagore (*Dastaan*)
Sumita Sanyal (*Sagina Mahato*)
Aparna Sen (*Sagina*)
Leena Chandavarkar (*Bairaag*)
Rekha (*Qila, Aag Ka Darya*)
Nirupa Roy (*Kranti*)
Rohini Hattangadi (*Dharm Adhikari*)

Of these, Nargis and Vyjayantimala jointly wear the crown of starring as leading ladies in the highest number of Dilip Kumar films, that is, seven each.

Markedly, the most captivating feature of the alluring serenades of Dilip Kumar was the sheer romantic intensity that oozed from every frame as he adoringly looked in the eyes of his leading ladies to set their hearts aflutter with that disarming smile. My wife, Kanika, and I have witnessed a live demonstration of this Dilipian magic when during one of our numerous visits to Dilip Saheb's abode, he, so very lovingly, held Kanika's hand, looked her in the eyes, and with that famous smile, would enquired, '*Kaisi hain aap?*' We were floored and Kanika was on cloud nine.

The romantic on-screen chemistry that developed between him and his heroines was one of the cornerstones of his incredible screen presence and those unforgettable performances. It is another matter that these 'reel' romances at the time led the grapevine about his 'real' romantic affiliations with Kamini Kaushal, Madhubala, (perhaps) Vyjayantimala, et al. But, it was anything but a natural corollary to his brilliant on-screen performances.

Mridula

Meera Misra

Swarnalata

Mumtaz Shanti

Initial Heroines

Dilip Kumar's first leading lady Mridula, who also made her debut with *Jwar Bhata*, had a winsome smile and confidence in her performance. But, her screen presence was laced with an air of artificiality—so very typical of that era—as opposed to Dilip Kumar's convincing romanticism even in his debut. The thespian had picked the right thread of expression from the word go to strike the correct romantic chords. Then, the second leading lady Swarnalata, wife of actor-director Nazir who later opted to move to Pakistan, was a big star then, but she did not have the fluency of expressions to match the natural flair of the megastar-to-be in their film *Pratima* (1945). The romantic chemistry with his third and fourth leading ladies Meera Misra and Ranjana in *Milan* (1946) did have the desired natural tinge, thanks to the balance struck by the great director Nitin Bose.

Senior actress Mumtaz Shanti, wife of producer-director-lyricist Wali Saheb, and a young Dilip Kumar were quite convincing as the lovers in *Ghar Ki Izzat* (1948). Irrespective of what critics of that era may have opined, it became clear from the first two films of Dilip Kumar that he was an actor of merit and had arrived to take forward the legacy of great actors such as Motilal, Ashok Kumar and Yaqoob. His third film *Milan* further established his acting métier.

Noor Jehan

The legendary singer-actor Noor Jehan and Dilip Kumar were paired in only one film *Jugnu* (1947) which set the box office afire to become a golden jubilee hit. Their romantic chemistry was best felt in the immortal Noor Jehan–Mohammed Rafi duet '*Yahan badla wafa ka bewafai ke siva kya hain'*, composed by Feroz Nizami. Noor Jehan did have large doses of theatricality in her performance as opposed to utterly natural emoting of Dilip Kumar, yet their romance came out on-screen. Noor Jehan and Feroz Nizami moved to Pakistan soon after partition but the singing legend and the megastar remained lifelong friends. In fact, when Noor Jehan re-visited India one last time in 1977, Dilip Kumar compèred a special show at the Shanmukhananda Hall in Mumbai and hosted a dinner evening in her honour. During his own couple of visits to Pakistan, Dilip Saheb always made it a point to visit Noor Jehan.

Dilip Kumar and Noor Jehan

The Shanmukhananda Hall programme

The dinner at Dilip–Saira's House

The press conference dinner

Kamini Kaushal

Kamini Kaushal and Dilip Kumar

A reigning queen of her times, Kamini Kaushal has the distinction of doing four quite remarkable films with Dilip Kumar. She struck a scintillating on-screen chemistry with Dilip Kumar which remains etched in the memories of fans. Dilip Kumar and Kamini Kaushal also shared a personal romantic fascination, more about which shall follow in the next chapter. Dilip Kumar in his autobiography has stated, 'I had an understanding and facile co-actor in Kamini Kaushal who was very attentive to the demands of the director and had the intelligence to grasp the intrinsic sensitivity of some of the more poignant situations in the script. She was an artiste who could perform with the required authority when needed. She was not new to the profession, having acted in Chetan Anand's *Neecha Nagar* (1946) earlier. Moreover, she was an educated person with whom one could have an interesting conversation.' Dilip Saheb has further touched upon his romantic involvement with great dignity in his autobiography to conclude on an intriguing note, 'Yes, circumstances called for us to discontinue working together and it was just as well because, after a few films together, star pairings generally tend to pall on viewers, which is bad for business.'

Nargis

Nargis and Dilip Kumar

As mentioned earlier, the legendary Nargis and Dilip Kumar acted in seven films together, and it was a treat to watch the pair in emotional and romantic scenes. Their performances peaked in Mehboob Khan's *Andaaz,* which also starred superstar Raj Kapoor—a casting coup of the time. The impact of stellar star cast was enormous; the film became a Golden jubilee hit and, subsequently, a classic. The magical on-screen chemistry of Dilip Kumar and Nargis was also seen in *Mela, Babul* and *Deedar,* while their powerful yet understated histrionics were witnessed in the avant-garde film *Jogan* (1950). This successful pairing, however, broke up in 1952 due to some differences that cropped up between them during the making of K. Asif's *Hulchul.* Whether there was an off-screen romance between these legends is a moot point but Dilip Kumar has said on record, with Nargis it was a no-holds-barred friendship. It was as though we were of the same gender because she was not at all hesitant to join the menfolk in their talks and was not one to be shocked if a bawdy remark was made in front of her. Her mother, Jaddan Bai, had become friendly with *Amma* and my elder sister due to her frequent visits to our home and later Agha*ji* came to know Nargis was an actress who feigned emotions while acting with me and there was nothing but a healthy friendship between us. Nargis was no doubt a very capable actress who was getting better with every film. I could see that she had improved vastly when we were cast in Mehboob Khan's *Andaaz* (1949).

Nalini Jaywant

Nalini Jaywant

In course of our numerous visits to the *Daulatkhana* of Dilip Saheb bungalow, it was our privilege to freely chat with him and reminisce about his work and old times. We once pointedly asked him as to which actress posed the toughest histrionic challenge as an artist. Without a moment's hesitation he, somewhat to our surprise, mentioned, Nalini Jaywant. *'Unke saath bahut sambhal ke kaam karna padta tha'* (You had be very careful while working with her). Coming from Dilip Kumar himself, it would be the ultimate compliment for any actor. That day, on returning home, we took another view at the Dilip–Nalini starrer *Shikast* (1953) and could instantly grasp as to where Dilip Saheb was coming from. The film is a treat for cinegoers in terms of a *jugalbandi* of marvellous performances of the two great artists. The other film the two were seen together was *Anokha Pyar (1948).* It is the loss of the film world that these two highly accomplished artists featured only in a couple of films.

Madhubala

Madhubala and Dilip Kumar

The reel and real romance between the ' Venus of Indian Screen' Madhubala and the 'Tragedy King' Dilip Kumar is the most often sung ballad of film folklore. The legendary on-screen romance and its resultant off-screen chemistry and affiliations could not fructify into its logical consummation due to a quirk of fate and conspiracy of circumstances which we shall dwell upon in the next chapter. Here, we shall restrict the elucidation to their cinematic captivation only. The marvellous Dilip–Madhubala chemistry evolved and took off in *Tarana* (1958), scaling bewildering romantic heights as they set a million hearts aflutter emoting on '*Nain mile nain huey baware*' and '*Beimaan tore nainva nindiya na aaye*'. They simply mesmerised their fans displaying true-to-life romantic fervour emoting '*Dil mein sama gaye sajan*' in *Sangdil.* But, these light-hearted romances were a springboard to the pair attaining unprecedented acting fete in Mehboob Khan's intense psychological drama *Amar* and K. Asif's timeless magnum opus *Mughal-E-Azam.* The incredible on-screen chemistry of the pair in the two classics made their performances immortal and the pairing, legendary. However, the personal relationship between the two, during its roller coaster ride, remained ambivalent but cordial right up to the end. Their officially parting of ways came about during the making of one of Dilip Kumar's greatest cinematic achievements, B.R. Chopra's *Naya Daur.* The film initially had Madhubala as the leading lady, only to be replaced by Vyjayantimala even after several reels were canned with the initial pair. Madhubala reportedly was not allowed to participate in a long and key outdoor shooting schedule of the movie by her father. A court battle ensued which was decided in the favour of B.R. Chopra. The episode made national headlines and was the flavour of film world's gossip for months, climaxing with Dilip Kumar's famous open declaration of his love for Madhubala in a court, 'I love this woman and shall love her till my dying day.' It is sad indeed that the most serious romantic involvement of the 'Tragedy King' himself ended in tragedy. But, more about that later.

Nimmi

Facile artist Nimmi featured in as many as five super-duper hit films of Dilip Kumar. Nimmi's brilliant emotional performances in *Daag, Amar* and *Deedar* were a treat to watch. She also has the distinction of co-starring with the thespian in the only fantasy film of his career, *Uran Khatola* (1955). The film had surreal overtones with a mesmerising musical score by maestro Naushad.

Nimmi and Dilip Kumar

Meena Kumari

'Tragedy Queen' Meena Kumari and 'Tragedy King' Dilip Kumar hit it off beautifully to give memorable performances in their four films together. It is amusing that while their light-hearted films *(Azaad* and *Kohinoor)* with comical overtones were run away hits, their serious movie (*Foot Path*) was only a moderate success. In any case, the pair complemented each other on-screen brilliantly, displaying great romantic fervour and terrific comic timing. Their romantic banters in *Azaad* truly charmed the viewers and the dialogue, *J'is dil mein aag lagi ho, woh waqt nahin dekhta Shobha!',* was on the lips of every romantic lover of that era. For that matter, the Marcus–Hannah romance in *Yahudi* was no less captivating and romantically enticing. But, their comic banter in *Kohinoor* takes the cake in showcasing how versatile Dilip Kumar and Meena Kumari were. Their subtle yet rib-tickling comic interludes in the film were outrageously funny. Off-screen, Dilip Saheb was very fond of Meena*ji* and personally supervised her funeral.

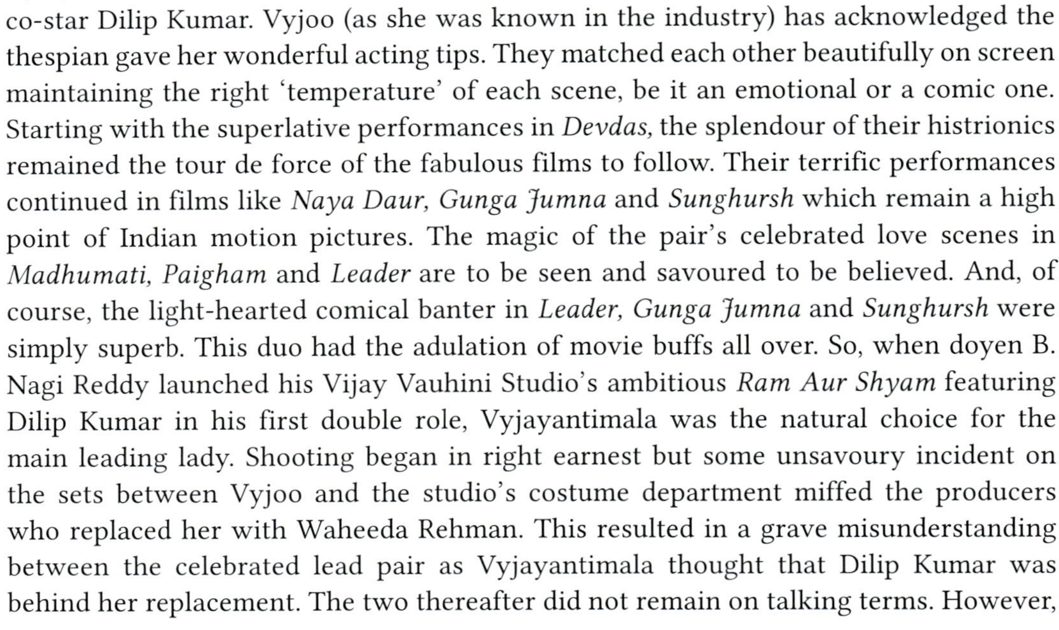

Meena Kumari and Dilip Kumar

Vyjayantimala

One of the greatest on-screen romantic pairs of Hindi cinema was the Dilip Kumar–Vyjayantimala combination. The pair displayed an unmatched chemistry in their seven films in which they starred together. The twinkle-toed dancing star Vyjayantimala owed her histrionic excellence to her talented co-star Dilip Kumar. Vyjoo (as she was known in the industry) has acknowledged the thespian gave her wonderful acting tips. They matched each other beautifully on screen maintaining the right 'temperature' of each scene, be it an emotional or a comic one. Starting with the superlative performances in *Devdas,* the splendour of their histrionics remained the tour de force of the fabulous films to follow. Their terrific performances continued in films like *Naya Daur, Gunga Jumna* and *Sunghursh* which remain a high point of Indian motion pictures. The magic of the pair's celebrated love scenes in *Madhumati, Paigham* and *Leader* are to be seen and savoured to be believed. And, of course, the light-hearted comical banter in *Leader, Gunga Jumna* and *Sunghursh* were simply superb. This duo had the adulation of movie buffs all over. So, when doyen B. Nagi Reddy launched his Vijay Vauhini Studio's ambitious *Ram Aur Shyam* featuring Dilip Kumar in his first double role, Vyjayantimala was the natural choice for the main leading lady. Shooting began in right earnest but some unsavoury incident on the sets between Vyjoo and the studio's costume department miffed the producers who replaced her with Waheeda Rehman. This resulted in a grave misunderstanding between the celebrated lead pair as Vyjayantimala thought that Dilip Kumar was behind her replacement. The two thereafter did not remain on talking terms. However, it is to the credit of Dilip Kumar and Vyjayantimala's professionalism that the duo did not let their acrimony come in the way of completion of their other film, H.S. Rawail's *Sunghursh.* They both reportedly told Rawail, '*Jhagda* Dilip Kumar *aur* Vyjayantimala *ke beech hai,* Kundan *aur* Munni *ke beech nahin.*' Kundan and Munni are the names of their characters in *Sunghursh.* Until 1964, when *Leader* and Raj Kapoor's *Sangam* were being shot almost simultaneously, the industry was abuzz with rumours of an affair between Dilip Kumar and Vyjayantimala, and later that year, of a Raj Kapoor–Vyjayantimala romance. Grapevine has it that Dilip Saheb did not like Vyjayantimala's closeness with his best friend Raj Kapoor and thus he distanced himself from one of his favourite heroines. However, the Dilip–Vyjayantimala friendship revived down the years but by then, the two greats had retired from films.

Dilip Kumar and Vyjayantimala

Waheeda Rehman

Consummate actor Waheeda Rehman offered sterling performances in all the four films that she featured in along with Dilip Kumar. In the super-duper hit *Ram Aur Shyam,* she displayed her flair for subtle comedy, essaying one of her most applauded roles. *Dil Diya Dard Liya, Aadmi* and, in later years, *Mashaal* were intensely dramatic films and she excelled with truly superlative performances. The Dilip–Waheeda pair was as well matched in terms of their acting prowess as any other celebrated pair in Dilip Saheb's films. Another splendid actress, Mumtaz starred opposite the thespian in *Ram Aur Shyam.* It was a role of a life time which Mumtaz performed with great élan and zoomed to the top artists' bracket.

Waheeda Rehman and Dilip Kumar

Nutan

The charming performer Nutan was a truly accomplished actor and early in her illustrious career, she got a plum assignment of co-starring with Dilip Kumar in a brilliant film '*Shikwa*' directed by Ramesh Saigal. It was a meaty role and the on-screen chemistry of the two greats in that movie was captivating. Sadly, as mentioned earlier, the film was shelved after being 99 per cent complete and it was a great loss for the Indian cinema. Nutan, however, did act with Dilip Saheb some years during the thespian's second inning in *Karma* (1986) and *Kanoon Apna Apna* (1989).

Nutan and Dilip Kumar

Saira Banu

Saira Banu's five movies opposite Dilip Saheb showcased her best performances, with the most notable ones being in the Bengali *Sagina Mahato* (a golden jubilee hit) and *Gopi* (a silver jubilee). The husband-wife pair evoked a hysterical response from their audiences with their first release *Gopi* in 1970. The personal chemistry of the most celebrated pair of the filmdom came across loud-and-clear on celluloid, in their other films as well, such as *Bairaag* and *Sagina*. Their last film together was *Duniya* in 1984, in which Saira*ji* made a special appearance.

Saira Banu and Dilip Kumar

Some One-Film Pairings

Dilip Kumar and Suchitra Sen

SUCHITRA SEN, the legendry Bengali beauty, essayed the role of Paro opposite Dilip Kumar in Bimal Roy's *Devdas,* and she gave a natural and convincing performance. She held her own in the classic film against the Filmfare Award-winning performances of Dilip Kumar as Devdas (arguably his best) and Vyjayantimala as Chandramukhi. But, the classic remained the lone outing of the great Suchitra Sen with the legendary Dilip Kumar.

Dilip Kumar and Munawar Sultana

MUNAWAR SULTANA was a highly rated actress of her time alongside Nargis, Suraiya and Kamini Kaushal. She had a string of hits such as *Khazanchi* (1941), *Pehli Nazar* (1945), *Dard* (1947), *Meri Kahani* (1948), *Raat Ki Rani* (1949), etc. to her credit. She even featured in the super-duper hit *Babul* (1950) co-starring Nargis and Dilip Kumar. She was an apt romantic foil to the love legend Dilip Kumar in the film. Who can forget the duo in the terrific Naushad melody, '*Nadi kinare saath hamare*' and in the timeless classic song '*Milte hi ankhein dil hua deewana kisika?*' The song was enacted with great romantic fervour by an extremely handsome Dilip Kumar with Munawar Sultana.

Usha Kiron, Daisey Irani and Dilip Kumar

USHA KIRON was the legendary director-editor Hrishikesh Mukherjee's first leading lady in his debut film *Musafir* starring Dilip Kumar. She delivered a good performance in the film in which Dilip Saheb was in his top form. But, *Musafir* remained the only film of the Dilip–Usha pairing. Usha Kiron, however, excelled in several other films such as *Badbaan, Patita, Adhikar, Badshah, Nazrana, etc.*

Nadira and Dilip

NADIRA, who made her debut with Mehboob Khan's classic mega hit *Aan,* played a haughty princess in the film, a role which made her an overnight star. She matched Dilip Saheb very well on-screen in the film. She later had a long career as a vamp and a character artist including her famous role against Raj Kapoor in *Shree 420.*

BINA RAI, an An artist of considerable merit and wife of the maverick actor Prem Nath, acted with two of the greatest legends of Indian cinema, Dilip Kumar and Dev Anand in *Insaniyat* (1955). She proved to be a good match to both the legends, essaying her part to perfection and measuring up to them, particularly the towering performance of Dilip Kumar as Mangal in the film. Regretfully, this was the only film in which this actress co-starred with Dilip Kumar (or even Dev Anand).

Bina Rai and Dilip Kumar

Other Prominent Actresses

The list of Dilip Kumar's other prominent leading ladies with whom he shared an effective on-screen chemistry is pretty long. Famous Kathak exponent Sitara Devi (first wife of K. Asif) also played a parallel leading role with vampish connotations in K. Asif's *Hulchul* directed by Shubh Karan Ojha. Similarly, Nigar Sultana, who was one of the top most stars of the 1940s and 1950s the and second wife of K. Asif, played a major character of Bahaar in *Mughal-E-Azam* with Dilip Kumar. She also had the opportunity to play the second lead in the Bimal Roy-directed *Yahudi* co-starring Dilip Kumar and Meena Kumari. Her performances as Bahaar in *Mughal-E-Azam* and a Roman princess in *Yahudi* won plaudits. Surya Kumari, a south Indian actress, gave a memorable romantic performance opposite the thespian in *Uran Khatola.* In *Kohinoor,* accomplished dancer and actress Kumkum got an opportunity to play the role of her lifetime as the second lead along with Meena Kumari, a role which she performed with great distinction. Another south Indian star B. Saroja Devi, who did lead roles in hit Hindi films such as *Sasural* (1961) and *Beti Bete* (1961), etc., played the second lead in Dilip Kumar's super hit *Paigham.*

Nigar Sultana

B. Saroja Devi

Kumkum

Surya Kumari

Sitara Devi

Sharmila Tagore did B.R. Chopra's *Dastaan* (1972) with Dilip Kumar. In that era, Rajesh Khanna–Sharmila was the most sought after hit pair. She tried to put her best foot forward in the film in which Dilip Kumar played a complex double role to perfection and had Bindu in the second lead. Leena Chandavarkar fulfilled her lifetime's ambition of starring opposite Dilip Saheb in *Bairaag.* She performed with a vivacious verve and panache with the thespian in the song sequences—*'Saare shaher mein aapsa koi nahin'* and *'Peete peete kabhi kabhie yoon jaam badal jaate hain'.* It was one of her best cinematic outings. Rekha also performed admirably opposite the megastar in *Aag Ka Dariya* and *Qila.* Many other well-known actresses who fulfilled their dreams of starring with Dilip Saheb include Mala Sinha (*Phir Kab Milogi*), Nirupa Roy (*Ram Aur Shyam* and *Kranti*) Nanda (*Mazdoor*), and Rakhee Gulzar (*Shakti*).

Sharing screen space with Dilip Kumar was the dream of every accomplished and celebrated artist of the Dilipian era. But, as Sharmila Tagore is believed to have said that **performing with Dilip Kumar in a movie was both a pleasure and a challenge**, actresses had to be on their toes to come close to matching the thespian in acting.

With Mumtaz

With Sharmila Tagore

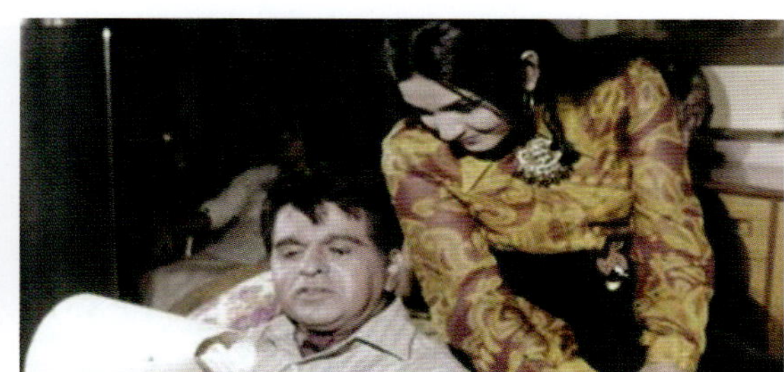

With Leena Chandavarkar

With Rekha

With Bindu

With Nirupa Roy

With Mala Sinha

With Rakhee

With Nanda

CHAPTER 6

REAL ROMANCE WAS IN THE AIR

In his illustrious and long career, megastar Dilip Kumar forged some fabulous romantic pairings with top-ranking and brilliant actresses such as Nargis, Kamini Kaushal, Nalini Jaywant, Madhubala, Nimmi, Meena Kumari, Vyjayantimala, Waheeda Rehman and others. The Hindi film industry's rumour mills worked overtime to romantically link Dilip Kumar with each one of them. The tabloids of that era had a field day gossiping to the hilt. We shall nevertheless confine this chapter to the duly authenticated real life romances of the thespian.

It was but natural that some of the on-screen magnetic charm of Dilip Kumar spilled over to his off-screen life. His disarming appeal rubbed off on his leading ladies who ostensibly looked for the romantic charm of Dilip Kumar in the real life Yusuf Khan. However, the introvert Yusuf, in his youth, was a die-hard romanticist and there is ample evidence of this little known trait of his in his autobiography titled, *The Substance and the Shado*w, where the 'Substance' (as Dilip Saheb likes to define Yusuf Khan) is juxtaposed against the 'Shadow' (as the thespian himself dubs Dilip Kumar, his screen self). Quite a few of the romantic interests of Dilip Saheb in his formative years did not see their desired fruition and those heartbreaks probably helped him deliver those terrific lovelorn performances which earned him the title of the 'Tragedy King'.

The Affairs and the Heartbreaks

The first romantic interest or infatuation of Yusuf Saheb was a beautiful young girl Kulsum in Deolali. She was the daughter of a Deccani Muslim woman Halima and a Turkish prisoner-of-war, and had lost her father long ago. Kulsum lived with her mother in a hut near Yusuf's house in Deolali. Enamoured by her beauty, many young men wanted to marry her, including a *hakim* from Lucknow (in Uttar Pradesh) and a handsome Christian ticket collector from the Deolali Railway Station. Yusuf's mother, out of compassion, often provided succour to Kulsum and her mother. Kulsum taught Yusuf how to climb trees and pluck mangoes and he, many a times, accompanied her as she took her goats for grazing. But, before an introvert Yusuf could express his fascination, the ticket collector converted to Islam and married Kulsum, leading to the first heartbreak of young Dilip. Years later, Dilip Saheb travelled to Deolali to perform a religious ceremony for his dead parents and ran into Kulsum, who was now a mother of half-a-dozen kids with *paan*-tainted teeth (which were pearly-white at one time). And, that was that.

Dilip Kumar and Kamini Kaushal

Hereafter, as Yusuf Khan became Dilip Kumar and the Shadow dwarfed the Substance, he shed his shyness in large measure to blossom into a heartthrob. After a somewhat tentative debut in *Jwar Bhata* and *Pratima,* the actor came of age in *Milan,* which was followed by the super-duper hit *Jugnu* opposite none other than Noor Jehan. Dilip Kumar had now hit the purple patch of his career and three mega hits followed in quick succession —*Shaheed, Shabnam* and *Nadiya Ke Paar.* The leading lady of all these hits was the comely Kamini Kaushal—reportedly Dilip Kumar's first flame and also his first serious heartbreak.

Kamini Kaushal's real name was Uma Kashyap. She was the daughter of Rai Bahadur S.R. Kashyap, a renowned Botanist, president of Indian Science Congress and dean of the pre-partition Punjab University. She was one of his five children which included three brothers and two sisters. She was very well-educated and had studied at Lady MacLagan School and Emily Kinnaird College of Lahore. She was also a champion swimmer. When her elder sister, who was married to B.S. Sood, a high ranking official of Bombay Port Trust, died in a car crash leaving behind two small kids, Uma married him and moved to Mumbai. It was here that legendary director Chetan Anand discovered her talent and cast her in his award-winning *Neecha Nagar* as Kamini Kaushal. As an actress, she quickly ascended to stardom with films like *Jail Yatra, Aag* (opposite Raj Kapoor), *Do Bhai,* etc. Soon, Filmistan's S. Mukerji signed her opposite Dilip Kumar in his *Shaheed* (1948) which was a box-office success. At that point in time and during the making of the film, Dilip Kumar gave a magazine interview saying and we quote:
I came out of my shell. I am desperately in love. The void, the vacuum in which I have lived all along, without knowing the meaning of life, is filled with warmth and an exhilarating happiness. A friendly hand is extended to me. It leads me from a jungle of doubt, fear and ignorance towards bright sunshine and confidence. This is the richest episode of my vaguely troubled existence. It gives me a sense of completeness and a new awareness. Life is not the same any more. But I must not speak about the glorious experience.

Although, Dilip Kumar did not name the 'friendly hand', the grapevine has it that it indeed was said for Kamini Kaushal. Famous Kathak exponent and actress Sitara Devi (who starred with Dilip in *Hulchul* and shared a sister-brother relationship with him) and producer-director P.N. Arora of All India Pictures (in whose super hit *Pugree* Kamini Kaushal starred) have been on-record authenticating the Dilip Kumar–Kamini Kaushal romance. It is said that Sitara Dev*iji* had met the rumoured couple huddled together and travelling aimlessly in the first-class compartment of Mumbai's local trains. P.N. Arora has said, on-record, that Dilip Kumar often visited Kamini Kaushal on the sets of *Pugree* and once Kamini's military-man brother strode on the film's sets, brandishing a pistol, threatening to kill Kamini if she did not call off her clandestine romance with Dilip Kumar. He also threatened to kill Dilip Kumar. Around that time, Shahi Latif–Ismat Chugtai's *Aarzoo,* in which Dilip–Kamini featured for the last time, was in the making. Ismat *Aapa* had reportedly warned Dilip Saheb against the futility of the said romance. The hot-headed brother of Kamini Kaushal reportedly shot himself, having failed to end the Dilip–Kamini romance. This came as a blow to Kamini Kaushal and Dilip Kumar and they put a stop to their romance. Of course, the death of Kamini's brother and her marital commitments must have been the determining factors. Sitara Devi stated that after the beak-up, Dilip Kumar had driven to her house and vented out his frustration and agony. Veteran journalists Shirish Kanekar and Ram Aurangabadkar have recorded interesting anecdotes stating that B.R. Chopra's super hit film *Gumrah* (featuring Ashok Kumar, Mala Sinha and Sunil Dutt) was reportedly based on this romance.

Dilip Saheb, however, has beautifully summed up the matter in his autobiography, saying: ***Stardom bothered me more than it pleased me and I guess I was drawn more intellectually than emotionally to Uma, with whom I could talk about matters and topics that interested me outside the purview of our working relationship. If that was love, maybe it was. I don't know and I don't think it matters any more. Yes, circumstances called for us to discontinue working together and it was just as well because, after a few films together, star pairings generally tend to pall on viewers, which is bad for business.***

The earlier elucidation very much puts all connotations of the famous affair in perspective. Years later, an incident occurred when Yash Chopra was shooting for B.R. Films' *Aadmi Aur Insaan* starring Saira Banu and Dharmendra in which Kamini was playing Saira's mother. Dilip Kumar, who was not involved with the film, came to meet his dear friend B.R. Chopra on the sets of the movie. For a moment, the Chopras were worried, but Dilip Kumar was his usual charming self, with his impeccable manners and gracious style. He gracefully conversed with Kamini Kaushal making her comfortable, along with other unit members.

Dilip Kumar by the flicker of an eyelid or subtle vocal resonance could effortlessly convey on screen intense romantic feelings and grave emotional turmoil. This trait of the actor reached perfection in the four films he did with the 'Venus of the Indian Screen' Madhubala—*Tarana, Sangdil, Amar* and *Mughal-E-Azam.* There was a stark contrast in the personalities of the first two loves of Dilip Saheb in terms of their markedly different educational and cultural roots. Hence, it was natural that there was striking difference in the relationship that developed between Dilip Kumar and Kamini Kaushal, and later with Madhubala. Kamini exuded urbane sophistication and bonded very well at an intellectual level with Dilip. On the other hand, both Madhubala and Dilip being Pathans shared a commonality of ethnic and cultural background. Thus, a vivacious Madhubala's ceaseless laughter became an ideal balm for Dilip Kumar's bruised heart.

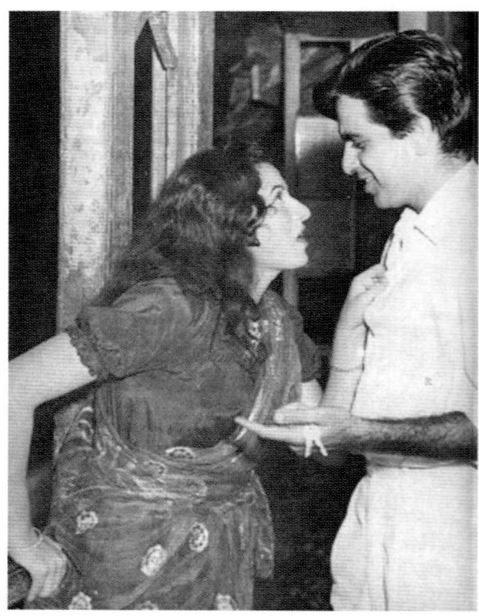

Dilip and Madhubala

Madhubala's real name was Mumtaz Jehan Begum Dehlavi. She was third born among the seven daughters (Kaneez, Fatima, Altaf, Chanchal, Zahida and Shahida being others) of a handsome Pathan Attaullah Khan and his beautiful Iranian wife. Her father was a headstrong, stubborn and egoistic man, and a harsh disciplinarian. Her mother was simple, illiterate and a homely woman. Attaullah Khan apparently had lost his job with the Imperial Tobacco Company, Delhi due to his arrogant, hot-tempered behaviour and attitude. He moved to Mumbai with his family but could not fend for them. He made his daughter work in films to make ends meet. After being introduced as a child artist by director Amiya Chakrabarty in his Mumtaz Shanti and

Ulhas starrer *Basant* (1942), Madhubala (the name given to her by Devika Rani) never looked back and embarked on a glorious career to become the sole breadwinner of the family. By the time she signed 'Har Singaar' opposite Dilip Kumar (which ultimately got shelved), Madhubala had a string of successful films to her credit. The impressive array of her movies included *Neel Kamal, Chittor Vijay, Dil Ki Rani* (all in 1947, co-starring Raj Kapoor), *Laal Dupatta* (1948), *Apradhi* (1949), *Singaar* (1949) and super hits *Dulari* and *Mahal* (both 1949). The pertinent point to be noted is that by the time (1949) Dilip Kumar was making rapid strides to be a superstar, Madhubala too was a star in her own right. So, it was just a matter of time before a Dilip–Madhubala starrer rolled. It soon did in 1951, as director Ram Daryani's *Tarana.*

The legendary Dilip Kumar–Madhubala romance is said to have took off on the sets of this film, as the duo hit the ground running, enacting the dulcet duet, '*Nain mile nain huey baware*'. One has to revisit *Tarana* to fathom the chemistry between Dr Motilal (Dilip Kumar) and Tarana (Madhubala) which even after six decades floors you with its innocent charm. They make the budding romance between the nubile village belle and the city-bred doctor absolutely convincing. Prior to being romantically drawn to Dilip Kumar, Madhubala was reportedly dating the leading man of her hit film *Badal,* the handsome Prem Nath. Grapevine has it that there was some time when Madhu was dating Dilip and Prem Nath simultaneously. Reportedly, when Prem Nath came to know that his friend Dilip (they struck a good friendship while working together in *Aan*) was seriously involved with Madhubala and that she was drawn to him as well, he withdrew and married Bina Rai, his charming co-star of *Aurat.* The Dilip–Madhubala romance was passionately emotional sans the intellectual angle. It is notable that *Tarana* was their first film together. They had previously shot a few reels together for Mahesh Kaul's 'Har Singaar', which was shelved. The seeds of the famous Dilip–Madhubala romance probably were sown on the sets of the shelved film itself. Interestingly, Bombay Talkies boss Devika Rani had chosen Madhubala to star opposite Dilip Kumar in his debut film *Jwar Bhata* but somehow the role went to Mridula. Anyway, Dilip Kumar and Madhubala's on-screen romances in their four films (ironically, the Dilip–Kamini pair also did only four films together) are cinematic landmarks, which include from the captivating *Tarana,* the alluring *Sangdil,* to the sublimely intense *Amar* and the magnum opus *Mughal-E-Azam.* The romantic sequences seemed to pick a leaf or two from their real life canvas. Madhubala's best work arguably was in those four films with Dilip Kumar (topped by her legendary portrayal of Anarkali in *Mughal-E-Azam*), and doubtlessly her performance peaked while acting opposite Dilip Saheb. On his part, Dilip Kumar never missed any opportunity to recommend Madhubala for a role opposite himself. The iconic *Amar* originally had Meena Kumari in the female lead, but she fell off with its renowned maker Mehboob Khan after the latter's squabble with her husband writer-director Kamaal Amrohi. Dilip Kumar promptly persuaded Mehboob Saheb to take in Madhubala. Similarly, when Nargis opted out of *Mughal-E-Azam,* Dilip Kumar convinced K. Asif to let Madhubala play Anarkali which ultimately became her best ever performance. The *mahurat* announcement of the celebrated classic *Daag* also had Madhubala's name as the leading lady but something went wrong and Nimmi played the part.

However, the perfect romance of this well-matched perfect couple did not culminate into marriage. Many were of the opinion that it was Madhubala's father Attaullah Khan who stood in the way of their marriage for the fear of losing the breadwinner for the large family. The truth lies somewhere around this premise. As the Dilip Kumar–Madhubala romance was peaking, Attaullah Khan once asked Dilip Kumar to star as the hero of a film he wanted to produce under his own banner and also had his daughter Madhubala in it. We believe that the moment Attaullah did that, he encroached upon Dilip Sahab's professional side via his personal life. Yusuf Saheb never wanted Dilip Kumar to be exploited for somebody's gain.

As is widely believed, Attaullah Khan was not opposed to the Dilip Kumar–Madhubala marriage but had his own axe to grind in the whole affair. He wanted the superstar of the era to work exclusively and on priority for his own home productions. On the other hand, Dilip Kumar, who had been positively considering marriage to Madhubala, was unwilling to tolerate any interference in his professional endeavours. Dilip Saheb reportedly laid down two conditions for getting married to Madhubala. One, he would financially support the Khan's family but Madhubala would have nothing to do with her father after wedding; and second, she would stop working in films. This was a clever killing-two-birds-with-one-stone strategy—if Madhubala agreed to quit films, her father's hold on her would automatically diminish. Both Dilip Saheb and Attaullah hardened their positions in the ensuing tug of war to the point that Madhu had Dilip's ultimatum to choose between him and her father. She opted for her father ending the fairy-tale romance.

Grapevine has it that on the sets of Madhubala–Kishore Kumar starrer *Dhake Ki Malmal* (1958), Dilip Kumar called famous comedian-producer-director Om Prakash to be a witness as he made a formal and final proposal to Madhubala, saying, 'I have a Qazi waiting at home, come with me now. I will marry you, my only condition is that you break all ties with your father.' According to Om Prakash, Madhubala on hearing this proposal-cum-ultimatum began to cry and Dilip Kumar, having failed to persuade his lady love, walked off in a huff. Apparently, this was not the first time Madhubala had let his proposal down. But, he had had enough and after this final proposal, Dilip Kumar never went back to her. Later, Madhubala reportedly did send him feelers through the well-known scribe Bunny Reuben but Dilip was unrelenting.

In the end, there was considerable acrimony on both sides as the affair was even talked about during the B.R. Chopra–Attaullah Khan court case. The climax, of course, was the historic courtroom admission of love by Dilip Kumar (mentioned in an earlier chapter). Both Dilip and Madhubala were Pathans and both were in the prime phase of their film careers. They were both single and therefore, there were no social complications in their union. What perhaps could have happened is that for Madhubala, the compulsions of family took over commitment of love. Dilip Saheb has shed light on the affair quite candidly and honestly in his autobiography and we quote:

Dilip and Madhubala

Contrary to popular notions, her father, Attaullah Khan, was not opposed to her marrying me. He had his own production company and he was only too glad to have two stars under the same roof. Had I not seen the whole business from my own point of view, it would have been just what he wanted, that is, Dilip Kumar and Madhubala holding hands and singing duets in his productions till the end of our careers. When I learned about his plans from Madhu, I explained to both of them that I had my own way of functioning and selecting projects and I would not show any laxity even if it were my own production house. It must have tilted the apple cart for him and he successfully convinced Madhu that I was being rude and presumptuous. I told her in all sincerity and honesty that I did not mean any offence and it was in her interest and mine as artistes to keep our professional options away from any personal considerations. She was naturally inclined to agree with her father and she persisted in trying to convince me that it would all be sorted out once we married. My instincts, however, predicted a situation in which I would be trapped and all the hard work and dedication I had invested in my career would be blown away by a hapless surrender to someone else's dictates and strategies. I had many upfront discussions with her father and she, not surprisingly, remained neutral and unmoved by my dilemma. The scenario was not very pleasant and it was heading inevitably to a dead end. In the circumstances, therefore, it seemed best that we did not decide to marry or even give each other a chance to rethink because my resolve by then had become strongly against a union that would not be good for either of us.

And that puts an end to the whole affair!

Madhubala was apparently deeply depressed after her break-up with Dilip Kumar and on the rebound married the legendary singer-actor-director-producer Kishore Kumar (who had at that time divorced his first wife Ruma Guha Thakurta). But, it turned out to be an unhappy marriage. Madhubala had acted in two of Kishore Kumar's hit home productions—*Chalti Ka Naam Gaadi* (1958) and *Jhumroo* (1961), but grapevine has it that she was persecuted by the legendary singer. The great composer Naushad Saheb himself told us that Madhubala had cried her heart out to him narrating terrible stories of Kishore Kumar's abuse on her. Madhubala sadly had a congenital heart problem which accentuated during the later part of her career. The first alarm bell of her ailment rang on the sets of Gemini's *Bahut Din Huwe* (1954) in Chennai when she fell seriously sick. Unfortunately, medical science had not advanced adequately at that point in time to successfully cure such heart ailment. Madhubala was treated by specialists in London, but that was of no avail. Dilip Kumar did meet Madhubala at her Arabian Villa residence in Bandra suburb of Mumbai during her illness and also after his marriage to Saira Banu. Reportedly, Madhubala was happy to see Dilip Saheb after his marriage and she congratulated him, saying, '*Hamarey shehzade ko unki shehzadi mil gayi hai, main bahut khush hoon'* (I am very happy that our prince has found his princess). What an end to a fairy-tale love story. Madhubala succumbed to her illness in 1969 leaving behind millions of grieving fans and a number of unfinished films including J.K. Nanda's 'Chalak', co-starring Raj Kapoor with music by Shankar–Jaikishan.

The Rumoured Romances

The twinkle-toed danseuse Vyjayantimala metamorphosed into one of the finest actresses this country has seen. She had a long association with Dilip Kumar spanning over seven films, beginning with *Devdas* (1956) to *Sunghursh* (1968). In between, there were five films—*Naya Daur* (1957), *Madhumati* (1958), *Paigham* (1959), *Gunga Jumna* (1961) and *Leader* (1964). The intense yet facile romantic portrayal that the pair cast on the silver screen became legendary. Expectedly, the honesty of their on-screen romance led to film industry's gossip mills working overtime to romantically link them in real life too. Whether there was a real life romance or not shall never be known since both the thespian and his famous leading lady are intensely private persons.

The same can be said about the consummate actor Waheeda Rehman who had four histrionic outings with the megastar in the films *Dil Diya Dard Liya* (1967), *Ram Aur Shyam* (1967), *Aadmi* (1968) and *Mashaal* (1984). The on-screen pair was so convincing that it had rumour-mongers swearing to their romantic involvement. There, of course, has not been and nor will there be any admission of real life romantic leanings. Nevertheless, both Vyjayantimala*ji* and Waheeda*ji* have had an excellent relationship with Dilip Saheb and Saira*ji* till today.

Dilip Kumar and Vyjayantimala

Dilip Kumar and Waheeda Rehman

However, there were other rumoured link-ups of Dilip Kumar even outside the film industry. The most famous one was his rumoured whirlwind romance with the dark-eyed, sensuous beautiful princess of a royal family from an obscure Indian state. Reportedly, Krishna Kapoor and her illustrious husband Raj Kapoor had made elaborate plans to welcome the newly-weds at the R.K. Studios but the thespian developed cold feet at the very last moment. Then, there were rumours of Dilip Kumar's involvement with a mysterious and fascinating Indo-French beauty. Grapevine has it that this rather serious relationship was closely guarded by the thespian and has remained a mystery till date. Similarly, during the making of his film *Leader,* there were rumours of a reported romance between him and a foreign dance instructor.

A diehard romantic and the most celebrated on-screen lover of a score of successful films, Dilip Kumar eventually settled for domestic bliss and married the beautiful Saira Banu—who was the daughter of 'Pari Chehra' Naseem Banu, a famous actress in her own right—on 11 October 1966 after a whirlwind romance. The Dilip–Saira marriage stood the test of time and has been one of the most successful star weddings of the Hindi film industry. Saira*ji* has and continues to take extremely good care of her nonagenarian husband. But, more on this shall follow in the latter chapters.

CHAPTER 7

DILIP KUMAR AND SAIRA BANU: A MATCH MADE IN HEAVEN

'*Pari Chehra*' (fairy-faced) actress, Naseem Banu (real name Roshan Ara Begum) was an extremely beautiful lady endowed with an innate and graceful charm. Daughter of classical singer Shamshad Begum and Nawab Abdul Waheed Khan, she was introduced in films by the legendary Sohrab Modi in his home production *Khoon Ka Khoon* in 1935. Her debut was followed by films like *Khan Bahadur* (1937), *Meetha Zahar* (1938) and *Talaaq* (1938). She won tremendous adulation for playing Empress Noor Jehan in Sohrab Modi's magnificent hit *Pukar* (1939). She soon married Mohammad Ehsan-ul-Haq, the son of Khan Bahadur Mohammad Suleman. The couple started their own home banner, Taj Mahal Pictures, and produced a handful of films including *Ujala* (1942) and *Begum* (1945). Many of these did not succeed at the box office despite filmmaker S. Mukerji's all-out support in scripting and making these movies. Mukerji, who had just branched off from Bombay Talkies Studios, then cast her in his film *Chal Chal Re Naujawan* (1944) opposite Ashok Kumar. She then went on to star in many more successful films such as *Door Chalen* (1946), *Anokhi Ada* (1948), *Chandni Raat* (1949), *Sheesh Mahal* (1950), etc. The couple had two children Saira Banu (the later day famous star in her own right) and Sultan Ahmad. Naseem Banu*ji* (whom the first author addressed as Roshan *Aapa* in my childhood during my couple of visits to her house) and Ehsan Saheb later separated. Roshan *Aapa* took great care of her children, Saira and Sultan, who later received their education in London.

At 16, Saira Banu made her sensational Bollywood debut with Subodh Mukerji's super-duper hit *Junglee* (1961), opposite the rebel star Shammi Kapoor, and never looked back. Among the big films she starred in thereafter included–Manmohan Desai's *Bluff Master* (1963, with Shammi Kapoor); Mohan Kumar's *Ayee Milan Ki Bela* (1964, opposite Rajendra Kumar) and *Aman* (1967, with Rajendra Kumar); Devendra Goel's *Door Ki Awaaz* (1964, with Joy Mukerji); Subodh Mukerji's *April Fool* (1964, opposite Biswajeet),

Saaz Aur Awaaz (1966, opposite Joy Mukerji), and *Shagird* (1967, with Joy Mukerji); Shankar Mukherji's *Pyar Mohabbat* (1966, co-starring Dev Anand); Mahesh Kaul's *Diwana* (1967, opposite Raj Kapoor); Manoj Kumar's *Poorab Aur Pachhim* (1970, opposite the actor-director himself); Lekh Tandon's *Jhuk Gaya Asmaan* (1968, with Rajendra Kumar); Yash Chopra's *Aadmi Aur Insaan* (1969, with Dharmendra); Mehmood's *Padosan* (1968, with Sunil Dutt); Hrishikesh Mukherjee's *Chaitali* (1975, with Dharmendra); Brij Sadanah's *Victoria No. 203* (1972, opposite Navin Nishchol); Aatmaram's *Resham Ki Dori* (1974, opposite Dharmendra); B.R. Chopra's *Zameer* (1975, Amitabh Bachchan); Raj Khosla's *Nehle Pe Dehla* (1976, opposite Sunil Dutt); and Prakash Mehra's *Hera Pheri* (1976, with Amitabh Bachchan and Vinod Khanna). Saira Banu was given the title of 'Beauty Queen' at the time of release of her first film *Junglee* and, quite deservingly, it stayed with her forever.

Dilip Kumar greatly admired Naseem*ji* for her dignity and self-reliance. Being close to the doyen S. Mukerji, Dilip Saheb was also close to the family of Naseem*ji*. Reportedly, Saira Banu had a crush on Dilip Kumar from her growing up years when she met the thespian on the sets of *Mughal-E-Azam*. While in London, Saira watched Mehboob Khan's *Aan* at the Scala Theatre and was mesmerised by Dilip Saheb's performance and personality. After completing her studies in England and upon her return to India, she engaged a scholarly Maulvi to make her proficient in Urdu and Farsi ostensibly to get closer to Dilip. There was some talk of Dilip Saheb accepting to cast Saira Banu as early as when *Gunga Jumna* was launched and later in *Leader* and thereafter for the second lead role of Shanta in *Ram Aur Shyam* (it eventually went to Mumtaz). At a party hosted by Mehboob Khan in those days, S. Mukerji had hinted to Dilip Kumar that the young girl Saira was crazy to work with him. Dilip Kumar reportedly told some scribes at that time that Saira Banu was too young to be cast opposite him. He also jokingly pointed to his greying mop of hair to dissuade Saira from pursuing ideas of starring opposite him. But, as Saira Banu's debut film *Junglee* became a stupendous hit, she became a much sought after actress. Saira*ji* was signed for films opposite virtually all the top heroes of that era including Dev Anand, Raj Kapoor, Shammi Kapoor, Rajendra Kumar, Sunil Dutt, Joy Mukerji, Manoj Kumar, etc., but a choosy Dilip Kumar eluded her. Saira Banu got so busy that she missed a few important films like S.U. Sunny's *Palki* (1967). Mehboob Khan, however, got her to commit bulk dates for his ambitious '*Habba Khatoon*' for which he had announced Dilip Kumar as the leading man way back in 1957 itself. But Dilip Saheb could not get himself to play Yousuf Shah Chak (husband of the poetess Habba Khatoon) which had negative shades. He differed with Mehboob Khan on some aspects of the script, and eventually withdrew from the film. Soon after, Mehboob Saheb passed away and the jinxed '*Habba Khatoon*' got shelved. But, Saira Banu kept sending frequent requests to Dilip Kumar via some popular producers for doing a film with her. On the other hand, Dilip Saheb kept sounding clapper boards at the mahurats of Saira Banu films. Dilip Kumar kept on working with heroines matching his age and maturity. Nevertheless, at that juncture Dilip Kumar did confide in S. Mukerji that he wanted to cast Saira in a subject specially written for her in a film titled 'Song of the Valley', which was set in the backdrop of the picturesque Kashmir Valley. But, the movie never took-off.

Dilip with Saira

Then, the unthinkable happened. Dilip Kumar was in Chennai shooting for *Ram Aur Shyam* when he received an invitation from Naseem *Aapa* to attend Saira's birthday bash in Mumbai on 23 August, 1966. Dilip Saheb decided to specially fly down to attend the event which later turned out to be the one that changed the course of his life. To quote Dilip Saheb, 'When I alighted from my car and entered the beautiful garden that leads to the house, I can still recall my eyes falling on Saira standing in the foyer of her new house looking breathtakingly beautiful in a brocade sari. I was taken aback, because she was no longer the young girl I had consciously avoided working with because I thought she would look too young to be my heroine. She had indeed grown to full womanhood and was in reality more beautiful than I thought she was.'[1] As Dilip Kumar shook hands with Saira Banu and congratulated her, time stood still and in that very propitious moment Dilip Kumar found his wife and Saira, her husband. They looked into each other's eyes and that was it. The celestial stars smiled on the star-pair and the moment froze.

The historic handshake

Later, ushered into the spacious drawing room of Saira's house, Dilip Kumar met many of his friends such as Dev Anand, Rajendra Kumar, music directors Shankar and Jaikishen, Manoj Kumar, Fali Mistry, Subodh Mukerji, R.K. Nayyar, etc., and exchanged pleasantries. But, Dilip Saheb's mind went racing back to the year 1955 when filmmaker S.S. Vasan had introduced him to an astrologer in Coimbatore who had predicted that he would marry in his forties and the girl would be extremely beautiful but half his age. He also said the girl would be from his profession only. His predictions were coming true, he felt.

If ever there was a whirlwind romance in Hindi film industry, it had to be Dilip and Saira's. Back in Chennai, Dilip Saheb kept regularly phoning Saira*ji* while she was shooting at Mehboob Studios for Lekh Tandon directed *Jhuk Gaya Asmaan.* One fine evening, he flew down to Mumbai and took Saira Banu out for dinner at the Sea Lounge of the Taj Hotel, followed by a drive to the Cuff Parade seafront where the most eligible bachelor of his time proposed to the Beauty Queen. The acceptance came readily. Then, Dilip Kumar lost no time in officially obtaining the consent of Naseem *Aapa.* The first person he informed in his own family was his younger brother Nasir Khan and in the film industry, he told his old friend Abhi Bhattacharya 'Gobindo'. All his friends were pleased to hear the good news except Naushad Saheb, a close family friend. Dilip Saheb did everything required to assuage the feelings of his family members particularly Sakina *Aapa.*

Dilip Kumar and Saira Banu got engaged on 2 October 1966. The engagement was a simple and private affair with only close friends and relatives attending the austere ceremony held at the Pali Hill residence of Saira Banu, which was smack opposite Dilip Kumar's residence. The guest list included S. Mukerji, Nasir Hussain, Sardar Akhtar, Mehboob Khan, Pran, H.S. Rawail, Abhi Bhattacharya, Subodh Mukerji, Joy Mukerji and an assortment of friends and relatives. Dilip Saheb wore an elegant suit and Saira*ji* wore a gorgeously sequinned white brocade sari presented by Sakina *Aapa.* At 7 PM sharp on that day, Dilip Kumar slipped in a diamond and ruby ring on Saira's engagement finger and she in turn slipped on a diamond ring on his. They then exchanged the traditional garlands of roses and jasmine completing the brief and solemn ceremony.

1. Dilip Kumar, Dilip Kumar: The Substance and the Shadow - An Autobiography (Hay House, Inc, 2014)

Dilip and Saira's Engagement

The wedding date was originally set as 4 November 1966. However, with the clamour of Dilipian fans reaching a crescendo and the couple getting mobbed at every public appearance, it became imperative not to wait so long. Eventually, the couple married on 11 October 1966 with much fanfare. Dilip Saheb's good friends Hiten Choudhary, Ramesh Saigal, Abhi Bhattacharya, Satish Bhalla and Balraj Kohli supervised the arrangements. Saira Banu's close friend Shibani (daughter of S. Mukerji) astutely handled the responsibilities at the bride's home.

The then Much-awaited Dilip–Saira Wedding

It was a fairy-tale wedding, the like of which had never previously been witnessed. Since the date was hurriedly fixed (the announcement was made only on the day of the engagement on 2 October 1966, barely nine days before the wedding), there was no time even to print formal invitations. Thus, the friends and well-wishers were invited on phone. Some 500 guests were expected but a huge number of celebrities, luminaries, politicians, media and friends turned up besides milling crowds which thronged the areas around the Pali Hills houses of the celebrated couple. Despite a police bandobast being in place, it was extremely difficult to control the crowd.

The Dilipian Baarat

Dilip Kumar's own luxurious limousine was tastefully decorated with flowers but the megastar was compelled to ride a mare from his house to Saira Banu's house, across the road, by his relatives. A huge contingent of famous personalities were present at the *baraat* which included Prithviraj Kapoor, Raj Kapoor, Dev Anand, Bharat Bhushan, Raj Kumar, Shashi Kapoor, Nargis, Nimmi, Nanda, Pran, Jairaj, Nanda, Sadhana with R.K. Nayyar, Shakeel Badayuni, etc. Dilip Saheb wore a *Kulla–Saafa,* the Pathani headgear. Prithviraj Kapoor led the *baraat* with Shashi Kapoor holding the reins of the mare. The *baraat* was scheduled to start at 5 PM but it got delayed by one hour since the bridegroom's apparel was not ready as the order was placed only one day before. The ubiquitous Raj Kapoor danced with gay abandon and energetic enthusiasm to heighten the revelry. *Qazi* Mugrey performed the *nikaah.* Shah Nawaz Khan, the then minister of labour, employment and rehabilitation, signed in as a witness to the marriage.

Raj Kapoor had once jokingly told media that the day his dear friend Dilip Kumar would get married, he would walk up the stairs leading to his house on his knees. To the great amusement and delight of all present, Raj Kapoor actually did that. When actor Raaj Kumar, who was a bachelor then, went to congratulate the newly-weds, Dilip Kumar asked for a glass of water and made Raaj Kumar drink it. He told him about a deep-seated belief that if a bridegroom offers a glass of water to a bachelor friend on his wedding day, he too would get married soon. Raaj Kumar was married shortly thereafter.

The wedding celebrations went on till the wee hours of the morning. Next day, a sumptuous *Dawat-E-Walima* (a wedding feast) was held which was attended by all the well-wishers, friends and luminaries including the then chief minister of Maharashtra Vasantrao Naik.

In a candid tongue-in cheek manner, Dilip Saheb has described the change in his life post-marriage as follows:
As a bachelor I would sit up with friends... We used to have sessions running deep into the night. So, often magnanimous friends would invade my austere little cottage in the middle of the night and out of pity for my 'insomnia ridden' loneliness drag me along, often in pyjamas, to informal get-togethers at their homes. Those delightful, mad sessions have ended.

CHAPTER 8

DRIBBLING WITH DIRECTORS

The most prestigious banners and renowned directors considered it their privilege to make a film with Dilip Kumar. The best directors in business in the film industry during that time were behind Dilip Kumar films, a majority of which included:

Amiya Chakrabarty (*Jwar Bhata, Daag*)
Paidi Jairaj (*Pratima*)
Nitin Bose (*Milan, Deedar, Gunga Jumna*)
M.I. Dharmsey (*Anokha Pyar*)
S.U. Sunny (*Mela, Babul, Uran Khatola, Kohinoor*)
Ram Daryani (*Ghar Ki Izzat, Tarana*)
Ramesh Saigal (*Shaheed, Shikast*)
Kishore Sahu (*Nadiya Ke Paar*)
Bibhuti Mitra (*Shabnam*)
Mehboob Khan (*Andaaz, Aan, Amar*)
Kidar Sharma (*Jogan*)
R.C. Talwar (*Sangdil*)
Bimal Roy (*Devdas, Madhumati, Yahudi*)
S.M.S. Naidu (*Azaad*)
S.S. Vasan (*Insaniyat, Paigham*)
Hrishikesh Mukherjee (*Musafir, Phir Kab Milogi*)
B.R. Chopra (*Naya Daur, Dastaan*)
Ram Mukerji (*Leader*)
A.R. Kardar (*Dil Diya Dard Liya*)
Chanakya (*Ram Aur Shyam*)
A. Bhim Singh (*Aadmi, Gopi, Sadhu Aur Shaitan*)
Jagannath Chattopadhyay (*Paari, Anokha Milan*)
H.S. Rawail (*Sunghursh*)
Tapan Sinha (*Sagina Mahato, Sagina*)
Asit Sen (*Bairaag*)
Manoj Kumar (*Kranti*)
Yash Chopra (*Mashaal*)
Ramesh Sippy (*Shakti*)
Subhash Ghai (*Vidhaata, Karma, Saudagar*)
Ramesh Talwar (*Duniya*)

Initially, the directors who influenced and shaped histrionics of Dilip Kumar were Amiya Chakraborty and Nitin Bose to whom he remained eternally grateful. Later, the best-in-the-business directors considered it a privilege to wield the megaphone for a Dilip Kumar film. According to the authors, the best work of the peerless actor was in his three landmark films with Bimal Roy. The other notable performances came in the films of Mehboob Khan, S.U. Sunny, S.S. Vasan, K. Asif, Ramesh Saigal and B.R. Chopra.

Amiya Chakrabarty

After the virtual closure of the iconic Bombay Talkies, director Amiya Chakrabarty floated his own production banner named Mars and Movies and went on to make some landmark films starting with *Daag* starring Dilip Kumar and Nimmi. The film was highly appreciated by both classes and masses and heralded as a classic with a refreshing newness. Reportedly, Dilip Kumar repaid his debt to the director of his debut movie *(Jwar Bhata)* by working for a nominal fee. The splendid director-actor rapport resulted in *Daag* featuring one of Dilip Kumar's most acclaimed acting triumphs. It was a complex role of a compulsive alcoholic who rediscovers his soul through the love of his devoted beloved. The cinegoers could identify and sympathise with the tribulations of the alcohol-addict Shankar played by Dilip. Amiya Chakrabarty made many a classics thereafter, namely *Patita* (1953) and *Seema* (1955). He was said to be toying with the idea of launching another Dilip Kumar starrer before his untimely demise in the midst of filming *Kathputli* (1957). His passing away was a big blow to Dilip Saheb who cried at the director's funeral.

The veteran actor Paidi Jairaj was the next director who wielded the megaphone for Dilip's second film *Pratima,* and the two actors formed a lifelong friendship. The executive producer of the film on behalf of Bombay Talkies was sound recordist M.I. Dharamsey, whose favour the megastar returned by getting him to direct Ambica Films' *Anokha Pyar* co-starring Nargis and Nalini Jaywant. Similarly, Dilip Kumar agreed to do *Tarana* for Daryani Bros as director Ram Daryani had signed him for *Ghar Ki Izzat* in the initial phase of his career. *Tarana* became the most lucid exposition of the remarkable romantic chemistry of the legendary Dilip Kumar–Madhubala pair.

One of the greatest contributions in honing the histrionic excellence of Dilip Kumar was by Nitin Bose. The actor-director duo together created three unforgettable films – *Milan, Deedar* and *Gunga Jumna.* Here is an excerpt from an interview given by Nitin Bose to Ali Peter John, the then editor of *Screen*:

Nitin Bose

At the time, I was directing a film called Mazdoor in which, I had cast Nasir Khan, Dilip's younger brother, as the hero on the recommendation of K.A. Abbas. The film dealt with the exploitation of workers by the companies, and the workers' right to participate in the functioning of the companies and their profits. I was always very fond of taking in young people and shaping them to my requirements rather than working with established artists, who might have preconceived ideas about acting. I noticed that a young lad of 22 or 23 was watching the rehearsals quietly and keenly from a corner. It was my practice to rehearse my artistes thoroughly with lighting and camera positions so as to save on valuable raw stock and time too. I asked Nasir who the young man was and why he came almost every day to meet him. He said it was his brother Yusuf Khan (Dilip Kumar) who was on the payroll of Bombay

Talkies. 'He wants to see how a great director like you works,' said Nasir. Mazdoor was released in 1945–46 and was a big hit. It also won the BJFA's award for the 'Best Hindi Film'. Soon after this, I received an invitation from Shiraz Ali Hakim (who was connected with Bombay Talkies) and when we were strolling in the garden after dinner, Mrs Hakim suggested that I do a film for them. Mr Hakim asked me if I had any good story in mind. I have always considered Rabindranath Tagore my Guru, so I said what about Nauka Doobi in Bengali and Hindi (Hindi title: Milan). When Mrs Hakim asked me if I had any particular artist in mind, I, on the spur of the moment, suggested Nasir, but Mr Hakim said why not try Yusuf Khan who was on their payroll? The rest of the cast was also selected from their company's artists. When the film was due to start, one day I was sitting down to dinner, when in rushed a distraught Nasir Khan, who asked me agitatedly, 'Dada, I hear you are doing Nauka Doobi. You had promised me the lead role. But now I hear you're giving it to someone else!' 'Yes, I have. But, wait, it is your own brother Yusuf Khan!' Nasir for a moment stood taking in this sudden and good news, and said happily, 'Oh, then I have no complaints. I am very happy about your choice. I must tell Yusuf about this good news.' He rushed out as quickly as he had come. Later, Yusuf told me it was Nasir who embraced him and told him the happy news first. When we started shooting, I decided to do the Bengali version first. Abhi Bhattacharya was in the technical department, but was very much interested in acting. He asked me, 'Dada, I want to act in this picture. Why don't you give me a break?' Since I liked to work with newcomers and Abhi had a good personality and was handsome too, I cast him in the Bengali Version. We started rehearsing for the Bengali version first. Dilip, as was his practice, watched everything closely. Once it so happened that the artist in the Bengali version just could not speak the lines as I had visualised it. The harder we tried, the worse things got. I threw away my kerchief in disgust and sat in my chair, smoking. Then my brother who was with me and others suggested, 'Why not start with the Hindi version?' I, too, was searching for a way to break the impasse and called to Dilip, 'Yusuf, you have been watching the rehearsals for such a long time. Have you understood what is required of you in this scene? Can you do it?' Dilip, with his eyes on the floor, quietly said, 'I will do my best, Dada.' Would you believe it, I did not even have to brief him–Dilip did everything perfectly, just as I had imagined it, in the first shot. I had, of course, noticed Dilip's intensity but to give a faultless rehearsal on the very first day (especially when the director is not in the best of moods!) indicated both guts and talent. I told Yusuf, happily, 'Well done, my boy' and looked around for the artist who had faltered so badly but he was already bounding down the stairs, pleading, 'Dada, don't be angry with me, please.' I can tell you without any exaggeration that from then on, there were hardly any retakes at all because of Dilip, in the whole of Milan. I knew there was an extraordinary talent in him and the film's thumping success proved this. By this time Dilip's talent had been recognised and he was doing a few films outside Bombay Talkies too.

Kishore Sahu

Dilip Kumar achieved his earliest super success at the box office with directors Shaukat Husain Rizvi (*Jugnu*), actor-director-producer Kishore Sahu (*Nadiya Ke Paar*) and Bibhuti Mitra (*Shabnam*), who got to do just one film with the legend. Veteran director Kidar Sharma also did one film *Jogan* with the thespian. The director and actor, however, had their disagreements during the making of the film and never worked together again. Producer-director R.C. Talwar was also destined to make only one film *(Sangdil)* with Dilip Kumar as their next announced venture 'Bank Manager' did not proceed beyond the *mahurat.* Veteran director Mahesh Kaul had announced an ambitious Dilip Kumar–Madhubala starrer *'Har Singaar'* which remained incomplete even after six reels were canned.

Dilip Kumar and Ramesh Saigal

Then, there was a close friend of Dilip Kumar, director-producer Ramesh Saigal who gave Dilip a box-office hit *Shaheed,* followed by a sensitively dramatic *Shikast.* The director-actor duo had launched two more films 'Kaala Aadmi' (which did not even start) and 'Shikwa' (which was shelved after being 95 per cent complete). Ramesh Saigal had some piquant observations on the actor, as quoted below:

Dilip gets terribly upset when anybody interrupts him on the sets. And I think that the serious, depressing and tragic roles that he is always called upon to play make him altogether a different man in the studios. But the moment he leaves the floors, he is his normal self again. Playing with children, talking to friends, and joking. The striking difference between the two Dilips–Dilip on the sets and the Dilip in real life–is a near approach to Dr Jekyll and Mr Hyde.

Mehboob, Nargis, Dilip and Jaddan

One of the most successful works in terms of high cinematic quality as well as box office success was by the director-actor duo Mehboob Khan and Dilip Kumar. Their films together—*Andaaz, Aan* and *Amar*—are replete with riveting drama and terrific performances. Strangely, Mehboob Saheb while viewing Dilip Kumar's *Milan* curiously asked Nitin Bose, 'Why did you take this new actor as hero instead of an established star? I am not at all impressed by him.' Nitin *Da* just grinned. Fate has strange ways to make what is ordained happen. After the success of *Milan,* Dilip Kumar bought his first car (a Fiat) and the cricket enthusiast that he always was, drove straight to the Brabourne Stadium after picking up family friend Dr Masani from Churchgate. They were specially invited by mutual friend and legendary cricketer Vijay Merchant to witness the second day's play of a test match from the special members' enclosure. In those pre-partition days, there used to be separate enclosures for Muslims. Dilip Kumar's seat was next to two very impressive looking gentlemen and the actor greeted them with a warm *Salaam Alaikum* and the greeting was reciprocated with equal warmth. After some time, one of the gentlemen introduced himself as Mehboob Khan and his companion as Naushad Ali to the pleasant surprise of Dilip Kumar. They had already seen a few Dilip Kumar films. This chance meeting was a precursor to two of the most enduring friendships and extremely rewarding professional associations in the future. Composer Naushad, who had written the story of Wadia Brothers' soon-to-be made *Mela,* invited Dilip to meet him and director S.U. Sunny (another deep friendship and long association in the offing) the following week. Dilip Kumar thus became the choice of the leading man for *Mela*–a resounding golden jubilee hit. Naushad was deeply impressed with Dilip Kumar's work in the film and strongly recommended him to Mehboob Khan who was then planning *Andaaz,* now a timeless classic. Post-independence, Hindi films were focussing more on youth and modernity. Although, Mehoob's last two films namely *Anmol Ghadi* and *Anokhi Adaa* were hits, the astute director had realised that it would be foolhardy to again cast ageing stars in the rapidly changing times. He decided to turn towards younger set of stars among the well-known actors and actresses. It was a clever move as it helped him impart freshness to his movie by using mouldable actors with a flair for natural acting. Meanwhile, Zia Sarhady also recommended Dilip Kumar. Thus, Mehboob Khan made the landmark film *Andaaz* with Nargis, Dilip Kumar and Raj Kapoor—the stars who became great legends in their own way and ruled the roost in filmdom. Dilip Kumar and Mehboob Khan developed a fabulous cinematic rapport and Indian cinema was the gainer. However, even after three grand cinematic triumphs such as *Andaaz, Aan* and *Amar,* the director-actor duo did not do any other film together. First, Dilip Saheb did not agree to play Nargis's son in *Mother India* (1957); and second, he pointed out the negative traits in the character of Yousuf Chak in Khan's ambitious *'Habba Khatoon'* and quit. Dilip Saheb has always waxed eloquent about his special relationship with Mehboob Saheb and held the iconic director-producer in highest esteem. 'Mehboob Saheb was a gem of a human being who took good care of his artists and technicians. He had an intuitive sense of good cinema and a sixth sense about filmmaking—one of our greatest filmmakers ever,' he said.

S.U. Sunny has directed Dilip Kumar in maximum number of films—*Mela, Babul, Uran Khatola* and *Kohinoor.* All of these were blockbuster hits. Sunny also wanted to film Naushad's story *Palki* with Dilip Kumar in the male lead but the actor pointed out a number of pitfalls in the storyline and declined the film. *Palki* was eventually made with Rajendra Kumar and Waheeda Rehman in the leads but S.U. Sunny died midway during the making of the film and Mahesh Kaul completed the picture which flopped at the box office. Still Dilip Kumar had a fine rapport with S.U. Sunny and the latter understood the actor's penchant for perfection. The duo truly enjoyed working together. There are some interesting and eerie anecdotes related to the actor-director duo. As per the grapevine, Sunny's wife practised witchcraft and the eerie anecdote relates to the time the light-hearted *Kohinoor* was under production. The incident is reported with all graphic detail in Dilip Saheb's autobiography (Pages 245 and 246):

S.U. Sunny

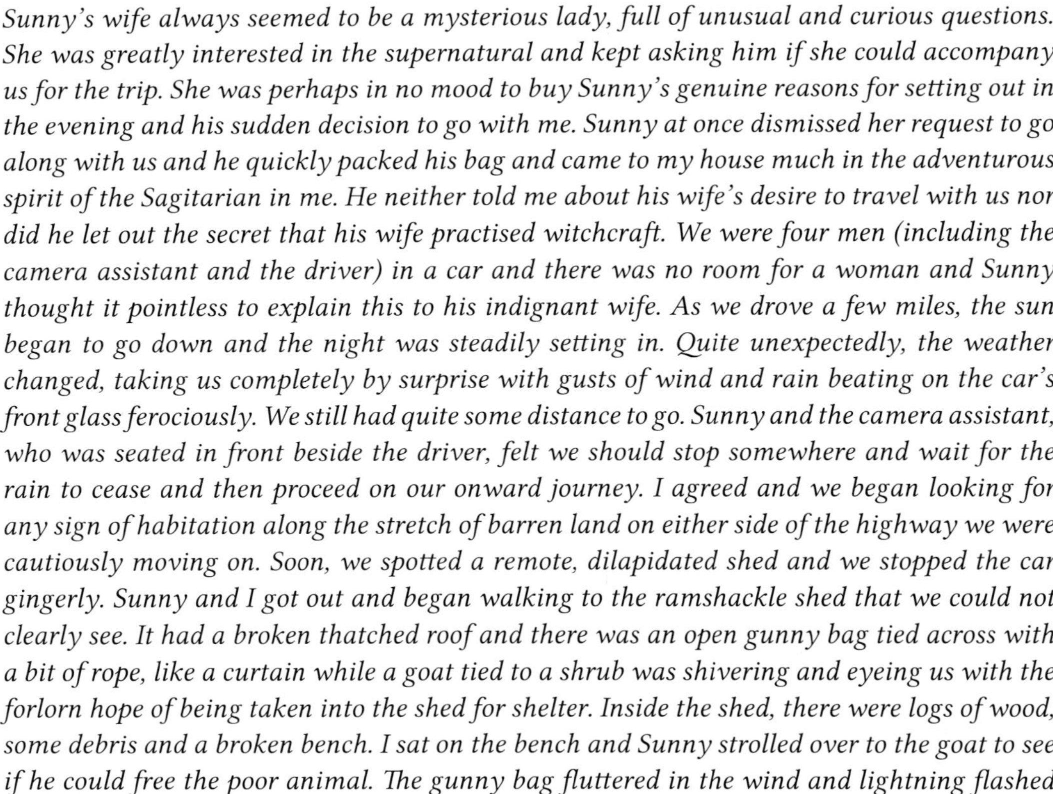

Sunny's wife always seemed to be a mysterious lady, full of unusual and curious questions. She was greatly interested in the supernatural and kept asking him if she could accompany us for the trip. She was perhaps in no mood to buy Sunny's genuine reasons for setting out in the evening and his sudden decision to go with me. Sunny at once dismissed her request to go along with us and he quickly packed his bag and came to my house much in the adventurous spirit of the Sagitarian in me. He neither told me about his wife's desire to travel with us nor did he let out the secret that his wife practised witchcraft. We were four men (including the camera assistant and the driver) in a car and there was no room for a woman and Sunny thought it pointless to explain this to his indignant wife. As we drove a few miles, the sun began to go down and the night was steadily setting in. Quite unexpectedly, the weather changed, taking us completely by surprise with gusts of wind and rain beating on the car's front glass ferociously. We still had quite some distance to go. Sunny and the camera assistant, who was seated in front beside the driver, felt we should stop somewhere and wait for the rain to cease and then proceed on our onward journey. I agreed and we began looking for any sign of habitation along the stretch of barren land on either side of the highway we were cautiously moving on. Soon, we spotted a remote, dilapidated shed and we stopped the car gingerly. Sunny and I got out and began walking to the ramshackle shed that we could not clearly see. It had a broken thatched roof and there was an open gunny bag tied across with a bit of rope, like a curtain while a goat tied to a shrub was shivering and eyeing us with the forlorn hope of being taken into the shed for shelter. Inside the shed, there were logs of wood, some debris and a broken bench. I sat on the bench and Sunny strolled over to the goat to see if he could free the poor animal. The gunny bag fluttered in the wind and lightning flashed

in the sky. The gale continued unabated. Sunny was walking back to where I was seated when the gunny bag parted and there in front of us was, suddenly, believe it or not, Sunny's wife. She was standing defiantly and staring at us puissantly with a victorious smile on her face as her hand crossed over her face to mysteriously wipe something crimson from her lips. If I remained unshaken by the sight of the woman who was physically miles away from us, it was because of my steely Pathan grit. The camera assistant was trembling and Sunny was rooted to the spot he stood on. The downpour ceased and we silently resumed our journey in the car. Sunny was speechless with shame or embarrassment and the camera assistant had no words either. The driver was oblivious of the whole episode since he had remained in the car. I tried to ease the chill I could feel by humming a song I knew in Pushtu.[1]

The doyen of south film industry and the boss of iconic Gemini Studios, S.S. Vasan developed a good rapport with Dilip Kumar while making his two hugely successful films with him—*Insaniyat* and *Paigham*. Often, there would be close consultations between the two for improvising and embellishing the films and the sharp director recognised the great prowess of Dilip in writing scenes. Many scenes of *Paigham* (including the captivating love scenes) were penned by Dilip Kumar himself. The ease and comfort of working in an unhurried yet efficient manner yielded extraordinary results, visible in both the films. Many brilliantly crafted scenes registered indelibly on the minds of movie goers with a telling effect. Their excellent teamwork is quite discernible as the scenes of these hit films unspool on the silver screen even today.

S.S. Vasan

Sriramulu M.S. Naidu, owner of the Coimbatore-based Pakshiraja Studios, could do only one film with Dilip Kumar—the super-duper hit *Azaad.* It is to the credit of S.M.S. Naidu that the producer-director made and successfully released *Azaad* in just around two-and-a-half months despite having the busiest and priciest stars (Dilip Kumar, Meena Kumari, Pran and Om Prakash) and music makers (C. Ramchandra, Rajinder Krishan and Lata Mangeshkar) in the cast and credits. By paying one rupee more than Naushad, Naidu could get C. Ramchandra to record nine super hit songs of the film in just about a week. He made the busy Rajinder Krishan write lyrics in cars, on sets and in hotels breathing down his neck, but the job got done. Then, he pulled off the real casting coup of sorts by persuading Dilip Kumar to play the title role of the swashbuckling Robinhood-inspired character who also masqueraded as an aged Khan Saheb. Grapevine has it that he offered Dilip twice the highest remuneration ever earned by the megastar and approached him through the friendly channel of Baburao Patel. Naidu's logic was that if Dilip Saheb could do a swashbuckling sword-wielding chieftain for Mehboob Khan in *Aan,* could he not do the same for him and that too at twice his price? Naidu sweetened the pie further by offering a large chunk of the lucrative amount upfront and the rest within just four months. Dilip Kumar consulted his trusted advisors S. Mukerji, Mehboob Khan and K. Asif and accepted the gauntlet thrown by Asif who with a provocative smile said, '*Kar ke dikhaiye*' (Show us that you can do it). The soundest advice came from the pragmatic S. Mukerji who opined, 'Go ahead and do it. An actor's job is acting and it should not matter whether he is enacting tragedy or comedy. What counts is the actor's ability and enterprise.'

Azaad was shot at a scorching pace and the film completed ahead of its schedule. It sported a slick look and was highly entertaining. Dilip Saheb won his second Filmfare Award for his virtual double role in *Azaad.* A press conference was held in Delhi by

[1] Dilip Kumar: The Substance and the Shadow – An Autobiography (Hay House, Inc, 2014).

Naidu in March 1955 at which both he and Dilip Kumar heaped praises on each other. But, grapevine has it that Dilip was quite miffed with Naidu's high-handedness in preventing him from urgently going to Mumbai during the shooting. Reportedly, Dilip vowed never to work again with Naidu and his Pakshiraja Studios, and kept his vow. Years down years and much after Naidu was gone, Dilip Kumar did shoot at the Pakshiraja Studios around 1994 for Premalaya's *Aag Ka Dariya* co-starring Rekha, Padmini Kolhapure and Amrita Singh.

S.M.S. Naidu and Dilip

The director Dilip Kumar revered the most and eulogised was Bimal Roy with whom he did some of his finest films—*Devdas, Madhumati* and *Yahudi.* Dilip Saheb had gone on record in 1968 to say that the director he misses the most is Bimal Roy. This is in-line our own belief that the cinema made by the duo was one of the finest. Undoubtedly, *Devdas* and *Madhumati* would make it to any list of the greatest Indian films compiled by anyone. Dilip Kumar has hailed Bimal Roy as one of the most significant filmmaker in the history of Indian cinema. He said that apart from being a great creative director and a man obsessed with cinema, Bimal *Da* was a wonderful person with a beautiful soul. A man of few words, Bimal Roy's subtle personality reflected in the classicism his movies exuded. On the sets of his films, there was no awkwardness or frenzy or loud communication with the affectionate and friendly director around. He and his team planned meticulously on paper and implemented it on to celluloid effortlessly. Bimal Roy's team had famous names including writers Nabendu Ghosh and Rajinder Singh Bedi, editor Hrishikesh Mukherjee, cinematographers Kamal Bose and Dilip Gupta, composers S.D. Burman and Salil Chowdhury, artists such as Dilip Kumar and others. They all had a terrific intuitive rapport with Bimal *Da.* The characters and ethos depicted in Bimal Roy's films grew on the movie goers and they could identify and live with the subtly unfolded narrative. Collectively, all these virtues were the USP of Bimal Roy's cinema. Dilip Kumar won his third Filmfare Best Actor Award for *Devdas.* Dilip Saheb had the following words for his favourite Bimal *Da* in an interview:

I have very fond memories of Bimal Roy. He had a gentleness and refinement in his speech and behaviour that was infectious. Whether it was Devdas or Madhumati or Yahudi, we worked with perfect understanding in a congenial atmosphere. His assistants and he conversed in Bengali and they chatted and laughed without any inhibitions. I knew some Bengali that I had picked up from Dadamoni (Ashok Kumar) and Sasadhar Mukerji Saheb and I made my own contribution to the informality by speaking in Bengali and they never tire of complimenting me for speaking Bengali the way it should be spoken. He never showed off his superior experience or his native sensitivity and intelligence. Instead, he was gentle and patient when he worked on artists and extracted the perfection he desired. In the making of Devdas, his aim was to convey the sense of hopelessness that pervades the relationship between Devdas and the two women as well as others who are a part of his doomed life without leading the more ardent viewers to cynicism and despondence.

Bimal Roy's protégée and editor Hrishikesh Mukherjee turned director at the insistence of Dilip Kumar who did his debut making *Musafir* (1957) for a token amount only. Dilip and Hrishikesh were close lifelong friends and later Dilip Saheb salvaged his stalled

The Bimal Da-Dilip rapport

Mala Sinha–Biswajit starrer *Phir Kab Milogi* by making a special appearance in it. Hrishikesh had planned to make a Dilip Kumar–Amitabh Bachchan starrer based on the famous play *Thank You Mr Glaad* but that was not to be.

With Hrishikesh Mukherjee

Legendary director-producer Baldev Raj (B.R.) Chopra and Dilip Kumar also famously got along together like a house on fire as a brilliant director-actor pair. The most noteworthy examples of this team's excellence is stamped on every frame of the super-duper hit *Naya Daur* (1957), which is one of Dilip Kumar's greatest histrionic triumphs and won him his fourth Filmfare Best aActor Award. Doubtlessly, *Naya Daur* was a deftly directed, brilliantly enacted, imaginatively written film with O.P. Nayyar's lilting hit music. The director-actor combo wanted to emulate the grand success of *Naya Daur* years later in *Dastaan* (1971) which was a remake of Chopra's earlier hit *Afsana* (1952) with Dilip Kumar playing a double role. But, despite a fine Dilipian performance and a slick look, the film failed at the box office as did *Mazdoor* (1983) directed by B.R.'s son Ravi Chopra. Later, B.R. Chopra and Dilip Kumar worked together again in Kishor Sharma's ambitious magnum opus '*Chanakya Chandragupta*' but after meticulous preparations the landmark film got shelved. B.R. Chopra also offered his eminently successful *Baghban* (2003) to Dilip Kumar but the deal did not materialise and eventually Amitabh Bachchan did the role. Nevertheless, Dilip Kumar and B.R. Chopra shared a lifelong mutual admiration and friendship.

B. R. Chopra, Dharam Chopra and Dilip Kumar

Veteran director-producer Abdul Rashid (A.R.) Kardar, owner of Kardar Studios, was keen to do a film with Dilip Kumar. He made *Dil Diya Dard Liya* with him in 1966. At that point in time, cinematic techniques had considerably advanced and Kardar's film filmmaking acumen was not in tune with modern practices. Moreover, the script of the film needed updating to come up to the standards of a Dilip Kumar film. Dilip Saheb provided full support in making the script crisp and interesting and also helped Kardar direct the movie in line with modern cinematic techniques. However, *Dil Diya Dard Liya* did not do too well at the box office. Kardar lodged a court case against the thespian which the latter won. Later, after making another outdated flop film, Kardar Productions folded up and the studios downed its shutters.

A.R. Kardar

Southern film director Chanakya did only one but highly successful film *Ram Aur Shyam* with the thespian. Chanakya did not know Hindi and grapevine has it that Dilip Kumar himself actually directed *Ram Aur Shyam.* Famous south Indian director A. Bhim Singh, a Sivaji Ganesan favourite, had developed a good rapport with Dilip Saheb while directing him in the classic *Aadmi* (1968) and their collaboration extended to the silver jubilee hit *Gopi* (1970).

A Bhim Singh directing Dilip and Saira

H.S. Rawail and Dilip with other luminary directors

Veteran Harnam Singh (H.S.) Rawail, after his biggest hit *Mere Mehboob* (1963), launched big-budget magnum opus *Sunghursh* (1968) with Dilip Kumar heading a formidable cast of great artists. According to us, *Sunghursh* is one of the best Dilip Kumar films and worthy of highest accolades. True Dilipian fans, till even to date, fondly watch *Sunghursh* on the DVD. H.S. Rawail got high praise as a director from Dilip Kumar during the making of the classic.

Legendary Bengali director Tapan Sinha convinced Dilip Kumar to play a very interesting and challenging role of an intrepid forthright but uncouth trade unionist in a Bengali film opposite wife Saira Banu. The result was the golden jubilee hit classic *Sagina Mahto* (1971) which won the thespian the coveted BFJA best actor Award and was India's official entry to the Moscow film festival. It was later remade in Hindi titled *Sagina* (1974) but the grand success of the Bengali super hit eluded the Hindi re-make. Dilip Sahab rated Tapan Babu as one of his best directors.

Dilip and Tapan Sinha

Actor-Director-Producer Manoj Kumar had been a Dilip Kumar fan and admirer right from his childhood and got the opportunity to play the second lead in the splendid *Aadmi* (1968) co-starring Dilip Kumar and Waheeda Rehman. When Dilip Sahab decided to stop doing romantic male lead roles the first principle character role he accepted was as the revolutionary Sanga in the magnum opus multi-starrer *Kranti* (1983). The film became a block buster hit to make an auspicious start to Dilip Sahab's second innings as a lead character artist in films. Prior to release of the over budget film Manoj Kumar was very nervous and Dilip Sahab comforted him saying *Yeh film Khuda ke hukm se bani hai. Tum fikar mat karo wohi isko chalayega* – prophetic words which proved so very true.

Dilip and Manoj

Veteran producer-director-distributor Gopal Das (G. P.) Sippy was a very close friend of Dilip Kumar. His son Ramesh Sippy became an illustrious director himself with a number of hit films like *Andaaz, Seeta Aur Geeta* and the timeless hit *Sholay.* When producers Mushir and Riaz (who had produced *Bairaag* with Dilip Sahab earlier) mooted the idea of making a Dilip Kumar – Amitabh Bachchan starrer *Shakti* based on a splendid Salim / Javed script Dilip Kumar's choice of the director fell on Ramesh Sippy. The Director-actor's team produced a classic silver jubilee hit heralded as an all time classic.

Dilip, Amit and Ramesh

Dilip and Subhash Ghai

Self styled Showman director-producer Subhash Ghai is the only director apart from the legends, viz., Mehboob Khan, Bimal Roy and Nitin Bose to have the distinction of making a Dilipian hat trick with *Vidhaata, Karma* and *Saudagar* – all major hits. The Dilip-Ghai chemistry was special and that can be seen in ample measure in their movies. Subhash Ghai had the gumption to pull off a casting miracle by having Dilip Kumar and Rajkumar work together after thirty three years in *Saudagar.* He also co-starred the consummate artistes Dilip Kumar and Nutan in *Karma.* Ghai had also made grandiose plans to star Dilip Kumar – Amitabh Bachchan and Shahrukh Khan in a highly ambitious venture titled *Homeland.* But the Project never got off ground. Incidently, Subhash Ghai while graduating from Film and Television Institute India (FTII) had written a thesis on Dilip Kumar's *Devdas.*

Dilip and Yash Chopra

The younger brother of B.R., Yash Chopra a legend in his own right was an assistant director in *Naya Daur* and became very close to Dilip Sahab. He fulfilled his life time's ambition of doing a Dilip Kumar starrer by making *Mashaal* (1986) under his own banner of Yash Raj Films. It was a remarkable film showcasing an awesome Dilip Kumar performance. The Dilip-Yash friendship lasted life long.

Among the other directors who did one film each with Dilip Sahab mention ought to be made of Asit Sen (*Bairaag*), Ramesh Talwar (*Duniya*), Jagannath Chattopadhyay (*Paari / Anokha Milan*), K. Raghavendra Rao (*Dharam Adhikari*), B. Gopal (*Kanoon Apna Apna*), K. Bapaiah (*Izzatdaar*), Umesh Mehra (*Qila*), S. V. Rajendra Singh Babu (*Aag Ka Dariya*) and Dilip Kumar (*Kalinga*) himself.

Dilip and Asit Sen

CHAPTER 9

THE SHARP MUSICAL EAR

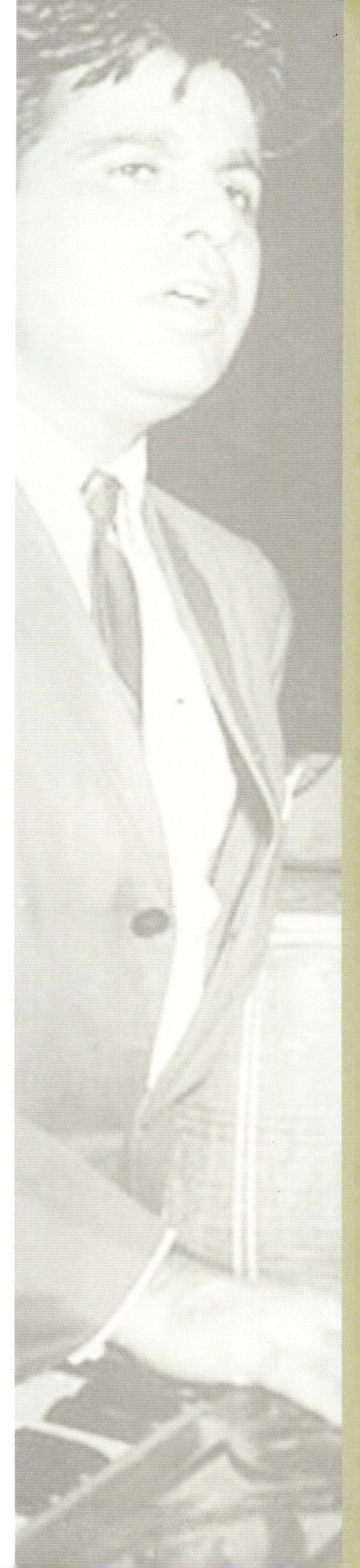

An inseparable and often a redeeming feature of Hindi films has been its music. Dilip Kumar's films, in addition to being embellished with powerful stories, magnificent performances, crisp dialogue, etc., invariably had lilting musical scores. Several of his numbers topped the charts and went on to become all-time hits. To score a Dilipian film was a prestigious assignment for the great composers of the era when the melody was a queen, and only the best in business got their chance. Here's a look at some of the well-know composers who gave music to Dilip Kumar starrers:

Anil Biswas *(Jwar Bhata, Milan, Arzoo, Tarana)*
Master Ghulam Haidar *(Shaheed)*
Pt Govind Ram *(Ghar Ki Izzat)*
Naushad *(Mela, Andaaz, Babul, Deedar, Aan, Amar, Uran Khatola, Mughal-E-Azam, Kohinoor, Gunga Jumna, Leader, Dil Diya Dard Liya, Ram Aur Shyam, Aadmi, Sunghursh)*
C. Ramchandra *(Nadiya Ke Paar, Insaniyat, Paigham)*
Sajjad *(Sangdil, Hulchul)*
Shankar–Jaikishan *(Daag, Shikast, Yahudi)*
S.D. Burman *(Shabnam, Devdas, Sagina)*
O.P. Nayyar *(Naya Daur)*
Salil Chowdhury *(Madhumati, Musafir)*
Khayyam *(Foot Path)*
Kalyanji–Anandji *(Gopi, Bairaag)*
R.D. Burman *(Shakti, Mazdoor)*
Laxmikant–Pyarelal *(Dastaan, Kranti)*

Legendary composer Naushad formed an unbeatable musical combination with Dilip Kumar, composing music for as many as fifteen memorable films of his. In some sense, his name is synonymous with Dilipian movies. The melodious musical scores of those landmark films are major milestones in the annals of Indian motion pictures. Also, one cannot resist the temptation of recapitulating a list of Dilip Kumar's films with the names of the lyricists and playback singers featuring in it. One such select list is as follows:

Mela (Shakil Badayuni/Mukesh)
Andaaz (Majrooh Sultanpuri/ Mukesh)
Babul (Shakil Badayuni/Talat Mahmood)
Aan (Shakil Badayuni/Mohd. Rafi)
Deedar (Shakil Badayuni/Mohd. Rafi)

Amar (Shakil Badayuni/no songs were picturised on Dilip Kumar)
Uran Khatola (Shakil Badayuni/Mohd. Rafi)
Kohinoor (Shakil Badayuni/Mohd. Rafi)
Mughal-E-Azam (Shakil Badayuni/no songs were filmed on Dilip Kumar)
Gunga Jumna (Shakil Badayuni/Mohd. Rafi)
Leader (Shakil Badayuni/Mohd. Rafi)
Dil Diya Dard Liya (Shakil Badayuni/Mohd. Rafi)
Ram Aur Shyam (Shakil Badayuni/Mohd. Rafi)
Aadmi (Shakil Badayuni/Mohd. Rafi)
Sunghursh (Shakil Badayuni/Mohd. Rafi)

As can be seen from the above listing, the Naushad-Rafi-Shakil combination ruled the roost in this glittering musical feast. The great Dilip Kumar–Naushad didn't work together after the 1968 classic *Sunghursh* for inexplicable and unknown reasons. However, in the later years, Naushad was signed to compose the music of two films of Dilip Sahab—Kishore Sharma's *'Chanakya Chandragupta'* (Director B.R. Chopra) and veteran producer-director-actor Sohrab Modi's remake of *Pukaar.* A few songs were recorded but alas both the films got shelved. Naushad Saheb knew Dilip Saheb's parents very well and was a regular visitor to the father (fondly referred to as Agha*ji*) by all and the two gentlemen hit it off very well. One among Dilip Saheb's close friends, Naushad was the only one who counselled the actor against marrying a much younger lady and did not attend the Dilip–Saira wedding. However, the close camaraderie, mutual respect and friendship between the two legendary stalwarts lasted a lifetime.

Naushad and Dilip Kumar

After Naushad, composer Anil Biswas has the distinction of scoring music for the second most number of Dilipian films—six of them, including the almost-complete-but-shelved *'Shikwa'* and his debut film *Jwar Bhata* (1944). The renowned composer also has another distinction to his credit—of discovering Talat Mahmood's velvet voice as the playback voice of Dilip Saheb in his Hindi film song *'Aye dil mujhe aisi jagah le chal'* in *Arzoo* (1950). The popular lilting melodies composed by Anil *Da* for Dilip Kumar would surely include *'Jeevan sapna toot gaya'* (*Anokha Pyar*, sung by Mukesh); *'Ab yaad na kar bhool bhi ja'* (*Anokha Pyar*, sung by Lata Mangeshkar and Mukesh); *'Nain mile nain huye bawre'* and *'Seene mein sulagte hain'* (*Tarana*, sung by Lata Mangeshkar/Talat Mahmood); *'Jali jo shaakh-e-chaman'* (*Tarana*, sung by Talat Mahmood), etc. Surprisingly, Anil Biswas very seldom recorded with Mohd. Rafi due to personal preference still Ramesh Saigal's shelved film *'Shikwa'* had several Mohd. Rafi numbers composed by Anil *Da.*

With Anil Biswas and Naushad

In the early phase of Dilip Kumar's career, some of the biggest musical names of pre-partition India such as Master Ghulam Haidar *(Shaheed),* Feroz Nizami *(Jugnu)* and Pt Govind Ram *(Ghar Ki Izzat)* composed music for his films. The extremely popular musical scores of *Shaheed ('Watan ki raah mein watan ke naujawan'* and *'Badnaam na ho jaaye')* and *Jugnu ('Yahan badla wafa ka')* are popular even to this day. Arun Kumar Mukerji also had the chance to compose the music for a Dilipian film, *Pratima.*

The first major musical success of composer S.D. (Sachin Deb) Burman, who later composed music for many super hit films of Dev Anand, was for Dilip Kumar's *Shabnam.* The film established S.D. Burman as a successful music director in Mumbai film industry. Dada Burman (as the legend was fondly called) used Mukesh as Dilip Kumar's playback voice in the movie and strangely enough never ever got the great Mohd. Rafi to sing for the megastar in his other landmark films such as *Devdas* (Talat Mahmood) and *Sagina* (Kishore Kumar). Dada Burman had, of course, put his best foot forward in giving memorable scores in all the three movies. He has the unique distinction of being the only composer who had Kishore Kumar sing for Dilip Kumar.

Dilip with S.D. Burman and Lata Mangeshkar

Nadiya Ke Paar, Azaad, Insaniyat and *Paigham* were the four highly successful Dilipian films which featured hugely popular musical scores by the legendary and inimitable C. Ramchandra. Anna, as he was popularly called, used Mohd. Rafi as the mainstay playback voice of Dilip Kumar (besides when he himself chipped in under the pseudonym Chitalkar). The music of *Azaad* in particular was on a par with the best ever scores heard in our films at that time.

C. Ramchandra

Dilip Kumar with Shankar Jaikishan and Sharda

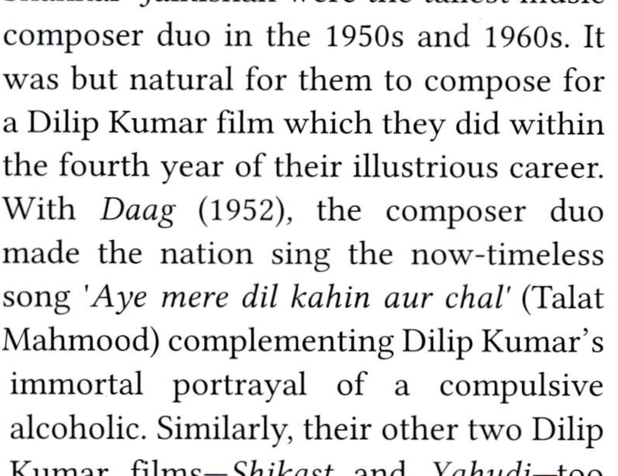

Shankar–Jaikishan were the tallest music composer duo in the 1950s and 1960s. It was but natural for them to compose for a Dilip Kumar film which they did within the fourth year of their illustrious career. With *Daag* (1952), the composer duo made the nation sing the now-timeless song '*Aye mere dil kahin aur chal*' (Talat Mahmood) complementing Dilip Kumar's immortal portrayal of a compulsive alcoholic. Similarly, their other two Dilip Kumar films—*Shikast* and *Yahudi*—too had spellbinding melodies. Surprisingly, like S.D. Burman, they too never got super-talented Mohd. Rafi to do a playback for Dilip Kumar. Under their able supervision, Talat Mahmood *(Daag* and *Shikast)* and Mukesh *(Yahudi)* rendered their golden voices for the thespian.

In *Naya Daur*, composer O.P. Nayyar gave one of his career-best scores with evergreen songs like '*Uden jab jab julfein teri, Yeh desh hai veer jawaano ka, Saathi haath badhana, Maang ke saath tumhara*', etc. Sadly, the super hit film remained the only one which Nayyar Saheb composed music for. Similarly, genius composer Sajjad Hussain (credited as Sajjad) scored music for only two Dilip Kumar starrers—*Sangdil* and *Hulchul.*

When music director Salil Chowdhury got a chance of composing music for Bimal Roy's *Madhumati,* he grabbed the coveted opportunity with both hands. He brilliantly collaborated with his favourite poet and lyricist Shailendra (they shared similar socio-political convictions too) and crafted a scintillating score replete with mesmerising compositions based on the folk treasures of Kumaun and Assam. Besides an unforgettable Rafi classic —*Toote huey khwaabon ne* —Salil *Da* chose Mukesh to be Dilip Saheb's playback voice. Of course, the classic film had one of Lata Mangeshkar's best songs.

Dilip Saheb not only had a sharp musical ear, but he was (and still is) an accomplished singer in his own right alongside being a connoisseur of fine arts and poetry. Salil Chowdhury also had the distinction of being the only composer who made Dilip Kumar sing a duet—*'Laagi nahin chhoote rama'* — with nightingale Lata Mangeshkar for Hrishikesh Mukherjee's maiden venture *Musafir.* Dilip Kumar and Lata Mangeshkar have shared a lifelong brother-sister relationship. Dilip Saheb's eloquent introduction of Lata*ji* at her maiden concert at the prestigious Royal Albert Hall of London is etched in the memory of all music lovers—it was oratory at its best.

With Salil Chowdhury

After 1968, Kalyanji–Anandji somehow became the favourite composers of Dilip Kumar and the music director duo composed songs for films such as *Gopi, Bairaag, Vidhaata* and the unreleased *'Kalinga'.* During his second innings, Dilip Saheb had Laxmikant–Pyarelal as the composers in his films—*Dastaan, Kranti, Karma, Izzatdaar, Saudagar* and the unreleased *'Aag Ka Dariya'.* Later, music director R.D. Burman scoring the music in *Phir Kab Milogi, Mazdoor, Shakti* and *Duniya.* The other music composers who gave music for Dilipian films include Bappi Lahiri *(Dharam Adhikari, Kanoon Apna Apna),* Hridaynath Mangeshkar *(Mashaal)* and Anand Raj Anand *(Qila).*

With Kalyanji–Anandji

Laxmikant–Pyarelal

With R.D. Burman

On the poetic side, the most eminent lyricists of the time put their best foot forward in writing captivating songs for Dilipian films. The list of such lyricists is akin to the 'Who's Who' of the song writers and includes Pt Narendra Sharma, Arzoo Lucknowi, P.L. Santoshi, Ishwar Chand Kapoor, Moti B.A., M.G. Adeeb, Asghar Sarhady, Raja Mehdi Ali Khan, J. Nakshab, Qamar Jalalabadi, Shakil Badayuni, Majrooh Sultanpuri, Prem Dhawan, Jan Nisan Akhtar, Kidar Sharma, Pt. Indra, Babu Ram Sharma, Himmat Rai Sharma, Kaif Irfani, D.N. Madhok, Rajinder Krishan, Shailendra, Hasrat Jaipuri, Sahir Ludhianvi, Kavi Pradeep, Indeevar, Santosh Anand, Anand Bakshi, Javed Akhtar, Dev Kohli, etc. The lyrics penned by these luminaries remain immortal.

With Lyricist Shailendra

One of the greatest singers ever, Mohd. Rafi, is quite correctly perceived to be the voice of Dilip Kumar for having crooned the lion's share of the songs picturised on the thespian. Rafi's voice suited Dilip's acting to a T. Personally, the actor-singer shared a lifelong fondness for each other and a very warm friendship. Likewise, Dilip Kumar and Talat Mahmood had a great personal equation and a long-lasting friendship. Mukesh also sang his heart out when singing for Dilip Kumar. Kishore Kumar sang for the legendary megastar in only one film *(Sagina)* but those songs became super hits. Regretfully, Hemant Kumar and Manna Dey (with the sole exception of *Jwar Bhata*) never got the opportunity to lend their voices for Dilip Kumar.

With Mohd. Rafi

With Talat Mahmood

Dilip, Talat and Mukesh

With Kishore Kumar

Dilip Kumar had a wonderful personal relationship of brother – sister with the celebrated Kathak exponent, singer and film artiste Sitara Devi (who at one time was married to the *Movie Moghul* K. Asif). Dilip Sahab and *Melody Queen* Lata Mangeshkar have been a mutual admiration society and Dilip Kumar addresses Lataji as his little sister.

With Sitara Devi

With Lata Mangeshkar

This chapter cannot deemed to be complete without a listing of the best solos (in Table 9.1) and duets (in Table 9.2) enacted by the great Dilip Kumar (as per our personal choice).

Table 9.1 Solo Songs of Dilip Kumar

S.No.	Song	Film	Singer	Composer	Lyricist
1	'Gaye ja geet milan ke'	*Mela*	Mukesh	Naushad	Shakeel Badayuni
2	'Watan ki raah mein'	*Shaheed*	Mohd. Rafi	Ghulam Haider	Raja Mehdi Ali Khan
3	'Aye dil mujhe aisi jagah'	*Aarzoo*	Talat Mahmood	Anil Biswas	Majrooh Sultanpuri
4	'Tu kahe agar jeevan bhar'	*Andaaz*	Mukesh	Naushad	Shakeel Badayuni
5	'Mera jeevan sathi bichhad gaya'	*Babul*	Talat Mahmood	Naushad	Shakeel Badayuni
6	'Huye ham jinke liye barbad'	*Deedar*	Mohd. Rafi	Naushad	Shakeel Badayuni
7	'Yeh hawa yeh raat yeh chandani'	*Sangdil*	Talat Mahmood	Sajjad	Rajinder Krishan
8	'Takra gaya tumse dil'	*Aan*	Mohd. Rafi	Naushad	Shakeel Badayuni
9	'Aye mere dil kahin aur chal'	*Daag*	Talat Mahmood	Shankar–Jaikishan	Shailendra
10	'Na toofan se khelo'	*Uran Khatola*	Mohd. Rafi	Naushad	Shakeel Badayuni
11	'Lagi re yeh kaisi'	*Devdas*	Talat Mahmood	S.D. Burman	Sahil Ludhianvi
12	'Apni chhaya mein bhagwan'	*Insaniyat*	Mohd. Rafi	C. Ramchandra	Rajinder Krishan
13	'Suhana safar aur yeh'	*Madhumati*	Mukesh	Salil Chowdhury	Shailendra
14	'Toote huye khwabo ne'	*Madhumati*	Mohd. Rafi	Salil Chowdhury	Shailendra
15	'Yeh mera diwanapan hai'	*Yahudi*	Mukesh	Shankar–Jaikishan	Shailendra
16	'Madhuban mein radhika naache'	*Kohinoor*	Mohd. Rafi	Naushad	Shakeel Badayuni
17	'Nain lad jaiyehein'	*Gunga Jumna*	Mohd. Rafi	Naushad	Shakeel Badayuni
18	'Mujhe duniyawalon sharabi na'	*Leader*	Mohd. Rafi	Naushad	Shakeel Badayuni
19	'Koi sagar dil ko'	*Dil Diya Dard Liya*	Mohd. Rafi	Naushad	Shakeel Badayuni
20	'Aaj ki raat mere'	*Ram Aur Shyam*	Mohd. Rafi	Naushad	Shakeel Badayuni
21	'Aaj purani rahon se'	*Aadmi*	Mohd. Rafi	Naushad	Shakeel Badayuni
22	'Jab dil se dil'	*Sunghursh*	Mohd. Rafi	Naushad	Shakeel Badayuni
23	'Na tu zameen ke liye'	*Dastaan*	Mohd. Rafi	Laxmikant–Pyarelal	Sahil Ludhianvi
24	'Sala main to Saheb'	*Sagina*	Kishore Kumar	S.D. Burman	Majrooh Sultanpuri

Table 9.2 Duest Songs of Dilip Kumar

S.No.	Song	Film	Singer	Composer	Lyricist
1	'Yahan badla wafa ka'	*Jugnu*	Mohd. Rafi / Noor Jehan	Feroz Nizami	Asghar Sarhady
2	'Main bhanwara tu hai phool'	*Mela*	Mukesh / Shamshad Begum	Naushad	Shakeel Badayuni
3	'Tumhare liye huye badnaam'	*Shabnam*	Mukesh / Shamshad Begum	S.D. Burman	Qamar Jalalabadi
4	'Milte hi aankhen dil hua'	*Babul*	Talat Mahmood / Shamshad Begum	Naushad	Shakeel Badayuni
5	'Dekh liya maine'	*Deedar*	Mohd. Rafi / Lata Mangeshkar	Naushad	Shakeel Badayuni
6	'Nain mile nain huye'	*Tarana*	Talat / Lata Mangeshkar	Anil Biswas	
7	'Dil mein sama gaye'	*Sangdil*	Talat / Lata Mangeshkar	Sajjad	Rajinder Krishan
8	'Seene mein sulagte hain'	*Tarana*	Talat / Lata Mangeshkar	Anil Biswas	Prem Dhawan
9	'Kitna haseen hain mausam'	*Aazad*	Chitalkar / Lata Mangeshkar	C. Ramchandra	
10	'Maang ke saath tumhara'	*Naya Daur*	Mohd. Rafi / Asha Bhosle	O.P. Nayyar	Sahil Ludhianvi
11	'Do sitaron ka zameen'	*Kohinoor*	Mohd. Rafi / Lata Mangeshkar	Naushad	Shakeel Badayuni
12	'Jawani mein akelepan'	*Paigham*	Mohd. Rafi / Asha Bhosle	C. Ramchandra	Pradeep
13	'Udein jab jab zulfein teri'	*Naya Daur*	Mohd. Rafi / Asha Bhosle	O.P. Nayyar	Sahil Ludhianvi
14	'Koi pyar ki dekhe'	*Kohinoor*	Mohd. Rafi / Asha Bhosle	Naushad	Shakeel Badayuni
15	'O chhaliya re chhaliya'	*Gunga Jumna*	Mohd. Rafi / Asha Bhosle	Naushad	Shakeel Badayuni
16	'Tere husn ki kya tariff'	*Leader*	Mohd. Rafi / Asha Bhosle	Naushad	Shakeel Badayuni
17	'Sawan aaye ya na'	*Dil Diya Dard Liya*	Mohd. Rafi / Asha Bhosle	Naushad	Shakeel Badayuni
18	'Ek shehenshah ne'	*Leader*	Mohd. Rafi / Lata Mangeshkar	Naushad	Shakeel Badayuni
19	'Main hoon saqi'	*Ram Aur Shyam*	Mohd. Rafi / Lata Mangeshkar	Naushad	Shakeel Badayuni
20	'Aaj kal shauq-e-deedar'	*Leader*	Mohd. Rafi / Asha Bhosle	Naushad	Shakeel Badayuni
21	'Ek padosan peeche'	*Gopi*	Mahendra Kapoor / Lata Mangeshkar	Kalyanji–Anandji	Rajinder Krishan
22	'Saare shahar mein'	*Bairaag*	Mohd. Rafi / Asha Bhosle	Kalyanji–Anandji	Anand Bakshi
23	'Tumhre sang to'	*Sagina*	Mohd. Rafi / Lata Mangeshkar	S.D. Burman	Majrooh Sultanpuri
24	'Peete peete kabhi'	*Bairaag*	Mohd. Rafi / Asha Bhosle	Kalyanji–Anandji	Anand Bakshi

CHAPTER 10

CONTEMPO-RARIES, COLLEAGUES AND THE CREW

In Chapter five, we have already dwelled on, at length, on the histrionic synergy and personal equations of Dilip Kumar with his leading ladies and therefore, this chapter shall focus (largely but not entirely) on his male colleagues, character artists and the people actively involved with the making of his films.

Dilip Kumar is perhaps the only leading actor to have shared screen space with the greatest actors that Hindi cinema had seen during his over seven decades long career. Among the most interesting histrionic confrontations seen on screen of the megastar were with: Prithviraj Kapoor *(Mughal-E-Azam),* Chandra Mohan *(Shaheed),* Yaqoob *(Hulchul* and *Deedar),* Ashok Kumar *(Deedar, Shakti* and *Duniya),* Motilal *(Devdas* and *Paigham),* Raj Kapoor *(Andaaz),* Dev Anand *(Insaniyat),* Prem Nath *(Aan),* Pran *(Madhumati, Dil Diya Dard Liya, Ram Aur Shyam, Aadmi, Gopi* and *Duniya),* Raaj Kumar *(Paigham* and *Saudagar),* Balraj Sahani *(Hulchul* and *Sunghursh),* Kanhaiyalal *(Gunga Jumna* and *Ram Aur Shyam),* K.N. Singh *(Hulchul* and *Shikast),* Jayant *(Amar, Insaniyat* and *Sunghursh),* Gope *(Arzoo* and *Tarana),* Johnny Walker *(Madhumati, Naya Daur, Dil Diya Dard Liya* and *Gopi),* Jeevan *(Mela, Naya Duar* and *Kohinoor),* Ajeet *(Naya Daur* and *Mughal-E-Azam),* Kumar *(Tarana* and *Mughal-E-Azam),* Nazir Hussain *(Devdas, Naya Daur, Gunga Jumna* and *Ram Aur Shyam),* Shammi Kapoor *(Vidhata),* Shashi Kapoor *(Kranti),* Dharmendra *(Paari),* Manoj Kumar *(Aadmi* and *Kranti),* Sanjeev Kumar *(Sunghursh* and *Vidhaata),* Amitabh Bachchan *(Shakti),* Shatrughan Sinha *(Kranti),* Naseeruddin Shah *(Karma),* Amrish Puri *(Vidhata, Shakti, Duniya),* Anupam Kher *(Karma),* etc.

Among the female character artists, Dilip Kumar's most memorable performances were with Leela Chitnis *(Shaheed* and *Naya Daur),* Lalita Pawar *(Daag),* Shobhna Samarth *(Insaniyat),* Durga Khote *(Mughal-E-Azam),* Leela Misra *(Ram Aur Shyam),* Nigar Sultana *(Mughal-E-Azam),* Nirupa Roy *(Ram Aur Shyam* and *Kranti),* etc.

With Prithviraj Kapoor

With Sohrab Modi

With Chandramohan and Leela Chitnis

With Motilal

With Ashok Kumar

With Yaqoob

With Raj Kapoor

With Dev Anand

With Pran

With Jeevan

With Jayant

With Lalita Pawar

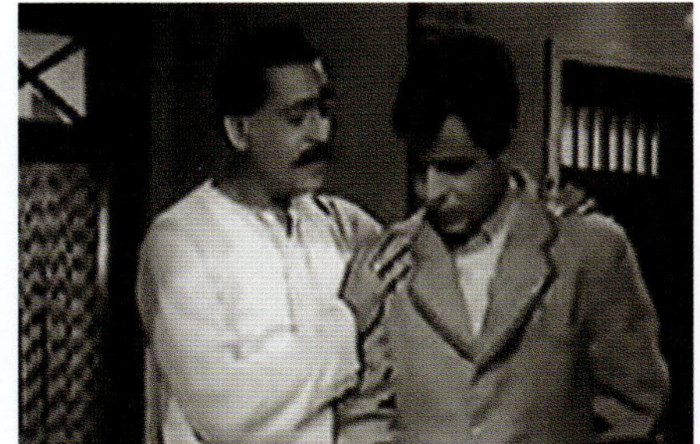
With K.N. Singh

With Kanhaiyalal

With Raaj Kumar

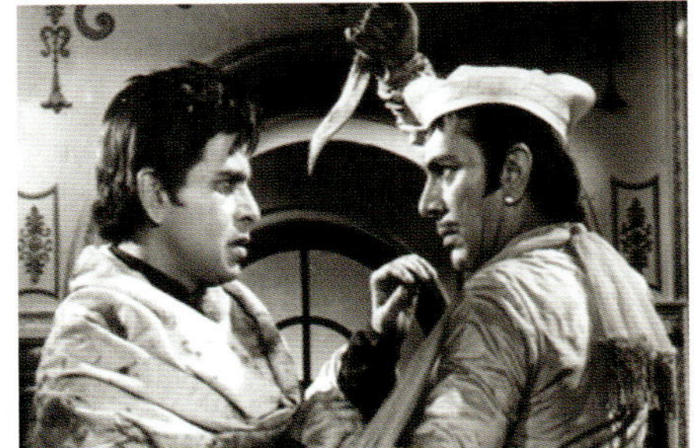
With Balraj Sahani

With Prem Nath

With Johny Walker

With Ajeet

With Nazir Hussain

With Shammi Kapoor

With Manoj Kumar

With Dharmendra

With Shashi Kapoor

With Amitabh Bachchan

With Sanjeev Kumar

With Shatrughan Sinha

With Anil Kapoor

With Amrish Puri

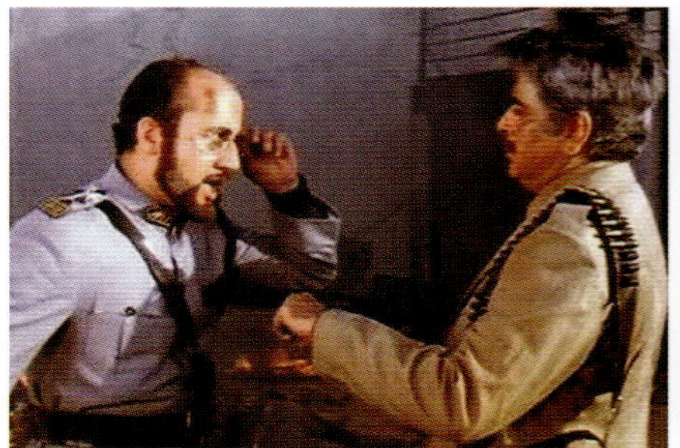
With Anupam Kher

Celebrated cinematographers, who were truly the best in the Hindi film industry, such as Faredoon A. Irani, Fali Mistry, Jal Mistry, V. Babasaheb, Dilip Gupta, R.D. Mathur and Kamal Bose got to train their lenses on the actor with a stupendous screen presence and the results on the silver screen were simply magical. The most opulent cinematographic creations which matched the thematic mood of those great Dilip Kumar starrers can be listed as:

R.D. Mathur *(Jwar Bhata, Mughal-E-Azam, Sunghursh)*
Radhu Karmakar *(Milan)*
Jaywant Pathare *(Tarana)*
Fali Mistry *(Mela, Babul)*
Faredoon A. Irani *(Andaaz, Aan, Amar, Aadmi, Gopi)*
Marshal Braganza *(Shaheed)*
Jal Mistry *(Anokha Pyar, Uran Khatola)*
K.H. Kapadia *(Nadiya Ke Paar, Shikast)*
D.C. Mehta *(Jogan)*
Dilip Gupta *(Deedar, Madhumati, Yahudi)*
V. Babasaheb *(Daag, Gunga Jumna, Leader)*
Kamal Bose *(Devdas, Musafir, Bairaag, Kalinga)*
M.N. Malhotra *(Naya Daur)*
Dwarka Divecha *(Dil Diya Dard Liya)*
Marcus Bartley *(Ram Aur Shyam)*
Bimal Mukherji *(Sagina, Sagina Mahato)*
Dharam Chopra *(Dastaan, Mazdoor)*
Joe D'Souza *(Kranti)*
S.M. Anwar *(Shakti)*
Kay Gee *(Mashaal)*
Kamlakar Rao *(Vidhata, Karma)*
Ashok Mehta *(Saudagar)*

With Naseeruddin Shah

Faredoon Irani

R.D. Mathur

Fali Mistri

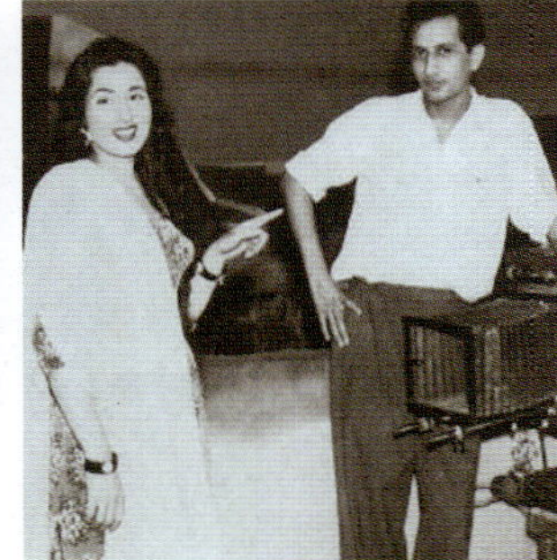

Jai Mistri with Madhubala

Dwarka Divecha

Dilip Gupta

Kamal Bose

V. Babasaheb

Ace Cinematographer Faredoon A. Irani has the distinction of capturing the maximum number—five—of Dilipian films.

Some the most eminent writers of all time pushed their illustrious pens to write some amazing screenplays and dialogues for Dilip starrers and the most applauded works were by Babu Bhagwati Charan Verma, Azm Bazidpuri, S.Ali Reza, Wajahat Mirza, Ramanand Sagar, Nabendu Ghosh, Rajinder Singh Bedi, Agha Jani Kashmiri, Abraar Alvi, Akhtar-ul-Iman, Rajinder Krishan, Salim-Javed and few others.

Rajinder S. Bedi with Other Writers and Poets

Wajahat Mirza

Ramanand Sagar

Agha Jani Kashmiri

Renowned editors who provided a cutting edge to the unfolding visuals of Dilip films included Moosa Mansoor, Kamlakar, Shamsuddin Kadri, J.S. Diwadkar, Shivaji Avdhoot, Hrishikesh Mukherjee, Pratap Dave, Vasant Borkar, Das Dhaimade, Pran Mehra, Dharmveer, Krishna Sachdev, M.S. Shinde, Waman Bhosle, Gurudutt Shirali, etc.

The list is endless and comprises the most respected names in the annals of Indian cinema in all departments of filmmaking.

CHAPTER 11

THE TERRIFIC TRIO

Between late 1940s and early 1970s, three megastars—Dilip Kumar, Dev Anand and Raj Kapoor—ruled the roost in Hindi cinema with their magnetic screen presence, superlative histrionics and ability to carry a film on their shoulders. The trio, popularly known as 'The Trinity' or 'The Big Three', enjoyed phenomenal popularity and a demi-God status amongst their fans.

The 'Big Three' carved their own niche in the film world from the point of their arrival on the silver screen itself. They worked hard to create an original image for themselves, individually crafted with care and stylised as the Hindi films' leading men who are often

The Terrific Trio

larger than life yet utterly credible, natural and relatable. The trio started their film journeys in the 1940s, with Dilip Kumar making his debut with *Jwar Bhata* (1944), Raj Kapoor with *Chittor Vijay* (1945) and Dev Anand with *Hum Ek Hain* (1947). The careers of the three stalwarts took very similar paths with a great deal of parallels—the films catapulting the 'Big Three' into the top league of superstars came around the same time. Dilip Kumar's first super hit film *Milan* from Bombay Talkies released in 1946; Dev Anand's superhit *Ziddi,* also from Bombay Talkies, came in 1948; and Raj Kapoor's *Barsaat,* made under his own banner R.K. Films, released in 1949. However, as expected, they went on to form their own individual camps with preferred producers, directors, writers, composers and lyricists, etc.; they also went on to achieve spectacular cinematic success in their individual careers. They intelligently took their careers to meteoric heights on the celluloid firmament to emerge as individual megastars who were heads and shoulders above their contemporaries including Motilal, Bharat Bhushan, Pradeep Kumar, Kishore Kumar, Prem Nath, Balraj Sahni, Shammi Kapoor, Dharmendra, Shashi Kapoor, Manoj Kumar and others and even the legendary actor par excellence, the indomitable Ashok Kumar.

The Trinity: Dilip Kumar, Dev Anand and Raj Kumar

The Dilip Kumar camp had luminaries such as legendary directors Mehboob Khan, Bimal Roy, Nitin Bose, S.U. Sunny, Amiya Chakrabarty, K. Asif, Ramesh Saigal, S.S. Vasan et al; music director Naushad; lyricist Shakil Badayuni, writers Wajahat Mirza, Rajinder Krishan, Akhtar-ul-Iman, Abraar Alvi and Rahi Masoom Raza; and cinematographers Faredoon A. Irani, V. Babasaheb, R.D. Mathur, Kamal Bose, etc.

Dev Anand's close circle had directors Chetan Anand, Vijay Anand, Raj Khosla, Shankar Mukherjee; music directors S.D. Burman, R.D. Burman and Jaidev; lyricists Sahir Ludhianvi, Shailendra, Majrooh Sultanpuri and Neeraj; cinematographers Fali Mistry, Jal Mistry, V. Ratra, and D.K. Prabhakar; art director T.K. Desai and writers (apart from Chetan, Vijay and Dev himself) Vrajendra Gaur, Suraj Sanim, K.A. Narayan, et al. The Raj Kapoor group had music directors Shankar–Jaikishan, lyricists Shailendra and Hasrat Jaipuri; writers K.A. Abbas, Inder Raj Anand and Arjun Dev Rashk; cinematographers Radhu Karmakar and Taru Dutt; art director M.R. Achrekar and sound recordist Allaudin, etc.

The camps followers or members were not assigned projects on an exclusive basis; rather, it was mutually inclusive. For example, Amiya Chakrabarty made two of his career best motion pictures *Daag* and *Patita* with Dilip Kumar and Dev Anand in the leads respectively. Similarly, Naushad Saheb scored the music of Raj Kapoor-starrer *Dastaan,* while Shankar–Jaikishan gave music in three Dilip Kumar starrers (*Daag, Shikast* and *Yahudi*) and six Dev Anand starrers *(Patita, Love Marriage, Asli Naqli, Roop Ki Rani Choron Ka Raja, Kahin Aur Chal, Pyar Mohabbat* and *Duniya).*

On the other hand, S.D. Burman composed music for three Raj Kapoor films *(Chittor Vijay, Dil Ki Rani* and *Pyar)* and two films starring Dilip Kumar *(Devdas* and *Sagina).* There was mutual respect for each other's craft and a healthy rivalry among the 'Big Three'. Moreover, at a personal level, they were great friends with an enviable camaraderie amongst them. There were several other common meeting grounds between the three. Each of them formed his own production company and went on to produce some landmark films. Dilip Kumar had 'Citizen Films', Dev Anand had 'Navketan Films' and Raj Kapoor, the 'R.K. Films'. In the aspect of film production, Dev Anand led the trinity, having produced forty films for Navketan Films. Raj Kapoor came a distant second with sisteen films for R.K. Films, while Dilip Kumar produced just one film—the super-duper Technicolor hit *Gunga Jumna*—for his Citizen Films. Raj Kapoor went on to become a director of great eminence and international recognition directing most of his home productions, while Dev Anand directed twenty of Navketan's films. Dilip Kumar never ever officially directed a film. The only film to which Dilip Saheb officially lent his name to as director was *'Kalinga'* but he has chosen never to release it. When we presented a collage of pictures of Navketan's films to Dev Saheb, he in an unguarded moment blurted out, *'Itna kaam kisi ne nahin kiya'* (No one has done so much work). Well, we vigorously nodded our head in agreement. While presenting a similar collage of his films to Dilip Saheb, his reaction was a typical disarming smile and a nod of appreciation. Meeting Dilip Kumar and Dev Anand were experiences in stark contrast—with Dilip Saheb time stood still as one got transported to an era of art, culture and courtesy whereas with Dev Saheb, time flew past at a tearing pace as he rolled out his charming hospitality and interaction.

In terms of acting prowess, the living legend Dilip Kumar got ensconced on a much loftier pedestal. While many performers may have charmed their ways into the hearts of their fans, Dilip went far beyond, mesmerising and captivating filmgoers across many generations with his unmatched histrionics in virtually all his films. His portrayal of vastly diverse characters in about fifty-seven films stand as shining testimonials of the exceptional performing calibre of the actor. Many of his films such as *Shaheed, Andaaz, Babul, Deedar, Aan, Azaad, Uran Khatola, Amar, Devdas, Insaniyat, Naya Daur, Madhumati, Paighaam, Kohinoor, Mughal-E-Azam, Gunga Jumna, Leader, Ram Aur Shyam, Aadmi, Sunghursh, Sagina Mahto, Shakti, Vidhaata, Mashal, Saudagar,* et al are heralded as landmark motion pictures in the annals of Hindi film industry. Dilip and Dev became and remained close friends and shared screen space in the film *Insaniyat* (1955).

They not only had a healthy professional rivalry but also shared profound mutual respect. Dev Saheb has spoken from his heart about colleague Dilip Kumar in his autobiography *Romancing with Life*[1] ***One day outside his home, Nasir Khan introduced me to his elder brother, who stood there looking very striking in a white shirt and white pants. He was doing his first film for Bombay Talkies at the time. His name was Yusuf Khan. The world knows him better as Dilip Kumar, the biggest and the most charismatic star of the Indian screen.***

Dev Anand's large-heartedness in openly acknowledging a professional rival as the biggest and most charismatic star speaks volumes of the legend's sheer honesty of character. In his autobiography, Dev Saheb has also mentioned nostalgically about Dilip Saheb attending his sister Usha's wedding and sitting on the ground with him with Dev's father sitting right behind in a chair to pose for a photograph. Dev Saheb admired the down-to-earth Dilip Saheb for making himself appear as a part of the family.

Dev Anand was a stylish actor with an urbane image. But histrionically, a magnificent

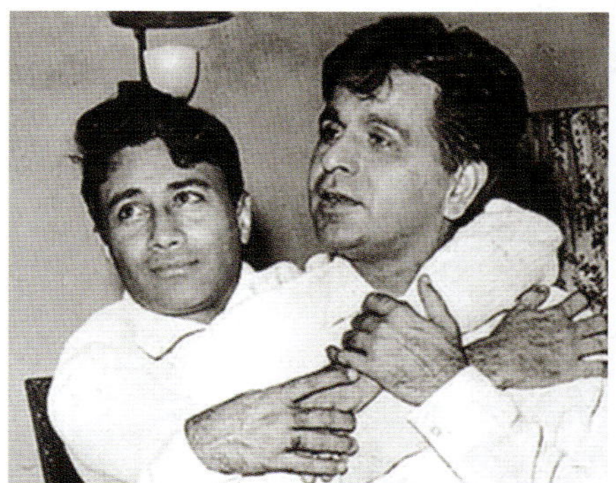

Dev Anand and Dilip Kumar: Circa 1964

Dilip Kumar with Dev Anand at a family wedding

Dilip Kumar and Dev Anand: Circa 2009

performer who never got his due as an actor perhaps due to his larger-than-life romantic image. Nevertheless, Dev Anand emphatically established his great acting capabilities in landmark films such as *Guide, Hum Dono, Kala Pani, Munimji, Taxi Driver, Baadbaan, Manzil,* et al. Of course, the endearing romantic serenades of Dev Anand in his films such as *CID, Baarish, Paying Guest, Nau Do Gyarah, Solva Saal, Kala Bazar, Jab Pyar Kisise Hota Hai, Tere Ghar Ke Samne, Jewel Thief* and *Johny Mera Naam* won the admiration and fanatic adulation of his fans.

Raj Kapoor too was an admirable actor, but the outstanding director in him (who went on to acquire unsurpassed international repute and stature) outstripped the growth of the actor. Raj Saheb acted in fifty odd films with sterling performances in *Gopinath, Awara, Aah, Shri 420, Chori Chori, Anari, Sharda, Jagte Raho, Jis Desh Mein Ganga Behti Hai, Teesri Kasam,* etc. As a director, Raj Kapoor's legacy includes landmark films like *Barsaat, Awara, Shri 420, Jis Desh Mein Ganga Behti Hai, Sangam, Mera Naam Joker, Bobby* and *Ram Teri Ganga Maili,* et al. Dev Saheb and Raj Saheb maintained good

Raj Kapoor and Dilip Kumar

1 Anand, Dev. 2007. Romancing with *Life: An Autobiography*. India: Viking by Penguin Books.

camaraderie but the relationship had a chequered phase, when the latter literally weaned away Zeenat Aman from the former's films and life, calling her a volcano of talent and gave her a plum role in his *Satyam Shivam Sundaram.* Dev Saheb said that his heart broke into pieces at that point and that Raj Kapoor grasped his hand in a very tight grip, as if trying to make amends for some wrongdoing displaying a surge of affection. Meanwhile, Dilip Kumar and Raj Kapoor did work together in Mehboob Khan's *Andaaz* but Dev Anand and Raj Kapoor never ever shared space on the silver screen.

Dilip–Dev–Raj held an incredible sway over the audience generating mass hysteria. When their films *Gunga Jumna* (1961), *Hum Dono* (1961) and *Jis Desh Mein Ganga Behti Hai* (1960) were running almost simultaneously, there were nationwide heated debates among fans as to who outdid whom. The subject saw animated drawing room discussions in virtually every home. When Raj Kapoor won the Filmfare Award for his performance in *Jis Desh Mein Ganga Behti Hai,* there were big protests, especially by Dilip Kumar fans. Still Dilip Kumar very sportingly presented Raj Kapoor his Best Actor trophy at the Filmfare Awards function. Similarly, when Raj Kapoor's *Teesri Kasam* (1966) performance did not get him the award, he presented the trophy at the Filmfare Awards function to Dev Anand (who won it for his performance in *Guide* (1965)), in a most sporting gesture.

Raj to Dev : The 'Guide' Award

Personally, the trio maintained a very cordial and affable relationship among themselves. Both Raj Kapoor and Dev Anand attended the Dilip-Saira wedding and Dilip Kumar attended wedding of Dev Anand's daughter as well as the marriages of Raj Kapoor's sons and daughters.

There shall never be another 'The Big Three or The Trinity' and there shall never be three outstanding contemporaries of the stature of Dilip Kumar, Dev Anand and Raj Kapoor who magnificently strode across the celluloid firmament as a colossal trio.

The Magnificent Trio

CHAPTER 12

THE OTHER SIDE OF THE STAR: DILIP KUMAR'S NATIONAL, SOCIO-POLITICAL AND PHILANTHROPIC ENDEAVOURS

Dilip Kumar has a very secular approach to religion and his firm conviction on this score is reflected amply in his statement: ***(The) God prescribed religion to bring harmony amongst men (and) not to disrupt and disintegrate them into militant factions. I am reminded of a verse in the Quran which virtually implies: This then is a confirmation of the teachings that have been sent before... this is nothing new... you will not distinguish between this and the other teachings.... You will not distinguish between this messenger and the messengers that have been sent before... those who do distinguish are the ones who divide...we hold them in contempt!***

An incident illustrating Dilip Saheb's secular bent of mind relates to the time when the classic *Madhumati* was being filmed in Nainital. The incident was narrated by the then production controller of Bimal Roy Productions, Premji (later secretary to Dilip Kumar and a producer in his own right with films such as *Mera Saya, Dushman, Dost* and *Meera* made under his banner of Suchitra Films). He said: ***One day, a priest approached Dilip Kumar and asked for help to repair a temple. Dilip called for me and asked to pay the priest ₹1,000. A few days later, a maulvi came to Dilip with a similar request, to repair a mosque. Dilip promptly instructed me to hand him ₹1,000. A thousand rupees was a huge amount in those days so I privately told Dilip to be careful about donating money. Dilip merely smiled and tilted his head upwards to indicate that whether it was Bhagwan or Allah, they were the same to him.*** A similar observation was recorded by journalist Vir Sanghvi, who mentioned, 'If you want an example of the success of Indian secularism, Dilip Kumar should fit the bill. He has been a truly patriotic Muslim. And India, in turn, has honoured him by treating him as a legend in his own lifetime.'

As is evident from earlier chapters, Dilip Kumar was, is and shall always be a diehard nationalist with strong secular beliefs and patriotic fervour. The inner fabric of the legendary megastar has been steeped in the purely Hindustani culture and the famed *Ganga-Jamuni Tehzeeb.* Dilip Saheb was born in undivided India and never believed in the two-nation theory. He still feels that people to people, the two nations are still one and it is just politics that has kept the people apart. He believes that political ambitions and not religious convictions caused the partition and vested interests gave it a religious colour.

Dilip Kumar always espoused national causes and identified himself with the political party of his choice based on his convictions. However, he never harboured any political ambitions and limited himself to pre-election campaigns. Despite innumerable opportunities, he never got involved in active politics unlike his peers and colleagues in the film industry like M.G. Ramchandran (MGR), N.T. Rama (NTR) Rao, J. Jayalalitha, Vyjayantimala, Sunil Dutt, Hema Malini, Dharmendra, Shatrughan Sinha, Govinda, Raj Babbar, et al.

MGR, NTR and Dilip

Dilip Saheb identified with and believed in the Nehruvian democratic socialism and the principles and policies of the Indian National Congress. He had a wonderful relationship with the then Prime Ministers Pt Jawahar Lal Nehru and his daughter Indira Gandhi which began when Dilip forcefully put forth his case during the *Gunga Jumna* fracas with the Censor Board. Pandit*ji* was deeply impressed with his rhetoric and requested him to canvass for the Congress party during the 1962 national general elections particularly in V.K. Krishna Menon's Mumbai constituency, which he did with great success (Krishna Menon defeated the veteran Acharya Kripalani aided by Dilip's hold over the masses) to become a regular feature of the Congress party's election campaigns down the years. His maiden speech was made at the Cooperage in South Mumbai to a tumultuous public response from the record public gathering. Dilip Saheb formed many lifetime friendships with many Congress Party bigwigs, among whom he was closest to the legendary Maulana Abdul Kalam Azad, Rajni Patel and Sharad Pawar. Over the years, he actively campaigned in numerous elections for the Congress party. He was particularly active in the campaigns for the Congress party candidates like Sharad Pawar in Baramati (Pune, Maharashtra), Shah Nawaz Khan in Meerut (Uttar Pradesh) and colleague and close friend Sunil Dutt in Mumbai.

Public Meetings with Pt Nehru and Dilip Kumar

Pt Nehru and Indira Gandhi with Dilip, his Sisters, Raj Kapoor and Motilal

Although Dilip Saheb was never interested in active politics, rumours of his political plunge continued circulating in the media. There was a time when *The Indian Express* newspaper carried a front page news item that Dilip Kumar is to be appointed an envoy in a plum posting abroad.

Envoy Dilip

By K. S. Ramkumar

Dilip Kumar is to become an Ambassador.

A highly reliable diplomatic source revealed on Monday that the handsome Pathan is to be posted in one of the Arab countries most likely in Kuwait.

The "tragedy king", who literally ruled over the hearts of millions of cine-goers for over three decades, has reportedly finally made up his mind about accepting the high honour.

Dilip Kumar alias Yusufkhan Sarvarkhan Pathan, whose latest film "Bairaag" (his 49th film in 33 years) was released only a couple of months ago, had been speaking out in film functions about his "bairaag" (renunciation) from the film industry following the release of the long-awaited film grossing well at the box-office.

Lately, his appearance in films had become rarer.

The news of his diplomatic assignment may come as a big shock to his innumerable admirers and fans as the appointment may virtually mean an end to the distinguished career of the highest ever paid star.

It was widely rumoured in recent times that this great film personality, often referred to as "the actors' actor", was to be nominated as a Member of Parliament. However, as he had announced two of his own films one of them titled "Kali Sarso", and accepted nearly five to six outside offers, it was presumed that he had either given up or put off the idea of pursuing a political or diplomatic career.

Of late, age was showing on his expressive face and even his staunch fans felt that it was time he had switched over to character roles like Ashok Kumar and Balraj Sahni. But instead, it seems, he preferred to quit films when he was still very much at the top.

So, the often hotly debated question "After Dilip who?" will loom large on the film industry and the cine-goers.

Dilip Kumar has been bestowed with the coveted civilian honours by the Government of India including the Padma Bhushan (1991), the Dadasaheb Phalke Award (1995) and the Padma Vibhushan (2016). The current Home Minister Rajnath Singh specially flew down to Mumbai to present the Padma Vibhushan to Dilip Saheb at his Pali Hill residence.

Lord Meghnad Desai, a member of House of Lords, UK since 1991, penned an interesting book on the star, titled *Nehru's Hero: Dilip Kumar, in the Life of India,* which is a collection of essays on the Indian cinema of the Nehru era. The Preface of the book candidly remarks, 'Dilip Kumar towered over that era and filled over lives. We emulated his dress, his hair, his mannerisms and his dialogues. But above all, the characters he played in the various roles portrayed ideals, which we absorbed.' Lord Desai went on to conclude his book with the observation: ***As Indians were defining themselves as individual men and women trying to fashion a new society with new approaches to personal and social morality and to place themselves as citizens vis-à-vis their fellow Indians, they looked to their Prime Minister's speeches for didactic guidance but to their film heroes and heroines for the models. Dilip Kumar reflected the best of this country at the best of its times. This is why he is still fondly remembered and regarded by generations after mine that thrilled to his young heroic portraits. He***

is the ideal of India of that age imaged in his many roles—rural and urban, active and quiescent, tragic and comic, rich and poor. In all his films, he was only trying to entertain, not preach. He can be proud that he was always a box-office hit and remains so to his last film. It is no mean achievement to please and to embody the aspirations and ideals of nation. Few have done it. Dilip Kumar a.k.a. Yusuf Khan is one of these few.

When Dilip Kumar was shooting for Manoj Kumar's super-duper hit *Kranti* (1981), Sharad Pawar and Rajni Patel prevailed upon him to accept being the Sheriff of Mumbai. The news created a real stir in the media as the coveted position of the city's Sheriff was awarded to an actor. Manoj Kumar was the first to get wind of the event and sought the permission of the Raj Bhawan to film the swearing in of Dilip Kumar as the Sheriff.

Governer Sadiq Ali swearing-in Dilip

During his tenure as the Sheriff, Dilip Saheb addressed large gatherings of professionals from such diverse areas as cardiology and poultry farming and conducted himself with great dignity and charm while discharging his duties as the Sheriff. The position also afforded him the rare opportunity to do social work which was so very close to Dilip Saheb's heart. Dilip Kumar nevertheless steered clear of active political involvement except for accepting the Congress's nomination as a Member of Parliament of the Rajya Sabha (2000–2006). During his stint as the Sheriff and later as a member of the Rajya Sabha, Dilip Saheb was extremely pleased to channelise government funds for deserving causes. He made contributions to improve hospitals, provide ambulances, finance building of primary schools in rural Maharashtra, provide computers and made monetary allocations for laying roads in Mumbai, Satara, Nashik and Nanded. He also contributed funds to construct modern clean public washrooms in the slum areas of Mumbai, beautified gardens and created new parks in Mumbai especially at  Bandra's Bandstand.

Dilip Kumar and Balasahab Thackeray

Dilip Kumar's popularity among and bonhomie with the political glitterati cut across political lines; for example, his friendship with Maharashtra's Sharad Pawar was as strong as with the Shiv Sena supremo Balasahab Thackeray. Grapevine has it that Dilip Saheb has spent many evenings on the terrace of Shiva Sena chief's residence *'Matoshree'* sipping beer in the company of Balasahab.

Dilip Saheb's popularity in the Middle Eastern countries and the Muslim world has been unparalleled with his films being particularly popular in Iran, Egypt, Afghanistan, Pakistan, Bangladesh, Turkey, Algeria, et al. He had a personal rapport with King Mohammed Zahour Shah of Afghanistan, Shah Mohammad Reza Pahlavi of Iran, etc., and visited many of these countries. When the thespian was conferred the prestigious Dadasaheb Phalke Award, the *Arab News* of Saudi Arabia carried the news on the front page. The Government of Pakistan conferred the *Nishan-e-Imtiaz* Award (the highest civilian honour) to Dilip Kumar in 1997, which stirred a controversy. The thespian accepted the same after seeking due approval of the then Indian Prime Minister Atal Bihari Vajpayee. Dilip Saheb flew down to Karachi accompanied by Saira Banu and friend Sunil Dutt to accept the award. The welcome reception he received was truly extraordinary. The then Prime Minister of Pakistan, Nawaz Sharif was a big fan of Dilip Saheb. A few years earlier, Dilip Kumar and Saira banu had visited Peshawar for the first time after partition to inaugurate the services of a blood bank. The then Pakistani President General Muhammad Zia-Ul-Haq converted the trip into a state visit by an Indian dignitary and hosted the celebrity couple.

At Gunga Jumna Premiere

Iranian Film Industry Meet

Hafiz Tomb Visit

Isfahan Visit

Persepolis Visit

Dilip with King Zahour Shah

Umrah in Saudi

Peshawar Visit

Dilip Kumar and Musharraf

Dilip Kumar and Nawaz Sharif

Dilip at the Front with Rafi

Whenever the country was faced with an emergency like a war or natural calamities (femine or floods or earthquakes), Dilip Kumar was always at the forefront of the film industry in generously contributing to the war or disaster funds by means of money donations, cultural shows, cricket matches, etc. After the 1962 war with China, Dilip Kumar alongwith Mohd. Rafi led a team of film industy artists to the front to entertain the Indian soldiers. On 17 March 1963, he arranged a charity cricket match at Mumbai's historic Gymkhana playground for collecting funds for the National Defence Bonds. In the match, Dilip Kumar scored 20 runs and captured 5 wickets showing his cricketing prowess for the Mayor's Eleven against the Chief Minister's Eleven. Legendary cricketer Vijay Merchant remarked in his running commentary, 'It was a great gesture on his part to have come forward to play here although he belonged to quite a different field.' Several such charity events continued under the patronage of Dilip Kumar in the years to come.

CHAPTER 13

THE PRIVATE LIFE OF A MEGASTAR: FADS AND FOIBLES

An uncrowned king of acting with a fan following of millions, a man with a peerless mystic aura and an icon placed on a lofty pedestal of stardom out of reach for peers—this is how Dilip Kumar appears from outside. However, in real life, he is a down-to-earth and affable individual with frugal needs but a fabulous taste in life. Those who have met him get infected with this disarming simplicity as it rubs off on them. Meeting the thespian is an experience to cherish as he makes you feel so very comfortable creating the feeling that the acquaintance has been truly a long one.

The greatest personal attribute of the living legend has been his firm unshakable belief in his convictions which has enabled him to stick to his principles while handling personal, private and professional affairs. In all probability, this self-inculcated personal attribute has helped him in portrayal of his on-screen characters with such immaculate sincerity and credibility. His face always exuded and still has a mirror-like honesty which commands instant admiration and catalyses eulogy. As a result, most of his screen appearances invariably struck a rapport with the audiences in a jiffy.

Dilip Kumar has always had a very secular approach to religion and his firm conviction on this score is reflected amply in his on-record statement:

Dilip – The secular Khan

God prescribed religion to bring harmony amongst men not to disrupt and disintegrate them into militant factions. I am reminded of a verse in the Quran which virtually implies: 'This. then is a confirmation of the teachings that have been sent before... this is nothing new... you will not distinguish between this and the other teachings.... You will not distinguish between this messenger and the messengers that have been sent before... those who do distinguish are the ones who DIVIDE....we hold them in contempt!' An incident illustrating Dilip Sahab's secular bent of mind relates to the time when the classic *Madhumati* was being filmed in Nainital and was narrated by the then Production Controller of Bimal Roy Productions, Premji (later Secretary to Dilip Kumar and a producer in his own right with films, viz., *Mera Saya, Dushman, Dost* and *Meera* made under his banner of Suchitra Films) who said '*One day a priest approached Dilip Kumar and asked for help to repair a temple. Dilip called for me and asked to pay the priest Rs. 1000. A few days later, a maulvi came to Dilip with a similar request, to repair a mosque. Dilip promptly instructed me to hand him Rs. 1000. A thousand rupees was a huge amount in those days so I privately told Dilip to be careful about donating money. Dilip merely smiled and tilted his head upwards to indicate that whether it was Bhagwan or Allah they were the same to him.*' A similar observation on record was made by journalist Vir Sanghvi who mentioned '*If you want an example of the success of Indian secularism, Dilip Kumar should fit the bill. He has been a truly patriotic Muslim. And India, in turn, has honoured him by treating him as a legen in his own lifetime.*' As is evident from the above, Dilip Kumar was, is and shall always be a die- hard nationalist with strong secular beliefs and patriotic fervour. The inner fabric of the legendary mega star has been steeped in the purely Hindustani culture and the *Gunga-Jamni Tehzeeb*. Dilip Sahab was born in the undivided India and never believed in the two nation theory. He still feels that people to people the two nations are still one and it is just Politics that has kept the peoples apart. Political ambitions and not religious convictions caused the partition although vested interests gave it a religious colour.

There are countless interesting anecdotes related to the fanatic adoration of Dilip Kumar fans for their favourite star. Some years ago in London, Dilip Saheb was taken aback when his chauffeur instead of taking him to India House (to attend a reception) drove to Liverpool where a smiling Sardar*ji* (called the Ice Cream King of Liverpool) apologetically but heartily welcomed and embraced him, saying, 'I will send you back immediately but *tussi pehle saadi ice cream kha lo*' (I will send you back immediately, but first please have my ice cream). Deen Mohammad, a sales assistant in a footwear shop, perhaps holds the world record of repeat viewings of Dilipian films with his scoreboard reading—*Mughal-E-Azam*: 275 times; *Leader:* 30 times; *Dil Diya Dard Liya:* 42 times; *Ram Aur Shyam:* 45 times; and *Dastaan:* 32 times, et al and all by encashing his leave. Trinetra Bajpai also has the distinction of viewing *Madhumati* 56 times in theatres. There are known instances of women in Chittor, Lucknow, Panvel and Juhu who passed away in their advanced ages believing Dilip Kumar to be their lost son. A couple of young girls in Bangalore had vowed not to marry till Dilip Kumar himself tied the knot. By the time Dilip Kumar got married at the age of 42 years, many of the girls had greyed and remained unmarried. Numerous such episodes abound in Dilip Kumar folklore.

Over the decades, the enviable mass popularity of the superstar never waned. On being asked by a scribe as to how he managed such fan reactions, Dilip Saheb's reply was simple: ***God is kind and I have taken my work seriously and accepted only a couple of films in a year. I have refused big money although that has led to my being hard up at times with a big family. But, I have felt stronger for having overcome the temptation of big money. I am happy with the respect and goodwill I hold. Sometimes I feel guilty that I do not deserve all this. As I always say—acting is easy, if Dilip Kumar can, act anyone can. At times when people break down after***

seeing my performances à la Devdas, I feel that I am a fraud, playing on their emotions. After all, it is that Dilip of the screen, that particular tragic character that has frozen a sad moment in their heart. What a viewpoint—steeped in sheer humility and completely devoid of any self-glorification.

The famous Dilipian hair style of twin veins forming a faint '*V*' on the forehead has stayed with him from the beginning to date and many opine that was one of the secrets of his massive popular appeal. His dress sense is immaculate. Wife Saira Banu had once asked a scribe, 'Have you seen Saheb in a dark suit? You do not look at the drapery and cannot take your eyes off the man.' Formal dressing apart, Dilip Saheb has over years stuck to his white t-shirt/shirt and slightly loose-fitting white trousers albeit after marriage, he did incorporate minor colourful variations wearing cream colour shirts and mushroom colour suits.

Dilip Kumar is a foodie—a connoisseur of culinary delights and likes to be served with Mughlai delicacies. He loves non-vegetarian fare and is reportedly a fine cook himself. But, apart from gorging on rich dishes (the famous Kodaikanal breakfast scene in *Ram Aur Shyam* comes to mind), he also likes eating simple fare. Be it chai, *khara* (salty) biscuits, an omelette in a little wayside tea shop in Khandala or the lavish spread at the Sea Lounge of the Taj Palace hotel—both are partaken with equal fondness. There is an amusing anecdote related to the love for food of Dilip Kumar. He was once feeling a wee bit sick and out of sorts while shooting for *Sunghursh* and producer-director H.S. Rawail came to his make-up room to suggest cancellation of the shooting for the day. Dilip Saheb promptly replied, '*Nahin nahin* Rawail Saheb! Shooting cancel *karne se bahot nuksaan hoga, maine thodi si fried fish mangai hai, khaate hi theek ho jaoonga*' (No, no, Rawail Saheb! Cancelling the shoot would lead to a huge loss. I have asked for fried fish, I will get well as soon I have it). It was Dilip Saheb's fondness for good food that probably led him to venture into the culinary business with his close friend J.K. Kapur to create the 'Copper Chimney' chain of restaurants.

Foodie Dilip

His grandfather's influence on Dilip Kumar led to his fondness for poetry and literature. He is an extremely well-read man proficient in Urdu, English, Hindi, Pushtu, Hindakoo, and Punjabi with some knowledge of Farsi, Bhojpuri and Marathi as well. Dilip Kumar's command of *shayrana* (poetic) renditions made him the cynosure of all eyes at *mushairas* where Urdu/Farsi poetry flows with captivating charm enthralling the hazareen. I have been truly fortunate that I could enjoy Dilip Saheb's delectable *Sher-O-Shayari* over telephone conversations during my Saudi Arabian sojourn. His poetic rapporteur is to be heard to be believed.

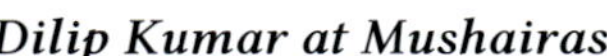

Dilip Kumar at Mushairas

Dilip Saheb is a self-professed lover of *Funoon-E-Latifa* (Fine Arts) and acquired amazing skills in the musical and allied fields. As detailed in the elucidation of the movie *Kohinoor,* Dilip Kumar actually learnt playing sitar from the legendary Ustad Haleem Zafar Khan and became so proficient in it that he actually played the instrument with great relish during picturisation of three songs of the film including the timeless Mohammad Rafi classic *'Madhuban mein Radhika naache re'* which is based on *Raag Hameer.* Being an insomniac, he was known to play sitar in the stillness of nights, though not any more. Very few friends know that Dilip Kumar has keen sense of choreography and is known to have regaled select friends at home gatherings replicating Gopi Krishna's dances of *'Jhanak Jhanak Payal Baaje'.* The Dilipian performances of just two songs *'Nain lad jaihein' (Gunga Jumna)* and *'Mere pairon mein ghunghroo' (Sunghursh)* are case in point to illustrate his dancing skills. Dilip Kumar's exceptional singing prowess is also well-known. As has been dwelled upon earlier, Dilip Kumar recorded his only film song—a duet with Lata Mangeshkar—under the music direction of Salil Chowdhury for Hrishikesh Mukherjee's *Musafir* (1957). He can brilliantly sing *ghazals*/*thumris* with great effect and enjoys singing for friends at private parties. He once sang the popular Mukesh number *'Waqt karta jo wafa' (Dil Ne Pukara)* playing a harmonium at a Filmfare Awards function years ago. Journalist Late Bunny Reuban had a cassette recording of Dilip Saheb singing a number of *ghazals* at a private party in Nairobi during the days when *Ram Aur Shyam* and *Aadmi* were premiered in Kenya. Reuban is no longer around and it is not known as to what happened to those precious recordings.

Dilip, Raj and Music

Dilip Kumar has been a keen sports enthusiast since his school days and played soccer for Wilson College and Khalsa College teams. He acquired great proficiency as an all-rounder

With Tenzing and his Wife

Gully Cricket

Painting

Dilip Kumar Playing Cricket

cricket player and participated in many matches for charity causes and loved watching test matches. I have a vivid recollection of his sweetly-timed cover drive and lofted shot while participating in the Mushtaq Ali benefit match at K.D. Singh Babu Stadium (Lucknow) circa 1970 when his *Gopi* was running houseful at the local Odeon theatre. Dilip Saheb also has been an accomplished Badminton player and used to play with Naushad Saheb among other colleagues at Khar Gymkhana. His penchant for kite flying is also well-known. He strove for attaining perfection in everything he did, be it strumming a sitar or wielding a cricket bat. Yet another hobby cultivated by the thespian was painting of myriad emotions on canvas.

BBC, 1953

The oratory skills of Dilip Kumar are truly legendary. He can mesmerise his audiences with his rhetoric in no small measure casting a hypnotic spell. He is a brilliant speaker and holds way over his audiences speaking with astonishing power of expression and fluency. Interviews of Dilip Kumar with BBC in 1953 and 1975 are cases in point. I have had many occasions of enjoying the laudable Dilipian speeches and two of them in particular were absolutely unforgettable—the 1970 Mushtaq Ali benefit cricket match at Lucknow and the annual day function of Rashtriya Chemicals and Fertilizers at Chembur on 26 January 1982. Dilip Kumar's introduction of Lata Mangeshkar at her international debut concert at the Royal Albert Hall (London) was the best ever eulogy to the legendary singer.

Dilip and Lata at the London Concert

In current times, movie stars make more money by featuring in advertisements, appearing as brand ambassadors, sponsorship, etc., than their compensation for actual work, that is, filmmaking. In the earlier era, big stars like Dilip Kumar never ever worked for the advertisement industry and their mystique and aura remained unaffected, since there was no overexposure. Dilip Kumar only helped close friends like the maverick journalist Baburao Patel (and that too free of cost) when he allowed his name to be featured in the promotion of some of the products of Patel's Mother India company such as Chilli Pickle and

Amrose Syrup. It is another matter that at the height of the popularity of the thespian, shopkeepers all over the country took pride in flaunting his photographs in front of their shops to attract customers.

Although, on screen, Dilip Kumar may have serenaded village belles, typist girls, homely middle-class girls, his choice of women has befitted a *nawabi* style. He may have once opined in print that 'Beauty lies in the heart of the woman, not the face' and it so happened that most of Dilip's women friends had more beauty on their faces. He had a rather extended bachelorhood till he was 42 years old in course of which his taste veered towards Maharanis, *Nawabzaadi*s, rich socialites and famous film stars. Apparently, his fascinations have been femme fatales or damsels in distress. They were chiffon-wearing, exquisitely-bejewelled women with arched eyebrows and beautifully manicured nails—delicate, mysterious, complicated, intriguing, sophisticated and pampered women of a bygone era. Reportedly, once while flying, Dilip Saheb poetically described the lotus like hands of the air hostess for the duration of the flight to his fellow passenger. But, post marriage, the megastar has remained pinned to his caring wife Saira Banu.

Dilip Kumar never lived alone. After his marriage, he moved, across the street, in to the house of wife Saira. But, before that he lived with the large retinue of his family in his imposing 48, Pali Hills mansion, which he had bought from a Parsi gentleman in 1953. He derived strength from his family. Dilip Saheb actually let his family use the sprawling mansion and he had his office as well as living quarters in the outhouse cottage of the mansion. The idea was not to let his family be disturbed by his activities and visitors.

Orator Dilip Kumar Paying His Tributes to Late Bimal Roy and Late S. Mukerji

Exuding measured bohemian warmth, Dilip Saheb is an intensely private person and values and cherishes the past loving to often revisit the by-gone era as is borne out by his famous quote:

I immerse myself in whatever I'm doing—a function, a charity cricket match, my nieces or nephews, my wife's wardrobe, a stanza of a poem, or just memories. I can live with memories alone. I paint and repaint the scenes of the past. I love trees, especially riding a bicycle under a banyan tree. Under the canopy of those rustling green leaves, I get an incomparable thrill.

Dilip At His Bungalow at 48, Pali Hills

EPILOGUE: THE MYTHS AND THE MAN

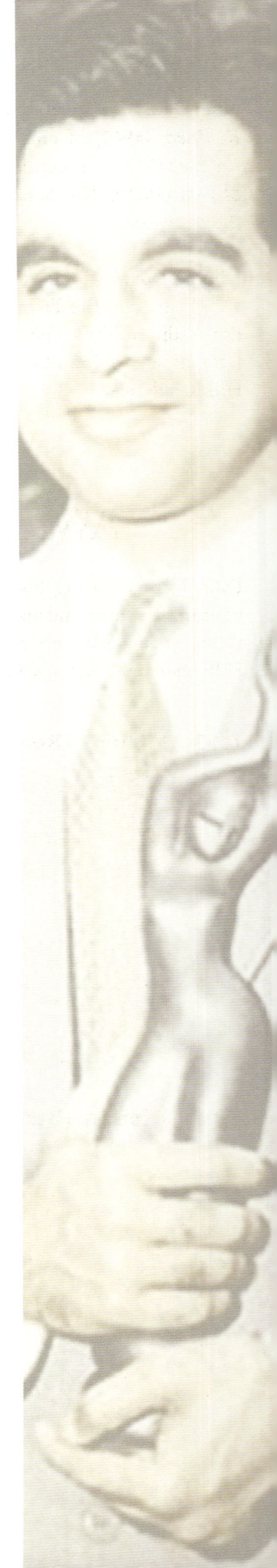

Peeping through the veil of time to revisit the enigma of Dilip Kumar and the mystique of his art, we find that the legendary supremacy of the actor continues to be widely acknowledged among not merely his legion of fans but also by the actor fraternity in the film industry as well as the younger students of Indian cinema. His legend lives on even in the twilight phase of the life of the megastar, shining as a beacon illuminating the paths of all and sundry aspiring to become names to reckon with in the celluloid world.

The principal reasons behind the everlasting appeal of the incomparable star are related to the myths or legends which have enveloped and continue to camouflage the flesh-and-blood form of the multifaceted persona of Yusuf Sarwar Khan alias Dilip Kumar. Dilip Saheb has, on one hand, projected a disarming personality both on and off screen to endear him to the masses and, on the other hand, equally charmed them with the aura of the mysterious shroud cleverly disguising the man behind the megastar.

One of the biggest factors catalysing the creation of the myths behind the man was that Dilip Kumar directed his own histrionic growth and engineered his own excellence. He harnessed his penchant for perfection to develop the most complex acting technique and mastered the art of unmatched portrayal of characters and their emotions. The result was creation of a wide range of portrayals of human emotions which are still etched in the minds of his fans. Dilip Kumar in that sense became an actor who was 'felt' by the cinemagoers. His acting style had evolved into an emotional experience, an intellectual exercise and an aesthetic delight—all at the same time. He gave torment, a face; grief, a voice; and emotion, a depiction which was beyond the level of a fine art. Even today, Dilip Kumar is the idol and inspiration of every aspiring undergraduate of acting.

The other factor contributing to the creation of the myth was that in his public appearances, interactions and orations, Dilip Kumar exuded sheer honesty of purpose and utter conviction of siding with the correct. The man's appeal was charmingly magnetic in every sense of the term. The mass adulation generated by the superstar was equally honest, sincere and deep-seated.

The artist, the man and the megastar has left indelible footprints on the sands of time. To say in terms of cinema, this *Mughal-E-Azam* (1960) of cinema has had a unique *Andaaz* (1949) and his *Aan* (1952) as an actor remains unmatched till date. The *Kohinoor* (1960) of cinema ushered in a *Kranti* (1981), through his *Shakti* (1982) and *Karma* (1986) of exceptional acting by playing everything under the sun, be it *Ram Aur Shyam* (1967). The *Saudagar* (1991) of cinematic dreams will remain *Amar* (1954) in the cineverse.

Dilip Kumar was conferred coveted civilian honours by the Government of India which include the Padma Bhushan (1991), the Dadasaheb Phalke Award (1995) and the Padma Vibhushan (2016). The current Home Minister Rajnath Singh specially flew down to Mumbai to present the Padma Vibhushan to Dilip Saheb at his Pali Hill Residence.

AWARDS and ACCOLADES

Dilip Kumar during his over six decades active film career has been bestowed with countless awards and accolades which he, of course, very richly deserved. Grapevine has it that the awards were so many that some of them were used as door-stoppers in his Pali Hills mansion. Meanwhile, here is a list of the major awards conferred on the thespian:

1953 Filmfare (Best Actor): *Daag*

1955 Filmfare (Best Actor): *Azaad*

1956 Filmfare (Best Actor): *Devdas*

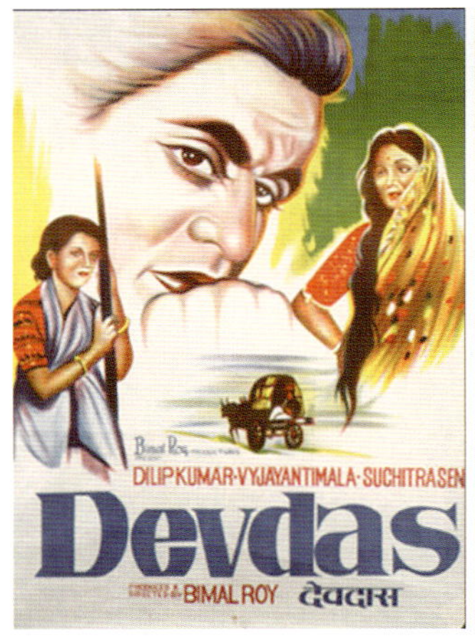

1957 Filmfare (Best Actor): *Naya Daur*

1960 Filmfare (Best Actor): *Kohinoor*

1964 Filmfare (Best Actor): *Leader*

1967 Filmfare (Best Actor): *Ram Aur Shyam*

1982 Filmfare (Best Actor): *Shakti*

1991 Padma Bhushan (awarded by the Government of India)

1993 Filmfare (Raj Kapoor Lifetime Achievement Award)

1995 Dadasaheb Phalke Award

Dilip Kumar after receiving the Dadasaheb Phalke Award (17 July 1995) at New Delhi. Also seen are Dr Shankar Dayal Sharma (the president of India) and K.P. Singh Deo (the Union minister for information and broadcasting).

1997 Nishan-E-Imtiaz (The highest civilian award of Pakistan)

1997 N.T. Rama Rao Award

1998 Ramnath Goenka Award

1998 Lux Zee Cine Awards

2000 Rajiv Gandhi Sadhbhavna Award

2015 Padma Vibhushan (awarded by the Government of India)

BIBLIOGRAPHY

Kumar, Dilip. 2014. *Dilip Kumar: The Substance and the Shadow—An Autobiography.* Hay House, Inc.

Desai, Meghnad. 2004. *Nehru's Hero: Dilip Kumar, in the Life of India.* Lotus Collection, Roli Books.

Reuben, Bunny. 2004. *Dilip Kumar: Star Legend of Indian Cinema—The Definitive Biography.* HarperCollins Publishers India.

Lanba, Urmila. 2002. *The Thespian: Life and Films of Dilip Kumar.* Vision Books.

Narwekar, Sanjit. 2004. *Dilip Kumar: The Last Emperor.* Rupa & Co.

Reuben, Bunny. 1993. *Bollywood Flashback: A Collection of Movie Memories.* Indus.

Bachchan Shrivastava, *Dilip Kumar* (in Hindi)

Old Issues of *Filmfare* Magazine

Old Issues of *Screen* Magazine

Old Issues of *Madhuri* Magazine

Old Issues of *Star & Style* Magazine

Old Issues of *Movie* Magazine

Old Issues of *Sports & Past Time* Magazine

Old Issues of *Cine Blitz* Magazine

Old Issues of *Picture Post* Magazine

BY THE SAME AUTHORS

Dev Eternal Anand

Those Magnificent Music Makers

Bimal Roy Productions
Madhumati
मधुमती
DIRECTION BIMAL ROY
MUSIC SALIL CHOWDHURY LYRICS SHAILENDRA
जेमिनी का
महान सामाजिक चित्र
पैग़ाम
REPUBLIC FILMS CORPORATION
DILIP KUMAR
MEENA KUMARI
कोहिनूर
DR. V.N. SINHA'S
KOHINOOR
DIRECTED BY S. U. SUNNY MUSIC NAUSHAD
K. ASIF'S
MUGHAL-E-AZAM
DILIP KUMAR
IN HIS FIRST DUAL ROLE
राम श्याम
RAM AUR SHYAM
EASTMANCOLOR
संगीत नौशाद
निर्देशक चाणक्य
DILIP KUMAR
MANOJ KUMAR
WAHEEDA REHMAN
PRAN · SIMMI
AADMI
आदमी
PRODUCED BY P.S.VEERAPPA · DIRECTED BY A.BHIMSINGH · MUSIC NAUSHAD · LYRICS SHAKEEL BADAYUNI
अपने समय का एक महान चित्र
दिलीप कुमार
वैजयन्तीमाला
बलराज साहनी
संजीव कुमार
एच.एस. रवैल
संघर्ष
DILIP KUMAR
SAIRA BANU
सगीना
J.K.KAPUR'S
SAGINA
TAPAN SINHA · S.D.BURMAN · MAJROOH
Bairaag
ASIT SEN
KALYANJI ANANDJI MUSHIR & RIAZ
क्रान्ती
MANOJ KUMAR'S
KRANTI
MANOJ KUMAR
DIRECTED BY
SALIM JAVED R.D.BURMAN
KRISHNAM RAJU PRESENTS
GOPIKRISHNA MOVIES
DHARM ADHIKARI
WHEN CRIMINALS BECOME SOLDIERS
KARMA
PRODUCED & DIRECTED BY
SUBHASH GHAI
LAXMIKANT PYARELAL · ANAND BAKSHI
KANOON
APNA APNA
DIVYA FILMS INTERNATIONAL PRESENTS
इज़्ज़तदार
SUDHAKAR BOKADE'S
IZZATDAAR
DIRECTED BY K. BAPAIAH
LAXMIKANT PYARELAL ANAND BAKSHI